Exploring Time and Place Through Play

Foundation Stage – Key Stage One

EDITED BY HILARY COOPER

 David Fulton Publishers

David Fulton Publishers Ltd
The Chiswick Centre, 414 Chiswick High Road, London W4 5TF

www.fultonpublishers.co.uk

First published in Great Britain in 2004 by David Fulton Publishers.

10 9 8 7 6 5 4 3 2

Note: The right of Hilary Cooper to be identified as the editor of this work has
been asserted by her in accordance with the Copyright, Designs and Patents Act
1988.

David Fulton Publishers is a division of Granada Learning Limited, part of ITV plc.

Copyright © Hilary Cooper and individual contributors

British Library Cataloguing in Publication Data
A catalogue record for this book is available from the British Library.

ISBN 1 84312 090 9

Typeset by RefineCatch Limited, Bungay, Suffolk
Printed and bound in Great Britain

Contents

Acknowledgements

The editor would like to thank all the colleagues at St Martin's College and the local education authority advisory teachers in Cumbria and Tower Hamlets, London who, despite heavy workloads, found time to work on the case studies described in this book. We are all grateful to the head teachers, teachers and other early years practitioners and of course the children with whom we worked in schools in Cumbria (Petteril Bank School, Appleby Primary School, Armathwaite School, Kendal Nursery School, Eaglesfield Paddle CE Primary School and St Mary's CE Primary School, Kirby Lonsdale), at St Mary and St Martin Primary School, Blyth, near Worksop, and in schools participating in the Oral Learning and Global Literacy Project, in Tower Hamlets, East London. Thanks are also due to Stuart Isley for interviewing practitioners in Tower Hamlets. Working together was for all of us a memorable pleasure. Also it made it possible to record real dialogue between children and adults; to analyse and reflect on how this was planned for and supported and how it developed. In this way we were able to find out about and build on the existing knowledge and understanding which real children had about time and place. Some names have been changed.

References are given at the end of each chapter, except for the following texts frequently referred to throughout:

Department for Education and Employment/Qualifications and Curriculum Authority (DfEE/QCA) (1999) *The National Curriculum: Handbook for teachers in England, Key Stages 1 and 2*. London: Stationery Office for DfEE/QCA.

QCA (2000) *Curriculum Guidance for the Foundation Stage*. London: QCA.

Siraj-Blatchford, I., Sylva, K., Muttock, S., Gilden, R. and Bell, D. (2002) *Researching Effective Pedagogy in the Early Years*, (Research Report 356). Annersley: Department for Education and Skills. (http://www.dfes.gov.uk/research/data/).

Notes on contributors

Jan Ashbridge

Jan Ashbridge is currently on secondment as a Foundation Stage advisory teacher in Cumbria. She has been an early years teacher for 13 years.

Cynthia Ashcroft

Cynthia Ashcroft is a principal lecturer and programme leader of the BA Hons with Qualified Teacher Status degree in Primary Education at St Martin's College, East London. She held a similar position at King Alfred's College, Winchester.

Vicki Boertien

Vicki Boertien recently qualified as a teacher. She specialised in the Advanced Study of Early Years on her degree course and was responsible for opening the early years unit in her school.

Veronica Broyd

Veronica Broyd is a very experienced nursery teacher who is currently seconded to Cumbria Local Education Authority as a Foundation curriculum co-ordinator.

Hilary Cooper

Hilary Cooper is Reader in Education at St Martin's College. Her doctoral research was on young children's understanding in history. She has published widely. Previously she taught at Goldsmith's College, London University and was for many years a class teacher across the 3–11 age range.

Sue Day

Sue Day is a principal lecturer in early years education at St Martin's College. She has been a reception class teacher, head of a nursery unit in a multicultural school, early years co-ordinator in a large primary school, head teacher of two very different nursery schools in Birmingham and early years advisor in Walsall.

Jane Dixon

Jane Dixon is a senior lecturer in primary education specialising in early years education at St Martin's College, Ambleside Campus. Previously she taught for 15 years in primary schools including an exchange visit to a school in Australia.

Alan Farmer

Alan Farmer is Head of the History–Geography Division at St Martin's College, Lancaster. He has written nearly a score of books on a variety of history topics.

Anne Heeley

Anne Heeley has taught for over 25 years and is presently Deputy Head at St Mary and St Martin Primary School, Blyth, near Worksop.

Sophie Mackay

Sophie Mackay is a qualified teacher and a project worker at the Humanities Education Centre, a development education centre which focuses on the global dimension in the curriculum, in Tower Hamlets. She has previously worked as a researcher and visiting lecturer in children's literature at the University of Surrey, Roehampton.

Hugh Moore

Hugh Moore is a senior lecturer in history education at St Martin's College, Lancaster. He is an experienced primary school teacher and previously worked in the museum education service.

Wendy Robson

Wendy Robson is an assistant head teacher in a primary school with responsibility for early years and Key Stage 1. She was seconded to St Martin's College as a lecturer in early years education.

Deborah Seward

Deborah Seward is a senior lecturer in history education at St Martin's College, Carlisle Campus. She teaches on a range of undergraduate and postgraduate courses and works with student teachers in schools. She taught classes across the 3–11 age range.

Nigel Toye

Nigel Toye is a senior lecturer in drama at St Martin's College, Lancaster, responsible for undergraduate and postgraduate and continuing professional development drama courses. His publications include *Drama and Traditional Story for Early Years* (2000), London: Routledge.

Jane Yates

Jane Yates is a teacher with a particular interest in early years education. She is currently working for Cumbria Education Service as an advisory teacher for multi-cultural and anti-racist education. Prior to this post she worked for Cumbria Development Education Centre on a school linking project.

1

Introduction

TIME AND PLACE are accepted dimensions of the early years curriculum. Children talk about past events in their own lives and those of their families, listen and respond to stories about the distant past and learn to differentiate between past and present, using time vocabulary (QCA 2000: 94–5). They observe, find out about and evaluate their own environment, identify features of the place in which they live, and they find out about different environments through story, using appropriate vocabulary, (pp. 96–7). The importance of learning through play runs throughout the *Curriculum Guidance for the Foundation Stage* (QCA 2000).

What practitioners wanted to know

This book emerges from an in-service course for early years practitioners, called 'Making Sense of My World', funded by Cumbria Early Years and Childcare Partnership. During the course, participants completed a questionnaire asking whether they thought that children could find out about time and place in play contexts. They thought that this was possible, but said that they would appreciate ideas about how to initiate and support such play.

The course had focused on the implications of *Researching Effective Pedagogy in the Early Years*, the 'REPEY' project (Siraj-Blatchford *et al.* 2002). Taking this into account we decided to set up a small project to see how we might help children to explore time and place through play. 'We' refers to three local education authority advisory teachers, nine tutors from St Martin's College and many practitioners working in early years settings, several of whom had been on the course.

Research underpinning our enquiry

Sustained shared thinking

The REPEY project was developed to identify the most effective strategies and techniques for promoting learning in the Foundation Stage. This study found that adult–child interactions which involved 'sustained, shared thinking' and open-ended questioning were essential in extending children's thinking. The adult is aware of and responds to the child's understanding or capability in the context of the subject or activity in question, the child is aware of what is to be learnt, (what is in the adult's mind), and both contribute to and are involved in the learning process. For the learning to be worthwhile the content should be in some way instructive. In effective settings almost half of all child-initiated episodes which involved intellectual challenge included interventions from a member of staff. However, the REPEY study also found that, while the most effective early years settings encourage such dialogue, it does not occur frequently.

Play within instructive learning environments

The REPEY project found that the most effective early years settings provided teacher-initiated group work, balanced with an 'open environment', where children had 'free' access to a range of instructive play activities in which adults supported their learning. In good and excellent settings equal numbers of activities were initiated by adults and by children, suggesting that effective settings encourage children to initiate activities and dialogue previously modelled by staff. Freely chosen play activities often provided the best opportunities for adults to extend children's thinking. Children's cognitive outcomes appeared to be directly related to the quantity and quality of teacher/adult planning in which activities and dialogue were differentiated to provide appropriate levels of challenge and children were formatively assessed and given feedback in order to plan for future learning. The best outcomes were achieved where parents and practitioners had shared educational aims and cognitive and social development were seen as complementary.

Practitioners' curriculum knowledge

In the REPEY project, practitioners' good curriculum knowledge, in addition to an understanding of child development, was found to be as vital in the early years as in later stages of education. It is necessary to know the questions to ask and the ways of answering, the key skills and concepts which are central, at any level, in different areas of learning.

Planning our project

First we agreed on the curriculum knowledge, the key concepts and skills which, at any level, lie at the heart of enquiries about time (pp. 8–10) and place (pp. 14–16). *Curriculum Guidance for the Foundation Stage* (QCA 2000) defines content (finding out about families and the distant past, about the place where children live and distant places), but is less clear about HOW to find out, the questions to ask and ways of answering them.

Then we agreed on a manageable scale and organisation for the project. Each of the advisory teachers and St Martin's tutors would work collaboratively with practitioners in a nursery or reception class. This would make it possible to work together, engage in discussion and joint exploration and draw on a rich variety of expertise and perspectives. It would also involve classes in schools of different types and sizes (a nursery school, nursery units, reception classes in infant and primary schools). The schools are in very different social, economic and cultural environments: tiny rural schools, schools in towns, in inner cities, including St Martin's partnership schools in the London Borough of Tower Hamlets. We hoped that this would provide some insights into the importance of the impact of social and cultural contexts on the ways in which learning objectives must be differently planned for.

In each class the visiting tutor or advisory teacher would work with the permanent staff to plan activities on a theme linked to either time or place, within their existing medium-term plans. The activities would include different kinds of play. They would include time for one or more of the adults to observe and engage in dialogue with groups of children. Their talk would be captured on video or audio tape or in field notes, so that it could be analysed later by all the adults.

Our questions

Our aim was to apply the key findings of the REPEY report to activities that would develop children's concepts of time and place. Through collecting empirical evidence from these different settings we wanted to gain some insights into:

- the curriculum knowledge – the questions to ask and ways of answering them, which adults need in order to interact with children to extend their thinking;

- planning skills – how to use the curriculum knowledge to plan for teacher-directed learning linked to free access to activities investigating time or place;

- dialogue – ways in which to engage in discussion with children about time and place.

The case studies

Chapter 2 explains why we think that finding out about time and place in play contexts is appropriate and important for young children, and identifies the key concepts and skills involved. Chapters 3 to 6 focus on time; Chapters 7 to 12 are about place.

In Chapter 3 Deborah Seward and Vicki Boertien explore ways of developing children's very limited social and communication skills and their self-esteem through play activities which encourage them to talk about themselves, 'then' and 'now'. In Chapter 4 Wendy Robson shows how skilful questioning enabled children to draw on what they already knew about castles and apply it to their imaginative play. Stories about the past raised questions for Alan Farmer and Anne Heeley, which they discuss in Chapter 5. Do imaginary times and places help children to explore concepts of time and place? Can young children differentiate between imagination and things that really happened? Does it matter? Should adults encourage them to move from fantasy to reality? Alan and Anne draw some conclusions, based on their discussions with children. In Chapter 6 Hugh Moore draws on his experience of teaching Key Stage 1 children, describing a rich variety of play activities which helped them to investigate life in the distant past.

Jane Yates in Chapter 7 reflects on questions which arose when a group of four- to eight-year-olds took her with them in their place capsule. In Chapter 8 children are observed playing freely in their own 'secret places' outdoors and explain why these are important to them. Jane Dixon and Sue Day show how opportunities for such play can be created and how it contributes to all the areas of early learning in the *Curriculum Guidance for the Foundation Stage* (QCA 2000). Respect for children's need for privacy, and also the rich knowledge many young children have of distant places is the focus of Chapter 9. Cynthia Ashcroft and Sophie Mackay show how story tents, inspired by the tents of Saudi Arabia, North American Indians, the Innuit and North African nomads were made and used in classrooms to develop imaginative play about journeys and other places, as part of the Tower Hamlets' Oracy and Global Learning Project. By contrast, in Chapter 10 40 nursery children go camping for a day in their local mountains in rural Cumbria and learn a lot about features of the landscape, recording routes so that they do not get lost on their adventures; they even catch a bear. In Chapter 11 children remember routes and landscape features as they help Bo Peep to find her lost sheep. Chapter 12 is about weather. A group of nursery children rebuild Percy the Park Keeper's shed after a storm and spontaneous conversations with adults about observations of ice and snow lead reception children to set up a role-play weather station.

We certainly did not embark on this project expecting to discover models of 'how to do it'. We expected that, like all good enquiries, it would raise more questions than it answered. We hope that you, the reader, will engage with our questions and reflections, in the light of your own experiences, as the case studies evolve. At the end of the book in Chapter 13 we draw together the strands which run through the book.

2

Why time? Why place? Why play?

Hilary Cooper

Why time?

EVERYONE LOVES A STORY ... stories 'open out fresh fields, the illimitable beckoning of horizons to imagination ... picturing the facts, lapping around them like seas around the rocks upon the coast ... essentially poetic' (Rowse 1946: 53–4).

All stories are about events and changes which happen over time, in our own lives and in the lives of others, whether recently or long ago in folk memory. Engaging with stories helps us to understand ways in which we are similar to and different from others, to consider why people behaved as they did, why there may be different versions of stories. Stories contribute to a growing sense of identity, an understanding of what it means to be human and of our place in the world.

Young children love to hear, to retell and talk about their own and their family stories: what they did as babies, what happened when Granny came to stay, when they got lost. Often events are linked to photographs or other records – baby books, birth tags, toys, birthday cards. In telling their stories children use the language of time: old, past, now, after, next. They talk about 'yesterday', 'last summer', 'when I'm five' (DFEE/QCA 1999: 104; QCA 2000: 94–5; 2003: 43, 46). They learn to put events in order, to clarify their thinking and ask questions (Why? How? Where? When?), in order to try to explain why things happened: we moved to this house after my brother was born, then I came to play school; I couldn't come to play school before because it was too far, but now I have lots of new friends (QCA 2000: 58, 62, 74; 2003: 21, 45) (see Chapter 3).

Young children pick up on our constant references to the passing of time. 'Piglet told himself that never, in all his life, and he was goodness knows how old – three, was it, or four? – never had he seen so much rain' ... (Milne 1926) and more recently, Isabel Allende recounts in *A Memoir* (2003) how her grandson Alejandro surprised her at the mirror 'scrutinising the map of my wrinkles', and said with compassionate commiseration: 'Don't worry Grandmother, you're going to live at least three more years.'

Kingsbury (1998) lists a variety of picture story books which can help young children understand why people and places change over time. Children can relate their own experiences to stories about growth and change in fictional families, for example *When I was a Baby* (Anholt 1988), *Grandpa* (Burningham 1984), *The Old, Old Man and the Very Little Boy* (Franklin 1992) and *The Hidden House* (Waddell 1992).

Salter (1996) gives an example of how children respond to true stories from the past. During their first week in school she told her reception class of four-year-olds that she was a visitor to the school from a long time ago and, dressed as Grace Darling the Victorian lighthouse keeper's brave daughter, told them how she had rescued shipwrecked sailors. Children accepted her in role, those who were usually restless sat perfectly still, and two weeks later were able to draw pictures and describe the main events of the story to a classroom assistant in role as a newspaper reporter. (Reception children in Chapter 5 discuss whether they think this story really happened.)

Children also enjoy traditional rhymes and stories set in the distant past and learn about sequences of events, motives, causes and effects in wider contexts, outside their direct experience (QCA 2000: 74; 2003: 20, 23, 27, 28). Nursery rhymes children learn are themselves historical sources found in children's books in the eighteenth century, when childhood was first recognised as a stage of development. 'Jack and Jill', 'Pussy's in the well' and 'Cross patch, draw the latch, Sit by the fire and spin . . .' were printed in *Mother Goose's Melody* (1765); 'Little Bo Peep' and 'Bye Baby Bunting' in *Gammer Gurton's Garland* (1748) (Knowles 1999: 547–52). Such rhymes are illustrated by pictures of hayricks and shepherdesses, cobblers, millers, pipers' sons.

'Fairy stories' are set in castles with coachmen, in forests with woodcutters. Through such stories children learn that some things were different long ago and that others remain the same (as they do in Chapter 4). Fairy stories may not be literally true but they are based on folk tales and oral history. These deal with central concerns of human life: 'Cinderella' for example, is about step-mothers and -sisters (Warner 1994). Folk tales are about rich and poor people, clever and foolish, good and wicked. Versions of traditional stories from around the world reflect such shared human concerns.

As children retell stories and decode pictures, using language of motive and of cause and effect (because . . ., so . . .), moving from simple predictable tales to more complex ones, they learn to create images of times and places which they have not experienced in reality. Holdaway (1979) describes how stories enable children to escape from the bonds of the present into the past and to extend their experience of the world, to explore emotion, intention, behaviour and human purpose.

Stories and play

As children get older they learn to recreate roles in their imaginative play (QCA 2000: 58, 62, 63; 2003: 20). Penelope Lively, who writes so vividly about her perceptions of time as a young child, in *Oleander, Jacaranda* (1994) says that she could 'slide off into another world at will . . . It can't be done now', and recalls how, hidden in the garden, she became Helen, lying in the arms of Paris, Achilles nobly dying, and how, as Daphne, she fled, feeling the wind in her hair and the strange shiver as she began to turn into a tree.

Sarra Garrs, the Bronte children's young servant, remembered how she was roped into playing a part in one of their plays, when Charlotte was five and Emily three. 'As an escaping prince, with a counterpane for a robe, I stepped from a window on the limbs of a cherry tree, which broke and let me down!' (Barker 1994).

Imagination seems to have been neglected in work on children's thinking (Meadows 1993: 361). Yet it involves the capacity to conceive what is not actually happening here and now and this requires knowledge and skills. Even if it transforms a story into the unreal and impossible the process is important. Such play involves concepts in which children are emotionally involved, such as good, evil, helplessness. It helps children to make sense of their world. These are the concerns of myths, legends, folk and fairy stories that once contributed to everybody's understanding of the world. And through 'let's pretend' play about stories children construct their own versions (QCA 2000: 25). This, in an embryonic way, is how all accounts of the past are constructed: by imagining, from what is known, how people in the past may have thought and felt and why they acted as they did. Garvey (1977: 32) found that children create appropriate behaviour for their role rather than simply imitate their own experience; they can become a princess or a knight or own a 'magic horse' – my son's favourite from a Russian folk tale ('Dun horse, magic horse come when I call you . . .') – and use experimental dialogue about supposed places and people in 'alternative worlds'. Children are also familiar with different interpretations in the style of illustrations of stories and different versions of traditional stories.

So do adults 'teach' about time?

Of course adults in educational settings traditionally build on or introduce children to stories about families, traditional tales and rhymes, images of past times; they help them to sequence, repeat, retell, and 'make up' stories long before they can decode text. They discuss what happens next and why, use the language of time and encourage children to explore stories through 'dressing-up' play. Traditionally they help children to mark and measure the passing of time:

morning, afternoon; day, night; days of the week, months and seasons. They do this in all sorts of ways, for example in cards and collages celebrating seasons, festivals, birthdays.

What more can adults do?

Maybe adults can best develop children's implicit awareness of and interest in past times and changes over time if they are themselves explicitly conscious of the skills and concepts that are central to the processes of finding out about the past, the questions to ask and ways of answering them. In this way children are gradually aware of the processes of their own learning and become independent learners. Discussion about the past is potentially a very powerful way of developing genuine extended shared thinking because usually there are no single correct answers and often children's ideas are surprisingly valid. And when children's 'guesses' are known to be wrong because of immaturity and limited knowledge, this does not matter. What is important is the process of guessing, listening to the ideas of others, and being prepared to change their own ideas, or to understand that sometimes there may be no 'right answer'. For young children, as for adult historians, finding out about the past involves:

- tracing causes and effects of changes over time; by
- making deductions and guesses about things which remain, for example asking why they were made and what they meant to the people who made and used them;
- understanding that there can be many different accounts of the past depending on what we know and how we interpret it and piece it together.

Such talk introduces the vocabulary of time.

Causes and effects of changes over time

We have already seen that adults often discuss time with children, in the context of their personal lives and of pictures, stories and rhymes. Maybe awareness just needs to be more explicit of possible open questions and knowing how to listen to children's answers and extend the discussion. Questions about changes over time involve reasoning about:

- causes and effects (why things may have happened or places changed);
- motives (why people may have acted as they did);
- similarity and difference (what was the same and what is different between 'now' and 'then'; why?);
- measuring the passing of time (time of day, days of the week, months, seasons, years);

■ sequencing events (in experience, in living memory and beyond).

Finding out about the past from things which remain

■ Knowing for certain – Sometimes photographs, artefacts, writing tell us things 'for certain'. We may be able to find out for certain: who is in the photograph, where it was taken, when and why; how the scrubbing board was used; how much we weighed as a baby.

■ Making good guesses – Often we cannot be certain and can only make 'good guesses' (I think, probably, maybe, perhaps). What are they saying, thinking, doing in the photograph? Who might have lived in the castle? What might they wear, eat? In this way children learn that there is often no single 'right' answer and that others may have different ideas, to which they need to listen and which may change their own ideas. They learn the language of hypothesis. What if? And they learn to explain their ideas to others.

John Betjeman's daughter Candida has written vividly about how her dad alerted her to 'the romance of the forgotten', how he 'created extra layers of wonder on top of what was already there'. He speculated about who might have made a building, who had leaned out of its windows to enjoy a view. This was not a boring academic exercise. 'It was the uncertainty of the information that made so many places come to life for me and convey the humanity of the place' (Lycett Green 2000: 156). Nulty (1998) describes how she used artefacts with her Key Stage 1 children (Arab clothes, replica Native American and Egyptian jewellery, a steel drum) in connection with stories about famous people, to stimulate problem solving, to help the children to hypothesise and to support their conclusions. Harnett (1998) has shown how she helped reception and Year 1 children make inferences about pictures with increasing skill.

Different 'interpretations' of the past

Stories, accounts of the past, are constructed by piecing together what we know and what we can 'guess' and filling in the gaps. Accounts of the past may vary depending on who does the selecting and what their particular interests are.

Children will come across different interpretations. Grandma may tell different stories about her childhood from Granddad. Two grandmas' accounts may differ, depending on where they lived, social class, how old they are, their personal experiences. Stories about long ago may change in the telling and retelling. They may be illustrated in different styles. Television versions of the stories of Robin Hood and Sherwood Forest reconstructions may be very different (see Chapter 5).

Children also create their own interpretations of the past in their play and in retelling stories. Of course small children's interpretations are immature and may be largely fanciful, but they are engaging with the process of imaginative interpretation which will become more likely with increased knowledge. Winnicot (in Bruce 1987: 71) suggested that adults are able to relate to powerful events, hero figures, music and paintings, if they have related to them and merged with what is important through play. Erikson (1965) found that if children were encouraged to reconstruct exciting scenes from folk tales through 'let's pretend' play, the stories they act out serve as metaphors for their lives, concerns and interests and help them to engage with the mainstream of human emotions in times and places other than their own. Langley Hamel (2003) gives excellent examples of how reception and Year 1 children understood that traditional tales become modified through the oral tradition, how they, in turn, modified them to reflect their own experiences and how this helped them to understand both familiar and unfamiliar worlds. Corbett (2003) has divided folk and fairy stories into categories. For example 'Little Red Riding Hood' is a 'warning' story; the main character promises to be good but soon becomes involved in the forbidden activity, something goes wrong, and rescue is needed. 'Cinderella' is a transformation story; a vulnerable character, mistreated in some way, overcomes the problem, often through kindness and is rewarded. In character stories a good character, set against the odds is heroic and is rewarded. Corbett shows how Key Stage 1 children can interpret these categories of story in the context of their own experiences and so become part of the mainstream of human experience over time.

There is a rich variety of opportunities for young children to engage with the past and construct their own interpretations of past times (Cooper 1998: 22–32; 2002: 64–94). Guest (1997) suggests how Littlenose stories (Grant 1990) can provide a starting point for making a role-play interpretation of a 'stone age shelter' (see Chapter 6). Bicknell (1998) describes role play in her nursery and reception class about a Victorian police station with Victorian photographs on the walls, after visiting the Robert Peel memorial in the locality. Alison Coleman (Cooper 2002: 36) found that a visit to Beamish Open Air Museum with a reception class led to discussion about how 'living history reconstructions' are made; the children needed help to understand that the staff did not really live in these conditions.

Using special vocabulary

In describing and making guesses about past times, children extend their vocabulary (QCA 2000: 52). They use words to describe:

- the passing of time (before, after);
- causes and effects of changes over time (because, so);
- similarities and differences between 'now' and 'then';
- the measurement of time (days, months, seasons).

They need to explicitly discuss:

- special words no longer used, which they encounter (tailor, chimney sweep);
- words still used but which may have had different meanings in the past, (princess, kingdom, knight).

Vygotsky (1986) showed that concepts are best learned gradually through use, trial and error, concrete examples and explicit discussion. Donaldson (1978) found that children rarely spontaneously question words or stories they do not understand.

Why place?

'The landscapes of infancy acquire a particular radiance which the passing of time brightens rather than dims', wrote Margaret Drabble (1979: 247) about the vivid descriptions of place many writers remember from their early childhood. Developing a sense of your environment involves observing and talking about its main characteristics, becoming articulate about what you like (or dislike) about it, maybe recording it in drawings, plans, models (QCA 2000: 96). Three- to four-year-olds will arrive in any early years setting with a huge amount of existing geographical vocabulary, experiences, knowledge and understanding which they can develop through play (Milner 1997). These skills are built on later. Children are increasingly able to relate plans and maps to photographs of key features, to use special vocabulary to describe places (river, stream; street, motorway; near, far; north, south) and to consider how the environment may be looked after. Children learn to find out about places, not just through experience but also from stories and information books; the people who live in them and the influence of the people on the place and vice versa (DfEE/QCA 1999: 110–11).

Why is it important for young children to find out about places?

Finding out about and identifying features in their environment, like developing concepts of time, is part of a child's developing sense of identity (QCA 2000: 96; 2003: 45). 'The immediate environment is a wealthy resource on which adults can draw if they are prepared to plan to do so' (Raikes 1991). To one head teacher it was part of her school's philosophy that learning, playing and dreaming have a unity which inspire each other, excite imagination and interest (Woods 1995). She went on to say that we learn about a place by touching, feeling, seeing and responding emotionally, then reinforce the experience through talking, writing, in art and in music. This, she said, provides concrete starting points for later symbolic and abstract thought.

It has also been argued that young children learn about their own environment by finding out about other places which are dramatically different and can be clearly contrasted with their own experience, although a visit to Oman in a 'place capsule' in Chapter 7 raises some questions about this. For some children and teachers with families who live or have lived in other parts of the country or the world this knowledge of other places may be innate; for others it needs to be planned (see Chapter 9).

Children construct their own sense of places

Although they may not be articulate about it, most young children seem to have an acute sense of place. Laurie Lee (1989: 7) writes about his first experience of long grass, aged three.

> The June grass amongst which I stood was taller than I was . . . I had never been so close to grass before . . . and all around me, each blade tattooed with tiger-skins of sunlight. It was knife-edge dark, and a wicked green, thick as a forest and alive with grasshoppers that chirped and chattered and leapt through the air like monkeys.

Children create their own fictional communities where endless adventure may happen. Robert Louis Stevenson (1885), ill in bed, created the 'land of counter-pane':

> I was the giant, great and still
> That sits upon the pillow hill
> And sees before him dale and plain
> The pleasant land of counterpane.

The Brontës' first plays were also 'Bed Plays'; The Islanders arose from 'several incidents which happened' (Barker 1994: 151–2). And before he was six C. S. Lewis created an 'Animal Land' in the attic, a Medieval world in which rabbits, in full chain-mail armour, rode out with great chivalry to catch cats. 'This invented world was – for me – full of interest, full of bustle, humour and character,' he later said (Green and Hooper 1974: 22). Similarly 'Julius', himself a fictional character (Burningham 1986), made himself a little home out of three chairs, the old curtains and a broom, then decided to dig a hole to the other side of the world, where he climbed the Chang Benang mountains and shot the rapids on the Chico Neeko River before returning for supper.

Children are aware of places different from their own through stories, from holidays and television. But without opportunities to talk about their experiences they may develop confused views. One reception class, during the war against Iraq, was helping the teacher make a 'beautiful beach', in a tray filled with fine, bright yellow sand on which they were arranging polished pebbles. When the teacher next looked it contained an ambulance, a helicopter and an army truck.

'Place' in educational settings

Traditionally early years settings include role-play areas, (QCA 2000: 25; 2003: 20). Usually these are linked to 'places' the children know which serve their community: home corners, shops, doctor's surgeries, hospitals, hairdressers. Or role-play places may be unfamiliar; it was a surprise to find a mosque in one Cumbrian reception class, containing informed and respectful worshippers (QCA 2000: 98). Places are sometimes imaginary, for example desert islands or caves, or places the children have visited, such as woods or beaches.

Outdoors may provide opportunities for larger scale play. I recently saw young builders working on a building site very similar to the one where the school extension was being built the other side of the safety mesh; the young builders were receiving sound advice from the professionals. Supplies were transported by a variety of vehicles made from giant construction kits to which cardboard sides, mirrors and battery powered lights had been added (QCA 2000: 50).

In another reception class the children made designs for their new nursery unit garden (see Chapter 8). Their teacher recommended Learning Through Landscapes as an excellent organisation which encourages the development of school grounds by the children (www.ltl.org.uk/schoolgrounds). The girls generally favoured tubs of sweet-smelling flowers while the boys preferred a quarry similar to the local quarry and a race track. (Some stereotypes resist contesting!) Designs were labelled: 'mtn-Aplan', 'Beni Da map', 'Matthew May plne'. Most (correctly) showed hills in the background labelled 'hills' or 'hilts'. Several had parking spaces for cars and bikes numbered one to five. 'Maybe it's because we'd just been doing one to five,' the teacher said. The children devised symbols to indicate their intentions. Tunnels had earth clearly shown on top and dots indicated gravel areas. A bike track had a wall around 'so that no one can get in'. Size was specified; Beni's sandpit instruction was 'big' (QCA 2000: 97). When I visited next term all of the children's ideas had been accommodated, albeit the quarry was only four foot high. Dean and Jackson (2003) write about ways of developing a sense of place through large scale, outdoor play: market stalls, petrol stations, tents.

On a visit to another school I was fortunate to find a workplace clearly meeting a need in the local community – a fashion designers' studio. (I ran one myself as a four-year-old and had hoped to train as a window dresser.) My preferences were discussed, material was chosen, and a design approved (QCA 2000: 90). Before I left I was presented with a velvet halter-neck top in a similar shade to my jacket (which was just as well since it did not quite meet at the back) and a wrap-around skirt with real buttons and buttonholes.

Weather, is a staple preschool interest – weather charts, collages showing sequences and characteristics of the seasons, and seasonal festivals (see Chapter 12). And of course adults read children stories and look at picture books about weather and places and journeys. *Dream Snow* (Carle 2000) is a magical book about when snow comes to a farm and *Cloudland* (Burningham 1996) and *Little Cloud* (Carle 1997) make us wonder what the ground looks like if you are flying on a cloud (see Chapter 10). *Where the Forest Meets the Sea* (Baker 1987) is a picture book conveying the beauty and the fragility of life and landscape on a small West Indian island, while following *Anno's Journey*, (Anno 1977) also a picture book, we can find out about the buildings in each of the towns and villages he passes through and about the work and leisure of their inhabitants. An excellent list of stories, rhymes and computer programs suitable as starting points for young children to find out about places can be found in *Geography in the Early Years* (Palmer 2003) and ideas for use of stories to develop a sense of place are discussed by Russell (2000) and by Rogers and Tucker (2003). Lewis (2003) shows how she used the story of *The Little Boat* (Henderson 1995) to develop awareness of other places with nursery children and Toye and Prendiville (2000) explore ways of developing stories about places as drama (see Chapter 11).

So how can adults further develop children's sense of place?

As with time concepts, adults need to be clear themselves about the content, vocabulary and skills associated with finding out about places. They need to be aware of the questions to ask and the ways of answering them, as a model for children to learn how to ask and answer their own questions about places.

Place

First, finding out about places involves finding out about:

- the features of places, both natural and man made;
- the people who live and work in a place and how they spend their leisure time;
- the way the environment influences their lives and vice versa;
- the services the community needs and about how goods and people are transported around the community and to and from other places.

Then it involves developing:

- an awareness of similarities and differences between places; and
- a sense of how you feel about a place, what you like and dislike and how you can look after the place.

Related themes include: how buildings are used; the kinds of work people do; types of transport; weather patterns; water in the environment (Raikes 1991).

How to find out about places

Skills involved in finding out about places include:

- observing and describing places (using all the senses);

- recording places and routes (real or imaginary), for example miniature land-scapes in sand and water trays or talking about positioning furniture in a dolls' house, making and reading simple plans and maps, recording as draw-ings, paintings, models or photographs; linking images to plans and maps (see Chapters 10 and 11);

- observing and recording patterns and processes, for example related to weather (Why is the sun not so hot today? Do you think it will rain? Why?), seasons (After winter it will be . . .?) and where things are located (If they build a lot of houses here what will the people also need close by?);

- understanding how the environment can be sustained, for example by not pick-ing wild flowers, not dropping litter (I watched one child assiduously cleaning the bird droppings from the nursery path with a yard broom and water!);

- using other sources to find out about places, for example stories, posters and information books.

As part of a whole-school (nursery–Year 2) topic on Africa, Langley Hamel and Hamel (2003) describe how they combined elements and universal themes of well-known western lullabies, stories and riddles with some broad aspects of African storytelling, both to enhance children's awareness of other places and to develop a rich variety of language work. For example Year 1 children made up a story about a lost elephant based on *The Hunter* (Geraghty 1994), then sang it as a Ghanean call-and-response game, 'Che che kole'. As part of the same project Toye (2003) developed teacher-led drama based on a traditional African story, 'Nnenna and her Udara Tree' (Izabezo 1993), which involved the nursery–Year 2 classes in exploring and discussing universal human themes in African contexts.

Using special vocabulary

The language involved in finding out about places includes:

- names of features – for example, tower block, cottage, lane, motorway, stream, river, shop, supermarket, church, fire station;

- language of direction – left, right, north, south, up, down;

- language of measurement – near, far, close, distant, big, small;

- positional language – above, below, beside;

- language related to weather and climate – sun, cloud, rain, wind, hot, cold, seasons;

- language of comparison – the same, different;

- likes, dislikes and explanations;

- language of sustainability and of hypothesis and argument – What if? I think . . ., because . . .;

- spatial patterns – moving vehicles around brick buildings on play mats;
- different viewpoints – What does it look like from the top of the slide?, from the pushchair?, the window of a high building?

Milner (1994) identifies a sequence of six types of question to ask nursery and reception children about place. The first questions encourage investigation, observation, description and information gathering, using appropriate vocabulary. 'What is this place like?' The next involve locational language and skills. 'Where is it?' 'How is it connected to other places?' Then, 'Why is it like this?' encourages children to formulate hypotheses from their knowledge and experience. 'What is it like to be in this place?' invites evaluation and a point of view and 'How is it similar to other places?' requires identifying similarities and differences. Milner emphasises the importance of effective planning of contexts in which to ask such questions, and the need to ensure that they are based in children's interests and personal biographies and encourage them to search for patterns, to act as travellers, explorers, investigators.

Why play?

As long ago as 1580 Montaigne, the French essayist wrote, 'It should be noted that most children at play are not playing about; their games should be seen as their most serious-minded activity' (Pal 1958). This was surprisingly long before the nineteenth-century pioneers of early childhood education, Montessori, Foebel, the MacMillan sisters, campaigned for play as central to learning, in reaction to rigid didactic teaching. Yet they all had slightly different ideas of what they meant by play. Long debates followed. Does play essentially involve imagination? Is it mainly concerned with exploring feelings – psychodynamic? Is it manipulative – model making and construction kits? Is it exploratory – finding out about materials and how things work? Where do games come in – chasing games, games of chance, matching games? If all these are different types of play what is the common factor? And underpinning all these questions: is play intrinsic – something children do spontaneously and in which adults should never become involved?; or is it extrinsic – a means to an end?; or something of both?

There is still no single theory which explains the significance of play in early childhood or the variety of activities and purposes which define play (Hughes 1991). Attempts to identify principles which underpin play (Bruce 1987) have been challenged by others (Macauley and Jackson 1992). Pellegrini's (1991) three dimensions provide a good basis for describing play activities: in play children are motivated; they make choices; they are disposed to explore, to be flexible, and are actively engaged.

Why is play important play?

Vygotsky (1978) convincingly explains the role of imaginative play in development. In play, he says, a child creates an imaginary situation in order to resolve the conflict between what they would *like* to do, but are constrained from doing and what they *can* do. Children's play, he suggests, is imagination in action, whereas adolescent imagination is play without action. In play a stick may become a horse. Therefore in play, objects and meaning are separated. This imaginative leap frees the child from the constraints of the immediate environment. A child is able to form new aspirations, in the role of a fictitious person. Children enjoy play so much that they learn to abide by the rules of the imaginary situation. For these reasons a child's greatest self-control occurs in play, and a child's greatest achievements are possible. In play, Vygotsky says, children always behave beyond their age and daily behaviour. Play, he says, is a leading factor in development. Play itself changes, beginning with situations very close to the real one (maybe in home-corner play). Gradually children consciously realise the purpose of play and creating imaginary situations as a means of developing abstract thought.

Imagining other times and places through play

This sort of imaginative play is particularly important in exploring concepts of time and place. It begins within children's own experiences, but extends to other times and places which can only be imagined. Moyles (1994) suggests that play builds a child's self-confidence in being able to learn about their world and Bruce (1987) contends that freeflow play – wallowing in ideas, feelings and relationships with competence – forms a fundamental part of fostering a child's creativity and wider learning, by supposing 'alternative worlds'.

Beetlestone (1998) sees play as a safe opportunity for risk-taking and testing out ideas. Moyles and Adams (2001) say that play can take children beyond any barriers to thinking; thoughts focus on pretence and endless possibilities. Children's recreation of other places and other times will inevitably rely to a great extent on pretence and imagination because they are immature, they do not understand the world from an adult's experience or point of view and their knowledge of the world is limited. But it is argued (Cooper 2000: 147) that children need to engage in the process of creating numerous imaginative suppositions about other times and places, through which, with maturity and greater knowledge, they are able to develop genuine imagination and empathy for people who live in times and places other than their own.

Time, place and broad holistic learning

Wood and Atfield (1996) emphasise the interaction of logic and reasoning with children's play. This enables them to construct 'what if' and 'as if' scenarios. Craft

(2002) suggests that all categories of play involve openness to 'possibilities' and Bruce and Meggitt (1991) suggest that a necessary part of children's play involves considering the possibilities through which the play may unfold. Such play involves not only creating interpretations or other times and places but also sequencing events over time and considering causes and effects, similarities and differences, reasons for people's actions. Moyles (1994) has suggested that the role of imaginative play in relation to learning is that through play children first explore, then use the knowledge they have. Later they recognise and subsequently transfer this knowledge to problem solve in other situations. Eventually they practise and revise the knowledge and skills involved, through play.

Garvey (1977) has emphasised the importance of play which reconstructs stories about the past or other places in social and emotional growth, since it involves experimental dialogue and allows children to explore emotions, relationships and situations, times and places outside their direct experience. Smilansky (1990 cited in Bennett *et al.* 1997) similarly says that social competence is increased by behaving in 'as if' and 'what if' situations, which sustain and convey pretence.

The role of adults in play

Some still claim that play is intrinsic and spontaneous and has an almost magical quality into which adults should never intervene and there is good evidence that this can be so. Penelope Lively (1994: 39) writes of her 'rich and creative life' with Steven, her neighbour in Egypt in the 1940s, who was a year older than she and how they 'pooled their respective skills'. She invented the games and he made the props. She shows us a photograph of them with bows and arrows and a wooden packing case. Penelope Lively says that they felt themselves to be involved in a 'mature preoccupation of significant business'. This play was rudely broken into by outsiders taking the photograph, and she still resents this. She still feels, despite the evidence, that it was not a packing case but a house with doors and windows and smoke coming out of the chimney and that outside the buffalo roamed. Sue Day and Jane Dixon (Chapter 8) have the greatest respect for such play.

However many children need to *learn* how to play – how to communicate verbally, to use material creatively, to think in divergent ways. Vicki Boertien (Chapter 3) and Wendy Robson (Chapter 4) realise that this is the starting place for the children in their classes. Meadows and Cashdan (1988: 39) found that sustained conversation and lively involvement which leads to creative, innovative play were rarely found in free play. Vygotsky (1976) and Bruner (1987) both say that social interaction with adults can enhance the quality of learning through play. Vygotsky sees this as helping children to create meaning from experience within a shared framework, to increase their knowledge and tools for thinking.

Bruner also sees adults, and children who are 'more knowledgeable others', both modelling learning skills and processes and transmitting relevant knowledge. Yet Sylva *et al.* (1980: 75) found that often adults are involved in managerial interactions, rather than providing cognitive challenge, and Ofsted (1993: 10) have concluded that 'in the poorer classes teachers over-direct work and under-direct play'.

Planning for play

Most teachers think that it is important to enable children to make choices and have a sense of ownership of their environment and their play (Bennett *et al.* 1997). This depends on creating environments with which children can actively engage, explore and take risks. It also depends on planning a rich variety of themes, play settings and experiences related to resources.

Play does need to be planned for, in terms of time, groupings, learning objectives, use of adults and quality interactions, while also remaining open-ended and integrated with the curriculum. (Examples of plans for the learning environment and for play activities in Chapters 3, 4, 7, 8, 9, and 12 show some of the ways in which teachers addressed this challenge.) Objectives need to be wide ranging and allow for different possibilities.

Children, if they are to feel ownership, need to be involved in negotiating and organising role play (Bennett *et al.* 1997). They need to learn to develop a story they know, to sequence ideas and adopt roles, take different roles and to take turns – the social skills necessary for making independent choices and decisions.

Time also needs to be planned for adults to observe and assess children's learning through play, so that they can feed back into curriculum planning. Jenny, one teacher who reviewed her practice, after watching videos of children in her class playing (Bennett *et al.* 1997), used a 'plan, do, review' planning model. She used review time to discuss planned play, to encourage children to make links and connections, experiment, initiate ideas, practise skills and to follow up ideas. She may, for example, teach them a new skill or a new song related to the play theme. Two other teachers participating in this project also assessed each of the National Curriculum subjects through play at Key Stage 1. They integrated play and teacher-directed activities through a topic approach, changing the topic each half term. The children were involved in the decisions. These teachers observed links between what the children were doing in play and when they were working with Jenny. These teachers were aiming for a curriculum model in which the adults' observations inform both child- and teacher-initiated activities.

Interactions

Shefatya (1990: 153) says that basic skills of play should be emphasised with younger children and that these seem to be the skills characterising the play of older children. For example, they may need to learn how to say what their role is, how to use objects as symbols, how to create and elaborate situations, how to co-operate. There seems to be a consensus that adult interventions should be in support of and in response to children's ideas. Children need to take roles and develop themes which interest them. However if there is a common ground of reci-procity between adults and children, and if the adult is sensitive to the meanings and intentions of children, adults can move their learning forward. Children between four- and five-years-old, for example, may ask for confirmation of events and experiences, through the questions they ask. Adults can encourage children to think about hypothetical experiences. In role, maybe for a short time, the adult is freed for real and meaningful discussion and can work collaboratively with children, listen to, value and preserve the authenticity of their ideas. Some adults are reluctant to participate in play unless children's ideas are flowing freely and they are invited to join in, in which case teaching during play is in response to the children's intentions.

Sensitive intervention allows adults to extend language, model, mediate, ask questions and focus children's attention on specific aspects. Adults may intervene to give some direction for a while, then withdraw.

The three teachers involved in Bennett *et al.*'s (1997) study all concluded that independence can only be achieved by both structuring play and by making teacher-directed activities more playful. They structured play by discussing stories with the children, letting the children set it up and make props, encouraging them to write and draw their story boards, as frameworks for play. They all came to realise that much of the curriculum can be taught through play. Hurst (1999) and Wood and Atfield (1996) all conclude that a proactive role in children's play is desirable.

Wood (1997) suggests that teaching children to become aware of the process involved in learning increases their ability to transfer learning to new situations. She suggests using circle time to teach children to be aware of the processes of their learning: to recall, reflect on action, evaluate, organise information, develop communication skills and learn forward planning. She thinks that children need to recognise the links between playing and learning, to become successful learners and that the knowledge and skills which children acquire through play form the building blocks of understanding, which can later be connected to the subject disciplines as an organising framework.

Curriculum Guidance for the Foundation Stage (QCA 2000: 25) represents a synop-sis of recent research. It states that through play children explore, develop and represent their learning experiences. This helps them to make sense of the world, to practise and build up ideas, concepts and skills, learn how to control impulses and understand rules, to co-operate and talk as they explore their feelings, take risks, make mistakes. In play children think creatively and imaginatively, and communicate with others to investigate or solve problems. The role of the adult is considered to be crucial in planning and resourcing a challenging environment, supporting children's learning through planned play activities, extending and supporting spontaneous play and extending and developing children's language and communication in play.

References

Allende, I. (2003) *A Memoir*. London: HarperCollins.

Anholt, C. (1988) *When I Was a Baby*. London: William Heinemann.

Anno, M. (1977) *Anno's Journey*. London: Bodley Head.

Baker, J. (1987) *Where the Forest Meets the Sea*. London: Julia MacRae Books.

Barker, J. (1994) *The Brontës*. London: Wiedenfeld and Nicholson.

Beetlestone, F. (1998) *Creative Teaching, Imaginative Children*. Buckingham: Open University Press.

Bennett, N., Wood, L. and Rogers, S. (1997) *Teaching Through Play: Teachers' thinking and classroom practice*. Buckingham: Open University Press.

Bicknell, G. (1998) 'Peel appeal: talking about the past with nursery and reception children', in Hoodless, P. (ed.) *History and English in the Primary School*. 8–19. London: Routledge.

Bruce, T. (1987) *Early Childhood Education*. London: Hodder and Stoughton.

Bruce, T. and Meggitt, C. (1991) *Time to Play in Early Childhood*. Sevenoaks: Hodder and Stoughton.

Bruner, J. S. (1987) *Making Sense: The child's construction of the world*. London: Methuen.

Burningham, J. (1984) *Grandpa*. London: Jonathan Cape.

Burningham, J. (1986) *Where's Julius?* London: Jonathan Cape.

Burningham, J. (1996) *Cloudland*. London: Jonathan Cape.

Carle, E. (1997) *Little Cloud*. Middlesex: Hamish Hamilton.

Carle, E. (2000) *Dream Snow*. London: Hamish Hamilton.

Cooper, H. (1998) 'Writing about history', in Hoodless, P. (ed.) *History and English in the Primary School*, 157–78. London: Routledge.

Cooper, H. (2000) *The Teaching of History in Primary Schools: Implementing the revised National Curriculum*, 3rd edn. London: David Fulton.

Cooper, H. (2002) *History in the Early Years*, 2nd edn. London: RoutledgeFalmer.

Corbett, P. (2003) *How to Teach Story Writing at Key Stage 1*. London: David Fulton.

Craft, A. (2002) *Creativity and Early Years Education: A life-wide foundation*. London: Continuum.

Dean, K. and Jackson, E. (2003) 'Geography and play: a sense of place in play', *Primary Geographer* **51**, 15–17.

Donaldson, M. (1978) *Children's Minds*. London: Fontana.

Drabble, M. (1979) *A Writer's Britain*. London: Thames and Hudson.

Erikson, E. H. (1965) *Childhood and Society*. London: Penguin.

Franklin, I. L. (1992) *The Old, Old Man and the Very Little Boy*. New York: Athenaum, Simon and Schuster.

Garvey, C. (1977) *Play (The Developing Child* series, Bruner, J., Cole, M. and Lloyd, B. (series eds)). London: Collins/Fontana.

Geraghty, P. (1994) *The Hunter*. London: Hutchinson.

Grant, J. (1990) *Littlenose Goes South*. London: Hodder and Stoughton.

Green, L. and Hooper, W. (1974) *C. S. Lewis, A Biography*. Glasgow: William Collins.

Guest, G. (1997) 'Developing design and technology through history', *Primary History* **17**, 4–6.

Harnett, P. (1998) 'Children working with pictures', in Hoodless, P. (ed.) *History and English in the Primary School*, 69–86. London: Routledge.

Henderson, K. (1995) *The Little Boat*. London: Walker Books.

Holdaway, D. (1979) *The Foundations of Literacy*. London and Sydney: Ashton Scholastic.

Hughes, F. F. P. (1991) *Children Play and Development*. Needham Heights, MA: Allyn and Bacon.

Hurst, V. (1999) *Planning for Early Learning: Education in the years before five*. London: Paul Chapman.

Izabezo, I. (1993) *Isimeme's Stories*. Barnstable, Devon: Spindlewood.

Kingsbury, B. (1998) 'Picture books for teaching history', *Primary History* **20**, 17–18.

Knowles, E. (ed.) (1999) *The Oxford Dictionary of Quotations*. Oxford: Oxford University Press.

Langley Hamel, K. (2003) 'Traditional stories and rhymes: Goldilocks don't do owt!' in Cooper, H. and Sixsmith, C. (eds) *Teaching Across the Early Years 3–7: Curriculum coherence and continuity*, 46–55. London: RoutledgeFalmer.

Langley Hamel, K. and Hamel, K. (2003) 'Out of Africa? Lullabies, riddles and stories', in Cooper, H. and Sixsmith, C. (eds) *Teaching Across the Early Years 3–7: Curriculum coherence and continuity*. 131–6. London: RoutledgeFalmer.

Lee, L. (1989) *Cider with Rosie*. London: Cresset Press.

Lewis, L. (2003) 'The Little Boat', *Primary Geographer* **51** (April), 24–5.

Lively, P. (1994) *Oleander, Jacaranda*. London: Penguin.

Lycett Green, C. (2000) *Over the Hills and Far Away*. London: Black Swan.

Macauley, H. and Jackson, P. (1992) *Educating Young Children: A structured approach*. London: David Fulton.

Meadows, S. (1993) *The Child as Thinker: The development and acquisition of cognition in childhood*. London: Routledge.

Meadows, S. and Cashdan, A. (1988) *Teaching Styles in Nursery Education: Final report to SSRC*. Sheffield: Sheffield City Polytechnic.

Milne, A. A. (1926) *Winnie-the-Pooh*. London: Methuen.

Milner, A. M. (1994) *Geography Starts Here! Practical approaches with nursery and reception children*. Sheffield: The Geographical Association.

Milner, A. M. (1997) *Geography Through Play: Structured play at Key Stage 1*. Sheffield: The Geographical Association.

Moyles, J. (ed.) (1994) *The Excellence of Play*. Buckingham: Open University Press.

Moyles, J. and Adams, S. (2001) *StEPS: Statements of entitlement to play: a framework for play*. Buckingham: Open University Press.

Nulty, P. (1998) 'Talking about artefacts at Key Stage 1: promoting and assessing listening and speaking', in Hoodless, P. (ed.) *History and English in Primary Schools*, 20–34. London: Routledge.

Ofsted (Office for Standards in Education) (1993) *First Class: The standards and quality of education in reception classes*. London: HMSO.

Pal, M. (ed.) (1958) *Essais* (translated by Cohen, J.M.), Harmondsworth: Penguin.

Palmer, J. A. (2003) *Geography in the Early Years*, 2nd edn. London: Routledge.

Pellegrini, A. D. (1991) *Applied Child Development: a developmental approach*. Hillsdale, NJ: Lawrence Erlbaum.

Qualifications and Curriculum Authority (QCA) (2003) *The Foundation Stage Profile*. London: QCA.

Raikes, J. (1991) *Planning for Geography in the National Curriculum, Key Stage 1*. London: The Geographical Association.

Rogers, S. and Tucker, K. (2003) 'Mind travel', *Primary Geographer* **51** (April), 13–14.

Rowse, A. L. (1946) *The Use of History*. London: Hodder and Stoughton.

Russell, K. (2000) 'Stories of place', *Primary Geographer* **47**, 34–5.

Salter, K. (1996) 'Grace Darling and reception children', *Primary History* **14**, 18–19.

Shefatya, L. (1990) 'Socio-economic status and ethnic differences in sociodramatic play: theoretical and practical implications', in Klugman, E. and Smilansky, S. (eds) *Children's Play and Learning Perspectives and Policy Implications*. New York: Teacher's College Press.

Stevenson, R. L. (1985) *A Child's Garden of Verses*. London: Gollancz.

Sylva, K., Roy, C. and Painter, M. (1980) *Childwatching at Playgroup and Nursery*. London: Grant McIntyre.

Toye, N. (2003) 'Finding a voice – drama and young children', in Cooper, H. and Sixsmith, C. (eds) *Teaching Across the Early Years 3–7: Curriculum coherence and continuity*, 106–19. London: RoutledgeFalmer.

Toye, N. and Prendiville, F. (2000) *Drama and Traditional Story for the Early Years*. London: Routledge.

Vygotsky, L. S. (1976) *Mind in Society: The development of psychological processes*. Harvard: Harvard University Press.

Vygotsky, L. S. (1986) *Thought and Language* (translated, revised and edited by Alex Kozulin). Massachusetts: Massachusetts Institute of Technology.

Waddell, M. (1992) *The Hidden House*. London: Walker Books.

Warner, M. (1994) *The Beast and the Blonde: Fairy tales and their tellers*. London: Chatto and Windus.

Wood, L. (1997) *Teaching Through Play: Teaching thinking and classroom practice*. Neville-Buckingham: Open University Press.

Wood, E. and Atfield, J. (1996) *Play Learning and the Early Childhood Curriculum*. London: Paul Chapman Press.

Woods, P. (1995) *Creative Teachers in their Primary Schools*. Buckingham: Open University Press.

Resources referred to in the text

Beamish Open Air Museum, www.beamishmuseum.co.uk

Learning Through Landscapes (the UK School Grounds Charity)
    3rd Floor, Southside Offices
    The Law Courts
    Winchester SO23 9DL
    www.ltl.org.uk schoolgrounds

All about us

Deborah Seward and Vicki Boertien

Introduction

THE AIM OF THIS CHAPTER is to illustrate how the 'embryonic capacity for historical thinking' (H. Cooper 2002: 2) can be fostered with children in the Foundation Stage through a study of the popular topic of 'Ourselves'. The teacher involved is a newly qualified teacher working in an early years unit in a school in a northern city, in particularly challenging circumstances. The chapter will outline her aims for the topic linked to Foundation Stage principles and planning requirements. Examples of planning and learning activities are included to illustrate the miriad of possibilities this topic has for developing children's historical knowledge, skills and understanding.

The school

Kestrel Bank Primary School is situated near the city centre in an economically and socially disadvantaged area. Many of the children have a statement of special educational need. The early years unit consists of children aged three- to five-years-old who need considerable support in developing their communication, language, literacy and mathematical skills and in accelerating their personal, social and emotional development. In the recent Ofsted Inspection (autumn 2002) the teaching in the early years unit was recognised as being consistently good, making a positive impact on pupils' achievement.

It was in this challenging context that a newly qualified teacher, Vicki Boertien, found herself working. Having established the unit and undergone an inspection during her first term of full time teaching, Vicki was concerned about the children's ability to work and play together and their limited communication skills. She wanted to develop a topic which would engage the children on an individual level, would motivate them to participate and encourage communication and social interaction. She decided on a popular topic, 'Ourselves', as she felt this was an area all children could participate in, whatever their level of competence. She felt it would build confidence and self-esteem by developing personal pride and encourage children to share what they already knew. In line with the best examples of early years practice she would be 'starting from the child'. She felt that in accordance with 'Principles for Early Years Education' (QCA 2000: 11) it would help to ensure that all children felt valued and secure in the setting. She was also keen to ensure that positive attitudes towards learning were established and felt that this topic would enable her to achieve this goal. The topic was undertaken in the spring term of 2003 when the children were well established in the unit and familiar with the routines of the school day.

The early years unit

The newly established unit caters for 26 children aged between three and five. Eleven are reception-aged pupils attending for the whole school week and 14 are nursery-aged children attending for afternoon sessions. The unit is large and spacious, bright and colourful. Distinct areas for activity are identified:

- a literacy area – a quiet carpeted area with books, story sacks, large beanbags, whiteboard and magnetic letters;
- a listening area with story tapes and books;
- a music area containing a range of large and small instruments and rhyme books;
- a 'topic' area which changes with each new topic, but currently contains a birthday display, balloons, parcels, books, the sorting activity described later and child-created objects, such as birthday cards and a birthday chart;
- a maths area with resources which include a number washing line, jigsaws, weighing scales, two- and three-dimensional shapes, threading equipment, pegboards, money, dominoes, unifix and compare bears;
- a large 'wet' area for messy activities, such as painting, model making, sand/water play;
- a role-play area, currently a home with 'party' resources;
- a large area with climbing frame and staging so children have space for large play equipment, including bricks, blocks and soft play equipment;
- a computer area containing three computers and two printers.

These areas are clearly separated by creative use of furniture and home-made wooden fencing. All equipment is labelled, tidy and easily accessible for the children as a means of encouraging independence and self initiated activity. The walls are brightly decorated with both teacher- and child-created displays, sending out the message that everyone's work is valued and highly thought of. These displays include a daily weather chart identifying the day of the week (basic beginnings of chronological understanding) and a birthday chart in the 'topic' area, showing the months of the year with children's pictures beside each month. Vividly coloured child-made mobiles dangle from the ceiling and sway gently in the draught. This is clearly a classroom where children are expected to be actively involved in the learning process and Vicki's beliefs that children need to be involved and valued are implicit in her classroom organisation. The areas are planned for in both medium- and long-term planning. An example of Vicki's planning for resources can be seen in Figure 3.1.

Planning

Before this topic was planned Vicki had spent a term becoming familiar with the children in the unit. She knew their strengths and areas for development and it was this that encouraged her to take on the topic, 'Ourselves'. She was aware of the importance of making learning meaningful and appropriate to the particular needs of these children, and of their limited concentration spans. As Fisher (2002: 15) states children need 'a learning environment that offers concrete experiences that are relevant, meaningful and worthy of active involvement'. This was one of the guiding principles underpinning the whole topic. Alongside this belief about the importance of active involvement was the identified need to develop children's social and communication skills. The opportunities offered by the topic for describing, questioning, investigating, explaining, sequencing and communicating match many of the processes involved in learning history. This meant that the topic would address many of the Stepping Stones and Early Learning Goals in Knowledge and Understanding of the World (QCA 2000: 95). As Purkis (1996: 295) acknowledges:

> The methods used by a historian or archaeologist are entirely consistent with the best teaching practice in the early years. The key words are exploration, investigation and problem solving. The learning objectives are to enable the children to both describe and explain the past.

As these elements are present in quality play, Vicki felt it was a very important aspect of her role to develop these skills through the resources and activities she used and in teaching. This was a significant focus of the topic she wished to develop with the children in the unit, so these would be highlighted in her holistic approach to 'Ourselves'.

The other area she wished to develop was children's use of language. This was an area for improvement for all the children and was a recognised weakness on entry to the unit. There is a consensus view that language is central to the development of historical thinking (H. Cooper 2002; C. Cooper 2002; Purkis 1996) and so

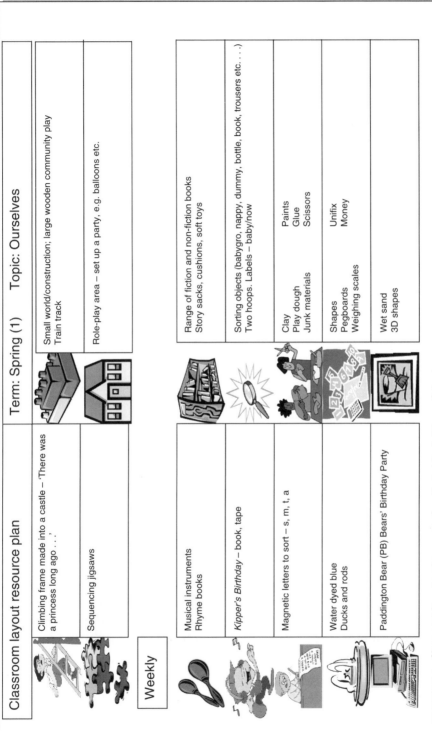

Classroom layout resource plan | **Term: Spring (1)** | **Topic: Ourselves**

Climbing frame made into a castle – 'There was a princess long ago . . .'

Sequencing jigsaws

Small world/construction; large wooden community play
Train track

Role-play area – set up a party, e.g. balloons etc.

Weekly

Musical instruments
Rhyme books

Kipper's Birthday – book, tape

Magnetic letters to sort – s, m, t, a

Water dyed blue
Ducks and rods

Paddington Bear (PB) Bears' Birthday Party

Range of fiction and non-fiction books
Story sacks, cushions, soft toys

Sorting objects (babygro, nappy, dummy, bottle, book, trousers etc. . . .)
Two hoops. Labels – baby/now

Clay   Paints
Play dough   Glue
Junk materials   Scissors

Shapes   Unifix
Pegboards   Money
Weighing scales

Wet sand
3D shapes

FIGURE 3.1   Classroom layout and resource plan, Kestrel Bank Primary School

the role of any teacher is to provide the context and model for correct use of vocabulary. As Fisher (2002: 296) highlights: 'It is the teacher who must ensure that there is something interesting to talk about, initiate and sustain the quality of language and steer discussion from mere observation and description to investigation and hypothesis.' Vicki felt the topic would be interesting and a focus of her role would be to encourage discussion, develop vocabulary and encourage the notion of hypothesis.

Vicki had also noticed the difficulty many of the children had in playing. Many had limited opportunities for quality play before entering the unit and playing together was problematical. She had discovered over the previous term that the children frequently required guidance and adult support if successful play experiences were to be established. These observations would be supported by Hilary Cooper (2002: 27) who states 'young children do not always find free play as easy and natural as theories suggest'. Vicki realised she needed to establish a context which was familiar to the children and so that they could use their existing knowledge and skills to play and learn together. She had to adopt a proactive role in creating meaningful play situations to stimulate curiosity, co-operation and problem solving. The crucial role of play in the Foundation Stage has been emphasised (QCA 2000: 25). It was important for Vicki to plan for play activities as there was the possibility little would be forthcoming from the children themselves, but equally she had to be open and responsive to suggestions which may be made by the children.

These then were the issues and aspirations Vicki had in mind when she began her planning. The completed detailed medium-term plans are shown in Figure 3.2 and examples of short-term planning for activities used are given in Figures 3.3, 3.4 and 3.5.

The activities

The following represent a snapshot of some of the activities that took place as part of the 'Ourselves' topic. In many ways Vicki achieved her aim of making the learning meaningful to the children and creating motivation. Throughout the activities the children were enthusiastic and well motivated. They encouraged their parents to find and provide photographs of them as babies to compare with current pictures taken by Vicki. This was a valuable, almost incidental, aspect of the topic as it established a dialogue with parents and encouraged them into the classroom. This helped Vicki develop a partnership with parents to support their children's learning. 'Parents are children's first and most enduring educators' (QCA 2000: 9). The children eagerly discussed their photographs and were keen to show and share them with the whole class which created enjoyment in learning.

Medium-term Planning: Kestrel Bank Primary School	Term: 2 (2)	Topic: Ourselves
Designing and Making Skills ■ Join construction pieces together to build and balance ■ Begin to try out a range of tools and techniques safely ■ Build and construct with a wide range of objects, selecting appropriate resources, and adapting their work where necessary	**Exploration and Investigation** ■ Show curiosity, observe and manipulate objects ■ Describe simple features of objects and events ■ Sort objects by one function ■ Talk about what is seen and what is happening ■ Find out about, and identify, some features of living things, objects and events they observe	**Sense of Place** ■ Show an interest in the world in which they live ■ Comment and ask questions about where they live and the natural world ■ Find out about their environment and talk about those features they like
Wooden construction – making bridges ('Billy Goats Gruff') and houses ('Three Little Pigs') Train track Make houses and bridges from Duplo/Stickle bricks Make 3D houses using inside out boxes, paint, stick straw	Spring work – look at real flowers, e.g. snowdrops and daffodils. Naming parts. Talk about function of parts Bake biscuits. Talk about the materials changing Bake porridge (Goldilocks) – talk about the change of materials, change of taste Look and sort sticks, cement, bricks, straw. Talk about the materials – which is best for a house? Why? (raining etc.) Talk about things that come out of eggs – observe tadpoles growing. Bring real chicks into classroom	Spring work – talk about the seasons, observe trees, daily weather chart Weekly visit to shop to buy snack – talk about journey, identifying features they observe on the way Visit to post office
Outdoors Trip to post office Walk to shops Spring trees	**KNOWLEDGE AND UNDERSTANDING OF THE WORLD** Assessment: Questioning/Discussion/Finished products	**Role play** Post office – calculator, birthday cards, different packages, scales, money, hats, shoes, posters, post box, black sack. Party corner – presents, balloons, invitations etc.
Cultures and Beliefs ■ Express feelings about a significant personal event ■ Describe significant events for family or friends ■ Gain an awareness of the cultures and beliefs of others	**Information and Communication Technology** ■ Know how to operate simple equipment ■ Find out about and identify the uses of everyday technology and communication technology and programmable toys to support their learning	**Sense of Time** ■ Remember and talk about significant things that have happened to them ■ Begin to differentiate between past and present
See 'Special things and harvest' medium-term plan Birthday work Easter work – Palm Sunday, Good Friday Make Easter cards	Listening centre Computer area – PB Bears' Birthday Party, Topsy and Tim etc.	Talk about birthdays – *Kipper's Birthday, Wibbly Pig Opens his Presents.* Make birthday cards Sequence literacy stories Change day of the week pointer Spring work – talk about the seasons, observe growth of animals Life sequencing jigsaws Sort objects that they had when they were a baby to objects that they have nowadays – nappies, bottle and cup, dummy, reins, clothes, book etc. Children bring in baby photographs. Sequence people photographs into chronological order Make a class birthday chart

FIGURE 3.2 Medium-term plans: Knowledge and understanding of the World

---

Activity Sheet

Class: Reception   **Teacher:** Miss Boertien

Date: 31/03/03

Learning area: Knowledge and Understanding of the World (sense of time)

Learning objective: To be able to place pictures from a baby to an adult in the correct order.

Resources:

- Each child has own baby photograph
- Photographs of teacher as baby, child and adult
- Old photograph – black and white
- Photo album

Description of shared activity:

Teacher spreads out range of photos on the table alongside photo album. Children are encouraged to help sort photos discussing similarity/difference, change. What are people in photo wearing? Can you tell who they are? Talk about how their appearances have changed (e.g. size, hair). Teacher can introduce a photograph of when they were a baby. Then the teacher shows a black and white photograph of own father. What is different about this photograph? (black and white, clothes etc.). Create the problem of needing to sequence three photographs of the teacher for the album. May want to use a washing line or Blu tac to display sequence. Use terminology such as 'then', 'now', 'baby', 'child', 'first', 'second' and 'last'. Why have they put photos in that particular order?

Follow-up activity (where appropriate): Explain to the children that now they are going to cut, order and stick three pictures of a person's life. The children will also be encouraged to write a caption underneath each picture.

Independently: Children sort sequencing cards.

Differentiation: Adult support during follow-up activity for less able children.

Success criteria: Children will be able to sequence the pictures in the correct order.

FIGURE 3.3 Plan for activity to order pictures from baby to adult

Using photographs with reception children

Prior to this activity the children and Vicki had shared the big book *My History* (Hughes 1997) in which they had examined pictures of babies and toddlers. They had had wide-ranging discussions about what they could do as babies and what they could do now and the vocabulary 'then' and 'now' had been introduced. To extend this activity and fire curiosity Vicki placed a range of photographs on a table. These consisted of photographs of the children as babies or toddlers and present day ones, photographs of Vicki as a baby, toddler and now and an older photograph of Vicki's father. The children were curious and wanted to know what she was doing. She said that she was trying to sort out the pictures for

---

Activity Sheet

Class: Reception   **Teacher:** Miss Boertien

Date: 01/04/03

Learning area: Knowledge and Understanding of the World (sense of time)

Learning objective: To be able to sort objects into those they used as baby and those that they use now.

Resources:

- Two hoops
- Labels – 'baby (then)'/'now'
- Bag of different objects – nappy, dummy, bottle, babygro, cup, child-sized shoes, toothbrush, pencil, book, potty etc.

Description of shared activity:

This activity will take place after children have read *My History* and talked about pictures and related these to the children's own photographs. They will have answered questions such as: Can they remember being that age? What can they do now that they couldn't when they were a baby? Two hoops will be placed on the carpet with appropriate labels 'baby (then)' and 'now'. The one labelled baby has a doll beside it as a prompt for the children. A big bag of objects is placed next to the hoops and children are encouraged to work in pairs to sort the items into the hoops. Children will support each other. To stimulate discussion, ask the children why they placed their object in that hoop.

FIGURE 3.4   Plan for activity to sort objects into those used as a baby and those used now

---

Activity Sheet

Class: Nursery   **Teacher:** Miss Boertien

Date: 02/03/03   **Teaching assistant:** Mrs Rose

Learning area: Knowledge and Understanding of the World (sense of time)

Learning objective: To be able to talk about their own birthday experiences.

Resources:

- Book – *Wibbly Pig Opens his Presents* (Inkpen 1995) and Wibbly Pig soft toy
- birthday banner; balloons; birthday cards; presents; card, glitter pens and foil paper

Description of shared activity: Stimulate discussion about birthdays by showing the children presents, cards etc. Show the children Wibbly Pig, explain that today is his birthday. Read book. Allow the children to sequence the story and talk about their birthday experiences.

Follow-up activity: Role-play area set up as a 'party corner' encourage children to write invitations, cards, bake cakes and hold a party. Children may want to make a birthday card for Wibbly Pig. Ensure resources are available, i.e. card, glitter pens and foil paper for children to decorate card. Encourage children to write name (mark-making) inside card. Use cards and objects from shared task to make a display.

FIGURE 3.5   Plan for activity to talk about birthday experiences

a photograph album, so creating a problem for the children to solve. A number of children said they would help and a wide-ranging discussion began.

Nick: Look this is me, I'm having dinner.
Vicki: How do you know that?
Nick: I've got a bowl!
Vicki: So you have. Is there anything else that tells us you are having dinner?
Nick: Yes, I'm wearing a bib.
Simon: (laughing) You've got food round your mouth!

It is clear from this discussion that the children were beginning to use the photographs as evidence and were making deductions from what they could see in the pictures. This ability would clearly be developed in Key Stage 1 where children are encouraged to work with a range of sources of evidence (DfEE/QCA 1999; Knowledge, skills and understanding (KSU) 4a). The conversations continued with Vicki providing 'scaffolding' and 'modelling' through her use of questions such as:

What's happening in this picture?

How do you know?

How can we tell?

Who took the picture?

Why?

Where was the picture taken?

How have you changed?

What's different?

Are all the pictures of babies similar/different? Why?

This use of careful questioning is appropriate not only to young children (QCA 2000: 84) but also to children in Key Stage 1 as they are asked to 'ask and answer questions about the past' (DfEE/QCA 1999: 104). The children responded positively and were genuinely interested in all the pictures and showed they were able to observe, hypothesise and explain – fundamental skills to be developed in history.

Sam: (squealing with delight) Look, it's me. I'm a toddler, I climbed the steps on my own. (This was clearly a significant moment for Sam.)
Vicki: Did you? That's really clever. How old were you? Can you remember?
Sam: I was two and it was at the park.
Vicki: (to all the children involved) I didn't recognise you. How has Sam changed?
Carla: He's got blond hair.
Shona: His hair is different now.
Vicki: Yes, what colour is it now?

Children: Brown.

Vicki: Yes, it has changed. Sometimes our hair changes as we grow older.

Carla: Babies don't have much hair; my sister hasn't.

Shona: Your hair grows like you.

It was clear from this activity that the children were aware of changes which took place as they grew up and they could identify differences in appearance and Sam was able to share his experiences. These are the beginning steps in being able to identify similarity and difference which is an important aspect of historical thinking developed in Key Stage 1.

During the activity the children discovered the old photograph of Vicki's father, which was black and white, and were intrigued by it.

Martin: (holding the picture for all to see): Look at this.

Children: Oh!

Vicki: Is there anything different about this picture?

Children: Yes.

Lisa: It's grey.

Vicki: Yes, it's black and white.

Martin: They didn't have coloured pictures a long time ago, they couldn't make them.

Sam: There are more children in the picture.

Lisa: And they're wearing different clothes?

Vicki: Yes, they are. This is my dad and his sisters.

Martin: Is it old then?

Vicki: What do you think?

From this short dialogue extract the children were clearly engaging with the picture and beginning to copy Vicki's model of questioning by asking their own questions, so laying the foundations for future development of enquiry skills (KSU, 4b) at Key Stage 1 (DfEE/QCA 1999: 104). It is also clear that these children were developing the 'language for communication skills' identified in Foundation Stage (QCA 2000: 49).

As the children were able to distinguish between photographs of 'then' and 'now' Vicki decided to develop this activity to see if the children could sequence three photographs, so she introduced a problem to be solved. She introduced three photographs of herself: one as a baby, one aged four (the same age as some of the children) and an up-to-date picture.

Vicki: Look, I've got three pictures of me here. I want to put them in the right order in the album. Can you help me?

Children: (chorus) Yes.

Vicki: Well which one should I start with? (Simon picks up the picture of Vicki aged four and places it at the left-hand side of the table.)

Vicki: Is that right, does this one go first?

Alex: No, it's the one where you're a baby.
Hope: Yes, this one (holding up the correct photograph).
Vicki: Alright, is it this one next (holding up her most recent picture)?
Children: No.
Vicki: Why not?
Alex: Because you're older in that one. It comes after this (pointing at
             Vicki aged four).
Vicki: Well done, put them in the right order. Yes, that's me aged one, then
             four and now.

Clearly Alex and Hope were beginning to sequence the three pictures with confidence and giving explanations as to why they had organised them in this way. It is notion of sequence, which is further developed in Key Stage 1, as children begin to develop a sense of chronology and time (DfEE/QCA 1999, KSU 1a & b). These activities were designed to stimulate early historical thinking with the conversations critical in helping Vicki identify what the children know, can do and understand. Indeed she was pleasantly surprised at the level of thinking and understanding taking place.

Mystery bag with reception children

This activity followed the activities above and numerous discussions about babies, change and differences between then and now. Vicki had a large sack filled with items belonging to a baby and a child of five. This was placed on the carpet along with two hoops labelled 'baby (then)' and 'now' and was an activity the children could attempt in pairs. The aim was that the children would discuss and support each other in sorting the items. This ability to sort objects and distinguish between 'then' and 'now' is fundamental to understanding change over time, as is the use of vocabulary and explanation as to why objects are sorted in a particular way. This was designed as an independent activity with an element of fun and mystery; children are 'highly motivated by novelty' Whitebread (1996: 12). The questions for Vicki were: will the children be drawn to the activity and will they complete it independently, supporting each other in the process?
    Two children were intrigued by the brightly coloured sack.

Children: Miss Boertien, what's in here?
Vicki: Would you like to find out?
Children: Yes!

Vicki explains that some things belonging to a baby and a five-year-old have been mixed up and need sorting into the hoops with the labels on. The children recognise the words 'then' and 'now' and offer to sort the items.

Taylor: (pulls out the first item) Look, it's a baby shoe, it's small. I'll put it in here
             (selects correct hoop).

Oliver: (pulls out second item then laughing) It's a potty!

Taylor: My baby sister has one of those, it's for babies (directs Oliver to the correct hoop).

Taylor: My turn. It's a wellie! (He places it in the wrong hoop.)

Oliver: That's not right, it's too big. I wear one like that (puts it in correct hoop).

The boys go on to sort a T-shirt, book, nappy and dummy into the correct hoops. Vicki returns.

Vicki: Well done. Why did you put this book in here?

Taylor: Because it's big.

Oliver: No, because babies don't read books. We do.

Vicki: (picking up the T-shirt) Why did you put this here, in the 'now' hoop?

Taylor: Because it's big.

Vicki: Would a baby wear it?

Taylor: No, it's too big, they wear babygros.

This dialogue indicates the boys were beginning to have an understanding between 'then' and 'now' and differences between the baby things and other items. However, Taylor seemed confused by 'now' and the notion of size whereas Oliver seemed much more confident in his interpretation of the terms. It was Vicki's thoughtful intervention and awareness of what the boys were doing that enabled her to assess what each understood. These are the kind of initial activities which are developed in Key Stage 1 as children move on to sorting more unfamiliar objects, artefacts or pictures and continue to develop vocabulary in communicating what they know.

Jigsaws and reception children

Another common article found in early years classrooms is the jigsaw, which helps to develop fine motor skills, problem solving, sequencing and provides a fun way of learning. The children in Vicki's unit enjoyed the challenge of a jigsaw so she ensured that for this topic she had a range of jigsaws available dealing with familiar sequences, such as getting dressed, daily sequences and growing up. The children frequently chose these as activities they wanted to engage in, but there was limited discussion between children about the sequence involved. They were more concerned with the practical problems of finding pieces and making them fit.

Andrew and David were working on similar jigsaws.

Andrew: I've done the baby.

David: I've nearly done mine.

Vicki: What comes next?

Andrew: A boy.

Vicki: Yes, you grow into a boy.

David: Mine has a girl next, then a lady.

Andrew: I have a dad next, after the boy, then it's the old man.

David: I have an old lady after the lady, she's like my grandma – she's old.

The boys were clearly aware of appropriate language, the sequence of growing up and ageing, even though this wasn't always verbalised and David had a definite idea that grandparents were old. This would link comfortably with Key Stage 1 work where children are encouraged to 'find out about the lives of members of their family and of others around them' (DfEE/QCA 1999: 104).

The nursery children and Wibbly Pig

Vicki decided to introduce the idea of 'significant events' to the nursery children through birthdays. She used a favourite story character, 'Wibbly Pig', who was a resident occupant of the classroom (Inkpen 1995). The soft toy version of Wibbly Pig was sat next to Vicki as well as a selection of brightly coloured, interesting objects all relating to birthdays. Vicki initiated the conversation with an element of surprise, which immediately stimulated the children's interest.

Vicki: Wow! Look at this, what are these?

                  Children name a balloon, present, card and banner.

Vicki: Elliot would you like to hold this? What does it say?

                  Elliot and Vicki hold up a party banner.

Children: (chorus) Happy birthday!

Emma: It's someone's birthday!

Vicki: Yes, whose birthday could it be? Is it yours Emma?

                  Emma shakes her head.

Vicki: What about you, Luke, is it your birthday?

                  Luke shakes his head.

                  The children look puzzled so Vicki suggests they look for clues.

Vicki: Look, this card has number three on it. Who's three?

Lucy: I'm three.

Katie: (proudly) I'm four.

Vicki: Can anyone remember their birthday?

Luke: I got lots of presents.

Daniel: I got dinosaurs.

Katie: I had a Barbie cake and lots of cards.

Vicki: (going back to the card) Let's see who this card is for. (She opens the card.)
                  Oh, it's to Wibbly Pig! I wonder what he will get for his birthday.

The children go on to predict items people receive on their birthdays and then Vicki reads the story, *Wibbly Pig Opens his Presents* (Inkpen 1995) inviting the children to predict and finally sequence events. This activity showed that the children were able to talk about their birthdays and had a sense of associated items relating to birthdays, the initial 'Stepping Stone' relating to 'a sense of time' (QCA 2000: 95).

They could make simple predictions and sequence the story; valuable early reading skills as well as an 'embryonic' chronological skill. This was further extended when the children, playing in the role-play area, which contained items relating to birthdays, decided to make their own birthday cards for Wibbly Pig. This child-initiated activity developed not only communication skills, but also designing and making skills (QCA 2000: 91).

These activities illustrated to Vicki that the nursery children were able to talk about their own personal birthday experiences, identifying key aspects relating to birthday celebrations and had a clear idea of themselves in time. They talked extensively about parties, presents and future birthdays and began to develop turn taking and responding to each other, especially through role play in the role-play area.

Extending the activities

The preceding activities are only a snapshot of some of the learning that took place in Vicki's classroom which related to the children's developing sense of time. Vicki went on to develop these in a number of ways through a variety of play-orientated activities which were both teacher- and child-initiated.

She extended the photograph activity by introducing more photographs of the children and keeping it relevant to them until they sequenced up to five personal pictures, one for each year, accompanied by captions. This notion of change over time was also extended by Vicki's holistic approach and the introduction of the life cycle of a frog, which the children were fascinated by as they watched tadpoles develop. An emphasis on sequencing stories further developed the Early Learning Goals for language and communication (QCA 2000: 53). This helped the children to develop the ability to observe, predict and sequence, all skills that are further developed through history at Key Stage 1.

Throughout the rest of the year the children continued to look at changes in the weather through the days and seasons; and birthdays, highlighted by the children's display, were celebrated. They sequenced their daily activities and discussed events that had taken place 'before' and 'after' play/lunch. They began to talk about 'in the morning' and 'in the afternoon' and 'yesterday', 'today' and 'tomorrow' were introduced and used. Such traditionally good practice in the early years classroom is an essential step in laying the foundations of secure historical understanding in later years.

During the summer term Vicki turned the role-play area into a castle and the children experienced a range of stories relating to castles, princes and princesses. They extended their vocabulary in relation to time with the introduction of 'a long time ago' and language relating to castles. They dressed up as princesses and knights and acted out familiar stories, thoroughly enjoying themselves and developing initial ideas about history. This emphasis on sequencing stories through actions also continued to develop Early Learning Goals for language and communication so vital for future understanding of chronology.

This valuable work will be developed in future in Key Stage 1 when the children move on to topics such as 'toys', 'houses and homes' and 'celebrations'. The language already introduced, relating to time will be consolidated and developed, as will the ability to sequence events and objects (DfEE/QCA 1999: 104; KSU 1a & b). Children will develop the ability to identify similarities and differences between objects used 'then' and 'now', experiencing 'wash days' in the past, working with artefacts and other relevant sources of evidence. They will continue to predict and hypothesise about evidence by guessing what objects were used for and interpreting pictures. Their ability to ask and answer questions will be enhanced by working with evidence and also experiencing oral history as they find out about the 'way of life of their family or others around them' (DfEE/QCA 1999: 104).

Conclusion

This case study illustrates that even in challenging circumstances young children can, and do, begin to formulate historical thinking and develop rudimentary historical skills. The important factor is that the learning taking place is relevant and meaningful to them, allowing opportunities for exploration, questioning, discussion and problem solving – popular approaches in early years classrooms. The role of the teacher is critical in establishing and developing opportunities for this to take place. As O'Hara and O'Hara (2001: 13) state: 'Effective provision in both foundation and primary settings offers children the chance to gain first-hand experience, ask questions, reflect and predict as well as to experiment and play with ideas.' It is this first-hand experience which is so instrumental in bringing the past alive for children. This was what Vicki concentrated on – personal, first-hand experience to stimulate discussion and thinking. Clearly the children in the unit are aware of past events in their own lives, can ask questions and are driven by a curiosity to find out more.

The holistic nature of learning in the Foundation Stage apparent in Vicki's classroom means that children do meet concepts of time, sequence, similarity, difference and change centred around their own personal experiences and it is this range of experience that lays the foundations of future historical thinking. The importance of personal history is noted by Purkis (1996: 296) who states:

> The growing awareness that each of us has a past as well as a present and a future extends knowledge of self and is a psychologically healthy sign of developing maturity.

Knowledge and understanding of history can help answer two key questions 'Who am I?' and 'Where am I?'

Not only did Vicki's topic develop historical skills but it helped develop personal, social, emotional and communication skills giving children a greater sense of self-worth and it is important to acknowledge this.

As this case study has shown if we ensure children are valued and develop self-esteem then they will ask questions and develop enquiry skills (KSU 4a/b). If we ensure there are opportunities to talk, discuss and predict then they will develop communication skills (KSU 5). If we ensure they work with a range of evidence then they will interpret and form hypotheses, valuable enquiry and interpretation skills (KSU 3, 4). Finally if we talk about special days, days of the week, months and seasons then they will develop a sense of time (KSU 1).

What is important is that we recognise that this occurs naturally in Foundation Stage settings through numerous play opportunities, but we need to seize the initiative to develop learning through questions and dialogue with the children, teasing out what they know and understand. However, much of this learning and teaching takes place through areas with labels other than 'history' and ultimately it is a cumulative result of good early years practice that children develop historical knowledge, skills and understanding. These may be labelled as communication skills, reading skills and/or observation skills, which are covered by a number of Early Learning Goals, but as O'Hara and O'Hara (2001: 17) state are a good example of 'history but not as we know it'.

References

Cooper, C. (2002) 'History: Finding out about the past and the language of time', in Cooper, H. and Sixsmith, C. (eds) *Teaching across the Early Years 3–7: Curriculum coherence and continuity*, 153–68. London: RoutledgeFalmer.

Cooper, H. (2002) *History in the Early Years*, 2nd edn. London: RoutledgeFalmer.

Fisher, J. (2002) *Starting from the Child*, 2nd edn. Buckingham: Open University Press.

Hughes, P. (1997) *My History*. London: Heinemann.

Inkpen, M. (1995) *Wibbly Pig Opens his Presents*. London: Hodder Children's Books.

O'Hara, L. and O'Hara, M. (2001) *Teaching History 3–11, The Essential Guide*. London: Continuum.

Purkis, S. (1996) 'Mrs Rainbow told us what things were like when she went to school. History in the Early Years', in Whitebread, D. (ed.) *Teaching and Learning in the Early Years*, 293–311. London: Routledge.

Whitebread, D. (ed.) (1996) *Teaching and Learning in the Early Years*. Routledge. London.

Kings, queens and castles

Wendy Robson

WHEN I VISITED the early years unit at Appleby Primary School, the children were enthusiastically playing in the role-play area, which was a castle with a dungeon. The concept of playing within a castle did not appear to have much relevance to the children. The queen, Olivia, wearing a long dress and crown was seated on her throne. Jamie-Lee, her 'baby', was crouching by her side. Jodie was pretending to feed the baby. Bethan was in role as a dog and was on all fours.

Baby: Mamma.
Jodie: Eat your dinner or I'll put you in the dungeon.
Baby: Mamma.
Queen: Bedtime – put baby to bed.

The dog crawls around on all fours woofing and rubbing its head on the baby. Jamie-Lee decides to be a dog as well and goes on all fours, following Bethan.

Jodie: Bedtime baby. You got to go to bed.
Jamie-Lee: Woof!

Jodie gets down on all fours and becomes a dog.

The *Curriculum Guidance for the Foundation Stage* (QCA 2000) states that, 'Well-planned play is a key way in which children learn with enjoyment and challenge during the foundation stage.'

Role-play areas are usually well planned and organised with resources that provide children with the opportunity to play in role, but how often does the teacher plan to work with the children in this area and how do the children utilise the resources provided? When the teacher plans an activity for children in the role-play area, it is often linked to a specific learning objective in mathematics or literacy. It is common to see a role-play area as a shop and the teaching is linked to an objective from the Numeracy Strategy. But can the role-play area also be used to extend the understanding of change over time?

How can we move beyond the familiar?

In recent research the home corner or the role-play area is frequently mentioned as an environment that both stimulates children's play and gives practitioners the chance to extend their play and so extend their children's learning. Most learning however occurs when an adult is present and is able to interact with the child.

> In the most effective (excellent) settings, the importance of staff members extending child-initiated interactions was also clearly identified. In fact, almost half of all the child-initiated episodes which contained intellectual challenge, included interventions from a staff member to extend the child's thinking.
>
> (Siraj-Blatchford *et al.* 2002)

Meadows and Cashdan (1988) found that when they investigated children's behaviour during free-play sessions, the children did not persevere with tasks and the conversation between adult and child was very limited. They too concluded that for most effective learning it was necessary to have a high level of adult–child interaction during play.

With these factors in mind the staff in the early years unit at Appleby Primary School planned for a teacher to observe and interact with children in the role-play area, to try to find ways in which this might extend children's learning. The focus for learning in the unit would be on using stories to introduce a sense of time and of people from the past, to enable the children to respond to stories and rhymes in play, and to respond to what they have heard with relevant comments, questions and actions (QCA 2000: 50, 95). The theme would be 'Kings, queen and castles'.

Planning: starting points, organisation and adult roles

The early years unit is part of Appleby Primary School. It is the only primary school in the small town of Appleby, which is noted for its castle dating back to the twelfth century. The River Eden flows through the centre of the town. There are also other castles in a state of ruin within a radius of 12 miles and it is likely that the children will have travelled past them on the way to the larger towns, or they may even have visited them with other adults.

There are 300 children on the roll from ages three to 11. The early years unit provides for up to 70 children aged between three and five years. The children of nursery age attend on a part-time, half-day basis whereas the reception-age children attend full time. The unit is run by five staff (two teachers and three teaching assistants) on a mainly high scope system.

There are approximately 20 planned resource areas providing activities linked to areas of learning across the early years curriculum. Following the medium-term plan, (Figure 4.1) the activities in most of these areas change weekly (Figure 4.2). Each week four of the staff work in a specific area on an activity linked to a key

- **Intended learning outcomes**
  to develop skills in collaborative play;
  to become aware of differences between the past and present;
  to become aware of changes over time;
  to use and understand language of time;
  to begin to hypothesise about social life in a castle in the past, supporting the hypothesis with reasons.

- **Sequence of activities**
  Week 1: Introduce castle. (Need card, bin bags for dungeon, bed, chair for throne, dressing-up rail
  with long dresses, waistcoats, cloaks, helmets.)
  Week 2: Role play using crowns made in technology. Introduce dungeon.
  Week 3: Using torches in dungeon, contrast of darkness and light.
  Week 4: As previous week.
  Week 5: With adult role play life in a castle.
  Week 6: Role play 'Sleeping Beauty'.

- **Links to Stepping Stones**
  Personal/Social
    Working with others as part of a group sharing resources
    Look after resources in classroom
    Begin to understand similarities in people and in their way of life.
    Select activities and resources independently
    Continue to be interested and motivated to learn
  Communication, Language and Literacy
    Interact with others, negotiating plans and activities and taking turns in conversation.
    Enjoy listening to and using spoken language in play and learning.
    Make up own stories
    Use language to recreate roles and experiences.
  Knowledge and Understanding of the World
    Find out about past and present events in their own lives and in those of their families and
    others they know

FIGURE 4.1 Medium-term plan for play in the castle over six weeks showing learning outcomes and links
to the Stepping Stones (QCA 2000)

learning objective with small groups of children, while the fifth member of
staff 'floats', monitoring and observing in the unit, generally targeting particular
individuals, assessing their level of play and learning (Figure 4.3).

All the children (both nursery and reception) have access to all the activity areas
or work stations within the adjoining rooms so it is common to find nursery- and
reception-age children involved in the same activity either collaboratively or in
parallel. The children choose their activities for the day, the only stipulation being
that no more than four children are in the same area at the same time.

Small world	Finger puppets of king, queen etc. Using puppets, children to make up stories and act them out
ICT	Using program PAINT children to draw a castle and print it out
Mark making	Pots of black poster paint and quill pens
Large construction	Using the large wooden bricks and planks to build a castle
Listening area	Tapes of fairytales
Water	Pulley over water tray with buckets to attach
Small construction	Using Duplo build a wall for Humpty Dumpty (Humpty egg, Duplo horses and people for King's horses)
Play dough	Making tarts for The Queen of Hearts
Easel	Painting a castle
Book area	Books displayed of traditional tales
Technology	Make a candle holder (junk modelling)
Jigsaw area	Nursery rhyme jigsaws
K & U of W	Display of non-fiction books displayed on castles
Language	Sequencing the story of 'Cinderella'
Sand	Sandcastles
Cutting and sticking	Collage a castle photocopy picture

Main adult-supported activities

Numeracy	Use cakes and tarts from role-play area for subtraction (Knave of Hearts steals tarts)
Baking area	Jam tarts
Music	'Hairy Scary Castle' with adult from *Three Singing Pigs: Music making with traditional stories* (Umansky 1994)
Outdoors	Build sandcastles in the sandpit, with adult act out and sing 'There was a Princess Long Ago'

FIGURE 4.2 Weekly plan (week 6) showing activities linked to theme: 'Kings, queens and castles'

Earlier in the term, the children had been working on themes related to a topic on 'Light and dark'. In the role-play area the interior of a 'castle' had been constructed, a section of which had been partitioned with card to provide 'a dark dungeon', which the children could go inside. In the main part of the castle there was a wooden bed with blankets, a chair made into a throne, and dressing-up clothes. These included long dresses, waistcoats, crowns, plastic swords and shields. Traditional tales and nursery rhymes had been read or sung to the children throughout the term.

For the planned week it was decided that other areas of the unit would link to the theme of 'Kings, queens and castles' (Figure 4.2). Throughout the week, the children would hear traditional tales involving castles, for example, 'Cinderella', 'The Princess and the Pea', 'Rumplestiltskin', 'Sleeping Beauty'. These would be

Role-play area: Castle					
	Mon	Tue	Wed	Thur	Fri
Teacher 1	Role play	Observations	Music	Mathematics	Baking
Teaching assistant 1	Mathematics	Mathematics	Mathematics	Observations	Mathematics
Teaching assistant 2	Baking	Baking	Baking	Baking	Observations
Teaching assistant 3	Music	Music	Observations	Music	Music
Teacher 2	Observations	Role play	Role play	Role play	Role play
Parent	Outdoor	Outdoor	Outdoor	Outdoor	Outdoor

FIGURE 4.3 Weekly plan for adults' observations of play in castle and intended learning outcomes

read to them by staff members or they would listen to the taped stories in the listening area. In the book area non-fiction books on castles were to be displayed alongside fictional texts in which there were pictures of castles.

A teacher, Louise, would interact with small groups of children within the castle. The aims were to assess the children's knowledge and understanding of time past, to see if they had any awareness of changes over time and to gauge their ability to use the language of time. Louise would also aim to extend the children's knowledge by using questioning to scaffold learning, to encourage the children to hypothesise about social life in a castle in the past, to listen to the ideas of their peers and be able to give reasons for their answers. Louise would not participate in role in the castle, but would question the children about their activities and their interpretation of life in a castle in the past, and through further questioning use her knowledge of the children to provide prompts that would enable children to give reasoned answers.

Then and now: exploring and extending thinking

Louise went into the castle and was followed by Katie and Olivia. The girls selected long dresses and asked for help with the fastenings. While helping the children, Louise talked with them, questioning them about life in the past.

> Louise: What do you think it would have been like living in a castle?
> Katie: It was dark and spooky. It was cold 'cos it's got no heating.
> Louise: How do you think people kept warm then?
> Olivia: They would go and find some heat – light a fire upstairs and downstairs – they didn't have carpets and nice things – just dark walls. There might be a fire in the kitchen.

Louise: Why would they have a fire in the kitchen?

Katie: They would get some fire and put a pan on – that's how they cook tea.

The children moved to an area in the castle where they decided the fire would be. They then acted out the role of cooking their tea. They selected a frying pan from the cupboard and added some plastic sausages. They then poured imaginary beans from a baked bean tin into the pan. Through their actions the children were modelling behaviour which supported Vygotsky's theory (1978) that in play children behave beyond their age and daily behaviour. Often in home-corner play children have access only to predetermined materials which allow only limited opportunities for imaginative interpretation.

In the castle the children were therefore given the opportunity for creativity within role play as the castle contained only the basic props. This enabled the children to use problem-solving skills to provide and improvise resources in order to act out a role. The pan and sausages had not been provided within the castle setting so the children had introduced them in order to act out the role. They were aware of the atmosphere within the castle and of fire as a source of heat and for cooking, although the food they selected to cook was to some extent contemporary!

The girls' activity provided a focus for other children. Joshua and Thomas came into the castle and went to see what the girls were doing.

Louise: How do you think they cooked in a castle?

Joshua: In a pot on a fire. They had porridge in those days 'cos I seen it on the telly.

Louise: How did they get water? Did they have taps?

Thomas: Naaa, they got it from the river.

Joshua: No, the well.

Thomas: No, the pool.

Louise: How did they carry the water from the well to the castle?

Thomas: In a bottle or a bucket.

Joshua: Yea – a bucket.

Louise, Thomas and Joshua went in search of a bucket, which was then placed in the area of the castle that had become the kitchen.

The children were therefore initiating the learning situation and the teacher was responding to the needs of the children. The conversation concluded with Louise asking: 'Who do you think did the cooking?'

Thomas: The women.

Joshua: No, a man.

Thomas: No the women and the queen.

Joshua: No, it was a man 'cos when I go to 'The Little Chef' it's a man.

Louise: Thomas, why do you think the women cooked?

Thomas: My mum cooks.

Extending children's thinking

The discussion between Joshua, Thomas and the teacher showed a clear awareness that water had not always been on tap, awareness of difference between life in the past and now. Joshua was familiar with artefacts and language associated with the past in his use of the word 'well'. He may have this knowledge from a nursery rhyme and the illustrations associated with it, perhaps 'Jack and Jill', or it may be that he had 'seen it on the telly' as in the case of the porridge, where he obviously has a visual image of the way food was cooked in the past. Both children used their contemporary experiences to hypothesise on who might have been responsible for cooking in the castle.

This discussion also shows how important it is not to underestimate the effectiveness of children learning from peers. In the role-play area the adult was able to extend learning within the group by questioning and allowing the children to listen to each other's responses, to reflect and select their own hypothesis. The more capable child was able to lead in the play, so scaffolding the thinking of his peers (Vygotsky 1978).

When Louise questioned Rob about living in a castle, he could describe, using his senses, how it might have felt, based on reasoning from what he knew: it would be cold because there was no glass in the windows.

Louise: What do you think it was like living in a castle?
Rob: It was cold.
Louise: Why was it cold in the castle?
Rob: It had lots of windows.

Louise used the example of a familiar environment to encourage Rob to explain his reasoning.

Louise: School has lots of windows but it's not cold here is it?
Rob: No – but they didn't have glass in so the wind blew in.

Rob demonstrated his knowledge of differences between living in the past and now. He was aware that castles did not have glass at the windows, so logically it would be cold. This interaction and questioning of the adult in the role play enabled assessment of the child's level of understanding, and showed Rob was also aware of changes over time.

On another occasion Ryan and Paul were observed playing in the castle. Paul and Ryan put on crowns. Paul sat on the throne, holding a plastic sword and Ryan went to lie down on the bed. Louise asked them if they thought they would have had beds like that in the past. Their response was:

Ryan: No they didn't have beds. They slept on straw and hay – they not much comfy – but a bit. (This answer possibly reflected the teacher's selection the previous day of the story of 'Rumplestiltskin', and Ryan is remembering how the miller's daughter slept in the story.)

Paul: (pointing to the cover) They were made of rags.
Louise: What do you mean?
Paul: You know – bits of stuff fastened together.
Louise: Oh do you mean a patchwork quilt?
         Thomas went to the book area and found a picture of a child in bed with a patchwork quilt over him.
Louise: What about the bed? Might they have had a bed made of wood? (looking exasperatedly at the teacher)
Paul: Yes!
Louise: But where would the wood come from?
Paul: Trees course!
Louise: But how did they cut down the trees to get the wood?
Ryan: With a sword. (He picks up the sword and mimes slashing at trees.)
Louise: Wouldn't that take a long time? Can you think of something else they might have used?

At this point there was silence as the child tried to rationalise an answer. Now as Louise was aware of Ryan's level of understanding, it was an opportunity to take the learning further. By providing a 'scaffold' for learning, the adult takes the child from their position of present understanding into the area or zone just beyond what the child could achieve alone, their 'zone of proximal development' (Vygotsky 1978). In this case Louise knew the children's previous experiences in the classroom and knew which stories were familiar to them. She helped them to transfer what they already knew to solve a new problem.

Louise: Do you remember the story of 'Little Red Riding Hood'?
Paul and Thomas: Yes.
Louise: Can you remember who saved Red Riding Hood from the wolf?
Paul: The woodcutter.
Louise: Well done, and what did he use to save Red Riding Hood?
                   Paul was quiet.
Thomas shouted: An axe! (He mimed chopping with an axe.)
Louise: That's right, well done. Now, he was a woodcutter, so his job was to cut down trees – so what did he use to cut down trees?
Thomas: His axe.

This demonstrates how familiar traditional stories can be used to develop an understanding of life in the past. It also shows how the teacher, through recapping on the story of Red Riding Hood, which she had previously read to the children, and by using effective questioning, was able to extend the children's learning. The children had seen the illustrations in the book, which they had compared and contrasted with illustrations in contemporary stories or with recent photographs. This raised their awareness of change over time.

The value of questioning

The use of open-ended questions allowed speculation and extended the imagination. Effective questioning from the adult, especially in role-play situations can often, 'provide the best opportunities for adults to extend children's thinking.' (Siraj-Blatchford *et al.* 2002).

A similar conversation to that with Paul and Thomas was recorded with Matthew and Dale. Matthew attended nursery in the mornings and was very chatty.

> Louise: Matthew, what do you think it was like living in a castle?
> Matt: It was cold. My daddy told me they used not light, they used candles. They kept warm with a fire.
> Louise: What did they burn on the fire?
> Matt: Burned wood.
> Louise: Where do you think the wood came from?
> Matt: Trees – they sawed them down.
> Louise: Dale, How do you think they cut down the trees?
> Dale: Chopped down branches with a sword.

Louise used the tale of Red Riding Hood again to scaffold reasoning to gain the answer woodcutter and axe. Therefore in each instance there was an opportunity to build on the children's existing knowledge, to promote learning and understanding of life in the past.

Interestingly, although the children all knew that there was no electricity for cooking, and that there was no electric lighting operated by switches on the wall, several of them had the misconception that battery-operated torches had been available. This was possibly because previously in the topic of 'light and dark' the children had been given torches to use in the dungeon part of the castle, so they associated torches with life in the castle and with the other resources that had been provided for play within the castle.

The children believed only kings, queens, princes and princesses and their servants lived in a castle, possibly because all the stories and nursery rhymes they were familiar with involved these characters. Yet when questioned about Appleby Castle, the local castle regularly open to the public, they did not think royalty lived there now and one child had been to a wedding there.

Mark's understanding of life in a castle came from the visual experience of television. He and Rob had put on crowns and had picked up swords and shields. Louise asked Rob what the weapons were used for.

> Rob: Hundreds of years ago they used a shield to stop bad guys hitting them.
> Mark: And from dragons.
> Louise: Are you dressed up as a king?
> Rob: No we's guards.

Louise: What's your job?

Mark: We fight dragons and bad guys.

Louise: How do you know that guards fought dragons?

Mark: I seen it on the telly.

Rob: They got the bad guys and put them in the dungeon.

Louise: What was it like in the dungeon?

Mark: Dark and scary 'cos there's ghosts and nasty people.

The boys, because they were in role, were automatically using language related to castles: dungeon, guards.

Louise: How did they cook food?

Mark: Cook it on a fire – didn't have gas not a stove like these days.

Rob: You had water in a stream – carried it in a bucket.

Louise: Who brought the water from the stream?

Mark: Soldiers carried it. Kings and queens didn't.

Louise: How did they get warm water?

Rob: They didn't. They just used cold water – very cold water.

A group of three children were playing in the castle. Alice, in role as the queen, was seated on the throne wearing a long dress and crown. Also in role as servant and baby princess were Jodie and Beth. Louise took this as an opportunity to interact with the group. This time she related the questions to travel in the past.

Louise: Hello. Are you visiting the queen?

Jodie: Yes.

Louise: How did you get here? How do you think you would have travelled in the olden days?

Jodie: Had taxis

Louise: Do you think they travelled in cars in those days?

Beth: No walk.

Louise: If they were going a long way it would take a long time to walk. Can you think of a way they could travel more quickly?

Beth: Run.

Louise used the same strategies employed previously and asked the children to recall a familiar story. This time the children were visualising the illustrations in the story as well as remembering the characters and plot.

Louise: Do you remember the story of 'Cinderella'? How did she go to the ball?

Beth: Went in a coach.

Alice: A coach with horses.

Jodie: Didn't have horses

Alice: Yes them did – them did.

Beth drew on her knowledge of contemporary life with horses and concluded the discussion by adding: 'If it was raining you would have a horse hat' (riding hat).

These interactions support the theories of Vygotsky (1978) and Bruner (1983), on the role of play in children's development. They illustrate, in a modest way, that through play and other experiences and interactions, children are able to discover new meanings, to develop more complex understandings and skills. The adult presence suggested ways in which progression in thinking depends on the correct kind and right amount of assistance at the right time.

Positioning a teacher in the role-play area had raised the level of learning. There were naturally strong links across the other areas of the Foundation Stage curriculum, in particular with the areas of language, literacy, communication and personal and social education. Questions had been linked to the children's own experiences, either through their visual images gained from books, from listening to stories, watching the television or video or from awareness of the castle building in Appleby itself. The children were to some extent allowed to determine their own learning, as the teacher's questions were decided by the children's play activities. The children's learning throughout was scaffolded by the teacher or by more able peers within the group, as they listened to the answers given and reflected on them in the light of their own knowledge and experiences. Where young children have freely chosen to play in a learning environment, there is a greater opportunity for effective adult intervention.

This case study considered how teachers could, through effective use of role play, develop an awareness of a sense of time in young children and enable them to differentiate between past and present. The benefits of play have long been recognised, but as reflected in Jamie-Lee and Jodie's role play at the beginning of this chapter, free play alone does not necessarily maximise cognitive development. The children were interacting socially but it was of little relevance to life in a castle. By positioning the teacher in the role-play area the learning of the children was increased and provided the teacher with insights into the children's understanding of change over time, and of their ability to use vocabulary related to the past. Words such as dungeon, well, carriage, woodcutter were introduced and these were used alongside the descriptive language of time, for example, the past, long ago, before and when.

Siraj-Blatchford *et al.* (2002) reported that teaching and learning were most effective in settings where there were cognitive interactions, including those which lead to sustained shared thinking. Learning was also found to be most effective where there was frequent use of questioning techniques by adults, especially in the context of children's play.

This was again reflected in the castle activity as, through questioning, the teacher was also able to increase the children's knowledge and understanding of life in past times. Many of the questions were open ended, therefore emphasising the value of the children's thoughts and providing the teacher with an insight into the child's ideas rather than, as in the case of closed questioning, providing an opportunity to possibly fail by incorrect answers. Asking the questions to small groups gave the children opportunity for discussion and to listen and learn from each other.

Continuity – Foundation Stage to Key Stage 1

There are several ways in which this theme could be developed, both in the Foundation Stage and into Key Stage 1 and Key Stage 2. The role-play area in the unit could have been constructed to focus on one particular room in a castle. If the kitchen had been selected, then there would have been more potential for a specific focus on the differences between preparing food then and now and even the sorts of meals created then compared with now. This could be continued through Key Stage 1 and even into Key Stage 2 where it could link to a study of local history, especially since the school is situated within close proximity to a castle.

At Key Stage 1 children could be encouraged to identify differences between ways of life now and then. They could visit a castle and examine artefacts demonstrating domestic life in the castle and, as with the examples from the early years unit, be encouraged to ask and answer questions about the past. In the breadth of study, they could be encouraged to show, in role, knowledge and understanding of the way of life of people in the more distant past, who lived in the local area or elsewhere in Britain. There is a close link with the QCA unit plans for history at Key Stages 1 and 2 (http://www.qca.org.uk), particularly with Unit 2: What were homes like a long time ago?

There is more potential for closer links with literacy through text level and traditional stories and for taking on a particular character's role at Key Stage 1. And, perhaps most importantly, learning through role is likely to provide children in Key Stage 1, and beyond, with enthusiasm for history.

References

Bruner, J. S. (1983) *Child's Talk: learning to use language*. Oxford: Oxford University Press.

Meadows, S. and Cashdan, A. (1988) *Helping Children Learn*. London: David Fulton.

Umansky, K. (1994) *Three Singing Pigs: Music making with traditional stories*. London: A. C. Black.

Vygotsky, L. S. (1978) *Mind in Society: The development of psychological processes*. Harvard: Harvard University Press.

Moving between fantasy and reality: sustained, shared thinking about the past

Alan Farmer and Anne Heeley

Stories about the past: probable? possible? impossible?

STIMULATING AND SUPPORTING PLAY based on stories set in past times raises a number of questions which we explore in this chapter. Story is central to children's developing awareness of past times; from a very young age children encounter stories from the past. Some of these stories are about real people and events. Others are make-believe – fairy stories. So how do children gradually come to know what is a 'real' story and what is a 'made-up' story? How do they come to know that Cinderella didn't exist but Florence Nightingale did? The fact that 'true' stories about the past are often vehicles for literacy and told in the Literacy Hour, alongside fairy stories, possibly compounds the problem for young children. Are they simply dependent on an adult telling them which stories really happened? Do children forget? Should adults help children to differentiate between 'true' and 'made-up' stories?

There is no doubt that young children, apparently universally (Brown 1991), delight in fantasy stories, dislocated from anything familiar in their everyday waking experience. They do not necessarily understand that some stories actually happened, some are fairy stories and some (like Robin Hood and King Arthur) are betwixt and between. The boundaries between imagination and reality are blurred for most four- and five-year-olds. (Think of Father Christmas and the Tooth Fairy!) But how blurred are the boundaries? To date (as far as we are aware) there has been no systematic study of children's ability to make inferences about real and made-up stories. Surely the question of whether a story set in the past is real or fantasy is an important aspect of children's developing intellectual independence: it is certainly the basis for developing genuine historical understanding later on. Young children gradually develop a sense of what is possible, probable and impossible.

We think there tends to be an assumption that this understanding is acquired naturally about the age of seven or eight – around the time that children realise that Father Christmas is a myth. But it may be that children begin this process much sooner. Should adults intervene to accelerate this process? What should that intervention be? Does society actually want such teacher intervention? This is a big question with far-reaching connotations. Do parents want teachers to cast doubts on Father Christmas or the miracles of Jesus? There are obviously dangers here.

Nevertheless we have dipped our toes in the water, conducted a small research project, and have some suggestions to make about how teachers might proceed. As long ago as 1978, Margaret Donaldson argued that children must be helped to make inferences, and to understand the nature of different disciplines, as early as possible. We agree. Children gradually become aware of the difference between 'histories' and stories and as they do it is the adult's job, with sensitivity, to support them in this process.

So who are 'we' and what axes have we to grind? We are brother and sister but we are not sure that that is particularly relevant. Anne is the Deputy Head of a primary school and teaches the reception class. Alan is Head of the Department of History and Geography in an institution of higher education. He is now more con-cerned with academic American history than with how young children learn. However, he has always been interested in how children learn about the past, and in particular in storytelling. Neither of us, as far as we are aware, has any particu-lar theoretical case to pedal. We are as different as most siblings. The only thing we really share is a commitment to education, a profession in which both of us have spent all our working lives. Our sympathies are with the practitioners, not the theorists. Some theory will inevitably intrude in this chapter, but we hope that most of what we have to say will be common sense.

Stories are an important way to find out about past times

Both of us tend to the view that story is the essence of finding out about the past for young children and indeed for people of all ages. The link between story and history is long established. For thousands of years communities learnt about their past through the medium of story – passed on from one generation to the next within families or by bards, poets and religious leaders. One of the twentieth cen-tury's best historians (and storytellers), stated that 'We shouldn't be ashamed to admit that history at bottom is simply a form of storytelling . . . there is no escap-ing the fact that the original task of the historian is to answer the child's question: 'What happened next?' (Taylor 1983). Undoubtedly in the early years, story pro-vides the ideal vehicle for helping children acquire an interest in – and begin to make sense of – the past, especially the distant past. Farmer (1990), Bage (1999;

2000), Cox and Hughes (in Hoodless 1998: 87–101) and Farmer and Cooper (in Hoodless 1998: 35–51) are among the most recent advocates of learning about past times through storytelling. They (variously) claim the following.

- Most children use and enjoy stories.

- Stories help children to learn and understand.

- Stories stimulate the imagination and inspire curiosity.

- Stories help children acquire some early 'time markers': the internal chronology and narrative form of story provide children with support to order or recount the past.

- Stories are the foundation of literacy: they act as a vehicle for specific historical vocabulary.

- If well told and actively experienced, stories help transmit enormous amounts of information.

- Through exploring the beliefs and actions of characters in stories, children can begin to appreciate the feelings and motivation of people.

- When stories are accompanied by illustrations, further information about the time depicted can be conveyed through the pictures, thus contributing to children's mental images of the past.

There are dangers. Children can be manipulated by storytellers. 'True' stories can be gross oversimplifications of reality. Real characters are often presented as little more than caricatures. Such can impose coherence where there is none. Thus 'true' stories may not be far removed from fictional stories set in the past. We accept the dangers. But we remain convinced that storytelling is or should be an essential component in developing awareness of the past. We think this is almost a fact! But it leaves much to interpretation – not least the quality of the story and the qualities of the storyteller. What makes a good 'history story'? Aristotle said that a story has a beginning which sets up expectations, a middle – or muddle – that complicates them, and an end that satisfies them. We think the best pure 'history stories' for young children have a relatively simple plot and one or at most two central characters. It should be said that many of the best 'histories' are not stories by Aristotle's definition: they are essentially anecdotal. But we think that any teacher talk about the past which captures the children's imagination, whether that talk is about gladiators in Ancient Rome or child chimney sweeps in the nineteenth century, has story overtones. The teacher can, of course, read from a book. There are plenty of history stories now in print. Children may gain a more varied vocabulary if the teacher reads rather than tells a story in his/her own language. However, we think that storytelling is generally better than story reading. There is no barrier between the teacher and the audience.

Good storytelling is not easy: it requires detailed preparation, good class control and a high standard of presentation in order to hold the children's attention. Essentially the teacher needs to see the action of the story happening and involve the children in that action. Was the 'hero' right to do as he did? What do you think is going to happen next? Involving children somehow adds to the vitality of the telling. It becomes a shared experience of teacher and class.

Stories, the past and the curriculum

So we have no doubt that retelling 'true' stories about the past is a good thing. We are not alone.

> Story has long been considered an appropriate method of teaching history to young children. A good, well-told story commands attention and can lead to discussion, question and answer. The attraction of story lies in its narrative power, through which it appeals to children's curiosity, emotions and imagination.
>
> (NCC 1993: 33)

The status of story within the Programme of Study for Key Stage 1 was clearly indicated by the opening paragraph which set out the Key Elements:

> Pupils should be helped to develop an awareness of the past through stories from different periods and cultures, including:
>
> ■ well-known myths and legends,
> ■ stories about historical events,
> ■ eye-witness accounts of historical events,
> ■ fictional stories set in the past.
>
> (DES 1991)

The National Curriculum does not establish an agreed starting point for Key Stage 1 history: the past can be entered at any point and in any place. The National Curriculum orders do say, however, that young children have to study aspects of the way of life of people in Britain in the past beyond living memory. The choice of precisely which time is left open to teachers. Undoubtedly commercially produced schemes have had some influence on that choice. Famous people (for example, Alfred the Great, Boudicca, Mary Seacole) have received particular attention from publishers. Famous events (for example, the voyage of the *Mayflower*, the Great Plague) have also been the subject of stories. These stories might be told as part of history or as part of the Literacy Hour. The National Literacy Strategy (DfEE 1998) has had wide-ranging implications for the place of 'histories'. It is now expected that children will be introduced to traditional stories throughout their early years. These will often include history stories of various types, including myths and legends. The Literacy Hour can thus provide a context for exposition concerning historical content and for developing children's basic historical skills. At the Foundation Stage (QCA 2000: 94–5) children find out about changes in their own lives and environments; they are encouraged to use time vocabulary and are introduced to a sense of time and people from the past through story and role play. Indeed the personal and social and communication skills this involves are integrated throughout the areas of learning.

Should we help children differentiate between fact and fantasy?

We suggest that it is not enough for children to be told that a particular story is real or made up: they need to develop some organising concepts – a tool kit for future understanding. It could be argued that young children will be unable to understand the difference between 'real' or 'made-up' before a certain age. The fact that most young children believe in Father Christmas may suggest that the majority are not ready to appreciate the difference between the various story forms until they reach a certain age.

The great debate about children's readiness to learn still rumbles on. Piaget's ideas on child development remain a crucial element in the notion of readiness. Piaget suggested that children develop according to an inherent 'natural' stage-wise progression, the course of which might be supported or enriched but not interfered with or forced (Flavell 1963). However, a host of researchers have questioned Piagetian theory. Many of the counter 'big hitters' (like Bruner 1975) have suggested that children are capable of intellectual achievements at an earlier point than that predicted by Piaget. In Bruner's model, facilitating a pupil's progress through the use of appropriate support materials and intervention will provide children with scaffolding upon which they can construct increasingly advanced ways of thinking. Our sympathies are with Bruner (rather than Piaget). We believe that good teaching helps. Passively waiting for children to become ready to learn might necessitate a very long wait indeed! The concept of readiness can easily lead to a lowering of teacher expectations.

Obviously teachers need to be sensitive to a child's personality, interests, cultural background, general life experience and abilities but they also need to be prepared to intervene through questioning, guiding and instructing, in an effort to extend thinking. There is plenty of evidence to suggest that young children can think and we should not underestimate their ability to do so.

Learning from children's thinking

Enough pontificating. It is time to see how some young children think. The only easy way to get at their thinking about real and made-up stories is to see what they say. Anne recorded children's responses to questions about real or made-up stories during the 2002–3 school year. Her pupils were aged four to five and of different abilities and gender.

How do you know if a story is true or not?

Anne first asked a small group of children this question. They all gave reasons for their replies.

Christopher:	If a story is a fairytale it has 'Once upon a time' and 'They all lived happily ever after' in it.
Alex:	If it's about dinosaurs it would be true because dinosaurs lived a long time ago. If it's like 'The Three Billy Goats Gruff' I know it isn't a true story because trolls don't exist.
Neil:	If the story was a monster one you'd know because monsters aren't real.
Abigail:	If it's real it will say beginning and end.
Katie:	I don't really know. If you see a play the people are dressed up, they're just pretending.

The children obviously had some mixed ideas. Christopher's notion that a story is a fairytale if it begins 'Once upon a time' and ends with 'They all lived happily ever after' is interesting. It suggests that teachers telling 'histories' must be careful. Stories often begin with the words 'Once upon a time . . .' or 'Long, long ago . . .'. History stories are more likely to begin with 'A long time ago'. But it could be that to young children's ears 'Once upon a time' and 'A long time ago' are not very different. It is also the case that many histories end on a high, implying that everyone lived happily ever afterwards. (How often do we tell the children of our heroes' and heroines' pains and tribulations later in life?) This too could confuse. Alex and Neil both recognise that if stories contain monsters then they are unlikely to be true. However, Alex has something of a Fred Flintstone concept of the past: he thinks there may have been a time when dinosaurs and people co-inhabited the planet. It should be said that adverts, films and cartoons all give some credibility to Alex's view. In many respects his view is far more rational than a belief in Father Christmas or the belief that Jesus fed 5,000 with a few loaves and fishes.

How do you know if a story from a long time ago is true?

When Anne asked the children this question they again gave reasoned answers.

Christopher:	If I've heard of the people, like Robin Hood, I know it's true. Also if the people are wearing old clothes.
Alex:	I'd know it was true if it was about something I know, like dinosaurs. I would look at the pictures.
Neil:	Pictures might tell or the words might tell. You think if the people can do things or not.

> Abigail: You can tell from the cover. If it's creased and dirty it's an old book but if it's new it would not be creased.
>
> Katie: I don't really know but I would try to think. I might ask my mummy.

Neil's view – 'You think if the people can do things or not,' – is surely the most perceptive. Alex's interest in dinosaurs is again apparent. But generally the children had trouble with the question. Christopher's answer provides a challenge to teachers trying to get across real history. Christopher was convinced that Robin Hood existed. He had been to Sherwood Forest and seen the Major Oak. Abigail and Katie are grasping at straws or, in Katie's case, her mummy!

Is the story of Grace Darling true?

So what do children make of a real story? Anne told the story of Grace Darling to the children as a group and talked to them individually. She did not tell them whether the story was real or made up but introduced it with the words: 'I am going to tell you about a person called Grace Darling who lived before your grandmas and granddads.' Throughout the story the children joined in with actions (for example, rowing the boat) and sound effects (for example, storm sounds) so they were actively involved. When the children were asked individually if they thought the story was real or made up these were their comments.

> Harry: The story was made up because of the storm.
>
> Ben: The story happened. (On further questioning, Ben was hesitant about his reasons and unable to express why he thought it was a true story. He just kept repeating, 'I think it happened.')
>
> Katie: I don't think it could have happened because the fishermen wouldn't have gone out in a storm. Nor would Grace. It was dangerous and her daddy would have gone on his own and not taken Grace.
>
> Hannah: It is a real story because the people are real. (When asked how she knew this she was unable to explain her reasons.)
>
> Richard: It is a true story because they rescued the fishermen. They rowed and rowed. (Richard had enjoyed the actions of rowing the boat and had thrown himself into the actions enthusiastically!)
>
> Neil: It's a true story because the Darlings saved the fishermen. They did really save them.

What can we make of this? Katie, the most able and articulate of the children, thought the story was made up. This was for a very good reason – her dad wouldn't have taken her out to sea in a storm! The other children simply had a kind of gut feeling it was true but were unable to articulate why.

Time talk between children

A lesson on dinosaurs provides another example of children's thinking. We agree that this is not exactly history but it does tell us something about children's thinking about the past. Many children are fascinated by dinosaurs. In many ways it is a pity that history has given them up! Christopher was telling the whole class about his visit to Florida where he had stroked a dinosaur. This sparked off a whole string of comments. Neil said that he couldn't have done because dinosaurs don't exist. They are extinct! Daniel asked what extinct meant and went on to say that Christopher could have stroked a dinosaur because he had seen a video of it. Neil explained that extinct meant there were no dinosaurs alive and anyway there hadn't been any people around when the dinosaurs lived so no one could have stroked one. Daniel retorted that there were people and dinosaurs because he had seen it on the video. He explained that there is an island where dinosaurs live and this is where Christopher had been. Neil insisted he knew everything about dinosaurs and Christopher didn't stroke a real one. He then asked Christopher if he'd stroked a lizard because they were related to dinosaurs. Christopher wasn't sure because his dad had said it was a dinosaur. The children were obviously unsure about what to believe because, as one child said, 'Christopher is a very clever boy and knows lots of things – so if he said he'd stroked a dinosaur he must have!' Other children sided with Neil because 'he knows all the dinosaurs' names and has lots of books'.

Anne asked how we could decide if something was true or not. Katie commented that if it was on the television it was true. Lots of children nodded in agreement. Anne then asked if all things on television were true. This had a mixed response. Some of the children thought everything on television must be true because they could see it. Others were not so sure but couldn't explain why. The conclusion seems to be that many children base their ideas on fact or fiction on whether someone they respect has told them or whether they have seen something on television.

Is the story of Princess Victoria true?

On a different occasion Anne read the story *Princess Victoria* (Mitchelhill 1991). She showed children the pictures as she read. Christopher had heard the name Princess Victoria as his mum had told him that Victoria was a princess of England. He also thought the rocking horse and toys looked real. Alex thought long and hard about whether it was a true story or not. Finally he said it was a true story because queens are real and Princess Victoria was a queen. John did not know how to tell whether a story was true or made up. He said, 'that it is too difficult a question for me to answer'. Abigail enjoyed talking about the story, particularly the clothes and the toys. She thought it was a made-up story because 'people don't wear clothes like that and don't have those sort of toys'.

The reason Anne chose this story was to see if the children commented about princesses in fairytales or made any comparisons. The fact that they didn't rather surprised her. She wonders whether this was because she showed them the book which wasn't like a typical fairytale book. However, the children were clearly undecided about whether Princess Victoria was 'true' or 'false'.

And George and the dragon?

On another occasion, Anne told all the class the story of Saint George and the dragon and discussed it with them. She asked the class if they thought the story was true.

> Harry: I've seen pictures in books of dragons guarding moats.
> Alex: Dragons lived a long time ago when there were knights.
> John: Dragons might have existed like the dinosaurs but they don't exist now.
> Hannah: It might be like the Loch Ness monster. It lives in Scotland.
> Katie: Loch Ness is true because George is going on holiday to look for it.
> Daniel: The story was made in England and Saint George was brave.

The children do well here. They are posing questions, sharing ideas and applying existing knowledge. Even so they are a bit unsure about the answer to the question asked. The problems that teachers face in trying to get across stories about events that really happened, as opposed to fairytales, are clear. The children's reasoning is sound. There are pictures in books of dragons! But not everything that is in a book is 'real'. Without a sense of chronology, it is difficult to say that knights and dragons did not co-exist. Dinosaurs certainly did exist and the Loch Nester monster might just exist.

What about King Arthur?

The final comments were made after Anne told the children a story about King Arthur.

> Richard: This is definitely true because there were kings and knights and castles a long time ago.
> Sandy: This is real because we have a queen and she lives in a castle and has special guards.
> Ben: I think I've seen this on television.
> William: It's very exciting. I like castles.
> Neil: Does it really matter if it is true or not?
> John: Yes because you've got to know about things or you won't know. Grown ups tell you things so you'll know when you're grown up.
> Harry: If someone wrote it down it must have happened.

Again many children believe things are true if they've seen something about the topic on television. Harry's view – that if someone wrote something down it 'must have happened' – seems to be a common misconception. Neil's question is a perceptive one. As is John's response. It should be said that King Arthur and the Knights of the Round Table is a difficult area for young children – and indeed for anyone studying Dark Age history. Historians continue to debate whether there was indeed a King Arthur.

Clearly the evidence above is very limited and we would not wish to judge the way that all four- and five-year-old children think on the basis of a few examples. Nevertheless we suspect that Anne's evidence could be replicated in most classrooms. So what does all this suggest?

Building on what children know

First, Anne believes the children enjoyed the various stories. Her questions also made them think. These points should not be missed! Second, most children are uncertain about which stories are true and which are made up. Interestingly, the brightest and most articulate are likely to be most wrong about a story's provenance. Children's understandings are unpredictable. Their various views are probably the result of different experiences. Children come to school with ideas formed from watching television, from visits, from talking with other children, and from talk at home. Children need a set of guiding principles so they can work things out themselves. So what might teachers do?

Recognise the power of myth

Kieran Egan may provide some answers. Egan is one of the major critics of Piagetian theory. In a number of books and articles he has argued that Piaget and other educational researchers have focused too exclusively on a narrow set of logico-mathematical operations and, in so doing, have ignored children's extraordinary ability to fantasise. Convinced that 'children's imaginations are the most powerful and energetic tools', he stresses the importance of story in teaching. Story, he thinks, is not just some casual entertainment; instead it reflects a basic and powerful form in which people of all ages make sense of the world. Egan celebrates emotion, imagination and morality as elements in, or aims for, teaching, argues that the story form has a central place in achieving them, and claims that the power of the story form enables a teacher to 'teach any content more engagingly and meaningfully' (Egan 1989: 2). Somewhat ironically (given his criticism of Piaget) Egan has developed an alternative theory of child development. He has outlined four educational stages of development through which children proceed but never 'leave': mythic (up to the age of eight), romantic (eight to 15), philosophic (15–20) and ironic (post 20).

Egan sees a major difference in the way most children think, and see the world, before and after the age of eight. He suggests that children aged between four and eight think in ways redolent of the old myth stories which are built on the conflict of opposites. Opposition, thinks Egan, is the key to mythic understanding.

Children bring some order into their world by dividing everything into opposites. Once the opposites are understood, children can use them to ascribe meaning to intermediary terms. (In other words, once children understand hot and cold they can understand warm.) Egan claims that children's love of fairy stories involving the deep opposite emotions of love–hate, joy–fear, good–bad should be fostered as this will engage their interest and attention most readily. He stresses the fact that young children imagine: they create other worlds alongside the real world. For youngsters magic is entirely acceptable so long as it moves the story along. At the mythic stage most children readily accept magic or fantastic elements. They are unperturbed by the process whereby Cinderella's Fairy Godmother suddenly appears and turns mice into footmen and a pumpkin into a coach. They accept that Father Christmas can fly around the world and pop down every chimney, distributing toys to everyone from the contents of a few sacks carried on one sleigh. Most children aged eight upwards will not accept this.

Egan is surely right when he stresses that young children's introduction to past times should be full of the most odd and exotic societies and emphasise dramatic personalities and events. He stresses the need for children to fantasise. He points out that the child 'who cannot on the one hand conserve measurements may, on the other, lead a vivid intellectual life, brimming with knights, dragons, witches and star warriors' (Egan 1983: 360).

It should be said that Egan thinks that mythic stage children can learn about the past, without too much respect for evidence. He suggests, for example, that with younger pupils Alfred the Great should be taught as a good thing/king, a genuine hero battling against adversity in the form of the Vikings. Although a mythic version may be a simplification of reality, it is not necessarily unhistorical. Most Anglo-Saxon scholars consider Alfred 'great'. If he was 'great', it was because the Vikings posed a real threat to Anglo-Saxon civilisation.

Egan's theory has another implication for finding out about the past. Given his emphasis on opposites, he would seem to indicate (we are not sure that he goes this far) that teachers do need to get across the extremes of 'real' and 'made-up' stories. Only when they have a thorough grasp of the extremes of fact and fantasy should they be introduced to the grey areas – the murky world of myths and legends and fictional tales based in a 'real-ish' past.

Which stories? which questions?

If this is correct, teachers need to give careful consideration to the stories that they employ and in which order. They also need to encourage children to ask questions about the stories. Is the story true? How do you know? How might you tell? Could this have happened to you or to your parents? Who might have made up the story? By using focused questions teachers can arouse children's natural curiosity and help them to interrogate stories. Our study suggests that young children can and do make valid inferences about stories and can support their inferences with arguments. But their opinions need to be founded on some basic understanding.

How do we know it is *not* true?

Children will need (eventually) to realise that history is based on sources left behind from the past. Young children do not have much concept of sources or evidence. Before tackling the difficult concept of evidence, children need to have grasped some basic principles to test for falsifiability. Four- and five-year-olds may have a very uninformed framework within which to relate true or untrue. But most appreciate that stories about magic spells, talking animals and monsters are untrue. Open-ended discussion with each other and with teachers (and parents) should improve understanding, allowing children to develop their ideas. Children's answers need to be listened to and encouraged. They must have confidence to form, explain and justify their opinions, and must also learn to listen to those of others. In this way, they should begin to recognise what is likely to be true and what is likely to be fantasy.

Moving from fantasy to reality

Should teachers help kick-start this process? Many parents might well oppose the idea of children questioning stories. Do we really want teachers to destroy children's illusions about Father Christmas and the Tooth Fairy? This might be perceived as an attack on the magic of childhood. There are also problems with religious stories. Are the various miracle stories from the Bible, the Koran and other holy scripts true or made up? What do young children make of them? Should they question them? Did Jesus rise from the dead? Was he able to turn water into wine? These are big questions for adults, never mind young children, who for many generations have been brainwashed into accepting religious 'truth'.

We are not advocating destroying children's illusions or arousing the wrath of evangelical parents. In our view teachers should leave controversial issues aside. (So should brothers and sisters: we have very different views on the notion of 'miracles'!) Teachers can ask questions of other stories and share other ideas. If children ask difficult questions about Father Christmas or religious stories teachers should deflect them as they do now. Cultural and religious concerns need not get in the way of teachers' efforts to enable children to think critically, to question and to discuss ideas, in order to begin to understand the past. Children do need to learn to grasp the most basic concept: at one extreme there is something that approximates to a real past; at the other there is a totally fictitious – fairytale – past.

Teachers need to encourage children to exercise their thinking skills by providing a wide range of appropriate stories from the past and allowing follow-up discussion. The job of the teacher is to ask the right, challenging questions that encourage the exchange of ideas, that push children towards speculation, and that ultimately result in greater understanding. By thinking about stories, and by being able to distinguish between fact and fiction, young children will begin to develop historical understanding.

References

Bage, G. (1999) *Narrative Matters: Teaching and learning history through story*. London: Falmer Press.

Bage, G. (2000) *Thinking History 4–14: Teaching, learning, curricula and communities*. London: RoutledgeFalmer.

Brown, D. E. (1991) *Human Universals*. New York: McGraw-Hill.

Bruner, J. S. (1975) *Towards a Theory of Instruction*, 7th edn. Harvard, Mass: The Belknap Press of Harvard University.

Department for Education and Employment (DfEE) (1998) *The National Literacy Strategy Framework for Teaching*. London: DfEE.

Department for Education and Science (DES) (1991) *History in the Natoinal Curriculum*, London: HMSO.

Donaldson, M. (1978) *Children's Minds*. London: Fontana.

Egan, K. (1983) 'Children's path to reality from fantasy: contrary thoughts about curriculum foundations', *Journal of Curriculum Studies* **15**(5), 357–71.

Egan, K. (1989) *Teaching as Storytelling*. London: Routledge.

Farmer, A. (1990) 'Story-telling in history', *Teaching History*. **58**, 17–23.

Flavell, J. H. (1963) *Developmental Psychology of Jean Piaget*. New York: Van Nostrand.

Hoodless, P. (ed.) (1998) *History and English in the Primary School: Exploiting the links*. London: Routledge.

Mitchelhill, B. (1991) *Princess Victoria*, (History Key Stage One Stories, Set A). Aylesbury: Ginn.

National Curriculum Council (NCC) (1993) *Teaching History at Key Stage One*. York: NCC.

Taylor, A. J. P. (1983) 'Fiction in history', in Fines, J. (ed.) *Teaching History*. 113–15. Edinburgh: Macmillan.

Ancient history: things to do and questions to ask

Hugh Moore

Why ancient history?

Dressing up

Grinding corn

Twisting and plying your own
  string and yarn

Gathering herbs

Natural dyeing

Weaving on a warp weighted loom

Making wattle and daub walls

Making clay pots

Casting bronze axes, daggers and
  spearheads

Site visits – to ancient settlements

I'VE ALWAYS ENJOYED 'doing' ancient history with young children and I've started this chapter with a list so that you can see what I mean – all the above activities could be part of it. As part of a previous job in a museum I was able to do such wonderful things: dress children in a wolf-skin (it died naturally), and put 3–11,000-year-old stone/bronze axes in their hands. I found that Key Stage 1 children do not have a problem with understanding ancient history. In fact they were interested and excited and could easily work out how the Stone Age got its name! However, I have a set of deeper reasons for thinking that life between 3 and 5,000 years ago, the Stone/Bronze Age, is a good Key Stage 1 project.

First, practicalities

The National Curriculum for Key Stage 1 (DfEE/QCA 1999) tells us to teach children 'about a way of life in the more distant past'. (I've always thought that – and here's the contrary thing – the closer to living memory you get, the more similar to our way of life things become and, therefore, the more confusing.) A topic on the Stone/Bronze Age is in the spirit of that document. The chronology is easy because the other topics children will cover (often in the wrong order) all follow. A recent Ofsted report on the teaching of history (Hampshire Inspection and Advisory Service 2002), discusses the excellent idea of having a whole-school time-line. This topic would enable pupils to have a firm basis for viewing all the later history.

Pupils are familiar with this topic from cartoons too (although at first they do get confused about the fact that there were no dinosaurs then and people didn't live in caves). Most of our representations of that period echo these cartoons – they are artists' impressions and, as such, are easy for pupils to understand and distinguish from the objects and excavations which form our only primary sources of information about the period.

Second, it's a good topic in its own right

There are plenty of exciting things for pupils to do while they learn about this period – many of which are simple and creative activities, which can become integrated into play. Let me elaborate on that. Stone/Bronze Age technology isn't difficult to understand. It is intuitive and easy to imitate. Grinding corn on a saddle quern, spinning and plying and, to an extent, natural dyeing are visible processes with tangible results. Dressing up in simple garments made from woollen cloth and animal skins – or fake fur – is fun and, unlike later costume, is easy to make.

Third, finding our roots

Let me begin by telling you a true story. I was once showing a group of children some eggs (I worked on a farm at that stage.) The eggs ranged from a quail's egg to a goose egg. While I was a talking about which bird had laid which egg I became acutely aware that the children were giving me strange looks, puzzled looks, 'I completely don't understand what you are saying' looks. So I asked them if they knew what a chicken was. They nodded. I asked them to describe one.

> 'A chicken is pink.'
> 'A chicken is frozen. You can buy a chicken in the supermarket.'

Do we really know that little about how we feed ourselves?

Four years studying for a psychology degree has left me with an abiding interest in the evolution of behaviour – the roots of our behaviour as human beings. Let me explain. Reynolds (1976: 58–61, 237), among many others, illustrates how our ancestor, *Homo erectus*, probably learned to use fire, made wonderful tools and began the process of modern social behaviour. Many of the things we have learned to do as human beings go back a long, long way. Human beings have grown up knowing how to feed and clothe themselves. We might observe that those children who thought chickens were frozen have lost touch with something important in human nature – they have to an extent lost their roots. However, as I found long ago when I used to work on that farm, once children rediscover those roots they seem to prosper as human beings. So, as Reynolds says, we must acknowledge the very real place of our biology in understanding the human condition.

Considering the lives people lived beyond 3,000 years ago is about understanding our lives in a naturalistic sense, about being able to understand the actual things that sustain us as humans. That's why this period is so important. It is not so long ago that *we* were hunter-gatherers – close enough to be recognisable. (We were farmers then. We had clay pots, a few bronze tools, many stone tools and we lived in small villages and there was a structure to society.) It is a simple period to understand.

Think about it. We modern people are completely detached from our environment – so detached that we've hardly any idea where our food comes from. If you stripped away all the trappings of our modern lives, we would have very little idea of how to survive.

What was it like in our locality in the Stone Age?

Discussing pictures

To start your project on the late Stone Age/early Bronze Age look at pictures of what a village in the ancient landscape looked like. Discuss why there would have been fewer people and lots of forest and marshes in those days. Look at a picture of the inside of one of the huts, discuss with the children why there was a fire inside: to keep the people warm, to produce light, for cooking.

Becoming archaeologists: looking for clues

Next you might make a series of 'site visits' (in role as archaeologists): first to a recently developed area of your landscape (site visit 1); second to a place where you can see evidence of past occupation (site visit 2); and third to a vantage point – a place from where you can see a large area of your own landscape (site visit 3).

Site visit 1 is to an area the children themselves remember being developed, perhaps to a new housing estate. Everyone can discuss their own memories of how the area looked before the changes and old photographs can be inspected. You can, of course, use other people's memories and talk about older developments. An older person can explain how the landscape looked in the 1930s, about buildings which have disappeared and others which have arrived.

Site visit 2 is to a place where evidence of the past remains in the landscape but the evidence needs interpretation. This could be a visit to almost anything. A generous farmer used to let me take groups to see the Bronze Age and Iron Age hut circles in the fields at Cowan Bridge in Lancashire. Maureen Grantham (1996) used to take her classes to see the settlements on Bodmin Moor. But the site need not be so old; a castle, a walk along an abandoned railway line, or a visit to an archaeological excavation. What clues about the past can we find? Why was it here? Why has it disappeared?

Site visit 3 is to a vantage point in your own landscape – a place where you can pause to imagine what it would have been like thousands of years ago – no cars, lorries, houses, shops. What might it be like? Why do you think that?

'Hang on', I hear you say. 'They can't do that! It's like Piaget's mountain task – you're asking a child of less than six to imagine something from another person's perspective' (Donaldson 1978: 22–5). That may be true, but as Hughes showed (Donaldson 1978), this kind of task is more about preparation and clarity. When children as young as three fully understand the mountain task, they are good at it. We can prepare the children to look at the distant past by getting them to understand that in the future people will have things we do not, and similarly we have things that people did not have in the past.

Making reconstructions – the wonders of information technology

With your help children can even make a photograph of what they think their landscape may have looked like in those days. They can take a digital picture of an area where they can see some houses and a road, but make sure there are plenty of trees and some green too. Now use a photo editing program, such as PHOTOSHOP, and 'rubber stamp' copies of the trees, green, marsh and so on over all the houses and roads in your landscape. You usually do this by activating 'rubber stamp' and then by selecting the areas you want to copy and stamping them over the bits you want to get rid of. Do not resize or crop the photograph as you do this, or the animation below won't work.

If you are familiar with PowerPoint then you can help children to animate the images and make all the buildings and roads seem to suddenly disappear from your original photograph. To do this, simply match up the before and after images on consecutive slides in PowerPoint; the photos must occupy exactly the same area of each slide – the modern one first. If you have done this correctly when you view the show and click the mouse button to bring on the next slide it seems as if all the houses and roads disappear but the areas of the photo you haven't worked on remain.

In case you are in any doubt about what the landscape would have looked like, let me explain. The physical landscape would be as it is now. There would be lots of woods, some cleared farm land with a few boundaries, small villages of round or possibly square huts, and a lot of marshland. There would be tracks which would have led to the fields, isolated dwellings and other villages. Some of the roads, fields and villages would have been in the same places as they are today.

The rivers were once great barriers because there were no bridges to cross them so the tracks would lead towards places where it was possible to wade through. When looking at their own landscape the children I worked with found no trouble in re-imagining the landscape of the past. They were happy about getting rid of cars and roads but were hesitant about getting rid of the houses – until I reminded them about the huts.

Making models

By the age of five or six a child is demonstrating a grasp of scientific concepts and measurement in play; role play is becoming more detailed and children are aware of the difference between fact and fantasy (Sheridan 1999: 32–3). Interestingly, towards the end of her book (p. 42), Sheridan describes a situation where children have been given models to make a town. She describes how the children, aged between five and six and a half, were able to arrange the buildings carefully and realistically.

Starting with now

Before you get the children to model the ancient landscape let them model your own. Give them something to represent houses and shops, the roads, bridges and rivers and cars, buses and lorries. The key to modelling our modern landscape is to encourage children to think about connectivity. Why does every house meet the road? Why do the roads lead to bridges? Are the houses connected by the roads to the shops and school? Where does our water and energy come from? How is it connected to our houses?

In ancient times

Oddly enough the ancient landscape is easier to model than our own. I have found that children were quite happy about the idea that these ancient people occupied the same places as we do. They can make huts with pointed roofs from card or bricks – a cone on top of a cylinder. To get the proportions right the roofs should be about three times the height of the walls and overlap them. They can paint the base green, add a few rough brown tracks to the fields and the next village and the river crossing. Children will understand about brown tracks because they will have seen short-cuts across grass areas. They can work out the routes people would have taken between buildings and other important areas and how their tracks would have worn into the grass. Ask them why they need to make a wood near the village (an important supply of firewood, berries and nuts). Have they included a nearby supply of water? They can put models of people, dogs, sheep and goats dotted around. Can children work out why models of wolves will be at some distance from the people? (They are the wild predators who will be watching from afar.)

Children can compare this settlement with the model of their locality today; explain how some of the tracks would have later turned into roads and the huts into houses. They can discuss why the huts would have been arranged as a protective farming settlement – not in streets of huts. They will also need to consider why there were not nearly so many people in those days – humans were quite rare in fact.

It may be possible to visit village recreations of prehistoric life, such as Castell Henlleys in Pembrokeshire, the Crannog on Loch Tay in Scotland or Butser Ancient Farm in Hampshire, or at least to visit their websites, which are given at the end of this chapter.

Creating an ancient hut in the home corner

What do we need to live? What are the essential tools of our present day lives? Young children are particularly familiar with these as much of their preschool young lives have been spent in the familiarity of their homes alongside their mother or father. To these children the rhythm of domestic life was doing the washing, shopping and the preparation of food. That is not to say that the fridge and the washing machine will be the most significant bits of the home to them. They might reserve the telly, bath and toy cupboard for this role. First children need to recognise these features of home life and to understand their roles. Only when they have done this can we take them away and begin the process of understanding that prehistoric people had very little except what they could make for themselves. So discuss why the accoutrements of modern life which litter the home corner – the washing machine, television, telephone – will have to go.

Sam wrote a poem about the hut his '250 times grandad and grandma' lived in after his class visited Castell Henllys prehistoric village in Pembrokeshire.

Sam's poem
I visited a hut in Wales.
Round with pointed straw roof.
The sort of hut my great (250 times) granddad and grandma lived in.
Imagine that – just like this hut.
This hut.
Where they cooked on a fire right in the centre – with the smell of smoke in their nostrils.
This hut.
Where everybody in the family slept in the same room because there was only one room.
This hut where there were dead fish and herbs hanging from the roof.
I found out other things too.
Imagine only having a bath in the summer – when you can wash in the stream!
Think about never going to school – because school doesn't exist.
No electricity so –
No telly,
Electric lights,
Game cube,
Fridge or freezer and ice cream,

Computer,

Microwave,

or lava-lamps with different colours (and little goldfish) that help me get to sleep.

No pipes so –

No toilet,

Bath,

Sink,

Washing machine to watch go round,

or ponds with fountains and goldfish.

No glass so –

No windows,

Glasses,

or fish tanks with goldfish.

They said.

No plastic so –

No plastic bags,

Plastic toys,

My sister's yellow plastic beads,

or, golden plastic goldfish for the bath.

And,

This is almost the worst bit,

No shops so –

No crisps!

Potatoes or chips,

Chocolate or fruity chews,

Beano,

Or cola.

And

No goldfish.

I'm glad I didn't live then.

Quite a concept isn't it, life without telly, packets of crisps, fruity chews and school?

So what shall we put in the new home corner? It needs a bed – how do we make a bed? – a pile of straw, animal skins, bracken – whatever. Somewhere to cook? They cooked over an open fire – make a model open fire, just a few logs and some shiny paper. They need pots – make clay pots. How did they cook their bread? They made the loaf and probably cooked it among the ashes of the fire.

There are of course many more things you can add to the corner: drying herbs, fleece for spinning, a wooden bucket for carrying water, lamps made with fat in a bowl with moss wicks, bundles of wood for the fire. How about a warp weighted loom (though it may have been a vertical loom), drop spindles, a saddle quern for grinding corn, and stone tools? I'll explain some of these later.

The concept of handmade

I feel uneasy about questions such as, 'Does it look handmade?' Not only is the word 'handmade' difficult to define but how does a child know about pole-lathes, hand looms, and all those things which are a part of the industry of handmade items? How can they tell if something is handmade? I think we need to define this idea early on in the process: 'Look, we can make this from wood; we can sew this; we can make this from clay,' and 'This is what the things we make for ourselves look like.' Remember that many children come from houses where even the food is ready made. I think this concept is fundamental to understanding this project – everything these people had was got by hand.

Make a model wall

A Stone/Bronze Age hut is made from wood, stones, reeds and clay – and we can make a model of one.

To make the model wall about 15 cm high use twigs of about 1–2 cm thick to make the uprights. Sharpen one end and then hammer them into a row of holes drilled every 6–10 cm into quite a thick and flat piece of wood – using a glue gun will secure these uprights well. Now weave thin twigs between the uprights (willow is good or prunings, but make sure you use them before they dry out). This is a hurdle. Hurdles were used in the construction of walls right up until recently. My mother's cottage has walls made in this way and that was only about 300 years ago. Now you need to daub the wall with clay – this was originally done with a mixture of dung and clay. You can make the daub with clay and chopped hay – it won't be as strong but it will work. It's a messy activity, but enormous fun.

Make flour, make bread

My son used to do this to me – Why is it raining, daddy? Because there are clouds in the sky. Why are there clouds in the sky? Because the sun shines on water and this dries up the water which gets into the air and goes up and then the air cools so the water comes out of the air again and it turns into clouds. Why does the sun dry up the water? And so we went on.

'How do we make a loaf of bread?' is a game of 'why consequences' too. The serious side of the game is learning to ask good questions: How do we make a loaf of bread? We get some flour. How do we get the flour? We have to get some wheat and crush it. How do we get wheat? How do we grow it? How do we crush it?

You can buy wheat in a health food shop. To crush it, make a saddle quern. You need a rounded river boulder, a bit bigger than your hand, and a stone slab (use part of a paving slab if you have to). Put the wheat on the slab and grind it with the boulder. If you want to try eating bread made from the wheat then grind it in a food blender – the flour from the saddle quern will be very gritty. They didn't use yeast for the bread.

Make yarn

How do we get clothes? We weave them. What do we weave them from? Woollen yarn. Where do we get the woollen yarn from?

To show the children how to make yarn don't try drop spinning with Key Stage 1 children as not only is it very difficult, it is complicated to understand how the short fibres of wool lock together to form a long thread. It is better to watch a demonstrator drop spinning and use some of the yarn for weaving when they have finished. If you want to demonstrate drop spinning yourself a good tip to make it easier is to add a small hook to the top of the spindle – loop the yarn around it to form the lock between the yarn on the spindle and the yarn you are spinning.

Try natural dyeing

Use unspun wool for dyeing as natural fibres take up natural dyes much better than artificial ones. Most early cloth in this country was probably woollen. They would have used plants like madder, weld and lichen to do their dyeing but I suggest you use onion skins which illustrate the process well and do not need a mordant. Wash the wool – they would probably have used urine to do this – and then simply simmer it with the onion skins for a very effective result. Use an old pan as the water which drains from boiled wool looks vile.

Weaving

Make a warp weighted loom. This is quite simple: two upright posts as tall as the user and a crosspiece. Then the warp threads are attached to the crosspiece and little clay doughnut-shaped weights (you can make these too) are attached to the bottom end of the warp. Put another cross bar across just above the warp weights to keep them steady. For an easy life make the warp threads about 1 cm apart – this is much coarser than they would have used. I would also suggest you use string for the warp as this will save you having to mend a lot of breakages. Then weave the weft thread through the warp.

Possible refinements are a shuttle, something long to wind the weft around and weave through the warp, and a beating comb, to squash the weft threads together.

Stone tools

Stone tools would still have been used in the Bronze Age – the later ones have holes drilled through them for a shaft. The earliest stone tools were made from flint. These were napped – shaped by chipping – and the resulting tools (knives, axes and scrapers) were beautifully made and sharp. Later polished stone tools were made from rock, such as slate. These were shaped and very smooth and the resulting axes, hammers and chisels were often quite beautiful. However, none of these tools are easy to make and the whole process can take a very long time and clearly there are safety issues. Finishing a flint tool was often done with an antler and a polished tool was finished by using a sanding process.

Children can carve and smooth the later, polished, stone axes from soap. These can even be tied to handles to imitate the finished product. If you want to try and make a real stone tool and you live in an area where flint is available, you can arrange small shards of flint along a split stick to form a serrated knife – you need to tie this together, but make sure you use blunt flint.

Bronze tools

Maureen Grantham (1996) came up with the wonderful idea of helping children to understand how metal is cast by casting 'tools' in chocolate. You can cast chocolate tools by forming the shape in damp sand, gently pushing silver foil into the hollow then pouring the melted chocolate into the mould. You can demonstrate how to cast straight into the sand with wax, although there are safety issues here. In both cases you will need to file the resulting tool to obtain the final form – but then that would have been a normal part of the process. Children should find out about the forms of bronze tools before they do this (a useful website is given at the end of the chapter). I suggest they try early bronze axe forms as these were flat and easier to cast. Later forms were much more complicated with hollows and loops. Common bronze tools were axes, daggers, swords and spearheads.

Food

Collecting natural food is difficult for us. Nowadays we find it hard to tell the difference between edible fungi and poisonous ones. We are not used to collecting nuts and berries in the autumn and the skills of making preserves and drying are rapidly disappearing. Most of the population live in urban environments where such things as giant puffballs, horse mushrooms, rosehips, sloes, hazelnuts and chestnuts are hard to find. It is certainly worthwhile looking at them in class and considering the expertise of the people who knew what could be eaten and what couldn't. How would they know?

I would like to concentrate on something early peoples ate which we don't think of as edible, something which is natural and very common and should be easy for your children to identify and collect – acorns. Acorns are a favourite food of pigs and rabbits. However, we can eat them too. Uncooked acorns are very bitter, but once roasted in a little oil they are like coffee and quite pleasant broken up and sprinkled on other food. Don't roast them too much as they go rock hard.

Clay pots

Clay of course is a natural material and comes from the ground. If you live in an area where there is clay bring some in and try to make a pot from it. Don't be afraid – I find that people often think that something won't work unless it has been bought. Shape the clay soil into a small thumb pot and bake this in a slow oven for several hours. It is magical to find it transformed into a hard, friable pot. Early pots were often of the coil type. If children want to concentrate on making 'Stone Age patterns' the pots could be made of bought clay (or any modelling material). Patterns were made in the clay with a stick or finger nails and by impressing cord into the surface and were carefully repeated all the way round the outside of the pot.

Dressing up and fur

Our abiding image of the Stone Age is of fur clad people hunting. And indeed 3,000 years ago fur was an important part of a person's costume – as well as woollen cloth and leather. It is good to discuss the wearing of fur with children – some of their reactions are amazing. One of the ways I have done so is in terms of waste, and how if everything is gained by the result of your own effort, you don't waste things like fur because you don't like them. The same was true for meat – when they killed an animal ancient peoples probably ate the lungs, brain and eyeballs as well as the steak. They even kept the guts, which they could turn into strong string. We, on the other hand, think nothing of throwing away vast amounts of perfectly usable things. What would an ancient person do with an empty can or a disused fridge? Fur is not hard to get hold of if you want to use it as part of an ancient dressing-up kit (you can often find it in charity shops). Fur is an outstanding material and incorporated with heavy woollen cloth will make Stone Age dressing up a memorable experience.

Conclusion

In deciding how to study life in the more distant past teachers have to weigh up their own knowledge and enthusiasms and take a serious look at the available local resources. Access to a museum loan collection on the Stone/Bronze Age, local archaeological sites and a relevant museum gallery all make this type of project much more viable. Finding out about the distant past through play activities is not necessarily better than, say, creating a Victorian kitchen, but it can be just as good. Remember creating 'an old kitchen' requires every bit as much subject knowledge and resourcing as this project. Life in the prehistoric past was in many ways simpler and activities connected with it really can be understandable, challenging, exciting and fun – and they do bring us close to our roots as a human being. What more do we want?

References

Donaldson, M. (1978) *Children's Minds*. London: Fontana.

Grantham, M. (1996) 'Pre-history on Bodmin Moor', *Primary History* **12** (March), 14–15.

Hampshire Inspection and Advisory Service (2002) 'Ofsted's 2002 report on history', *Primary History Matters* (Spring) **34**, 5.

Reynolds, V. (1976) *The Biology of Human Action*. Reading: W. H. Freeman and Company.

Sheridan, M. D. (1999) *Play in Early Childhood: From birth to six years*. London: Routledge.

Resources referred to in the text

Bronze age axes and stone age axe moulds, www.darwincountry.org/explore

Butser Ancient Farm, Hampshire, www.butser.org.uk

Castell Henllys prehistoric village Pembrokeshire, www.castellhenllys.com

Crannog prehistoric village, Loch Tay, Scotland, www.crannog.co.uk

7

Time and place capsules

Jane Yates

Armathwaite School

ARMATHWAITE COMMUNITY FIRST SCHOOL is a small rural school in the Eden Valley. It is one of only two first schools in Cumbria that cater for children from reception to Year 3. Children move on to primary schools in neighbouring villages for the rest of Key Stage 2. Although there are fewer than 30 children, you might be misled into thinking that the school is bigger than it actually is, by the large number of staff you may see in the school. However, the head teacher, Jenny Dixon, is the only full-time member of staff. There is also the equivalent of just over a full-time post, but this is shared between several part-time staff, each with a different curriculum specialism. Although the school is divided in to two classes, reception/Year 1 and Year 2/3, all teachers spend time teaching both classes. This means that individuals have responsibility for planning their curriculum specialist areas, but all staff share in the planning and delivering of independent learning for the Foundation Stage. During the last year a large new nursery has been built next to the school through a community lottery bid.

The school has a strong policy on independent learning and creativity. The week is structured around a balance of teaching knowledge/skills and independent learning. Independent learning is planned through a plan, do, review approach as a progression from reception through to Year 3. In reception and Year 1 there are much shorter planned activities. In Year 2/3 the children undertake their own projects in self-selected groups or as individuals. The adults interact with the children helping them to apply their knowledge and skills and use creativity to extend their projects. At the end of the week, on Friday afternoon, a cross-age review session takes place where children share their projects in small groups.

Each term a new role-play area is developed to link in with the topic. The role-play area is always constructed by the reception and Year 1 children during independent learning time. Working with the teacher at the beginning of each half term the children plan how they are going to develop the role-play area and then make changes while in role during the week. Many of the ideas suggested by the older children during review sessions are taken on board in its construction.

During independent learning, there are no boundaries within the school. The children freely move between the two adjoining classrooms and other rooms according to the resources and space they require. It is not uncommon to find Year 2/3 children spending time in the role-play area. This is encouraged by the school and has a very positive impact on the younger children.

How do I know the school?

I had worked with the school over the past couple of years on a variety of projects. The first was a Philosophy for Children (P4C) project with the Year 2/3 class. P4C aims to help children become more open in their thinking, to give them the skills to reason, to develop understanding and to value what others say. The staff at the school had reported on the positive way the skills developed in the P4C project had impacted on other lessons. This had a knock-on effect on the younger children in the school, as the Year 2/3 children modelled open-ended questions and ways to answer them. The school has subsequently trained all their staff in P4C and is developing a whole-school approach to this area.

Secondly, one of the staff had been involved in a Foundation Stage project I had been co-ordinating in 2003 for Cumbria Development Education Centre (CDEC) called Making Sense of My World. This had been funded by the Cumbria Early Years and Childcare Partnership. It allowed us to work with practitioners from all over Cumbria in exploring Knowledge and Understanding of the World (QCA 2000). The project had very much focused on the process of enquiry and how children 'make sense of the world'. We had been looking in particular at the concept of sustained shared thinking and open-ended questioning. Sustained shared thinking is a process that had come to our attention on reading the *Effective Pedagogy in the Early Years* project (Siraj-Blatchford *et al.* 2002). The project outlines five areas of interaction in sustained shared thinking – playing, modelling, discussing, extending and scaffolding. It also highlights the importance of having subject knowledge for practitioners in Foundation Stage settings. It was my intention to explore the ways in which adults might interact with children in these ways in setting up and supporting role-play situations.

The time capsule concept

The topic for the term was homes. There had been all sorts of discussions among staff as to how the role-play area could be used. Should there be a home from a particular country? Should there be a home from back in time? There were some reservations on having a single home as it might be limiting for the children and may lead to stereotypes. One of the teachers, Helen Hepworth, a specialist in design technology, suggested constructing a device which would enable the children to choose which places and times to go to. It was felt that this idea was very open-ended and would allow the children to use their imagination in order to visit other places and times. It was hoped that this would give us the opportunity to interact with a variety of situations.

Preparation and planning

A planning meeting was held between Jenny, Helen and myself. In this meeting we shared and explored ways we could introduce the children to the idea of travelling through time and place. Helen came up with an excellent idea: to introduce the concept through a story the children were already familiar with, such as the *Oxford Reading Tree* series *The Magic Key* (Hunt 1986–2003). In these stories the characters go to different times and places when the magic key 'glows'. The series offers a progression of stages where the concept of the magic key is introduced and developed to fire children's imagination with fantasy and adventure. The books are suitable for readers in Foundation Stage and Key Stage 1.

Then we wondered what factors would influence the children's choice of locations. Would they go to places and times based on their personal experiences? Would the places and times be imaginary or would they be real? What if they wanted to go to dangerous places and times? Would children want to go to different places and times simultaneously? Would they need real objects, or could they pretend?

Our heads were full of questions and ideas as we tried to put ourselves in the shoes of the reception children and how they might view the idea, but being a five-year-old was such a long time ago to us. So we decided to ask the experts!

As the Year 2s and 3s sat around the table expectantly the following week, we carefully explained our idea for constructing a role-play area with the younger children that would allow them to travel to different times and places. We suggested that their experience of 'pretending' was so much more recent than ours. They certainly seemed to have a lot more answers than we did.

'The role-play area needs to be much bigger, you end up banging your head'.
'You need different areas for the role play, not just one room, especially if you want to travel to different places.'
'We think you should move the role-play area to the Yellow room.' (This was a spare room used for music lessons.)

The children's initial concerns seemed mostly to do with the size and location of the role-play area. We decided to try out their ideas. This would mean careful planning for supervision by a rotation of adults, but with several students and parent helpers this would be possible.

We then asked the Year 2/3s which times or places they thought the younger children would want to go to. They thought that a castle was a likely choice, although there were suggestions of other real and imaginary places. We asked the children if we needed to put anything else in the role-play area. At first they started to list the things that could be there, then they realised that without knowing the destinations, it would not be possible to predict what would be needed. They all agreed that if there were boxes and objects available it would be possible to pretend what they were. One child made an interesting comment: 'If you had all the stuff, then it wouldn't really be pretend.' The Year 2/3 children left the session very excited about the project and asking if they would be able to travel to different places and times too!

Introducing the idea

The next day the idea was introduced to the reception and Year 1 class. A book from *The Magic Key* series was read and then children were asked for suggestions about where they could go. These were some of their ideas (see Figures 7.1 and 7.2):

Legoland	Blackpool beach
Scotland	Puppy world
Pony land	Africa (Kenya)
Lapland	Egypt
Person world	Charnborough
Oman	Back in time

It was interesting to see the range of places. Like the Year 2/3s, there was a mix of real and imaginary places. There were no distinct references to destinations relating to time, except for the idea of 'back in time'. No one mentioned going forward in time. Most real places seemed to be based on the children's own experience. None of the children had actually been to any of the places themselves, except for Blackpool beach, but they had heard about them from others or seen them on television. When the children were asked how they might get to these places and times, they decided they needed some kind of 'transport'.

Constructing the capsule

Children were presented with two child-height boxes from a delivery that had luckily just arrived containing some kitchen equipment. They agreed these could be made into transport for travelling to the times and places they had suggested in the previous session. They discussed a variety of names for the transport: portal,

FIGURE 7.1 Laura's list of places to visit in the time and space capsule

capsule, magic box. They settled on the idea of capsule. During the next couple of weeks the children were busily involved in deciding how to turn these boxes into the capsules (see Figure 7.3). This included the construction of a swing door that could be shut when someone was inside and holes at the sides so you could stick your arms out and hold the other person's hand, 'So you didn't feel alone or scared when you're travelling.' Inside, a variety of dials had been put for selecting places, seasons and dates. They decided to put the dials inside as otherwise they

1. casel un fold the casel· when yoy have finfst foldup the casel and roll up the carpet and take down thee bake g rond

2. Scret door wlak thow and have a sprise set like say on wensday it was fairy wold· and on friday il was a jungel

3. in the wold have a big big big big ball looking like a a wold· wlak thow a door and go in to opset wold

secret door   opset word

casser

FIGURE 7.2 Tom's ideas for the capsule – a castle, fairy world, jungle and alternative world

were worried that someone could change the dials when they were inside, so they would go to a different place. They decorated the boxes and added a light on top, 'So you can tell when someone is inside the capsule.' There had been much discussion as to how the time capsule would actually work. Would each person go to a different place? How would they play together if they all went to different places?

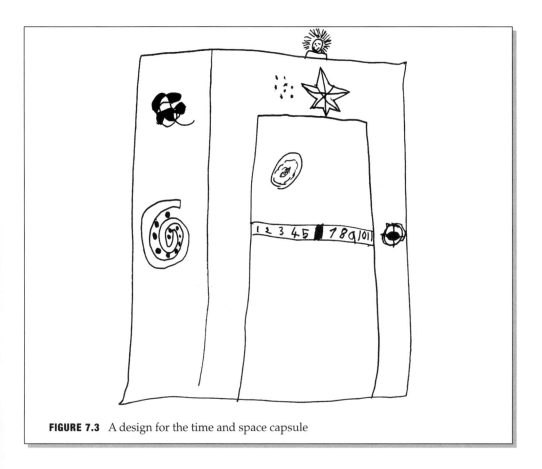

FIGURE 7.3 A design for the time and space capsule

They decided they all needed to agree on the destination before they took turns to use the capsule.

The two capsules were placed in the middle of the room, so that once they had been in the time capsule, the whole room became the new time or place, rather than leading into a separate room. Following up the Year 2/3 children's suggestion to provide more space for role play, the music room had been divided into three distinct areas with furniture – two smaller areas behind the capsule and a larger area in front. There was a feeling of real ownership of the capsules and great excitement at trying them out for the first time.

I had arranged to visit the school once the capsules had been completed, for two sessions on consecutive Friday afternoons. This also enabled me to take part in the review session at the end of the day. The aim of my visit was to explore ways in which we can effectively interact in a play situation to help children make sense of time and place, particularly looking at the different aspects of sustained shared thinking: playing, modelling, discussing, extending and scaffolding.

Oman

When I entered the 'capsule' room on the first Friday I stood at the door trying to take a guess at which time or place the children were in. It was certainly not immediately obvious as the children were involved in a familiar role-play situation preparing a meal in one of the smaller areas that had become a kitchen. The teacher, Helen, whispered to me that they were in Oman and it was the second time they had visited that week. She said they were in a hotel in Oman. I was excited by the idea they had chosen Oman, as it was certainly not somewhere I would have expected them to choose! Helen explained that the father of one of the girls worked in Oman. She said that the children had spent a considerable time in packing their bags before they went to Oman and there had been lots of discussion on whether they would need clothing for hot or cold weather.

As I stood at the door my initial urge was to go over to the children and ask them all sorts of questions. Why have you chosen Oman? What can you tell me about Oman? However, I knew that this would probably distract them from their play. This is a dilemma facing many of us in early years when interacting in play as our interactions can often hinder play rather than develop it. I also wondered how I would be able to extend and scaffold the children's knowledge and understanding when I knew very little about Oman myself.

I stood there for what seemed like ages, trying to think of open-ended questions so that I could discuss what the children already knew about Oman. I needed questions that would allow me to join in with the play, but not to hinder the flow of play.

Eventually I went over and introduced myself, within the role play. I said I had just arrived at the hotel and was really hungry and wondered if they knew where I could get some food. The children immediately welcomed me and said I could eat with them and suggested I sit at the table. I asked them what they were cooking. I was somewhat surprised when they replied 'pizza and chips'. I then asked if this was the only option and whether there was any Oman food. The children stopped and looked at me blankly, not sure what I was asking, then served me my plate of imaginary pizza and chips.

As the play progressed I could see that the social interaction of the children was excellent, but it was devoid of the context of Oman. It was almost as if they had decided to go to Oman, but once they were there, they carried out their traditional role play of the home corner, taking on roles of mother, father, children and preparing food.

Once I had finished my meal I told the children I was going to find my hotel room and would see them later. I went into the other smaller area in the room. I sat alone and frantically began to think how I could interact again. I began to wonder if it was right to interact in this way and whether instead I should stop interfering with the children's play and just go along and join in 'playing', rather than thinking about discussing, extending or scaffolding their sense of time and place. I was confused that they did not seem to exhibit a sense of the place they had chosen to visit. However, on reflection, I considered whether this was a good thing. What had I expected to find? With my limited knowledge of Oman, who was I to know that the goings on in a hotel in Oman would be any different from a hotel anywhere else? Maybe it was a good thing that the children seemed to play in this generic way, rather than latching onto the expected stereotypes one might expect. I wondered if this might be the case if the children were encouraged to leave the hotel. I decided on another line of enquiry and went back to the kitchen.

I decided to join in

Jane: 'You know I've just arrived at the hotel – has anyone been outside yet? What's it like?'
  'It's very hot – we've been drinking lots of water.'
  'Shall we get you some?'
Jane: 'Oh, yes please, it was a long flight and I am thirsty now.' (Two children go off to get water from drinks fountain.)
Jane: 'But what's it like outside?'
  'It's hot outside.'
  'There are some palm trees and it is sandy.'
  'There are camels on the beach.'
Jane: 'Has anyone been to the beach yet?'
  'No, not yet.'
Jane: 'How do you know there are camels here if no one has been out yet?'
  'I saw them out the window before.'
Jane: 'Is anyone planning to go out? I'd really like to explore.'
  'Maybe later, we've got to finish cooking.'

The children seemed intent on staying inside the hotel and carrying out their chores of preparing food. I had managed to discuss a little of their knowledge of Oman, which seemed to be mainly focused on the fact that it was hot and therefore had a landscape that depicted this.

The children seemed obsessed by the hotness of being in Oman. There was a constant stream of children going to get water from the water dispenser in the other classroom. One of the boys had picked up a fan and was fanning himself.

Jane: 'That's a good idea. It is so hot in here.'
  'Do you want me to fan you as well?'
Jane: 'Yes, please. Why do you like to do so much fanning?'
  'I'm a servant.'
Jane: 'That sounds like hard work. Do you like being a servant?'
  'Yes.'

Jane: 'But are there some times when you would like someone to do something for you?'

'Well, only when I get tired. I'm all right now. They only have servants in hot places.'

Jane: 'Do they? Why is that?'

'Because people get too tired to do things in hot places.'

Jane: 'So does everyone in a hot place have a servant?'

'No, not everyone, only if you are rich – people had servants in the olden days.'

Jane: 'So are we in the olden days now?'

'No, we are in Oman.'

At last . . . a sustained dialogue involving discussing as well as extending!

Reflecting on the play

I could see that the dialogue had not only given me insight into the children's understanding of place, but also of time, cultures and beliefs. It made me question the interrelated nature of time, place, cultures and beliefs and how children don't distinguish between them in the same way as older children or adults.

At break time as the children came out of role I stopped to talk to Jodie, the girl whose father worked in Oman. It became evident that her experience of Oman was based on the stories her father had told about the hotel, so it was not surprising that the context of the role play had been focused mainly on being in the hotel.

At the end of the day the review session was held. This consisted of a group of seven children from across the full age range from reception to Year 2. There were three reception children in my group who had taken part in the role play to Oman. I was really looking forward to the chance to talk to them about their knowledge and understanding of Oman more directly now they were out of role. However, I was surprised to find that when it came to their turn the three reception children who had been part of the role play did not even mention the play they had been so engaged with all afternoon, but started showing a model they had made earlier in the week. Although frustrating and overwhelming, this was a great learning experience for me. It made me realise how we make assumptions that children who have been to places or heard about a place from a family member, automatically gain knowledge and understanding of that place.

It also made me realise the importance of subject knowledge. It would have been interesting to have shown the children photos of Oman from books or the Internet, or to have asked the father to come in and talk about his visits, to see how that would have influenced their play in future.

Blackpool beach

When I arrived the following Friday afternoon, the children had again spent considerable time packing their bags, this time to go to Blackpool beach in the capsule.

All the children were reception except for Joanne, a Year 2 girl who had asked to join in the role play. Again, I tried a similar line in my introduction.

> Jane: 'I've just arrived and I need to buy some lunch for my picnic.'
> 'You need to go to the shop. It's down there.' The child pointed down the corridor to another classroom.
> Jane: 'Mm, it looks quite a long way. What if I get lost?' (I was hoping that one of the children would suggest coming with me.)
> 'We could draw you a map.' (This was Joanne from Year 2.)

Joanne drew me a map, while two reception children watched, absolutely fascinated. I decided I would use this as a modelling opportunity, encouraging Joanne to do the modelling.

> Jane: 'So can you describe what I'll see as I get there?'
> 'You will pass two lamp posts and a house, then the shop.' (Joanne points to each feature on the map as they describe the route.)
> Jane: 'Thank you very much. I'll see you later.'

I could never have planned or predicted the opportunity with the map. Later I noticed Patrick, one of the reception children, drawing another map for someone else. The reception children did know what a map was and had drawn simple maps before, but not in a play situation. It made me realise that it is not that the reception children had no knowledge and understanding of maps, but they had not yet had the experience of applying their knowledge and understanding within the role-play setting. It also made me realise the potential for involving older children in role-play situations to model their knowledge and understanding. They could interact and introduce new ideas far more naturally than I ever could.

Although I was very pleased that there had been an incidental use of a map, this meant that I would still be on my own going to the shop. I was pleased when Lisa caught me at the shop, complete with a pushchair. There were some old coins in the till. I picked one up and said I didn't recognise these coins. Lisa explained that they were old coins. I asked her if we were in Blackpool now or back in time. Suddenly it was as if I had unleashed a new idea. Lisa replied:

> 'We can be back in time now.'
> Jane: 'So are we still in Blackpool or are we somewhere else?'
> ' We're still in Blackpool, but we are back in time.'
> Jane: 'How do you know if we're back in time?'
> 'There aren't any cars. They have horses to pull you. Can you be the horse and take me back to the beach in my cart?'
> Jane: (I pulled out the map and showed it to Lisa.) 'I've got this map to show me the way back to the beach. You can see the shop, a house and the two lamp posts. Can I use this map to get me to the beach again if I am back in time?'
> 'No, they didn't have lights on the street then. Come on, let's go back to the beach horsey.'

Lisa then got in the pushchair and I pushed her back along the corridor. She was worried about the cobbles on my poor hooves!

In the review time, I found out that Lisa knew about Blackpool beach in the past because she had seen a video in school called *Seaside Holiday with Magic Grandad* (BBC TV 2003). It was interesting that her association with 'back in time' was related to within 100 years ago. Later, Robbie showed another map the reception children had drawn. They were obviously very pleased with themselves.

Further thoughts

On reflection, it was not surprising that Lisa had related her experience of back in time to within 100 years. If we look at the *Curriculum Guidance for the Foundation Stage* (QCA 2000) which encourages practitioners to provide opportunities for children to explore their understanding of changes over time, it seems to refer to time within the recent past. Yet, although children may not understand chronology they may have the capacity to imagine distant times and places more vividly than older children.

Conclusions

At the end of the summer term, Jenny, Helen and I held a meeting where we discussed our learning from the capsule project. It had certainly made us think further about what the role of adults should be in planning for, extending and reviewing learning through play and the challenges and difficulties involved. It clarified a number of points for us.

- Subject knowledge
  Adults need to find out themselves about the times and places children visit in their play if they are to extend it. I should love to have been around longer to have found out more about Oman with the children. The subject knowledge children had already, for example about Blackpool beach in the past, had been integrated into their play. The planning and review sessions could have involved children and adults in finding out more, which may have been internalised in subsequent play.

- Setting up the role play
  A great deal of sustained shared thinking and problem solving between adults and children had taken place in setting up. The older children had advised the adults on the need to create more space for their play, how to resource it and the kinds of play younger children might enjoy. The reception and Year 1 children had plenty of suggestions of their own. They were all involved in deciding on the capsule idea and designing and making these involved sustained problem solving and discussion over two weeks. Maybe finding out

more about possible time and place locations for when the capsules were completed could have been woven in here.

- Concepts of place and time
  Since other times and places cannot be directly experienced they are an ideal way of developing imaginative thinking. It seemed, at least in the 'capsule' play, that children needed to visit other places first, before they thought of places in other times. But the boundary between concepts of time and place seemed blurred and flexible. The 'servant' in Oman talked about his role in past times; the pushchair on Blackpool beach became a horse and carriage! The Oman play also highlights the importance of linking cultures and beliefs as an intrinsic part of time and place concepts.

  There also needs to be a greater emphasis on the explicit teaching of skills and knowledge associated with time and place which can be applied during independent learning. The good practice of the school in encouraging literacy and numeracy skills (see medium-term planning grid shown in Figure 7.4) to be applied in role-play situations could be developed to include skills related to time and place.

- Preparing for travelling
  Opportunities for assessing knowledge and understanding of places and times is particularly appropriate during the activity of bag packing in preparation for travelling to a particular destination. For both Oman and Blackpool, the children had enjoyed spending a considerable amount of time in packing their bags before they went into the time capsule. Unfortunately I had not been present at this stage, but was informed by Jenny and Helen that there had been a lot of sustained discussion on what was relevant to take to the place, especially in terms of the likely climate. This type of discussion would help assess the children's knowledge and understanding of both places in order to be able to extend and scaffold their sense of time and place once out of the capsule.

- Adult–child interactions
  We might assume that the interaction with young children in play is easy for early years practitioners. While this can be the case when 'playing' along with the generic 'home-corner play' of children, it was certainly more challenging when embarking on sustained shared thinking. My confidence increased from one session to the next and made me realise that sustained shared thinking can only be improved through regular practice, both for adults and children. This was also emphasised in the Making Sense of My World project at CDEC in 2003, where teachers embarked on setting up focused enquiries on a weekly basis through a chosen stimulus such as a story, artefact, using puppets or within play.

ARMATHWAITE SCHOOL	MEDIUM-TERM PLANNING FOR INDEPENDENT LEARNING THROUGH PLAY		RECEPTION–FOUNDATION STAGE					
Area of P&L	Foundation Stage Early Learning Goals	Organisation	Main provider	Is the area literate?	Is the area numerate?	Resources	Links to NC foundation subjects	Assessment opportunities
Role play	**Personal, Social and Emotional Development** **1: Dispositions and attitudes** a: Continue to be interested, excited and motivated to learn. b: Be confident to try new activities, initiate ideas and speak in a familiar group.	Homes link *Phase one* Start with two homes with a dividing wall, so that children can phone, visit and have a next-door neighbour if they want!	All			Everything you need in a home – ask children to make a list of the things they would find useful.	Design and technology Unit 1D – Homes	
	2: Self-confidence and self-esteem a: Respond to significant experiences, showing a range of feelings when appropriate. **3: Making relationships**		All	Phone books, address book, house name/no. shopping lists, message board.	Telephones, clocks, purses, money.	Include dressing-up clothes.	History – Homes	
	b: Work as part of a group or class, taking turns and sharing fairly, understanding that there needs to be agreed values and codes of behaviour for groups of people, including adults and children, to work together harmoniously. **5: Self care** a: Dress and undress independently and manage their own personal hygiene. b: Select and use activities and resources independently.	Adapt to children's ideas if needed.	All	Postcards, maps, compass, tent instructions, first aid book.	Camp site fees etc.	A tent and camping gear, sleeping bag, map, compass, first aid box.	Geography – Homes	
	Communication, Language and Literacy **1: Language for communication** a: Interact with others, negotiating plans and taking turns in conversation. b: Enjoy listening to and using spoken and written language and readily turn to it in their play and learning.	*Phase two* Introduce a tent to the role-play area, so that children can plan and take a camping holiday in their play. Loads of literacy/numeracy links here!	HH JD	Opportunities for children to make own labels and captions/ instructions for time capsule etc.	Year, month, day, hour, minutes, seasons, destination settings.	Structure for the time capsule.	Art and design – sculpture	
	2: Language for thinking a: Use language to imagine and recreate roles and experiences. b: Use talk to organise, sequence and clarify thinking, ideas, feelings and events. **5: Writing** a: Attempt writing for different purposes, using features of different forms such as lists, stories and instructions. c: Write their own names and other things such as labels and captions and begin to form simple sentences, sometimes using punctuation.	*Phase three* Introduce a magic/time capsule, so that children can travel to magic/fantasy places and forwards and back in time! This will give them opportunities to create and visit an environment of their choice, which we hope will provide many opportunities for free use of their imaginations – i.e. they may travel to a land of dogs and cats, land of the dinosaurs, the strange world of the Fimbles! Or back in time to when they were a baby, forward in time to when they are an adult, back to a home from the past, or to a magic castle, etc.		Also any other links children come up with. Any books which would provide a stimulus – i.e. the Ahlberg baby books, home from the past books etc.		Dressing-up clothes we think of – to update if possible as children require. Books		
	Mathematical Development **3: Shape, space and measures** d: Use everyday words to describe position. e: Use developing mathematical ideas and methods to solve problems.							

FIGURE 7.4 Part of the medium-term planning for independent learning through play

It is easy to make the assumption that if adults are present in play, they need to be interacting continuously, when perhaps their time would be more valuably spent observing and thinking about how they can effectively interact next. This is supported by Siraj-Blatchford *et al.* (2002) who suggest that most of children's time in play should not be dominated by adults, but that any involvement with children should be in a planned and focused way to encourage shared thinking.

- Play: reception–Year 2
  Collaboration between children across the three to seven age phase, in planning, participating in and reviewing their play added to the learning potential. The older children were more able than the adults to decide on suitable play contexts and to design the resources. And they modelled their skills, in map making for example, for the younger children, who copied them with enthusiasm.

- Consult with older children
  The potential for successful play was much enhanced by the older children's suggestion that the play space should be bigger, with fewer boundaries. It is easy to assume that adults are the experts in creating role-play environments, when perhaps we need to consult more with older children, who have certainly been there more recently than we have!

References

Hunt, R. (1986–2003) *Oxford Reading Tree: The Magic Key Series* (Stages 4–9). Oxford: Oxford University Press.

Resources referred to in the text

(BBC TV 2003) *Seaside Holiday with Magic Grandad* (part of the *Watch* series)

Useful websites

www.bbc.co.uk/schools/magickey

www.sapere.net

www.yahoo.co.uk and www.google.co.uk to search for images of Oman

8

Secret places: 'You're too big to come in here!'

Jane Dixon and Sue Day

Outdoor play matters

SINCE THE INTRODUCTION of the Foundation Stage in 2000 the push for quality outdoor play has been high on the early years agenda. The outdoor play area can provide the perfect medium through which the key principles of active and exploratory learning take place. The outdoors affords opportunities for children to work freely, on a large scale, in a challenging and stimulating environment. The division between indoor and outdoor play should become blurred, as more practitioners see how children can access a whole curriculum just as effectively outside (Bilton 2002). Indeed, for many young children being outdoors is more appropriate for their stage of development and learning. Working outside enables them to make choices, take risks, work collaboratively, and follow through their own ideas, without the constraints of lack of space, timetables and the ever present adult.

The need for such outdoor experiences has never been greater. Today we live in a society that is often reluctant to let children play outside, fearful of physical and moral dangers. There are also fewer opportunities for children to play outside, as providers of public play areas are increasingly mindful of litigation. As a result we have a generation of children growing up denied the excitement of outdoor adventures, dens and secret places that many of us remember from our own childhood. We enjoyed both freedom and independence, which gave us the opportunities to develop all six of the areas of learning identified in the Foundation Stage (QCA 2000) long before this document was ever thought of! With increasing lack of opportunities for children to be physically active, we are now seeing for the first time, children with adult type diabetes, obesity and even cases of agoraphobia. It is clear that there is a need for quality outdoor play and an increasing onus on early years settings to consider and adapt their current practice to address these pressing needs.

Outdoor play at Brantfield Nursery

Kendal Nursery School, Brantfield, in Cumbria has taken to heart the notion of bringing the 'indoor classroom' outdoors. This focus on outdoor education is in line with current thinking, but also echoes the philosophy of the McMillan sisters (Bilton 2002) in the early twentieth century. They advocated learning outdoors as a way of improving children's health and of encouraging learning developed from the children's own interests. Practitioners today should be aware of the opportunities afforded by outdoor provision, not only in terms of developing children's learning, but also with regard to the positive benefits to their health. Ironically, the health issues for the McMillan sisters were quite different from those we face today!

The staff at Brantfield have invested a lot of time and energy in developing their outdoor play provision and the school has been identified as a model of good practice. The outdoor play is not a 'fair weather' experience here. The children and staff go out daily, whatever the weather. The rows of wellies, splashsuits and cagoules (in both child and adult sizes) were evidence of the school's dedication to outdoor play. Safety is a key issue, but is balanced with the concepts of 'risk taking' and challenge. Head teacher, Sue Matthews, stressed the importance of having parents on board with this philosophy. She spends time with new parents at induction discussing the importance and value of learning outdoors in line with the principles of the Foundation Stage (QCA 2000). This enables staff, parents and children to have a shared understanding of outdoor play.

This nursery is fortunate to have a large, verdant, natural outdoor setting that has been thoughtfully enhanced to maximise children's freedom of movement and learning. Specific areas have been created, such as the mark-making, gardening, sand, climbing and music areas. The well developed outdoor environment ensures that all the areas of learning in the Foundation Stage can be successfully met. A striking feature at Brantfield is the extensive provision of constructed dens such as a tree house, huts, hides and willow wigwams.

Secret places

Our own childhood memories of dens and secret places, made us wonder whether there was still the opportunity for children today to have the thrill and excitement of hiding that we enjoyed. Are early years settings today able to offer such opportunities, or is the concern for a total 'risk-free environment' denying children this experience?

Brantfield was the ideal setting for us to investigate children's secret places and how they were used. We wanted to know what learning opportunities the secret places promoted and how they related to specific areas of learning. We observed the children's use of secret places and talked with them about their play.

The use of the phrase 'secret places' has not been without controversy. Some early years practitioners are very much against using the term, fearing it may be misconstrued. Such belief reflects the present climate of heightened awareness of child protection issues which makes people wary of children having secrets. Our observations suggest that the term 'secret places' is part of children's everyday language, and with this in mind, some schools are happy to use it. The decision to use it or the substitute phrase 'special places', needs to be agreed locally by school, parents and children.

Secret places and holistic learning

In early years education, we are now at the exciting stage where outdoor play is recognised as being as effective as indoor play, in providing opportunities for learning across the whole curriculum. The Foundation Stage curriculum officially recognises that a rich and varied outdoor environment is important for young children and so requires practitioners to go outdoors with the children and create opportunities for play.

Young children seem to be forever on the move. This is a characteristic of how they learn best. Opportunities for play outside in the wider environment help develop the whole child emotionally, socially, cognitively and physically. Drummond (1995: 9) paints a vivid picture of this holistic development of children in the context of outdoor play.

> When children play out of doors, they are exercising their growing intellectual and emotional muscles, as well as their physical ones. They are developing their powers to think, to feel, to do, to see and understand, to represent and express. They are imagining, puzzling, wondering, exploring, befriending and sharing.

Although the focus of this study is 'secret places', relating particularly to Knowledge and Understanding of the World (QCA 2000: 86–96) and Personal, Social and Emotional Development (QCA 2000: 32–8)), we were mindful of the holistic way in which children learn and so expected a wide range of learning to take place (Figure 8.1).

We set out to discover which Foundation Stage areas of learning specifically related to children's play in their 'secret places'. Our findings held some surprises for us! We found a distinct difference in gender play. The focus of the children's play was imaginative play, with active and sustained play in fantasy roles (Hutt *et al.* 1989). Their sense of 'place' and 'hiding' also related significantly to a wider knowledge and understanding of the natural environment, including plants, minibeasts and weather. During their play children confidently used language which demonstrated an understanding of space and position. Our study involved us observing children at play, asking questions, listening to their conversations and even following them deep into the undergrowth. Such was our interest and

	Early Learning Goals	National Curriculum Programmes of Study
Personal, Social and Emotional Development	**Dispositions and attitudes** ■ Continue to be interested, excited and motivated to learn (P.32) ■ Be confident to try new activities, initiate ideas and speak in a familiar group (P.32) **Making relationships** ■ . . . understanding that there needs be agreed values and codes of behaviour for groups of people to work together harmoniously (P.36) **Behaviour and self-control** ■ Consider the consequences of their words and actions for themselves and others (P.38)	**PSHE and Citizenship** ■ Developing confidence and responsibility and making the most of their abilities ■ Developing good relationships and respecting the difference between people
Communication, Language and Literacy	**Language for communication** ■ Interact with others, negotiating plans and activities and taking turns in conversation (P.48) **Language for thinking** ■ Use language to imagine and recreate roles and experiences (P.58)	**English** En 1 Speaking and listening
Mathematical Development	**Shape, space and measures** ■ Use everyday words to describe position (P.80)	**Mathematics** Ma 3 Shape, space and measures
Knowledge and Understanding of the World	**Exploration and investigation** ■ Investigate objects and materials by using all of their senses as appropriate (P.86) ■ Find out about, and identify, some features of living things, objects and events they observe (P.86) ■ Look closely at similarities, differences, patterns and change (P.88) **Sense of place** ■ Observe, find out about and identify features in the place they live and the natural world (P.96) ■ Find out about their environment, and talk about those features they like and dislike (P.96)	**Geography** Geographical enquiry and skills Knowledge and understanding of places Knowledge and understanding of patterns and processes Knowledge and understanding of environmental change and sustainable development **Science** Sc 1 Scientific enquiry Sc 2 Life processes and living things Sc 3 Materials and their properties
Physical Development	**Sense of space** ■ Show awareness of space, of themselves and of others (P.108)	**PE** Acquiring and developing skills
Creative Development	**Imagination** ■ Use their imagination . . . in imaginative and role play and stories (P.124)	

FIGURE 8.1 How specific Early Learning Goals relate to secret places

commitment, that we endured prickles, insect bites and bad backs without a word of complaint!

The nursery grounds consist of deep undergrowth, mature shrubs and trees of all sizes, with pathways leading in and around the garden. The garden has the advantage of being on different levels, which adds interest and a further dimension to children's exploration and play. The grounds are interspersed with a number of purposefully constructed 'secret hiding places' for the children to play in. These include a willow wigwam, a tree house, an animal hide, a wooden cottage, a wooden rowing boat and a grass-covered hummock with tunnel entrance.

What did we find?

Constructed dens

During our observations, the tree house was transformed into a jail, fire station and home, as different children adapted it to their own play agendas. The play was noticeably gender specific, with boys boisterously acting in their roles of police officers and fire fighters, while the girls played more sedately in traditional home roles. There was a distinct difference in the amount of time spent in this and other 'secret places', with the girls spending considerably more time in them. The nature of their play was also very different. The girls tended to chat comfortably with one another in a relaxed, unhurried manner – 'We come in here to pick leaves and talk.' This provided great contrast to the boys' play, which always seemed to have an air of urgency, with the boys constantly on the move from one secret place to another.

> 'Quick, in here. Close the door – no one can get us now!'
> 'Come on you men! We need to find a hiding place.'
> 'Into the police station, all right?'

A large part of the boys' play involved running together, to and from their hiding place, and considerably less time actually in it. However, the girls on their own seemed to use the hiding place for sociable play. We noted the boys would often not speak to one another in the secret place, as they used it as somewhere to hide away and not be seen. They would only spend a short amount of time before running off to the next part of their adventure. Their choice of play roles and the way they enacted scenarios, meant that there was an edge of tension and 'danger' to their play. When we tracked them down in their lair and asked what they talked about, one little boy remarked, 'We talk about dangerous things.' To any worried reader, 'dangerous things' meant 'robbers' and 'houses on fire'!

The wigwam was set up with traditional home play equipment. This secret place was mainly used by girls, although some boys were allowed to join them.

The girls seemed to have the upper hand however, dictating the direction and rules of the play.

'You have to be the baby.'
'You can't bring this in here.'

At one point a group of girls excluded other children. 'We live in here.' It took sensitive adult intervention to help the children resolve the conflict, allowing play to continue. Both the boys and the girls stayed in character for some considerable time. The girls wanted the play to be contained within the wigwam, and this was the case until the baby (boy) made a bolt for freedom. He was successfully tracked down in the undergrowth by 'Mum and Dad' and returned home, still in character. He was later spotted 'running a criminal to ground'. It would seem that the need to run was strong for this boy in every play context.

Both boys and girls demonstrated evidence of their own experiences through their conversations in role:

Mum (girl): Are you going to do that job now?
Dad (boy):   No. Let's go out.

Our faith in equality of the sexes was restored by another 'Mum' (girl) who demanded to know 'Is tea ready yet?' after her hard day 'at work'.

The animal hide was a long, open shelter which allowed the children to observe sheep and other animals in the field beyond, while remaining hidden from view. During our observations, the children did not play in this structure, but rather chose to play 'underneath', 'behind' and 'next to' it, demonstrating through their use of these words, a sound knowledge of mathematical vocabulary in a real context. They found their own secret places around this structure, which were out of bounds to adults.

'Natural' dens

'You can't get down here.'
'You're too big to come in here,'

These were the taunts as we attempted to squeeze behind the animal hide.

While the structured dens encouraged the children to use them as their own special 'secret places', the most used 'secret places' were the ones the children created themselves from the dense undergrowth. This was particularly true of the boys. They took great delight in forging their way through the leaves and branches to specifically identified dens, completely out of view of the adult (Figure 8.2). They called out specific directions to each other as they raced to their chosen destination

'It's there.'
'OK, we'll meet you there.'
'Follow me – this way.'

FIGURE 8.2 Connor's 'entrance hole that leads to secret places'

The need to remain hidden from others was evident through the boys' language.

'No one can get us now.'
'No one will know where we are.'

The children were very aware of the different types of vegetation around their secret places in the undergrowth. They knew that some plants were prickly and that they must be careful of these. 'That's holly – it prickles.' They knew the names of various plants and trees and used these naturally in their conversations. One girl's favourite hiding place was 'in the trees'. She took us deep into the garden to show us which was 'her' tree. She was very definite about which was hers, dismissing one tree because 'it has pricklies in' and another because 'it's too big'. She came to a small tree and pointed to the height she would climb to; well within her safety limit. 'I just go up to this bit.' (See Figure 8.3.)

Two girls were observed hiding behind some trees. However, while they referred to this as their secret place, they were still visible to others. This did not seem to worry them and the emphasis seemed to be on having a quiet place to play and talk, rather than being completely hidden from others. They had quite

FIGURE 8.3 Georgia's secret place is half way up a tree

clear rules of admittance to their secret place: 'Boys aren't allowed in here – it's the girls' secret hiding place.'

Gender differences

In all the secret hiding places, both natural and constructed as explained above, clear distinctions between boys' and girls' play were observed. Boys used the secret hiding places as their base for sustained co-operative fantasy and superhero play, with lots of action and movement. Often early years practitioners tend to assume that boys cannot concentrate for any length of time. However, our observations concurred with Hutt *et al.* (1989) who found that boys' concentration span was longer when engaged in outdoor rather than indoor play. Secret places provide an opportunity for boys to be successful in deep, purposeful and sustained play and should therefore be considered a valuable part of outdoor play provision.

The notion that boys and girls play differently is supported by Sayeed and Guerin (2000) and Ouvry (2000) who found that boys often in engaged in fantasy play such as cops and robbers, while girls focused more on play based around the home setting. Our observations also showed girls' domestic play in their secret places was less action based than the boys. Girls' play was more contained within a small area and a single secret place, such as the wigwam, while the boys raced from one secret place to another.

Child-initiated and teacher-initiated play

Through our observations, we noted that the play within the secret places, both constructed and natural, was very much child initiated, with opportunities for the children to develop their own play agendas and rules. We also observed teacher-initiated play based around the notion of 'hiding places' when one teacher organised a large scale game of 'hide and seek'. Some children needed adult support to find appropriate hiding places. Others seemed to need the security of being alongside the adult to experience the delight of 'hiding'.

The sense of being 'hidden' seemed to be important for the boys, as evident in their choice of dense undergrowth to hide in, and the way they used the constructed secret places to remain out of sight. The girls we observed seemed to be content for their secret places to be visible, and even being under the eye of an adult did not seem to alter their play. The notion of being completely hidden did not seem as important to them. Perhaps they even felt more secure, knowing that others could find them. Our findings would suggest that most children enjoy playing in secret places, but that they might have a very different understanding of what it is to be hidden. Practitioners need therefore to ensure that provision of secret places is varied and will appeal to both the adventurous and timid child.

Noise levels

We found there was a distinct gender difference in noise level (Thorne 1993 in Sayeed and Guerin 2000) associated with secret places. Boys playing on their own, shouted commands and directions to one another on their way from one secret place to another, but remained silent when hiding in their den. The girls' talk within their secret place, however, was quietly conversational. The staff at Brantfield recognise the need for boys at times to play at 'full volume' and the out-door setting facilitates this. This very natural way for boys to play should not be discouraged or feared by practitioners. There is sometimes an assumption that boisterous play is out of control and not educationally appropriate.

Our study suggests that secret places have a significant part to play in outdoor play provision (Ouvry 2000; Edgington 2002). It is important children feel there is a place they can call their own and reflect their own identity. At home, this may be a bed-room or playroom. In the early years setting secret places can fulfil this role, allowing children to feel safe and secure, and able to take charge and set their own agendas.

Secret places and the curriculum

There are clear links with the Foundation Stage but in particular, with regard to 'sense of place' in the areas of Knowledge and Understanding of the World and Personal and Social Education (QCA 2000). These are shown in Figure 8.1. Secret places encourage true child-initiated play in terms of the depth of absorption and involvement of children. They foster independence by allowing choice and con-trol, and help build confidence and self-esteem. They promote social interaction and negotiation, developing more complex use of language for both thinking and communication. Secret places can provide a rich context for holistic learning. It might appear that much of this learning goes on without any overt adult input. However, the adult's indirect role in facilitating this wealth of learning is fundamental.

The role of the adult

Supporting the play

The depth and range of learning that can come from secret places needs to be made explicit to all those involved with children such as parents, support staff and governors. Induction of new parents is one important way in which this may be achieved. Open days offer the chance for interested parties to come and see the children at play for themselves, and gain an understanding of the value of such play. A written policy makes clear how individual settings put their principles of outdoor play into practice.

Promotion of secret places will be of limited value, unless there is a real conviction and commitment from practitioners. There has to be real understanding of the important learning that can take place through provision of secret places. Whole-school staff development can help practitioners begin to develop a shared philosophy of their role in outdoor play, and move away from the notion of adults as simply supervisors. While there is still a supervisory element, practitioners also need to be educators, facilitators and motivators. Time to reflect on current beliefs and attitudes will help to move practice forward and develop a genuine enthusiasm for outdoor play that can be infectious!

Safety

The freedom provided for children by a stimulating, outdoor learning environment, raises the serious issue of risk. The Play Safety Forum (2002) states how fear of litigation has led many providers to limit children's activities outdoors, while Stephenson (2003: 40) warns of the effects of making a setting risk free: 'In making a centre hazard free, inadvertently it will also be made challenge free.'

The role of the practitioner is to get the balance between challenge and safety in the context of a thorough risk assessment of the setting. The pressure to provide a 'safe' setting can result in a sterile environment, so empty of challenge that it stifles curiosity.

By their very nature, 'secret places' are usually out of view and sometimes found in wild terrain. Dens deep in the undergrowth or up a tree may present elements of risk. The role of the adult is to make an assessment of the level of acceptable risk, based on their knowledge of the individual child and setting. In today's climate it is all too easy to focus on what Stephenson (2003: 42) terms 'the darker side of risk'. However, she also impresses upon us the positive aspects of 'risk' such as being 'adventurous, daring, brave, strong, confident and successful'. Such bold words are rarely heard in the context of early years outdoor play.

The skills and dispositions involved in children's risk taking such as problem solving, thinking, independence, confidence to try new things and initiate ideas, can lead to successful learning in other areas. Indeed, Stephenson (2003) suggests that there is a link between physical risk taking and children developing confidence and competence in other areas of learning.

The Play Safety Forum (2002) recognises that children need and want to take risks in their play, and thrive on the stimulation that challenge provides. Stephenson (2003: 40) suggests that where a setting is 'too safe and restrictive' not only will children become bored but, in an attempt to create their own challenge, may use the equipment in unexpectedly dangerous ways. The challenge then for the practitioner is to provide challenging activities that will stimulate and interest children, but are balanced with the need to keep children safe.

Consideration must be given to the individual needs and development of the children, the environment and the level of staff training. Practitioners should highlight any potential risks to children and talk to them about safe practice in play. We found evidence of children's own understanding of safe play at Brantfield, as evidenced by the little girl climbing the tree who played within her limits. The Play Safety Forum statement (2002) provides valuable guidance on managing risk in play provision and is used by Brantfield staff.

Learning from free play

Practitioners perception of the role of the adult has ranged from minimum intervention (Fisher 2002) to more direct support (Fisher 2002; Moyles 2002). Today's practitioner is probably very conscious of the pressure to be seen to be actively involved in extending children's learning through play. Active involvement can lead to a higher level of learning in many contexts, but careful consideration must be given to the adult role in secret places, to ensure they do not hijack the children's play. Our findings highlighted this need, when we tried talking to some children in their secret place. They were perfectly polite, but it was clear they were simply humouring us! As soon as we walked away, the children reverted to 'role-play voices' and got back to their own 'business' of play.

Practitioners often worry that the depth of learning is missing unless there is significant adult presence. When children are playing in their secret places, we need to be very careful that intervention does not become interference and change the nature of the play. Bruce (2001) reminds us to 'know when to take a back seat, and let children develop the play without invasion or adult domination.'

Practitioners need to get the balance of support right, between being involved and giving children space when they are engaged in secret play. If the quality of the provision, for both indoor and outdoor play is conducive to deep learning, then we should have confidence that the secret play is also of value. When we managed to eavesdrop on children at play in secret places, we noted how the children negotiated clear rules and direction for their play, conversed with each other and discussed the need to share and let others join in. The play was sustained over a considerable period of time, with the children staying in character. Clearly they were incorporating prior learning and adapting it to their current play situation. Had we not overheard these children, we might have been tempted to assume that as there was no overt adult input, the play was of a low level.

Scaffolding

Brantfield had a planned programme in place to support and scaffold children's play outdoors over the year, relating to secret places. When children first start at the setting, they are introduced to the grounds and how they might be used. At this early stage teachers would use the constructed dens and share stories related to secret places, for example *We're Going on a Bear Hunt* (Rosen and Oxenbury 1989), and *Can't You Sleep Little Bear?* (Waddell 1999). Staff actively used vocabulary related to secret places, and encouraged children to do so as they explored the outdoor area together.

By the time we observed the children in the summer, the practitioners' role had evolved. Most children were able to use secret places independently and so the role of the adult meant taking 'a back seat' (Bruce 2001), rather than being actively involved. A large part of the practitioners' role for these children was to assess their learning. They then used this knowledge to extend the play by adding an extra dimension of challenge.

Some timid and reluctant children still needed support and scaffolding in playing in secret places. We observed the staff at Brantfield consciously scaffolding this play by organising large-scale hide and seek games for the children to play with adults. Another game was to hide and find a favourite toy. These activities helped to ensure all children were included in this 'hiding' play. Clearly staff need to make professional judgements about which children need adult support, and how and when this is carried out (Fisher 2002).

Modelling

It is important that staff are enthusiastic about outdoor play and the enjoyment and thrill of secret places, in order to enthuse children in this type of play and encourage further exploration. They should not be afraid to delve into the undergrowth or get themselves dirty and wet! Adults need to use the language and vocabulary of secret places in context and draw children's attention to such language in books and stories. Through modelling, staff can add a layer of language and help children verbalise their play, in terms of positional language for example. Secret places act as a stimulus for children to discuss environmental/seasonal changes and features of interest.

Secret places – planning, assessing and extending the play

There is a place for adults to support children in 'secret play', but it must be done sensitively and with a secure knowledge of the individual child's stage of development and learning, and own interests.

Planning

Planning needs to be both long and short term. Long-term planning needs to be a staged process over the year, enabling progression and development of play in secret places. During the first term children are helped to find and use secret places outdoors. In the second and third term children are encouraged to gain independence, to find and create places in which to hide and develop as their own bases for play.

Short-term planning is concerned with current interests, themes and topics, linked to seasonal changes and events, focusing on a sense of place (Knowledge and Understanding of the World; personal and Social Education). Resourcing should be identified to support these themes, and the needs and interests of the children.

Planning should:

- reflect the interconnectedness between the outdoor and indoor environments;
- include regular opportunities to review play during circle or small-group review time;
- make relevant links to other areas of learning.

Assessment

Due to the nature of secret play, it is important that assessment is non-invasive. This is not to say assessment will not be valid or rigorous. Individual children should be carefully observed to enable the practitioner to identify significant learning that has taken place and record this against the curricula framework. Video footage or photographs of children at play can also be used to assess learning. We found questioning children during their play to be of limited use as it interrupted their imaginative flow. However, during a review time, the children were keen to share their ideas. Such a review time provides the opportunity for gathering useful information about the level and understanding of the children's play. In the light of these assessments, the practitioner can plan and extend the next stage of learning by providing activities to further challenge the children.

Ways of extending the play

After observing children's play in 'secret places' and reviewing it with them, adults may suggest and introduce children to the skills of, for example:

- drawing maps and following them;
- giving directions;
- creating a display of plans, building designs and atlases;
- adapting secret places, for example, adding a roof;
- talking about their likes and dislikes, and different types of secret places;
- identifying similarities and differences between secret places;
- considering how children's natural den changes over the year, for example dense foliage provides greater cover in summer;
- examining photographs of the outdoor environment and discussing where and how they could create secret places;
- raising awareness of conservation issues through caring for secret places, for example introducing litter patrols;

- making food for picnics in secret places,
- drama enactment of stories in secret places such as 'Three Bears';
- 'writing' stories of things that happen in the secret places;
- adding props to the secret places to further develop imaginative play;
- making signposts;
- writing invitations to visit secret places;
- making model representations of secret places, using natural materials where appropriate;
- painting and drawing secret places;
- exploring feelings related to secret places – 'What does it feel like in the dark?'

Links to Key Stage 1

Many of the themes that secret places address in the Foundation Stage, such as caring for the environment, and looking at similarities and differences, are continued in Key Stage 1. The thrill and excitement of hiding in secret places and the opportunities for learning through such sustained play are still important for older children. The issue then, is not that the curriculum links are not there (Figure 8.1) but that often the outdoor provision in Key Stage 1 settings is inadequate. It is not unusual for it to be little more than a tarmac rectangle, with little or no natural foliage in which to hide. Time, space and staffing difficulties can further limit opportunity to develop 'secret play'. Despite these constraints, Key Stage 1 settings can begin to introduce the concept of 'secret places' with a limited budget.

Getting started

Although many early years settings will not be in the fortunate position of Brantfield with its extensive grounds and abundance of secret places, there are still things they can do to create some secret hiding places in their own settings. Creating places for children to crawl into or under and be 'hidden' away from the gaze of adults may have to be temporary and regularly refurbished where necessary. Giving children the opportunity to be involved in planning and creating their own play environment will give them ownership of their secret places from the start. They can create secret places from, for example:

- cardboard boxes of various sizes;
- tarpaulin sheets/blankets to sit on or cover tables, climbing frames and/or bushes, to create hidden dens;
- neatly trimmed hedges and bushes which allow children to hide within or behind them;
- where there is no foliage or plants, buy potted real or artificial plants and place strategically outdoors for children to sit among;

- logs can be used to define paths and areas;
- cheap fencing panels can be strategically placed to create hidden places;
- willow fencing is light and flexible and could be used to enclose an area, or as roofing;
- play tents and tunnels.

Conclusion

Secret places promoted many opportunities for learning, in particular Knowledge and Understanding of the World and Personal, Social and Emotional Development (QCA 2000). The main features of the play we observed were high levels of concentration, exploration, co-operation and imagination. The children used knowledge of prior learning and skills and transferred these into their play. Secret play not only has benefits to children's current level of confidence, but also in the longer term and across other areas of learning. Secret places provide curriculum links between Foundation Stage and Key Stage 1 which allow for continuity and progression. However, issues of time, space and facilities may make this difficult.

We explored the tension between 'challenge' and 'risk taking' and concluded that practitioners must find a balance between the two, to encourage children to be independently adventurous in their learning. Safety is a key issue in secret play. The role of the practitioner is to undertake risk assessments and also to ensure that children have an understanding of safe practice in play.

Significant differences were noted between the secret play of boys and girls, in terms of action, volume, and movement. Therefore there is a need for varied provision to accommodate these differences.

There is a definite role for the practitioner within secret play, which may not always be obvious to the casual observer. They need to strike a balance between being involved and giving the children space to play, through a flexible and responsive approach.

The children we observed used both constructed and natural secret places, but we noted their preference was for natural hiding places that they found for themselves. The rich learning opportunities afforded by secret play provision are such that all providers should consider including them in their settings. While it is recognised that a setting may have limited outdoor facilities, some form of secret play can still be developed on a budget.

Our time at Brantfield showed us that children can still enjoy the thrill and fun of secret play, that we remembered as children. The depth of the learning surprised us, and convinced us of the value of secret places within the outdoor curriculum.

References

Bilton, H. (2002) *Outdoor Play in the Early Years*, 2nd edn. London: David Fulton Publishers.

Bruce, T. (2001) *Learning Through Play: Babies, toddlers and the foundation years*, London: Hodder and Stoughton.

Drummond, M. J. (1995) *Can I Play Out?* Bradford: Bradford Education Committee.

Edgington, M. (2002) *The Great Outdoors: Developing children's learning through outdoor provision.* London: BAECE. (*www.early-education.org.uk*).

Fisher, J. (2002) *Starting from the Child*, 2nd edn. Buckingham: Open University Press.

Hutt, S., Tyler, S., Hutt, C. and Christopherson, H. (1989) *Play Exploration and Learning: A natural history of the pre-school*. London: Routledge.

Moyles, J. (ed.) (2002) *Beginning Teaching: Beginning learning in primary education*, 2nd edn. Buckingham: Open University Press.

Ouvry, M. (2000) *Exercising Muscles and Minds: Outdoor play and the early years curriculum.* London: National Early Years Network.

Play Safety Forum (2002) *Managing Risk in Play Provision: A position statement.* Children's Play Council, National Children's Bureau, http://www.ncb.org.uk/cpc Accessed December 2003.

Rosen, M. and Oxenbury, H. (1989) *We're Going on a Bear Hunt.* London: Walker Books.

Sayeed, Z. and Guerin, E. (2000) *Early Years Play.* London: David Fulton Publishers.

Stephenson, A. (2003) 'Physical Risk-taking: dangerous or endangered', *Early Years: An international Journal of Research and Development* **23**(1) 35–43.

Waddell, M. (1999) *Can't You Sleep Little Bear?* London: Walker Books.

Story tents: an oracy and global learning project

Cynthia Ashcroft and Sophie Mackay

Why story tents?

THE HUMANITIES EDUCATION CENTRE is part of the Tower Hamlets Library Service. It supports local schools in East London to include global dimensions in their curriculum planning, through the production of resources, the delivery of in-service training, and by running projects such as 'story tents'.

With story tents we wanted to create a resource for use in early years classrooms which would stimulate teaching about 'time and place' and enhance opportunities for oracy. We decided on the idea of a tent as it readily gave us the opportunity to explore different types of dwellings from around the world. As a safe, enclosed and stimulating environment, the tent was an ideal place to learn about different cultures and listen to stories from other places.

A child of four is about half the size of an adult and so everything, especially the classroom, appears twice as big. The size of the story tents – large to the children, small to us – gives a sense of awe and excitement, while at the same time providing a room within a room, where small-group activities can be carried out. We hoped it would be a 'relief' to enter into this smaller 'world'.

> In Saudi Arabia, 'Curtains are hung as surrounding walls and as panels of materials . . . they . . . (delineate) . . . the interior space . . . the "majlis" . . . which is a public space for receiving visitors . . .'
>
> (Tents in Saudi Arabia, website accessed 2003)

The tents we made are based on a garden gazebo frame that is reduced in height by cutting down the length of the legs. The floor space is 2 metres square and the height is 1.72 metres to the apex of the roof, which is made from coloured calico. The sides of the tent are formed of eight double-sided calico panels. The panels are decorated on one side by children from participating schools, using appliqué, fabric collage, paint and block printing. (The idea for decoration was inspired by a colleague's visit to refugee camps in the western Sahara, in Algeria, where she saw murals, painted by the children, of their dream homeland.) The blank side of each panel has large buttons to hang things on. The panels are easily reversed to alter the appearance of both the inside and outside of the tent.

'The Kiyowas of the southern plains and the Blackfeet far to the north, were best known for heraldic "murals in the round".'

(Tent decoration in Encyclopedia of North American Indians architecture, website accessed 2003)

The decorations on each of our tents have a theme: homes, journeys, play, the environment. These were chosen to enable children to look at the links between their everyday life experiences – where they live, what they eat, the games they play – and the day-to-day activities of people in other places.

Schools who chose to decorate panels selected one of the themes and then worked independently or with support from the Humanities Education Centre. In all, 12 schools participated in the decoration stage which led to the production of ten complete tents. The tents are now part of the London Borough of Tower Hamlets Library Service loan collection. The tents and support materials can be borrowed by schools. In this way, art work done by a few schools can be seen by a wide audience of children in East London.

Story tent resources

Each story tent comes with a wide range of back-up materials. These include a teachers' pack. This has instructions for assembling the tent and suggested activities covering storytelling, role play and working with photographs. The activities in the pack are matched to the learning outcomes for communication, language and literacy from the Foundation Stage curriculum (QCA 2000) and to the National Literacy Strategy learning outcomes for speaking and listening for Key Stage 1 (DfEE 1998). Each pack includes:

- vocabulary cards – a set of laminated picture and world vocabulary cards that cover target language associated with the planned focus;
- texts – a set range of fiction and non-fiction texts, including photopacks linked to the theme of the tent. The texts and photographs are selected to support and stimulate language work;
- collections of artefacts linked to the theme of the tent;
- a log book – this is designed to record how different schools and groups use the tent. Borrowers are encouraged to record activities, examples of children's work, photographs and examples of planning. Each log book will grow to be a resource in its own right.

All participating schools found the teachers' pack useful, particularly as a starting point.

Language for communication

In many cases schools took ideas and exemplars and customised them to meet the needs of their children. A number of strands ran through the resource packs. One strand was communication (Figure 9.1). So, following a path trodden by North American Indians and North African nomads, among others, we are using tents

The Early Years Curriculum   *Communication, Language & Literacy*
Strand A – Language for Communication (continued)
Activities correspond to *Planning for Progress 2*, Tower Hamlets Early Years Service
LFC 1–5: Language for Communication 1, 2, 3, 4, 5

The Early Years Curriculum & activities	In-role	Home	Community debate	Telling stories	Tableaux	Music activities
To be involved in communication as a two-way process using voice, facial expression, body language to communicate (LFC 1)	✻	✻	✻	✻	✻	
To want to communicate and enjoy conversations (LFC 1)	✻	✻	✻			
To respond appropriately to gestures, images, songs, simple stories (LFC 1)	✻	✻		✻	✻	✻
To know that there is a variety of ways to communicate in order to meet needs, to convey thought, intentions and feelings (LFC 1)	✻	✻	✻	✻	✻	
To use intonation, rhythm and phrasing to make meaning clear to others (LFC 1)	✻			✻		✻
To use intonation and gesture, extending vocabulary and exploring meaning and sounds of new words (LFC 2)						✻
To be able to listen and respond to the speech of others in one-to-one/small groups (LFC 3)	✻			✻		
To interact with others and initiate conversation (LFC 3)	✻		✻			
To enjoy using language and exploring the meanings and sounds of new words (LFC 3)						
To know what it is like to be listened to and listen to others (LFC 4)	✻	✻	✻	✻		✻
To speak clearly and confidently, showing an awareness of the listener in small then larger groups (LFC 4)	✻	✻	✻	✻		

FIGURE 9.1 Communication skills developed through story tent activities

and storytelling as a way of learning about different cultures and times – deepening our knowledge and understanding of the world – and about the magic and power of the spoken word.

'The shaking-tent was one of the most important rituals of the Innu people of Québec and Labrador. It was . . . an important method of direct communication with . . . Innu people in distant groups.'

(Kushapatshikan: the shaking tent, website accessed 2003)

Using story tents in schools: oracy, travel and the wide world

In this section we draw together some of the imaginative work done in participating schools. There are two types of school in our survey: those that made and used a tent, and those that received a ready-made one. Of the latter group, we noted that many saw the added opportunities for developing artistic skills, by making and decorating the side panels, as well as the potential for developing oracy skills. For example, we tape-recorded Pia explaining how she developed the use of story tents with colleagues and children in her school.

Pia

Pia is the teacher in charge of the early years unit. This is what she said.

We took 'Journeys' as our overall theme. For a while after erecting the ready-made tent, activities were quite teacher directed, but as time went on and the children became more and more involved in the planning and use of the tent, they became less so. Initially there was just the tent. It was really important to us to have the tent as a central feature in the planning and in the teaching area, and so, because it was the summer term, all sand and water activities were moved to outdoor provision.

Once everybody was comfortably in and around the tent we extended the activities. In small groups in the tent and in whole-class discussions we talked about going on a long journey and everything that is involved. We talked about, for example, packing a case, buying tickets, methods of travel, places to visit, and what we might see on arrival. Each of these actions was written on a piece of card, and the resulting 'card pack' was used as a stimulus for activities. We added suitcases and travel equipment to the dressing-up materials. Tickets to various global destinations, a till with real money, travel posters and a world map (Peter's projection) were put in the shop.

All journeys took place inside the tent and light Club-class snacks and refreshments were served. The destination was reached via an exit at the back of the tent. The destination, which we changed each week, was decorated with appropriate artefacts: plants, pictures and books. To return home the process was reversed. Instead of coming home via the shop the children had to come through customs where their bags were searched and they were required to justify why, for example, they had a red and gold sari. 'I wore it at my cousin's wedding,' was enough to get you back into the country!

At the beginning we noticed that the children spontaneously removed their shoes before entering the tent. It also became clear that the children never left the inside of the tent untidy, and apart from one instance of creative hair cutting, being hidden from staff was never a problem. Indeed the thought that they might be banned from the tent modified behaviour.

The story tent appeared on the offered plan both as a creative-play area and an area used for special occasions. Careful timetabling meant it was used in one form or another throughout the day.

The tent became popular very quickly. We were a little alarmed when the children started to ask for another one. However, with the help of some climbing frame equipment and a wonderful schoolkeeper we made some extra room and built our own. This way we got the best of both worlds: the experience of a ready-made tent and the experience of making and decorating one for ourselves. We noticed the tent built by the children was the most used.

Pia shows how effective the story tent was in providing an environment which enhanced opportunities for oracy, while learning about travel and the wider world. However, it was very clear to us that just putting up the tent and leaving out some interesting artefacts was not enough in itself. Indeed, in the few schools where this happened the story tent became sadly marginalised and unused. The careful and thoughtful approach of Pia and her colleagues, where the story tent is central to planning and organisation, allowed the story tents to work.

Neena

Neena is a learning support assistant, who works with groups of stage one English learners. She explained how she used a story tent with Foundation Stage children. She began by telling us about Rabia, who is four years old.

Rabia and her group 'travelled' to Bangladesh in the story tent. While there they talked about who they missed at home and how they could contact them to let them know they were all right. Rabia wanted to send a postcard (a variety of these had been put in the arrivals area) and make a phone call (there was a phone there too). She knew that she needed extra numbers to dial London and then her home phone number so she used all the numbers she knew. Somehow a picture of the place and the phone call merged into one.

Neena showed us an example of Rabia's confident mark making (Figure 9.2).

I started by observing the children playing in and around the story tent. I saw how much they enjoyed going in the tent. Inside they never stopped talking, so I decided to plan to work with my groups in there (Figure 9.3). After a few times I noticed that the concentration levels, especially from the boys, was much better than when we sat at a table. I think it is because they are not distracted by what their friends are doing nearby. This week the children have been bringing in photos of family members. My oracy and mathematics focus was on the language of relations and relationships and I also wanted to look at

FIGURE 9.2 Rabia's postcard from Bangladesh with her home phone number

family here and family elsewhere in the world. Joan, the secretary, scans and enlarges the children's photos to A4 size for me. I stick string loops on the back and the children love hanging them on the large buttons on the panels. It is like being in an art gallery.

Neena demonstrates clearly the importance of unobtrusive, structured observations. After the story tent had been erected she planned observations into her weekly timetable. It was then that she realised the amount of talk, in both Bengali and English, that went on when the children thought they couldn't be seen. After discussions with fellow team workers, she decided to timetable herself to work with groups and individuals in and around the tent. The large buttons sewn onto the inside of each panel allowed her to hang a new 'exhibition' of photographs each time.

Starting points:	ourselves	new life	journeys
	I am special	toys and games	living things
	where I live	machines	food

Spring.week 26 **week beginning** **24/03/03** **tactile (kinaesthetic) learning** – touching, doing, being physically involved **auditory learning** – talking and listening **visual learning** – seeing, observing, recording, writing	**Indicate functions of language.** describing, comparing, sorting and grouping, exploration and investigation, observing change, pattern seeking (generalising), evaluating, explaining, inferring, deducing, predicting, hypothesising, recalling, giving instructions, recounting, wondering, wishing, hoping, asking for help, suggesting, warning ■ **Use the detailed 'developing questioning' sheets to plan for these**

Focus 1	Describing	Resources
Adult: Shefa **'making passports'** ■ construct with a purpose in mind using a variety of resources ■ use equipment competently and appropriately ■ have awareness of and interest in cultural differences	What is your passport like? Do you think paper or card is the best material for making the passports? Explaining/recounting how and when passport made	'Passport' on 1 card × 4 sets 'My name is' on separate cards Passport-size photos of children

Focus 2	Describing	Resources
Adult: Rehana **'family photos'** ■ show interest in ICT ■ show understanding of family relationships ■ have awareness of other countries – family ■ collaborate to make the 'best' exhibition	How did Joan make a copy of their photo? Is the A4 copy bigger or smaller than the original? 'My photo *is next to* Jamal's.' (opposite, under, above, before, after)	Atlases Family photos A4 paper Tape and string Large felt pens

FIGURE 9.3 Foundation Stage: focus activity plan for story tent journeys

A little privacy

As we developed the story tents we worried about children being out of sight of a supervising adult. We needn't have been concerned. Although children at the Foundation Stage seem to think adults don't know what they are doing if they can't be seen when enclosed, the adults always had a very good idea about what they were up to. We felt that the increase in quantity and quality of talk, interactive and social play and concentration levels that were reported was to do with having a little 'privacy'. For most of the day these children are watched very closely and the story tents were a place to escape, as the children thought, this surveillance.

During the work with participating schools we found that the story tent not only provides opportunities for developing work in Knowledge and Understanding of the World but also in four of the other five areas of learning in the guidance for the Foundation Stage. (Any ideas for using story tents in PE lessons, would be gratefully received!)

> 'When extra coolness was desired in the tents, they would be doused with buckets of water so that the subsequent evaporation would cause temperatures inside to drop on even the hottest day.'
>
> (Encyclopedia of North American Indians, architecture, website accessed 2003)

Is this an early version of the early years curriculum: sand and water section?

References

Department for Education and Employment (DfEE) (1998) *The National Literacy Strategy*. London: DfEE/QCA.

Encyclopedia of North American Indians, architecture, http://college.hmco.com/history/readerscomp/naind/html/na_002600_architecture.htm Accessed December 2003.

Kushapatshikan: the shaking tent, http://www.innu.ca/shaking.html Accessed December 2003.

Tents in Saudi Arabia, http://www.saudiembassy.net/publications/magazine-96/blending.html Accessed December 2003.

10

We're going camping

Hilary Cooper

You'll go where laurel crowns are won, but – will you e'er forget
The scent of hawthorn in the sun, or bracken in the wet?

Rudyard Kipling: 'The Roman Centurion's Song'

WHEN I VISITED Eaglesfield Paddle Nursery they told me that they were all going camping in June and that I could come too. They showed me their book of photographs from last year's camp: brightly coloured tents pitched in a circle, balloons, flower windmills, bubble blowing, a sausage barbecue, pony rides, and everywhere four-year-olds and their parents laughing, despite their waterproofs. Some children were smiling from their tent entrances, where they sat chatting, reading stories (by torchlight), making kites, or even sleeping, boots in neat pairs outside. Going camping with them seemed a good opportunity to explore their concepts of place! 'We go every year,' Gill Brown, told me. (Gill is responsible for the nursery, which is part of Eaglesfield Paddle CE Primary School. Two groups of children come to separate sessions in the morning and the afternoon.) 'The Chair of governors lets us use her farm a few miles away; it's no longer a working farm – and there are no sleepovers I'm afraid.' (That was a relief!) 'Concepts of place', Gill mused, 'that's interesting, I don't know that we do much about place – but some of them need a challenge. You can come as long as you don't spoil the fun!'

Map sticks

So I visited the nursery for three afternoons to get to know the children and to introduce some 'games' I devised, which I hoped we could play at the camp. Each visit was video-recorded. The children were used to being photographed and ignored the camera completely. The first game was 'map sticks', reputed to be an Australian Aboriginal custom to find places in a society without means of map representation. I am not totally convinced, but it is a nice story! Map sticks was a structured activity in an imaginary context, aiming to scaffold children's learning and to encourage them to become independent investigators and problem solvers.

My aim was to help a group of four-year-olds to observe, investigate and describe their environment. I also wanted them: to record a trail, in sequence, of places visited on an 'adventure' as a linear map and to see whether they could trace the same way back by reversing the sequence; to see whether they could explain what was distinctive about each of the places and represent it as a symbol; to encourage them to use positional language; and to consider environmental issues, if opportunities arose (Raikes 1991; Milner 1994). Sounds a bit ambitious?

Everyone listened intently to my story of the 'adventure' I had the previous evening. They knew about adventures because they had just heard a story about an adventure. My adventure was described with great drama and illustrated by the stone, grass, ivy, twig and moss which I had stuck along my map stick (one of a collection of short, 'safe' sticks I had found on the ground in a nearby wood). I had attached them with what Aileen recognised as 'Glutac', so that I should be able to find my way back. The children guessed that I had first walked *along* a stony *track*, then crossed a grassy *field*; this gave rise to some discussion about the difference between a *field* and a *farm*, and whether the field was for animals or growing things. This was finally concluded to be an 'animal field' because I had grass on my map stick, 'because cows eat grass', 'and sheep do too'. I explained that the ivy was climbing up a wall which I had passed next. The idea of ivy climbing up a wall caused incredulous giggling until Lindsey told us that her mummy said that sweet peas can climb up walls and fences; this gave rise to further discussion about whether plants can climb and how. After the third symbol, the ivy, children were keen to suggest where I went next. They guessed that the twig was 'to show you went through a *forest*'. This was a word they knew from visiting Whinlatter Forest at Christmas, whereas *wood* was not familiar to them. After a brief diversion recollecting the excitement of seeing Father Christmas in the Whinlatter Forest – although he had run away along a *path* – they recognised moss as 'stuff that grows on stones where it's wet'. (Who would not in the Lake District?) They could explain why I had used it to show that I had crossed a *stream*, 'cause you can't put water on a stick!

It was agreed that Charlie, Michelle and Aileen should be the first group to take me on an adventure. (Charlie had come into the afternoon session declaring that he was bored.) As they stuck the Blu-tack on their map sticks they discussed what maps are for.

> Aileen: My mummy and daddy use a map to find out where to go.
> Michelle: Or you could ask for information from someone who's been there.
> Charlie: Pirates had maps to search for treasure.

I advised that we should all stick together on our adventure so that no one got lost, to which Charlie replied indignantly, 'I thought that's what we were making map sticks for.' No doubt that Charlie had grasped the concept!

And so we made our intrepid way into areas far outside the familiar nursery garden. The children wanted to record the adventure on their individual sticks. They stuck on the symbols they selected in sequence. When Aileen realised she had left some spaces and started to fill in the gaps Charlie pointed out to her why 'she must not miss any lumps'.

We recorded our journey, describing it in locational language and recognising changes in terrain. We began, as before with a stone (*down* a stony path), a leaf from an elder tree (*through* the wild garden), buttercups and daisies (*across* the school field – a wonderful 150 metres scamper), a piece of brick (from the farm track next to the school), bark (from the adventure playground) and sand (from the long-jump pit). Michelle had the imaginative idea of drawing an arrow pointing to the way we were going, 'in case they come to search for us'. So she did, at least to some extent, feel in role as 'an adventurer'.

We had three interesting discussions on the way. This involved abstract reasoning to discuss characteristics of places we had been through and how they could be represented as symbols. On the brick farm track Aileen had wanted to attach to her stick a piece of red plastic which had attracted her. Eventually Charlie (almost) explained why it was no good. 'There's only one bit and you've got it. How can we find our way back if you've taken it?' Aileen also, in her great excitement and to everyone's amusement, found 'a piece of pant'. It certainly did seem to be part of someone's grey trousers! This gave rise to some discussion of safety issues: it's not always a good idea to pick things up – and – as Charlie said, 'It won't help us get back anyhow.' We also talked about flowers, and concluded that it is, 'OK to pick buttercups and daisies because there's millions of them on the field', and 'anyway they'll get mown down when they cut the grass' but the flowers in the nursery garden have been planted specially for everyone to look at. 'Zeb picked one the other day so Mrs Brown put it in a bowl so we could still enjoy it, and we painted it too.'

When we returned to the nursery each of the children stuck their symbols in sequence on a strip of paper as a permanent linear map. They shared their account of their adventure with the rest of the class at the end of the afternoon and asked them to guess where they had been. With a little prompting they did. (Prompting was partly necessary because Aileen's independent choice of adhesive proved to take a long time to dry and her symbols slid around a bit.) The last thing I remember was Charlie explaining his adventure and the meaning of his map and his map stick to his delighted mum.

Cloud children

On my next visit I wanted to see whether the children could imagine a perspective different from their own, a bird's-eye view. It is now generally agreed that children are able to envisage perspectives different from their own if they are interested and related to their experience (Wiegand 1993). For example Halocha (2003) shows how he developed a project involving perspectives from a visit to a model village. Plesterer *et al.* (2003) made model landscapes with three- and four-year-olds, then they progressed to interpreting aerial maps and finally to a treasure hunt using them. MacKintosh (2003) bought large aerial photos of the school and the children's houses made into a mat as a basis for talking about the locality with Reception and Year 1 and 2 children.

I read the children two stories about clouds. *Little Cloud* (Carle 1997) is about a cloud which changes into different shapes and, after drifting across roof and tree tops, finally turns into rain. In *Cloudland* (Burningham 1996) a boy walks through clouds in the high mountains and finally meets the children who live in the clouds and joins in their adventures, making thunder music, walking along vapour trails and painting rainbows. These stories invite discussion, using language to describe places (city, farm, village house, trees), weather (clouds, rain, lightening, thunder, rainbow) and position (up, down, high, low, far away). I also wanted to see whether, having read the stories and looked at the illustrations, children would be able to imagine what it would be like to look down on the Earth from above – as clouds, to imagine a 'bird's-eye view', necessary for making and reading maps. Milner (1994) suggests that children can describe different viewpoints – from the top of a chair or a ladder or from the baby's pushchair – but would a 'cloud child's viewpoint' be overtaxing their cognition and imagination? If not, would they identify real or imaginary features? Which features? How far away?

After listening to the stories the children were anxious to talk about their experiences of air, wind and clouds.

David: Air balloons go up in the sky.
Michelle: When it was very windy my kite broke.
Fran: I've seen monsters in the sky.
Michelle: I wonder what clouds are?
Lizzie: They're made of coccon wool.
Michelle: No they're not. They're made of steam.
Lizzie: They're coccon wool.
Michelle: It's steam, like from the kettle. It's all around us and it goes up in the air.
           Clouds aren't rain, because rain is . . . rain.
Patrick: Are you a scientist?
Hilary: What's a scientist?
Patrick: Someone who knows everything. Steven's mummy is a scientist. She knows everything.

Despite Steven's mum's superior knowledge, I did not feel that it was appropriate to do more than listen to the children talking and ask the odd question, for example, 'Has anyone ever been in an aeroplane and seen the clouds – or up a very high mountain?' Some had, but no conclusions were drawn.

Gill had given me a large piece of white fabric from which to cut 'clouds', drawn with a silver pen. I asked her what it had been originally intended for. She gave me a long look. 'I was told it was for shrouds', she said, 'but they may have been winding me up . . .' Hm. Let's hope so.

The video records a perfect June day, strong gusts of warm wind, small white clouds scudding across a clear blue sky, and the school set in rolling green hills, about two miles from the nearest town. Will, Jon, Noelle, Helen and Becky said that they would like to be one of the cloud children and spent some time running around the field, floating and flying their white fabric clouds. When they grew tired of this we sat down on our clouds on the grass and pretended we were floating up higher and higher in the sky. 'It's so windy I really think I am a cloud in the sky,' Becky said opportunely. 'What can you see when you look down?' I asked. The first ideas were things clearly visible from where we sat: the playground, children playing, cars going along the road. Then the children seemed to understand the idea of an imagined perspective. 'I can see the tops of the trees,' Will said, 'And the top of the school' added Jon. I extended this by saying, 'Let's go up really high. Can you see Cockermouth?' 'Yes', said Helen. 'I can see children going into the shops – and grandmas.' 'Your grandma?' 'Lots of grandmas.' I imagine this was based on what she thought her grandma would be doing. In spite of gentle prompting no further features of Cockermouth were mentioned. Will said, 'Because I'm so high up I can see Eaglesfield – right over there.' Eaglesfield was certainly not visible. (The school, paradoxically is in a field about two miles away.) This prompted Noelle to say that she could see 'fields, with tractors in them'. This was a common sight at that time of year but there were none within view, so she must have been imagining this scene based on what she had previously noticed. Whether or not the children had detailed images of the places they talked about from above it was difficult to know.

Preparations for camping

What shall we take to camp?

The children were very much involved, in practical and concrete ways, in discussing with Gill their preparations for camp, taking ownership within an agreed framework. This resulted in making an ongoing list of things they would need on a flip chart, which became organised in categories. They discussed the variety of experiences they wanted to have, the resources this would require and who would provide them.

- Things we want to do: otter game, jigsaws, books, drawing, feely bag, duck duck goose, heffalumps and woozles, football, races.

- Songs to sing: 'One, two, three, four, five, Once I caught a fish alive'; 'One finger, one thumb keep moving'; 'Doctor Knickerbocker'; 'Bones'. (I did not ask what woozles or Dr Knickerbocker meant.)

- Things to take: tents (Twelve small tents were lent by parents. Gill had made a plan showing where to pitch each tent. Children were allocated three or four to a tent and chose tent names such as foxes, mice, badgers, otters, frogs, deer. The tent occupants, the parent or other adult linked to the group, the tent owner and the name of the person providing transport were all written on labels for each tent on the plan); sleeping bags; blankets; pillows; map; back-pack; compass; collapsible chair; picnic and drink; plates; wellies or walking boots; trainers; cooker; barbecue; walkie-talkie; my favourite dog; flags for tents.

- What we want to eat: barbecue sauce, mustard, baps, sausages, pancakes, sausage rolls, salad cream, organic apples (so we can eat the skins) biscuits.

When I arrived on the third afternoon Patrick was standing on a chair telephoning the head teacher, who usually went on the camp but this year was recuperating from surgery, to ask if the nursery may borrow his barbecue and a large tent. Patrick made sure that he did not pass over the phone to Gill until he had enquired, 'And how is your plastic hip getting on?'

How shall we get to the farm?

Five children were sitting around four pieces of A1 paper which were stuck together, with an aerial photograph of the school and its immediate environment stuck in the centre. They had decided to make a map to show how to get to the farm. They used symbols – lines to represent the roads and tracks and patches of green to represent grass and pictures of their houses. I decided a good starting question would be, 'What does your map show?' The children explained familiar features: the cross-roads outside the school; and a road with a broken white line down the centre, which after several twists (the roads around here certainly do twist a lot) faded into narrow tracks with no road markings (also true of most of the roads in this agricultural area). There were other features on the map:

'a pond'
'and a river'
'and you go across the river to the mountains'
'That's a high, high mountain.'
'No it's not a mountain, it's triangle.'
'That's to show it's a high, high mountain.' (Was Ellie introducing her own symbol or had she seen it on a map?)
'And that track shows you where you go to the farm.'

The other features which were pointed out to me were all related to the children's perspectives from their own houses. They tried to explain to me, logically, how the road led to their houses. Ian's house was surrounded by grass, Katie's was 'in the high, high mountains' (and she was still talking about when Father Christmas came!). Garry's house was distinguished by a 'road which goes in a circle' and Ellie's by her big garage. 'That's my window. You can see the road from my window – and I've added a monster you might see on a bear hunt.' Only Rowena's house was not on the map, but was 'close by the pond.'

The children did not know the route to the farm but they could certainly describe and record key features of their environment, although I did not know how correctly they were located in relation to each other.

Extending spontaneous play

Meanwhile a bus queue was assembling in the corner, tickets were being issued and eventually the driver arrived with his wheel under his arm, got into his cab, and traced his route in the air, before 'revving up'. The bus journey continued for some time with tickets being issued, bells being rung and several incidents were skilfully handled by the conductor and passengers: a dog was turned off the bus for misbehaving, a lady and crying baby got on and caused a disturbance. Eventually the bus became extremely long and crowded, and the play appeared about to disintegrate when Gill leapt on board. 'I want to go to Bramley Farm please', she said, bursting into song with, 'The wheels on the bus go round and round and round'. The passengers soon joined in with suggestions for 'What shall we do at Bramley Farm?' Before long Gill announced that they have arrived at Bramley Farm and led the passengers to an area outside the classroom. She asked the children where they are going to pitch their tents, then quietly withdrew.

This was a good example of combining free and directed play, linked to a shared experience. Gill intervened when play was floundering, redirected it, then withdrew; play continued to develop spontaneously. The idea that in play children cannot fail needs qualification. Purposeful intervention, which responds to the children's interests, extends play (Bennett 1997).

The children, having arrived in 'the country' talked about the video camera and took turns in looking through the viewfinder. Then Teresa got a cylindrical wooden brick and decided that she would make a video with her 'camera'. She embarked on a long description of what she could see through the camera. Patrick decided 'to write it all down' in his note book: 'fields, a cow, a horse, a sheep – the horse is in a barn – and there's a moo cow in the barn too; I can see a bear in a cave'. This is a good example of play creating a zone of proximal development (Vygotsky 1978). Patrick initiated the idea to 'write it all down' and pretended to do so. He was using reading and writing for a purpose in play although he could not yet read and write. I responded within the play framework. 'I can see the mountains.'

'And crocodiles',
'And a town from the top of a hill'.

Did the bear in the cave come from the bear hunt poem (Rosen and Oxenbury 1989), which they had been learning, prior to a bear hunt planned for the camping day? And did the idea of looking down on a town from the top of a hill originate in the cloud game – or was this my wishful thinking? The crocodiles sighted suggests how similar fantasy and imagination are.

Camping, June 21 – the longest day!

At 9.30 a.m. the cars set off in convoy. Rain threatened. We sang weather songs. 'What will the weather be today? It's a rainy day today.' But the lanes were effulgent with ragged robin, dog roses, cow parsley, the woods were dark and damp and the fields full of buttercups, daisies and clover. When we arrived Gill's husband Kit had erected the big tent and arranged the small tent bags according to the plan. Two nannies, who had first come last year and asked if they could come again, had set up tea, coffee and soft drinks and the dinner ladies had sent some tray bakes. I was very grateful for the help of Charlie, David and Vanessa in erecting our tent; at four-years-old they were much better at it than I was and, as rain approached, they found my ineptitude slightly irritating. 'You'll be better next year, Hilary,' they reassured me, as they arranged their blankets, cushions, toys and food comfortably in the tent and settled down to their first snack from their picnic boxes. It was ten o'clock.

After a while the sun came out. 'What will the weather be today? It's a sunny day today.' Children emerged from tents, queued up to use their pony-passes for a ride on Pixie, flew kites, played football or sat on their small folding chairs and chatted or read.

Bear hunt

The children had practised, learned and enjoyed the poem, *We're Going on a Bear Hunt* (Rosen and Oxenbury 1989). So a bear hunt had been organised for half the children in the morning and the others in the afternoon. We wanted to give the children the experience of describing different environments as well as following a trail and using positional language. Children's memory for a route can be significantly improved if their attention is drawn to features along the way. Kit, Gill's husband, had stuck small teddy bears printed on laminated, bright-coloured card about 12 centimetres square at intervals along the hunt track, on trees or gates or stuck in the ground. The trail was at least a mile long but no one complained that it was too far because it was so exciting. We hoped to give the children direct experience of the different environments described in the poem – excluding the deep,

deep river – and also to include some new environments. We wanted to encourage them to make up some of their own words to describe these.

Kit told us that he had seen the bear.

'How big is it?'
'Bigger than you, I think.' (We started warily.)

Nevertheless Patrick, who had not been comfortable with the poem, asked if he could join in. We set off.

'We're going on a Bear Hunt.
We're going to catch a big one.
What a beautiful day!
We're not scared . . .
Uh-uh!'

The 'long, wavy grass' was so long and so wavy that children who bent down disappeared. But we had to go *through* it. As each new bear sign was sighted we chanted the next verse of the poem. Our first addition to the poem was:

'Uh-uh! – big silver gate,
Can't go *over* it, (although someone tried)
Can't go *under* it, (ditto)
Got to go *through* it!
Creak click, creak, click.'

Then someone shouted, 'I can see a red bear in the forest!' So there was – but it was laminated. Everyone had to clamber over a stile, into the forest, which was wonderfully dark and mysterious, with mossy roots everywhere and a great deal of genuine 'stumble, trip; stumble trip'. Michelle's poetic addition here was, 'Stumble trip, cuckoo spit, stumble trip'. Noelle's was, 'Stumble trip, stumble trip, I've found munchrooms.'

After scrambling over another stile on the other side of the wood we came to – 'a big squelchy bog'. Jon's modification here was, 'Big squelchy bog. I've found bear snot.' Well he was not quite making up his own rhymes and poems (QCA 2000: 50) but the repeated 'b' and 's' were getting close! Next we had to climb up a really steep pasture – 'huff puff, huff puff', or if you prefer Aileen's graphic version 'Oh-ooh; Cow poo'. Oh well, such preoccupations are developmental stages – and this did rhyme.

Jo, having got first to the top of the hill, came running back in total amazement. 'Come and look at this.' He took my hand and with awe, led me to look down from the summit. 'It's the deep, deep river. It's enormous.' I shared his awe. 'I think it's a lake. It's too wide for a river.' 'Yes it must be a lake,' he agreed with relief. 'It's huge.' We should not have to go through it. Phew! Just over the top of the hill we waded through bracken – 'springy, curly bracken', then we sighted one small brightly coloured tent. Everyone charged over. Someone peeped inside – and there was the big cuddly bear from the nursery, protected from the elements, and happy with his bowls of food and drink. There were squeals, screams and shrieks of delight!

'Teddy's made a camp, camp, camp,
So he doesn't get damp, damp, damp.'

'Make up your own songs and rhymes' (QCA 2000: 50) is going well.
Beneath us, very tiny, we could see:

'People riding on Pixie' (a pony leant by a parent),
'Clouds, birds, cars going along the roads',
'Tiny trees, three windmills',
'Fells and – OUR tents'.

It was almost impossible to believe that it was *our camp* beneath us. We experienced a real bird's-eye perspective. Everyone was allowed to scramble down however they liked. Michelle climbed a tree on the way, which delayed her considerably and for Garry the best bit was, 'rolling down the hill with my friend and getting a dirty bum'. All good ways of exploring the area using all the senses. The bear hunt was one of the highlights of the day. It combined active learning, first-hand experiences and intrinsic motivation.

Kit cooked sausages for lunch on the barbecue and after lunch Gill read a new story *Frog in the Wide World* (Velthuijs 2000), a wonderfully illustrated big book, full of place concepts, in which Rat and Frog go out into the big wide world for an adventure. They experience excitement, novelty and fear before eventually returning safely home.

After lunch

The afternoon included requests to play the 'cloud game', while waiting in the pony queue. Having played it in the nursery, and particularly after climbing up the big hill, the children did seem to have a genuine understanding of different perspective. This time in the 'cloud game' they 'saw' things seen from the hill in the morning and also as far afield as the school and the town. Steven even saw a big city a long, long way away where his mum used to live.

Another group asked me to go with them on a 'map stick adventure'. We did not get further than the hay meadow, which Ella had delayed having cut until after the children's visit. They could not make a linear sequence to show where they had been; indeed this was not necessary as their tracks could be seen through the long grass. So they modified the game. They collected flowers from the same environment to fix on their map sticks, 'to show what it's like here'. They learned new names – speedwell and pink clover; buttercup they knew. Ellie and Katie mismatched, then correctly matched flowers and their leaves in pairs on their sticks – more spontaneous cognitive challenges, combined with a vivid experience of place! Vygotsky (1978) stressed the importance of social interaction with peers and adults to create meaning from experience within a shared framework in order to develop the knowledge, information and skills for independent learning.

Other activities continued freely. Everywhere children were discussing what to do, demonstrating their sense of ownership of the place and the day, engaging with their environment in different ways as they preferred; many chose to explore and enjoyed the freedom to take risks. A group of boys spent ages cleaning Gill's car, filling and carrying bowls of soapy water and sponges. Michelle tried swinging the giant bubble maker too energetically and was caught emerging naked from her tent, to put her clothes to dry in the sun. She was of course 'learning by trial and error'. At four o'clock, after a few camp songs and a relay race, we thanked Ella for allowing us to camp at her farm and the convoy wound back to school. It was Friday.

Camping in the nursery garden

Many writers have suggested that through play children first explore, then use knowledge, and subsequently use it to solve new problems (Moyles 1994). The following Monday when I visited the nursery the children had decided to set up a play tent in the nursery garden with picnic basket, barbecue, and folding chairs. During the afternoon, play seemed to move in and out of the tent, as it had done at camp. Children came in for a while, had a cup of tea and a chat, then left to play on the bikes or to dig in the garden. The adults were occasionally brought a 'cup of tea, raspberry juice or ham and cheese sandwiches'. Inside the tent (I'm afraid I eavesdropped), roles and story lines were allocated for 'mums and dads'.

> 'Who wants to be a baby? You're my little girl, OK? You're both sisters. The little baby is poorly. Lie down. It's very windy outside. I don't want anyone to go outside.'

Themes were collaboratively elaborated (Shefatya 1990: 153). Map sticks became integrated into this play throughout the afternoon, as children enjoyed using their newfound skill independently. Almost everyone, at some point went on a map stick adventure. Children were sometimes seen arranging to go on a journey together, discussing what to put on their map sticks.

> Teresa: I want to make a map for a long journey.
> Jon: I'll start you off.

Or they asked someone to guess where they had been.

'I've been on an adventure.'
'I can tell where you went.'

Correct names were used: clover, dandelion, bush, field, road. The sticking properties of goose grass were discovered.

Adventurers usually returned to the tent for a cup of tea and a rest.

Steven: I'm going to set things up to eat. That's what camps are for after a long journey.

Heard from within the tent, where there was always great attention paid to closing the flaps securely, and the baby was now crying:

'Now I'm going on a long journey.'
'Oh no *you're not* – not in that cold wind. It's terrible out there.'
'Oh yes I am.'
'Well be *very* careful.'

At one point the group in the tent decided to visit granny and took a map stick so that they could find their way back!

Looking back at the camp

Looking back at the video extracts of the camping day, the preparations for it and the play afterwards showed what a rich and complex learning experience it had been, although much of it may have seemed spontaneous.

What did children learn?

The overall learning objectives for the camping day were very wide ranging and open ended, reflecting the idea of planning for possibilities and the unpredictable. They could be shown to reflect each of the areas of learning (QCA 2000) and, in particular, personal and social education: negotiation, co-operation, organisation, turn taking, problem solving. These were required in pitching the tents, deciding how to spend the time, waiting for pony rides and sharing picnics, to name but a few activities. Language development was integral to the activities and included familiar stories listened to as a group, the bear hunt poem and stories read in the tents. The following Monday Gill even had photographs of the children in each tent, linked to the tent plan, on the wall for use as a number line.

Roles of adults

The roles of adults were varied as occasion demanded. Gill had set up the broad context in which other ideas took root, with enormous organisational flair. The parents had worked hard with her to make camping day a safe and a rich shared experience.

The theme had involved both adult-initiated and planned group work and a variety of freely chosen, but potentially instructive, play activities (Siraj-Blatchford *et al*. 2002). The adult's role in the three games to extend children's concepts of place was to design 'games' with precise learning objectives. There was shared thinking between the adult and children in the map stick game, for example when they discussed what makes appropriate symbols. There were also examples of the adult scaffolding learning in different ways: for example demonstrating how to make and read a map stick, asking the whole group to hypothesise about her adventure, suggesting that the children try to use the map stick to make a permanent map. Children then took initiatives, for example deciding to make a map stick to represent just the flowering plants in one hay meadow at camp. They also scaffolded each other's learning (Charlie explained why a 'piece of pant' was not a good symbol) and helped each other. In their subsequent spontaneous play they made, used and invited hypotheses from each other about the meanings of their map sticks.

Gill had also intervened to extend imaginative play before the camping day when she saw that the spontaneous bus play was disintegrating and took the bus to the farm where it continued without her. Gill was good at seizing such opportunities. She initiated the weather songs at camp and encouraged the children to wash her car! She exploited more formal opportunities, involving everyone in shared decisions about what to take to camp and expecting them to pack their bags and pitch their tents themselves. Afterwards she encouraged Lianne, the trainee nursery nurse, to follow up the camp experience with a story and games that would extend the camp theme to a distant place; this was one of Lianne's assignments. So Lianne read the children *We're Going on a Lion Hunt* (Axtell 2000), which has almost identical words to *We're Going on a Bear Hunt* (Rosen and Oxenbury 1989), but is set in Africa, with African illustrations.

Play

However we define 'play' plenty of different types of play emerged within the camping theme. There was quite specific learning set in imaginative contexts: map sticks, cloud children. There were child-initiated activities: making the map showing how to get to the farm. There was child-initiated role play on the bus and making the imaginary video of the farm. Both of these activities drew on what the children already knew about their area. And in the spontaneous, imaginative camp play in the nursery garden after the camping day, children were revisiting and integrating all of their camping experiences, in a familiar play situation. A rural environment may be helpful if you want to go camping or bear hunting or on journeys into the unknown, but is not essential. This type of bear can also be found in parks and even in school grounds.

References

Axtell, D. (2000) *We're Going on a Lion Hunt*. London: Macmillan Children's Books.

Bennet, N. (1997) *Teaching Through Play: Teachers' thinking and classroom practice*. Buckingham: Open University Press.

Burningham, J. (1996) *Cloudland*. London: Jonathan Cape.

Carle, E. (1997) *Little Cloud*. London: Hamish Hamilton.

Halocha, J. (2003) 'It's a small world', *Primary Geographer* **51**, 18–19.

Kipling, R. 'The Roman Centurion's Song', www.poetryloverspage.com/poets/kipling/roman_centurions.html Accessed December 2003.

MacKintosh, M. (2003) 'Up in a helicopter', *Primary Geographer* **51**, 22–3.

Milner, A. M. (1994) *Geography Starting Here! Practical approaches with nursery and reception children*. Sheffield: The Geographical Association.

Moyles, J. R. (ed.) (1994) *The Excellence of Play*. Buckingham: Open University Press.

Plesterer, B., Richards, J., Shevelan, C., Black, M. and Spencer, C. (2003) 'Hunt from above', *Primary Geographer* **51**, 20–1.

Raikes, J. (1991) *Planning for Key Stage 1*. Sheffield: The Geographical Association.

Rosen, M. and Oxenbury, H. (1989) *We're Going on a Bear Hunt*. London: Walker Books.

Shefatya, L. (1990) 'Socio-economic status and ethnic differences in sociodramatic play: theoretical and practical implications', in Klugman, E. and Smilansky, S. (eds) *Children's Play and Learning Perspectives and Policy Implications*. New York: Teacher's College Press.

Velthuijs, M. (2000) *Frog in the Wide World*. London: Anderson Press.

Vygotsky, L. S. (1978) *Mind in Society: The development of psychological processes*. Harvard: Harvard University Press.

Wiegand, P. (1993) *Children and Primary Geography*. London: Cassell.

Resources referred to in the text

Model villages (Halocha 2003):

www.beech-end.co.uk

www.babbacombemodelvillage.co.uk

http://ukmodelshops.co.uk

http://clon/ie/mvillagehtml.

Aerial photograph play mats from Wildgoose Products, www1.getmapping.com/home.asp

Where are my sheep?

Nigel Toye and Veronica Broyd

HOW DO YOUNG CHILDREN see places? Can they relate a place to a map? Can they create an imaginary place from a model and use it? How does this learning fit into the curriculum?

Four years' research exploring the use of drama with nursery children (Toye and Broyd 2002; Toye 2003) shows that drama can help children to achieve many of the aims of the Foundation Stage curriculum.

> The curriculum for the Foundation Stage should underpin all future learning by supporting, fostering, promoting and developing children's knowledge and understanding of the world, with opportunities for all children to solve problems, make decisions, experiment, predict, plan and question in a variety of contexts, and to explore and find out about their environment and people and places that have significance in their lives.
>
> (QCA 2000: 10)

One goal for early learning is for children to learn to 'observe, find out about, and identify features in the place they live in and in the natural world' (DfEE /QCA 1999: 36). In our study children solve problems, making decisions, predict, plan and question, all within the context of a variety of fictional contexts.

For the fifth year of study we wondered how they might understand and describe their environment and places through the guided imagination approach of educational drama. We wanted to consider what children could grasp of spatial relationships, of a sense of place and 'finding our way'. The dramas we had been evolving lent themselves to considering how the children would respond to pictures and picture maps.

We had been using pictures of places and objects to stimulate talk and give the children a sense of the imagined places where dramas took place. We found that they were very responsive to this visual and imaginative approach. In a drama which involved setting up a party in the living room of a house, the children were asked how they wanted to 'see' the room in the empty space. They were shown a number of pictures of common features, for example seating, windows and doors, which we placed around the working space, guided by what children suggested.

One week later the more mature children could not only remember where they had placed the pictures the previous week, but called out what the objects were even before the pictures were shown. The less mature group could remember some of the locations but needed the pictures to help them remember.

Our aims

We wanted to take this further. We wanted to see to what extent the children could demonstrate:

- a sense of place through the story of the drama, in which we use a model to describe the place;
- a sense of place in imagination, creating ideas of the place;
- the application of previous place knowledge to the story, teaching another about the place;
- links between the story, people and place.

We used a map/model of an imaginary place (but the sort of place the children would know, with features they might recognise) to see if they could sequence a journey, and to see how far they could recall and interpret information they had been given based on the map/model.

Process drama

It is important to realise that in this work we were using process drama, described as:

> a whole group drama process, essentially improvised in nature, in which attitude is of great concern . . . it is essentially, as the great drama teacher, Dorothy Heathcote, has frequently described it, lived at life-rate and operates from a discovery-at-this-moment basis rather than being memory based.
>
> (Bowell and Heap 2001: 7)

The drama is not performance based, but concerned with exploring situations. It is akin to the pretend play that children naturally adopt. As such, they understand the way it works and are able to accept stopping and starting in order to recall and reflect on what is going on in the drama. The one element that is different from their own play and something that can be difficult for some of the children to accept initially is that an adult is going to structure and lead by taking roles in this drama (teacher in role).

We are using the power of role play:

> Children learn many skills and attitudes in well-planned role play. It encourages individual and cooperative play and gives children opportunities to express feelings, to use

language, to develop literacy and numeracy skills and to learn without failure. Role play gives children the opportunity to make sense of their world.

(QCA 2000: 32)

This 'sense of their world' is enhanced and extended by the teacher in role approach, allowing the opportunity to plan, structure and intervene most powerfully.

Bo Peep

Preparing for Bo Peep

The set of dramas introduces the methodology to the children and gradually becomes more complex. The study concentrated on one class, split into two groups, one more mature and one less mature group, based on their teacher's assessment of confidence and language. The four introductory dramas are based on Percy the Park Keeper stories, such as *One Snowy Night* (Butterworth 1989) and *After the Storm* (Butterworth 1992). Through the teacher in role as Percy, the children are introduced to problems that arise: a tree has blown down in the park, or the big boy bullying a little boy. In the bullying drama this year we introduced the idea of a map to the children by using a picture map of the play area in the park where the incident takes place. We talked about pictures of play equipment in the playground and then showed the children the playground plan with smaller versions.

The photographs of play equipment were taken in a local park. Interestingly, although we did not say that, both the groups had children in them who recognised the pictures, saying 'I've been there.' So their memory of that place was very strong. It was surprising because the playground as a whole was not shown, so they must have recognised the particular slide or roundabout.

Bo Peep

The drama which was the main focus of this study concerned new characters and lasted for two half-hour sessions. It was based on the nursery rhyme 'Little Bo Peep' and the teacher played two main roles, Bo Peep and the farmer, her uncle, who had sent her to look after the sheep in one of the distant fields of the farm. However, she cannot find the right field, so when the children meet her she is unhappy and needing help to find sheep.

Creating the place

The 'map/model'

We chose to use a play mat with three-dimensional models placed on it as the map. The drama needed a countryside setting so we found a suitable mat, which had a pond, a road, a river and green areas surrounding these features. We added a range of easily recognised and universal features that the children would know. This would promote the use of words and ideas about place, as required by the Foundation Stage curriculum. We used models of two bridges across the river, a church, a farmhouse, some fences, a stone wall, a tree, some sheep, a horse, the farmer and the farmer's dog. They were not to scale, but they were all sufficiently small to fit.

We ended up with part map and part model. Many of the children would be used to having play mats, the majority of which tend to be townscapes. They would all be used to models of figures, houses and trees. We were very pleased with the final look of the map/model. It is difficult to know what to call it because it is not strictly a map and does have models on it, being partly three dimensional, and partly two dimensional.

Photographs

It was decided to support the map/model with photographs of the features. In practice it was important to link the models to pictures to help the visualisation. The models were representations and not realistic. In fact one child, when asked what she could see, called the model of the church 'a house'. If we compare the rather crude wooden model of the church with the picture we can see how the two visual stimuli were different and yet reinforced each other.

The characters and their problem

The two characters the children would encounter in this landscape were the farmer and Bo Peep. The problem in the drama was to help Bo Peep find where the sheep were, when she'd been sent to look after them but could not find her way. The structure outline for the drama is given in the Appendix.

Recording the project

Our analysis is based on the evidence from Nigel's field notes, observations made and recorded by Veronica and a video taken at each session by a third person. We spent two half-days analysing this evidence and drawing our conclusions. The two main focus groups were also compared with two other groups with whom Veronica did the same work.

The children's responses

Familiarity with the process

The groups were very familiar with the drama process by this time as was shown by Alan in the mature group. When the stimulus was introduced, a picture of the farmer with sheep dog and sheep, he pointed out, 'You're going to be the farmer.' He is predicting what is likely to happen in the drama and the fact that the teacher would take key roles. Both groups were fascinated by the map/model. They showed great interest in the model from the moment they came into the room, even before it was introduced. They were constantly looking over at it and clearly wanting to find out about it. Louie made a connection between the picture and the model, showing just how closely he was looking at the pictures and the model. He asked, 'Where's the other horse?' This was a very important transfer, as in the stimulus picture there were two horses, but only one on the model. It is a classic example of a child giving the teacher support and co-construction in drama. We had not thought of putting two horses on the model and certainly not of connecting the missing horse with the story. His contribution suggested the idea that the missing horse had hurt himself breaking the fence, which they were going to be requested to mend as part of the story anyway. Confidence in what they could do in the drama showed again immediately the broken fence was introduced. 'I think we can sort that out,' said one child.

One of the things that surprised us was that children did not tamper with the model. Having been asked by the farmer to look after it as it was his pride and joy and been shown everything that was on his farm, they seemed to respect that. Only one boy made his way to the model and touched anything. Even then he only stood a horse up that had fallen over and picked up one or two items to look at.

Introducing the place

How to introduce the children to the map/model was a challenge. With the first group Nigel found himself telling them all about the model and the pictures. When he realised this he slowed down and began to allow the children to describe what the pictures were and where they could see those on the model. With the second group he was slower from the start, allowing the children to talk about the pictures and map. However, as they were the less mature group, they needed more support anyway. All of the pictures were connected easily with the models on the map, except for the photograph of the pool, which was not a good choice.

The second main stage in using the model was to introduce the route the farmer would take from the farm to the Oak Tree Field, the location of the sheep. As he told them the route, there was great concentration from the children as he laid down footprint cards to show the stages. A notable in-put, as the farmer talked the mature group through the route, was Alan suggesting there was a waterfall somewhere on the river. He was bringing his own ideas to the context. Interestingly, it had originally been planned to have a waterfall on the route, but this was removed from the sequence because we thought there were too many landmarks. We responded to Alan's suggestion and added a waterfall in the second session.

Retracing the farmer's route

Now to see how well the children could recall the route the farmer had told them about. With the mature group their recollection of the route was tested out by interposing the activity of mending the fence, an activity that demanded co-operative pretend play and the language of planning and selection of activities and equipment. In the less mature group, it was thought best to let the children retell the route immediately after the farmer introduced it, to help fix it in their minds.

In both cases it was clear that children could recall the route, helped by the footprint cards still on the map. In fact we were delighted with their ability to retain the sequence, having been told it. All the children watched very carefully and certain key people in each of the groups described the stages. In the mature group almost all of the children were involved, whereas in the less mature group it was two or three leading children who were instrumental. Does that mean the others could not do it or that they did not have the confidence to speak out?

The mature group chose the first move as going over the footbridge and had to be slowed down by Veronica who asked, 'What did the farmer cross first, before the footbridge?' When they saw that he had crossed the road first their account became slower and more careful and deliberate. Alan put in one of the more subtle stages without being bidden, 'He follows the stream.' Carol also remembered to call the second bridge 'the old bridge'.

Meeting Bo Peep

At the very end of the first session Bo Peep was introduced to the children. They were asked to watch her and report what they saw; what she was doing. They saw a flustered and worried Bo Peep muttering about being late and not knowing which path to take. Before Veronica even stopped to talk about it, there were spontaneous comments such as, 'We know where they are,' from more than one child. They were clearly quite confident about knowing the farm, knowing where places were and Bo Peep's problem. They had to question Bo Peep to establish more about the situation.

Helping Bo Peep find the sheep

The main challenge for the second session, a few days later, was to see whether the children's confidence translated into clear directions for getting Bo Peep to the sheep. Each group was first asked to talk through the route from the farm to the field, putting the footstep markers for each stage of the journey. For the mature group, who had quite a number of their members missing in session one, this took the form of explaining to the newcomers the route to the farm and Bo Peep's problem. The amount of recall here was significant and the newcomers asked questions. Overall, the mature group, as expected, were quicker and remembered more, but the less mature group could surprise, as when Alice remembered that farmer John owned the land next to farmer George's, something that had not been remembered by the mature group.

The children walked around the room with 'Bo Peep' helping her to trace her route. Both groups contained children who were able to retell the correct sequence of landmarks passed as they guided Bo Peep on her walk to the field. Some children led Bo Peep, holding her hand and talking to her about where they had to go together. This allowed Bo Peep to respond to and enlarge on their visualisation of the route. In retrospect this 'seeing' the landscape could have been developed, the children describing more of what they could see.

In both groups there were children who were looking back at the map to check what the next landmark was. In the less mature group Carol stayed near the map and shouted over each time what the next landmark was. She was clearly using the map as the guide. With the mature group there were times when they jumped one of the landmarks, but were able to correct themselves easily if simply challenged, 'Is that the next one?' They were never asked more than once and they didn't need any more prompting than that, nor need any clues as to which the next feature was. The model worked very well as an aid to remembering, which the children used skilfully.

The less mature group had a much less strong grasp of the sequence of the route and there was much more random shouting out of 'bridge', 'pond' at the wrong times. 'Bo Peep' asked the children to check, saying 'I can't see the church', and 'Are you sure that this was what we should be looking for?'

On the other hand, with the less mature group, when Bo Peep heard the sheep were at the church she had to be led back but they did manage to come up with some key landmarks. In both groups even the quieter children were able to contribute. John was the only child (and he was in the less mature group) who remained on the outside and seemed very uncertain in all of the drama sessions. He spent most of his time supported by the nursery teacher.

How is it that children of this age are able to accept this way of looking at the farm and pretending they are there? What previous experience are they bringing to it? Veronica commented that there were a couple of children whose parents are very outdoor minded and would probably have seen maps and used them with the children. The other connection the children could make was that the map is based on the sort of play mats they were familiar with, although usually town-based layouts. We were using two media they were used to, tuning into familiar ideas: small world play and role play. However, playing with a mat and using one as a map to follow and interpret are two very different things.

When we got to the field and discovered that the sheep had gone, Alan suggested that they might have 'fallen over the waterfall'. Alan had introduced the waterfall in the first session, and picked up on it at this stage in the story.

Dealing with the angry farmer

At the moment the mature group were faced with the angry farmer who wanted to know why Bo Peep was not with the sheep, their explanations definitely centred on excusing Bo Peep because she did not know the place:

'We've seen her, but she ran away.'
'We showed her where to go.'
'She hadn't been there before.'

They showed great ability to deal with this angry adult in both groups and empathised strongly with Bo Peep.

Other evidence of how the lead children were committing to the map-based context, came with the resolution of the problem. Having caught the sheep Ellie suggested to the farmer, 'Why don't you tell her the sheep are back and she should look after them?' Barry picked up on this when the farmer had gone and Bo Peep came out of hiding. 'Go back to where you work and look after them,' he told Bo Peep. The language here shows children looking, unbidden, to solutions, to the future.

Follow-up ideas

Veronica was interested in seeing how the children would respond to a plan of a real area that they knew, so in consecutive weeks after the drama she planned two activities that were not dramas, using outline plans of the classroom and the garden area.

Hunt the strawberry

In the first activity Veronica used an architect's type plan of the classroom and had photographs of different workstations and places around the room to help children orientate themselves.

To test out their understanding of the plan she placed a strawberry on a table in the room and put a red spot on the plan, showing where the strawberry was. The children enjoyed the game of finding it. There was a lot of dashing about. Some of them clearly did relate the plan to the layout of the room, whereas others would look around to see if they could see the strawberry to locate it, rather than use the drawing. Then Veronica had volunteer children hide the strawberry in different parts of the room and see if they could place the spot on the drawing in the appropriate position. Some did manage, but this was a much more difficult task.

Treasure hunt

In the second activity the map of the garden at the nursery was used to set up a treasure hunt for the children, marking X on the map, which was a diagram of the layout with pictures of various parts of the garden attached to it. Some of the children in the garden simply looked at the picture and went to the feature without using the plan as a way of finding it. One girl was able to look at the plan and work out exactly where to go from it. However, she seemed to be the exception. Quite a number of the children sustained their concentration and stayed with the teacher to do this. Others merely looked at the plan and walked away, perhaps showing that it did not make sense to them?

Comparing the drama work with these activities

It is difficult to know if the drama work using the model prepared them for the use of these plans, in fact whether there was any relationship at all, because there are interesting differences between the activities and the drama. The plans were much more abstract than the model of the farm. On the other hand, the room and garden drawings were of a real place with which the children were acquainted and should be able to interpret as they stood in it. With the model of the farm, they were working purely with what their brains could imagine from the model and the pictures, and so were reliant totally on the model. Here there are two different types of learning about place – these activities being about their immediate environment, whereas the farm story is taking them elsewhere in their perceptions of place. With the farm they are using their previous encounters with such places and bringing them to this fictional place in their imaginations.

The use of plans differs in a second way from the drama, where the map has a purpose in relation not only to the child, but to someone else, Bo Peep and her problem. In the drama the map becomes a way of looking at problem solving for someone else, not finding a treasure or a strawberry for yourself. This contextual purpose provides a very different way of using the map because it relates to people and story. The map leads to the children empathising with Bo Peep, understanding her situation, before moving to the second stage of empathy, acting on that understanding in order to help/support her with her problem. Children are picking up this sense of place related to a story, related to events and attitudes and behaviours.

The use of the map in the garden or classroom is intrinsic and 'for me'. Embodying the map within a story is a more important objective. It should encourage the children to use their imaginations in their own small-world play or role play, to develop situations and events out of models or resources. To develop their ability to know or create, to expand on experiences is very important. Interestingly after the drama was finished the map/model was left out and children did continue to play with it.

Conclusions

The main objective of the drama work was to see whether the nursery children had a sense of place, of the farm and its landmarks from a pictorial map/model and whether they could understand a given route and could recall it. It was clear that they were fascinated by the map/model and very keen to use it. We showed that a notable number of the children of different levels of maturity could sequence an idea of place on a pictorial map and retain that and use it. Both groups had a very clear idea of what they were dealing with, constantly referring to the map as 'the map'.

How are the children seeing this imaginary place? When Alan is adding the waterfall to the context he must be seeing other possibilities. One of the children in the afternoon group, when asked what he enjoyed about it, said he enjoyed 'being on top of the bridge', which he never did in reality but was part of the imagined walk when taking Bo Peep to the sheep on the hill. Some clearly visualise strongly, but we don't know what they're seeing. Another example of the visualisation was when Michelle said of Bo Peep that 'She's gone down the hill,' accepting the idea of the Oak Tree Field being at the top of a hill.

The surprise for Veronica was:

■ that some children at this age could understand maps and diagrams as much as they did; and

■ that in such a static drama the children retained their interest throughout, even though most of the work was done in our heads and with words rather than with activities. If they had not been interested by the map/model it might well not have worked.

The model of the farm was crucial in both achievements and helped focus the work. The pictures and the model provided visual stimuli for the imagination. We can see that the use of pictures and visual stimulation is necessary to help language development, because for young children with limited vocabulary it's important that the building of the drama context is supported with other signs as well as the words.

The children were able to identify what each of the objects represented – farmhouse, farmer, horse, fence, footbridge, church, wall, old bridge, oak tree and sheep. This map worked well because we were using simple, generic features, not too demanding and complex and from a familiar setting. The same could be done with a townscape if you were to use broad generic landmarks, such as fire station, police station, sweetshop, supermarket or clothes shop.

An important question is whether this particular place drama would work with children from an inner-city environment who are not as familiar with fields, rivers, hills and sheep. Would we have to use a different environment or would it be important to use one like this, with which they were not familiar, but that they could learn about?

Other evidence of engagement with the work came from several parents, who commented on their children's enjoyment of the drama. One particular example came from a confident, but thoughtful and quiet lad. When the teacher talked to his mother she pointed out that he hadn't said much about the drama specifically, except that he had enjoyed it. However, some time after doing the drama, he was leaving the house to go to school, having been playing with his farm. He seemed worried that his brother wanted to play with the farm while he was gone. Then he said, 'I'll draw a plan.' He did this so that he would know what his farm looked like if his brother moved or changed things while he was away. Here we see transferring of the learning. Drama has the capacity to generate this sort of development.

You may like to develop some drama work yourself. Toye and Prendiville (2000) describe drama using traditional stories in the Foundation Stage and at Key Stage 1 and Baldwin and Fleming (2003) explore using a good range of texts across Key Stage 1 and Key Stage 2. If you would like to try out this drama, or modify it, a detailed plan is given in the Appendix.

References

Baldwin, P. and Fleming, K. (2003) Teaching Literacy through Drama: Creative approaches. London: RoutledgeFalmer.

Bowell, P. and Heap, B. (2001) *Planning Process Drama*. London: David Fulton Publishers.

Butterworth, N. (1989) *One Snowy Night*. London: Collins.

Butterworth, N. (1992) *After the Storm*. London: HarperCollins.

Department for Education and Employment (DfEE) (1999) *Early Learning Goals*. London: DfEE.

Toye, N. (2003) 'Finding a voice – drama and young children', in Cooper, H. and Sixsmith, C. (eds) *Teaching Across the Early Years 3–7*, 106–19. London, RoutledgeFalmer.

Toye N. and Broyd V. (2002) 'Drama in the nursery for Language and Personal and Social Development', *Drama, the magazine of National Drama*. **10**(1), 9–15.

Toye, N. and Prendiville, F. (2000) *Drama and Traditional Story for the Early Years*. London: RoutledgeFalmer.

Weather girls and boys

Jan Ashbridge

ST MARY'S PRIMARY SCHOOL is a one-class entry school in a rural community in South Cumbria. The children come from a variety of backgrounds and nearly all enter the reception class from the school's own nursery class. The nursery classroom was opened in 2000 and was built next to the reception class with both groups having access to a shared outdoor area. This arrangement has provided a valuable opportunity to develop close relationships between the staff and the children; and the teachers plan together to ensure continuity and progression of provision throughout the Foundation Stage.

The activities focused on in this chapter were part of the topic 'Changes', which was planned for the children across a half term. Weather formed one of the themes in this topic. At St Mary's there is a commitment to 'well planned play, both indoors and outdoors' and a recognition that play 'is a key way in which young children learn' (QCA 2000: 25). The staff were keen to explore the children's awareness of weather and how it affects their lives and their environment. Using this school, where there is such close collaboration between the Foundation Stage classes, gives a good opportunity to observe children's understanding of weather and the ways in which the staff take understanding of that theme on to the next level.

Nursery

Children in the nursery class were exploring the theme of weather through story. During the previous sessions they had been introduced to the story *After the Storm* about Percy the Park Keeper (Butterworth 1992). A small group role-play activity was set up following this, drawing together experiences that the children had been given access to.

Every day, when the parents bring children into the classroom they are encouraged to settle their children into an activity chosen by the child. On this particular morning, after this initial session, the teacher, Pauline Robson, brought the children together to reread the story, talk about the things they had done around the story that week and introduce the activity (Figure 12.1).

The activity took place outdoors with two separate groups of six children. Jane Hogarth, who works in the nursery, had provided equipment for the children to set up the scenario and helped the children to negotiate roles. The children decided that the playhouse would be Percy the Park Keeper's shed and they put the wheelbarrow and the tools there for him to use. There were various musical instruments available to encourage the children to recreate the noise of the storm,

Key Experience/Activity		
Adult led X Adult involvement Child independent	**Resources:** Book *After the Storm*, climbing frame, playhouse, animal puppets, wheelbarrow, mats, tools, instruments	Individual Pairs Small group X Whole group

Early Learning Goal/Stepping Stone:
K+U Exploration and Investigation – Blue Stepping Stone *Talk about what is seen and what is happening.*
Green Stepping Stone *Show an awareness of change*

Activity:
- Reread the story *After the Storm* to the whole group.
  Key questions/concepts: What different sorts of weather were in the story? What changes did the different weather make? How did the different weather affect the animals? How could they solve their problems?
- Adult will support a small group of children as they use the story outdoors in a role-play situation. They will help children to negotiate roles and begin to use the story as a starting point for their role play. They will encourage children to extend the story by developing their own ideas.
  Key concepts: Using the instruments to recreate the sounds of different weather. Discussions, observations of how the weather changes and how that changes the lives of the animals.

  Vocabulary: rain, wind, sun, storm, thunder, lightning, damage, clean

Evaluation/Assessment of learning:

Most children were able to use the weather vocabulary accurately. They could identify the types of weather involved in the storm. They were able to talk about what the weather did in the story and the problems it caused the animals. They could identify the changes in the weather.

FIGURE 12.1 Nursery activity plan for play 'After the Storm' identifying key learning experiences

and animal puppets were placed near the climbing frame, which had been turned into the tree by the addition of a few branches. A peaked cap was used to show which child was Percy.

Both groups of children thoroughly enjoyed using the instruments to make the sounds of the storm while 'Percy' slept. They spent several minutes exploring the different sounds before deciding which instruments sounded best.

Alison: Listen (shakes the tambourine)! I can do the lightning.
Milly: No, no, um, it's the thunder.
Alison: It sounds like lightning!
Joe: I don't need an instrument. Whooooooo, whooooo. I am the wind.
Jane H: What do you think of this Joe (shows him the swannee whistle)?
Joe: Nah, I can do it myself.
Kevin: (shakes the maracas right next to the playhouse) The storm is really near now . . . it's very loud.
Jane H: Goodness, that's very loud! What sort of weather are you making?
James: (banging a drum) It's the thunder.

After a few minutes of this, Jane Hogarth intervened in role:

Pauline R: Percy, come and see what the storm has done!
Ian: Yeah Percy! You'd better bring your tools.

The play then moved on to the effects of the storm and the problems facing the animals.

The children who took on the roles of the animals showed that they had a good understanding of how they might feel after the storm had damaged their homes in the trees. They used words directly from the text, but also talked to each other about their reactions to the storm and its devastating consequences.

Annabel: This'll be better than our old house won't it?
Kevin: Yeah! The rain won't get in, will it? . . . My rabbits live in the burrow . . . um . . . at the bottom of the tree . . . um . . . all safe from nasty storms.
Annabel: Squirrels live up the tree. It's better this one. Not broken. My babies don't like noisy thunder and lightning.

Both groups of children loved using the tools to help Percy build the new tree house for the animals. In the first group however, two girls, Anna and Alison, were very dominating. They tried to speak for all the children and found it hard to get in role, preferring to be themselves and organise everyone. They eventually decided that Percy's hut had also been damaged in the storm and went to repair the broken slates on the roof. Once they had moved on, the remaining boys and Milly started to play more freely and develop their animal roles further. Molly, Joe, and Ian were 'finishing off' their new homes when Christopher brought the rain stick over and played it next to the 'tree'.

Molly: What's happening?
Joe: Oh no, not again!
Christopher: That's the rain.
Ian: Quick, into our homes!
Molly: Mine's not finished.
Joe: Come in with me.

These children explored not only the facts they knew about storms (there is rain, strong wind, thunder and lightning), but also the effects the weather conditions might have on their environment (damage to the environment and property) and the effects on the people and creatures involved.

Later, while all the children were involved in child-initiated outdoor activities, a group of children noticed that there was ice around the outdoor area. They recognised that it was ice and came to get their teacher, Pauline, to show her what they had found. They collected pieces of ice to look at more carefully and talked with Pauline about how the ice looked and felt and how and why it might have formed. It was a cold but sunny morning, the perimeter of the outdoor area was still in shade, but the centre of the area where the slide is was not in shadow; it was bathed in bright sunlight.

Pauline: I wonder why there is ice round the edge but not in the middle of the outdoor area?
(The children couldn't think of any answer.)
Pauline: What would happen to the ice if we put pieces of it in different places around the outdoors?

The children were initially not sure, although they agreed that it would all probably melt. They all broke off a piece of ice and talked with Pauline about where they might put it. Joe decided to put his near the slide in the sunshine. After talking with the children about what might happen to the ice, Pauline concluded that all the children knew that their pieces of ice would melt and she was using this as an opportunity to take on their understanding of the link between warmth from the sun and the melting of the ice. Shortly after, Joe came to her in tears, complaining, 'Someone's stolen my ice! There's just water where it was.' Pauline's assumption that Joe understood what would happen to the ice was mistaken. When talking with her Joe knew that ice melted as a learned fact. But he didn't understand what that actually meant! This highlights the point that we often make assumptions about children's knowledge and understanding on the basis of what they say in response to quite closed questions. We must provide opportunities such as this for children to be able to explore what that knowledge actually means. Children need to be able to make sense of the world around them by doing, not just talking and watching. It wasn't until Joe held another piece of ice and felt it melt and drip from his hand that he actually made the link between the warm sun and the disappearance of his ice. The experience of Joe and his piece of ice illustrates clearly Helen Bilton's point that 'Children need to have a multisensory experience of these weather forms – not be inside looking out at the weather!' (Bilton 2002: 62). This is reinforced in the *SPEEL* report, which states that:

> Effective practitioners value and believe in teaching and learning practices which [. . .] make full use of a range of open ended, active, hands on, multi-sensory learning experiences through which children can [. . .] explore concepts and interests [and] reinforce and consolidate knowledge.
>
> (Moyles 2002: 54)

During the same session Alison and Anna were looking in the pots at the bulbs they were growing; the crocuses were flowering. Anna called me over.

Anna: Look what happens to our flowers in the sunshine.

Anna and Alison took me to look at the pots against the wall. One pot was in sunlight but the other was still in shadow.

Alison: The sunshine ones are different . . . bigger . . . it's opened out. I have those in my garden.
Jan: I wonder why that's happened?
Anna: Um . . . I think . . . um, they like the sun.
Alison: Yeah it makes them grow.
Jan: What else do they need to help them grow?
Alison: I know . . . rain.
Jan: Do you think the flowers open up in the rain too?
Anna: No, just the sun. It, like, wakes them up. These are still asleep. (She points at the ones in the shade.)
Jan: Do you like the sun? How does it make you feel?
Anna: Warm, warm like summer.
Alison: Flowers wake up in the warm. Wake up flowers. (She pulls the pot from the shade into the sunshine.)

The girls were encouraged to think more carefully about what they had observed. Open-ended questions were used to encourage them to think through the problem of why the flowers were different. Their thinking was supported by adult intervention which helped them to talk through their ideas. As the EPEY project found, in the most effective settings 'The adult interventions were most often in the form of questions that provoke speculation and extend the imagination' (Siraj-Blatchford *et al.* 2002: 47). The example above of Anna and Alison shows the benefits of this questioning where guidance is combined with questions that encourage exploration of ideas.

These children in the nursery were working on particular learning objectives taken from the Knowledge and Understanding of the World area of learning (QCA

2000). The staff planned for them to visit these concepts in a cross-curricular way. The use of the story (Communication, Language and Literacy) immediately put the learning in a meaningful context and the fact that the characters and settings in the story were already well known to the children meant that they were already able to empathise with the animals and had some ideas about how they might respond (Personal, Social and Emotional Development). This provided support for the children as they set about exploring the effect of weather on the lives of the animals and ultimately their own lives. Using the musical instruments to help create the sound effects for their role play (Creative Development) enabled the adult to question the children and explore their existing awareness of the sounds that we associate with weather.

The children explored the effects that severe weather can have on their environment and what problems that can cause by playing through the situation using the climbing frame as the tree and the tools to help build new homes for the animals (Physical Development).

The importance of offering children an outdoor curriculum that is mutually supportive of the curriculum on offer indoors, is key to ensuring that all children have the opportunity to learn in a way which suits their learning style. Some other children could listen and learn that warmth will make ice melt, but Joe needed a real situation that came up naturally and was sparked by his own interest and experience to fully understand what he had learned. Similarly, without the facility to observe at close hand the effects of the sun on the flowers they had planted, Alison and Anna may not have been able to make the connection between the weather and the sprouting and flowering of the plants and flowers around them in such a meaningful way. In these situations the learning came, not from the prepared planning of the teacher, but the interest of the children. Because of this the children had the independence and confidence to know what they wanted to learn about and the adult's role was to support them and scaffold their learning. Indeed the *SPEEL* report endorses the point that 'when children's learning is sensitively modelled and scaffolded they are likely to engage in complex thinking and problem solving' (Moyles 2002: 109 citing Bowman 2001).

Reception

The role-play area in the reception class is always linked to the topic the children are exploring. It is an area that is planned and created with the children so they are fully involved in its development and are able to think and talk through how they intend to take the play forward (Figure 12.2). In keeping with the theme of weather, their role-play area was a weather station/studio. The area is used to help children develop their knowledge and understanding across the curriculum

Opportunities for developing Language and Literacy	Creative opportunities	Developing Personal and Social skills
Provide a range of reference books on the weather. Provide a range of writing equipment to encourage mark making and a board to display and value contributions. Model writing weather reports for newspapers and scripts for TV. Use guided writing time to encourage children to write for a variety of purposes in role.	Making maps to use in the role play. Make props to use in the role play: microphones, pretend video recorders etc. Develop roles for themselves and act out narratives co-operatively. **Imaginative Play Area Term: 3 Theme: Weather station/studio**	Working together to create a 'TV' weather forecast. Sharing resources. Negotiating roles.
Recording the weather over a period of time, making charts and analysing data. Positional vocabulary.	Looking at maps, using maps to make weather forecasts. Introduce the words north, south, east, west. Use video camera to record forecasts. Use computer for making charts of the weather and typing the scripts etc. Identify other uses of ICT in the study of the weather.	Use range of equipment to find out about the weather, thermometer rain gauge etc. Operate video equipment.
Opportunities for Mathematical thinking	**Developing our Knowledge and Understanding**	**Physical opportunities**
Vocabulary list: north south east west forecast script change rain wind thunder snow sun frost icy report symbol research gauge thermometer chart degrees centigrade	**Props and accessories:** Range of non-fiction books about the weather Variety of atlases Maps of the world and the UK on a variety of scales Maps for children to draw on Weather symbols Writing equipment Notice board Computer and printer Tape recorder for radio forecasts ICT equipment – real and made by children – video, microphone etc. Equipment for measuring the weather, e.g. rain gauge, thermometer Newspaper weather forecasts Clothes to dress up in	**Possible characters:** Camera man Researcher Forecaster Script writer Sound recorder **Possible scenarios:** Weather research station – observing and recording the weather over a period of time, using non-fiction books and making charts of the weather. Writing reports and making newspaper forecasts. Radio/TV weather forecast – script writing, recording the bulletin.

FIGURE 12.2 Reception class plan for imaginative play area: weather theme

and these links are carefully planned. By making these links explicit, children are encouraged to use skills gained in one area and apply them to different situations. The children had been using the weather station/studio for about a week and had developed their learning in a variety of different areas.

During this session the children were involved in their own independent activities, so the children who were in the role-play area had on this occasion chosen to be there. The scenario during the session was a television weather studio. The children had previously watched weather forecasts together and discussed the content and style. There was a real camcorder for the children to use as the television camera and also a camera that the children had made out of boxes. Six children spent time in the area during the session.

They were quickly able to negotiate roles with each other, not needing adult support as the nursery children had. Georgia became very involved in writing scripts for the others to use. She had previously been involved in playing along side her teacher, Miss Waller, during a literacy focused session looking at script writing and was eager to try this out herself. Brendan, not usually a very confident boy, later took on the role of the presenter and enjoyed dressing up and performing to the camera. Some other children were more self-conscious and didn't want to be videoed. Edward wanted to be the researcher and spent time looking through the books and making notes on the computer using his own emergent writing. He was more than eager to talk about his work and what he had found out from the books, but didn't engage much in the role play except when he was being the cameraman and could take charge!

When Georgia had written her first script she called everyone together to begin the first recorded forecast. Edward started off using the homemade camera and pretended that he was videoing me, videoing him!

Edward: Have a go with mine. (He offers to swap.)

Edward knew he needed to have earpieces and wires attached to his ears. He took off his lens cap as he had seen me do and started videoing Georgia's report.

Rachael: Good morning. Today it's going to be cloudy over here and up here with snow right up here! (She sticks on the right symbols on the map of the British Isles.)
Georgia: And then later, the sun will come out and it will be much nicer.
Rachael: It's sunny in England and snowy in the North Pole.
Georgia: Tonight it's going to rain all over the country.
Both:　Goodbye, hope you have a nice day.

The girls had a good idea which part of the map was England and knew they lived there. They had previously been shown the area in which they live and made a point of putting a symbol there. They placed the snowy symbol on Scotland.

During the session I became involved in the play as a scriptwriter and Rachael and I were looking at weather forecasts from newspapers which were cut out and put up in the area.

Rachael: In the newspaper it says 'rainy in the south'.
Jan: Hmm, I wonder which way is south on our map?
Joel: Here! (He points to Scotland.)
Rachael: (chants) North, south, east, west.
Jan: Joel thinks that this is south Rachael, what do you think?
Georgia: That's the way to the North Pole not the South Pole! It's north I think.
Jan: Gosh, how are we going to remember that?
Joel: I'll write a notice. (He writes N at the top of the map.)
Rachael: South's down then.
Joel: Down here? S-s-south. (He writes S.)
Rachael: North, south, which is east, there or there?
Jan: (points) That's east, that's where the sun comes up in the morning.
Rachael: So that's west. (She takes the pen and writes E and W on the map.)

It was not planned for the children to be introduced to the concept of the points of the compass at this time but as the children seemed to be trying to use some of the words they had obviously heard before, for example, North Pole, it was a good opportunity to introduce a new idea in a meaningful context. The learning was initiated by the adult involved. The EPEY report notes such adult involvement when it states that 'The majority of episodes occurring in reception classes were initiated by adults, and the episodes of high intellectual challenge to the child occurred in teacher initiated episodes, a very different approach to that of pre-school settings' (Siraj-Blatchford *et al.* 2002: 13). This report also noted that:

Effective practitioners assess the children's performance to ensure the provision of challenging yet achievable experiences, they model appropriate language, values and practices, they encourage socio-dramatic play, they also praise and encourage, ask questions and verbally interact with the children to encourage sustained shared thinking.

(Siraj-Blatchford *et al.* (2002: 13)

As this suggests, adults have to be involved in children's playful learning, talking with them about their learning, encouraging them to be actively involved. It is also important that children get the space and time to make sense of this new learning in their own way, as is seen in Georgia's play following this session. She carried on in the role-play area and used the new idea of points of the compass and associated vocabulary independently, both in her script (Figure 12.3) but also on a map of the UK, by drawing weather symbols to represent what she had written (Figure 12.4). She wrote the script for Brendan, who had just joined the play. Georgia read the script to Brendan so he would know what to say.

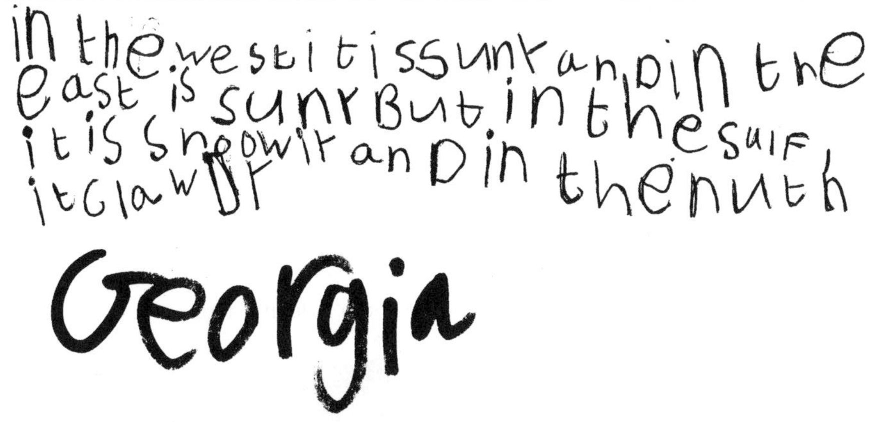

FIGURE 12.3 Georgia's script for weather presenter, done independently after compass points were introduced

Rachael: Tell him about the north, south, east, west so he knows.

Georgia: North is up this way, um . . . the way to the North Pole. South is down there, look at the S. E is the east way um . . . direction. The other is W for west. Look, it's in my script.

Brendan: Is that the way to the South Pole (points to the south)?

Rachael: I suppose so but it's sunny there today.

Georgia: (looks at adult) It's not sunny at the South Pole. The South Pole must be a different way.

Jan: It can be sunny at the South Pole but it's always very cold I think. Shall we look in the atlas and see where the South Pole is?

We looked together and decided that Brendan was right, it was the way to the South Pole but the South Pole was a lot further south than their map went.

The adult involvement during this episode was minimal, the children were cascading new knowledge and information down to each other. As often happens, children asked questions when they reached the limit of their understanding. Georgia requested my intervention to scaffold her learning.

A further example of this occurred with Rachael and Edward.

Rachael: The weather's changing a bit cloudy now.

Edward: How do they (the clouds) get here?

Jan: The wind blows them across the sky. Have you ever watched them on a windy day? Is it windy today?

Rachael: Let's go and see. (She goes to look out of the window.) Edward, look, the clouds are moving.

Jan: Wow! I wonder why they are going so fast?

Edward: The wind must be going fast too mustn't it? They're all going over there.

Rachael: That's the way the wind's taking them isn't it?

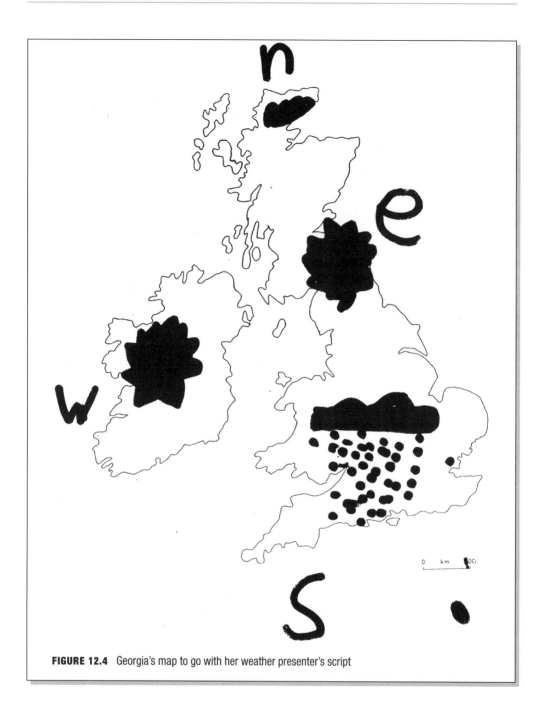

FIGURE 12.4 Georgia's map to go with her weather presenter's script

Jan: I don't think it'll be cloudy for long. What do you think?

Rachael: It'll change back to sunny.

This was a good time to help the children find out and understand that the wind could make a difference to the weather they experienced and not just be seen as a kind of weather in itself. The opportunity came from the children's interest, arising naturally from the situation. They needed a combination of information and open-ended questions to help them think through the implications of that information and begin to make sense of it in their own way. These adult–child exchanges help to show the importance of supporting and extending their learning by sharing ideas and working together in both adult-initiated and child-initiated contexts. There is almost a separation between knowing and finding out. 'Direct teaching should be complemented by dialogues between children and adults which centre on sustained shared thinking. There should be an equal emphasis on free play and direct teaching' (Siraj-Blatchford *et al.* 2002: 12). So, the knowledge that comes from direct teaching, for some children, cannot have true meaning unless that child has also had the opportunity to use the information for themselves and test it out in a meaningful context. The example earlier of Joe in the nursery class, who *knew* that ice melted but did not *understand* it is another clear example. If children like Joe, Rachael and Edward are to truly learn and understand, we must marry direct teaching with meaningful, child-initiated dialogues.

The planning for this role-play area, Figure 12.2 shows how important cross-curricular links are in helping children explore a range of new knowledge, skills and understanding within the theme in a meaningful, playful context. In the sequences illustrated above the main focus is obviously Knowledge and Understanding of the World, particularly the Early Learning Goal for a sense of place. Throughout the play, however, children were developing their skills in other areas of learning. These include all areas of Communication, Language and Literacy, most predominantly the goals for language for communication and language for thinking, where children interacted and negotiated well. They used language to think through their learning and organise and sequence the play. There were many opportunities in this situation to develop aspects of the children's Personal, Social and Emotional Development. This was shown clearly as they worked together in a group to negotiate and share equipment and information. There were many more examples where the children's learning in the focused area was supported and enhanced by their learning in other areas of learning.

Another situation illustrates this well. While the other children played in the role-play area, Carly had decided that she would use the data that the class had collected and put it onto a weatherboard. She used it on the computer to make a bar chart of the weather over the past two weeks. She thought 'It might be good for the weather presenter to have and it might go in a newspaper.' Learning about collecting data and making bar charts had been an adult-initiated mathematics focus the week before, using the same software, and Carly had enjoyed it. As the previous learning had also taken place within the meaningful context of the role-play area, Carly was now able to use this learning to independently meet the

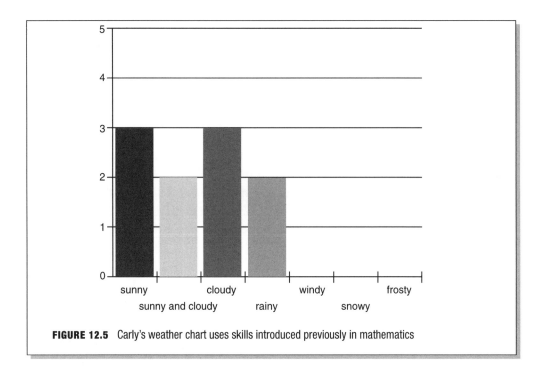

FIGURE 12.5 Carly's weather chart uses skills introduced previously in mathematics

demands of her self-chosen task. There was no adult involvement or support; Carly knew what she wanted to find out, knew what she wanted to do with the information and she had the tools at her disposal to carry out the task (Figure 12.5). She was able to talk about her work and describe what the data told her.

The task Carly had set herself was to find out about the weather. To do this she needed to use learning she had acquired in other areas of learning, primarily mathematics and Information and Communication Technology. This shows the importance of planning for learning to happen in meaningful contexts across the areas of learning.

Teaching and learning

There are two strands running through all of the children's experiences in the Foundation Stage classes as described above: first, what and how the children are learning; and secondly, what and how the practitioners are teaching.

Learning, in St Mary's nursery class, was a combination of adult-initiated activity, such as the role play, and child-initiated learning coming directly from their interest, such as Joe with the ice and Alison and Anna with the flowers. The children had taken control of what they wanted to learn and the adult was in a supportive role. The balance in the nursery was towards child-initiated learning. In the reception class, the learning came out of the more structured and carefully planned situation of the role-play area. Whereas the role-play area often allows the children to play and learn freely, with the only structure provided being the area itself and its resources, the examples explored above show the adult actively involved in the children's play situations. The children are offered experiences in which they can 'explore, investigate, discover, create, practise, rehearse, repeat, revise and consolidate their developing knowledge, skills, understanding and attitudes' (QCA 2000: 20).

As for teaching in the nursery, the adult responded to the children and followed their interests. In the reception class the balance has shifted slightly and although the teaching is not formal, the adult is using more opportunities to model ideas and new vocabulary. So, the adult is more overtly making connections for the children, modelling them and scaffolding the children's learning. In both nursery and reception, open-ended questions, conversations, suggestions, sharing of information and modelling were all used as strategies by the adult to develop children's understanding and make links between learning from different areas and situations. As the Curriculum Guidance for the Foundation Stage puts it 'Teaching means systematically helping children to learn so that they are helped to make connections in their learning and are actively led forward, as well as helped to reflect on what they have already learnt' (QCA 2000: 22).

Our challenge as early years educators is in recognising the learning that is happening and supporting and encouraging it through a developmentally appropriate curriculum and sensitive adult intervention.

References

Bilton, H. (2002) *Outdoor Play in the Early Years*, 2nd edn. London: David Fulton Publishers.

Butterworth, N. (1992) *After the Storm*. London: HarperCollins.

Cooper, H. and Sixsmith, C. (2003) *Teaching Across the Early Years 3–7*. London: RoutledgeFalmer.

Moyles, J. (2002) *Study of Pedagogical Effectiveness in Early Learning (SPEEL)*. London: HMSO.

13

Reflections on our project

Curriculum knowledge

THE FIRST OF THE QUESTIONS underpinning our project was:

> What curriculum knowledge do adults need in order to interact with children in ways which extend their thinking about time and place?

The case studies showed how a shared understanding of the key questions to ask and ways of answering set out in Chapter 2 enabled all the practitioners involved to stimulate, support and extend play-based activities investigating time and place. However, this knowledge did not need to be extensive or specialised.

This shared understanding made us explicitly aware of the considerable knowledge that many three- to five-year-olds have about place and time and to create opportunities to extend it. For example, children in Chapter 3 knew implicitly that they had grown and changed over time. Using evidence in photographs they were able to explain how and to sequence their lives. They could sort into categories of 'then' and 'now' and measure the passing of time through birthdays. These may be traditional early years activities, but because Vicki, their teacher, was able to identify key concepts within these activities (similarity and difference, sequence of changes over time, inferences from evidence), and to model questions using these concepts, a group of children who were described as having poor social and communication skills learned how to ask each other questions which led somewhere. Discussion based on these key thinking skills was progressively built upon through the play activities.

The teacher in Chapter 4, Louise, recognised that children had implicit information about ways in which the past is different from the present in familiar nursery rhymes and stories (for example Jack and Jill got water from a well, Little Red Riding Hood's father was a woodcutter), then through questioning children about their play in a 'castle', Louise helped them to become aware of what they already knew, to reason from it and to apply this knowledge to extend their play.

By helping children to make map sticks in Chapter 10, to find Bo Peep's sheep in Chapter 11, and journey to distant lands through the back of a story tent in Chapter 9 adults were able to find out, and to make children aware of what a lot they knew about features of familiar, and in some cases unfamiliar places, and about maps and routes, then to extend this understanding.

Planning for play activities to explore time and place

Our second question was:

How can practitioners use curriculum knowledge to plan activities investigating time and place and how do adult-directed and freely accessed activities link together?

The importance of a rich, free-access learning environment

All of the time-and place-focused activities described occurred within settings providing a rich variety of free activities. Figures 3.1 and 4.2 provide examples of such learning environments. Children were trained to be independent and so could draw on these resources and their skills in using them in their play. In Chapter 10 Aileen selected her paper and adhesive to make her linear map to record her adventure and the bear hunt at camp was one of a myriad of freely chosen possibilities. In Chapter 12 Carly knew how to use the computer when she had the idea of making a bar chart for the weather presenters.

Planning for holistic learning

The time and place activities were planned within integrated areas of learning. In Figure 3.2 activities described are set within a wide ranging theme on Knowledge and Understanding of the World (QCA 2000). Figure 12.2 shows how the weather studio drew on each of the areas of learning and Figure 8.1 shows how spontaneous outdoor play, which was not planned for, nevertheless provided opportunities for observing, promoting and assessing children's development in each of these areas.

Planning for focused learning about time and place

Within such rich physical environments and as part of an integrated curriculum teacher-led activities to find out about time and place were planned. These depended on clear curriculum knowledge, as set out in Chapter 2, to identify the learning intentions, possible questions and the role of the adult.

In Chapter 2 we said that finding out about the past involved making 'good guesses' about things from the past which remain and tracing changes over time, in order to construct interpretations of the past. The case studies provide many examples.

- Making deductions and 'good guesses' about sources, traces of the past which remain.

There are examples of children using oral sources in Chapter 3 ('All about us'); written sources in Chapter 4 and in Chapter 5 (nursery rhymes and stories); visual sources in Chapter 3 (photographs) and Chapter 4 (story illustrations); artefacts in Chapter 3 (baby's and children's things) and in Chapter 6 (bronze age tools and pots); and archaeological sites in Chapter 6.

■ Tracing changes over time

Sequence, similarity and difference are the focus of activities in Chapter 3; then and now (Chapter 4); causes and effects and motives (Chapter 5).

■ Interpretations

The past is reconstructed through story in Chapter 5, in the castle role play in Chapter 4 and in the reconstructing life in a Bronze Age hut in Chapter 6.

We identified the skills involved in finding out about places. Many of these were reflected in the case studies.

■ Naming features (as in the bear hunt in Chapter 10 and Bo Peep's route in Chapter 11).

■ Observing, comparing and describing places (as in the visit to Oman in Chapter 7 and the map stick activity, Chapter 10).

■ Observing, explaining and recording weather patterns (Chapter 12).

■ Tracing routes (for example Little Bo Peep's route).

■ Making maps (linear as in map sticks; plans, as in the journey to the camp in Chapter 10) graphs and diagrams (weather charts, Chapter 12).

■ Comparing places; communication between places (for example journeys to distant places, Chapters 7 and 9).

■ Expressing likes and dislikes about places (secret places in Chapter 8).

■ Using locational and positional vocabulary (Chapters 8 to 12).

■ The influence of their environment on people's lives and vice versa and (for example in the Bronze Age, Chapter 6 and in the same locality today).

■ Sustainability (whether or not to pick flowers was discussed in Chapter 10 – that's a start!).

■ Communities, work and leisure activities; the services a community needs and how goods and people are transported around the community and to and from other places; (Well we did go in a 'place capsule to Oman and Blackpool in Chapter 7 and on a bus to the farm in Chapter 10, but there is plenty of room for development here.)

There are of course plenty of opportunities for development in each of these strands.

In spite of the references to play based on workplaces, which was described in Chapter 2, none of the case studies involved such play. This may be because it often arises spontaneously and is not planned for. The visits to schools on particular scheduled days may have made it elusive.

Teachers' plans show how they planned play activities to develop these concepts. (The aims in Figures 3.3 and 3.4 were 'to order photographs from baby to adult' and 'to sort objects into those used by a baby and an older child'.) The intended learning outcomes for the play based in a castle are shown in Figure 4.1: to become aware of differences between past and present; of changes over time; to use the language of time and to begin to hypothesise about life in a castle in the past, giving reasons to support these. The aims for the focused activity plan for journeys (Figure 9.2) include developing an interest in cultural differences and of other countries. The aims of the play based on the storm (Figure 12.1) included discussing effects of weather changes, using specified vocabulary. Because these plans, although flexible, clearly identified concepts, skills and questions it was possible to assess what the children knew, to extend this and to assess what they learned.

Although play usually focused on either time or place, in several chapters the distinction between the concepts is blurred. In Chapter 6 children model, observe and discuss their locality and life today before reconstructing it in the distant past and in Chapter 7 one child goes to the shop 'today' and returns with a Victorian horse and cart – prompted by the old pennies in the till!

Personal and social education and communication skills

It was interesting that the activities to investigate place and time were seen by all the practitioners as powerful contexts for developing self-esteem, personal and social skills and communication skills. This was particularly emphasised in Chapter 3 and the aims in the medium-term plan for play in a castle (Figure 4.1) illustrate how social and language skills can be developed through play. The castle play aims to help children to interact and work as part of a group negotiating plans and taking turns in conversation; to select and look after resources; to be motivated; to enjoy using spoken language, listening to stories and recreating roles. Figure 9.1 shows how a key strand of the story tent project was to develop language for communication.

Links between adult-directed learning and free-access activities

The REPEY project (Siraj-Blatchford *et al.* 2002) suggested that effective settings encourage children to initiate activities modelled by staff. Our case studies provide many different examples of the subtle relationship between adult-initiated activities and children's play. Sometimes adult-initiated activities become models for free play; setting up camp and making map sticks in Chapter 10 become integrated into free play later. Sometimes an activity which needs to be adult led is seen by children as spontaneous. For example Vicki Boertien, in Chapter 3, gives herself problems to solve which the children voluntarily want to help her with: how to arrange photographs in her album; how to sort children's belongings. In some instances adults talk to children about their play and so extend and enrich it, without participating in it (in the castle, for example). In Chapter 7 Jane Yates is invited by the children into their hotel in Oman. Sometimes adults move in to sustain play which is about to disintegrate, then move out again when roles, scenes and purposes are re-established (as when Gill redirects the bus in Chapter 10). Or they seize on opportunities that arise; Gill cheers up the campers with songs about the sun coming out – soon! When Jan Ashbridge became involved in the weather station play as a script writer (Chapter 12) this enabled her to collect and display weather forecast maps which stimulated a long and complex discussion about the poles and points of the compass. In some cases the adults frame the play, as in the Bo Peep process drama but create possibilities for the children to assume ownership; finding ways to solve Bo Peep's problems (Chapter 11). In Chapter 6 Hugh Moore introduces the skills necessary for play about the distant past.

Yet none of the case studies provides an example of extended, rich, free, imaginative play of the kind Penelope Lively, the Brontë children, C. S. Lewis and Laurie Lee describe in Chapter 2. It is interesting to speculate why. Is it because they were unusually imaginative literary children? Is it because they were isolated, with limited alternative entertainment that their imaginations had free rein? Do children today have too many stimuli to develop their imaginations? Is it because such play is inhibited in educational settings? Are three- to five-year-olds simply not mature enough for such play? If Kieran Egan is right, as Alan Farmer and Anne Heeley suggest in Chapter 5, and the golden age of mythic play continues until eight-years-old there are very strong implications for teachers of Key Stage 1 children about the rich opportunities found in play to explore other times and places in valid but imaginative ways. It may be, too, that social, cognitive and communication skills and prior knowledge are necessary for such play to flourish. Do we need to introduce children to these prerequisite steps, to stimulate such play? Certainly the nursery children in Chapter 11 developed the play the teacher had introduced to rebuild Percy the Park Keeper's shed and the children who began with the teacher-directed play about 'ourselves' were said to be ready for role play based on fairy stories by their third term in school.

Working with parents

Several of the case studies show how parents and practitioners shared educational aims. For example the theme, 'All about us' (Chapter 3) was an ideal way of involving parents who might not otherwise have been involved in their children's learning. 'The children encouraged their parents to find photographs of them as babies and to talk about them.' When the nursery went camping (Chapter 10) families were involved in all stages of the planning and worked collaboratively with the school staff both in the preparation and at the camp, on organisational matters, from toilets to transport, and in providing and enjoying the activities together and with their children, whether hunting for bears or blowing bubbles. Indeed two grannies who had first 'camped' three years ago now came every year. Family knowledge of other places is central to the story tent project in Chapter 9.

Dialogue which extends thinking

The third question we set out to investigate in our project was:

> How do practitioners engage in dialogue about time and place with children?

Everyone working on the case studies had a shared understanding of the key time and place concepts they wanted children to develop, planned for activities to support this and planned time for adults to observe and interact with children involved in the activities, whether teacher directed or 'free access'. This made it possible for each case study to capture examples of adults talking to children about time and place, to see how discussion was initiated and extended and how children used it as a model for asking each other questions. In Chapter 3 we see how Vicki, the teacher, structured questions so that children gradually learned in simple ways, to observe and to make inferences about photographs, to give reasons and to comment on each other's decisions and question what other children said. In Chapter 4 Louise helps children to move beyond the familiar, to listen to each other, to draw on what they know and to share ideas; to make links between their own experiences and other times, to challenge each other's ideas. ('Cooks aren't always women. I went to a Little chef and the cook there was a man.') In Chapter 5 there are many examples of children developing and contesting and reasoning about each other's ideas in response to Anne Heeley's open questions about whether a variety of different stories are true. Anne only asked the questions which were followed by long sequences of children's views. While in Chapter 12 we are reminded of the importance of doing, as well as talking, when Joe, who took part in a reasoned discussion about melting, is later distraught because someone 'stole' his piece of ice. Jan's participation in the weather play as a script writer in this chapter illustrates how well she was able to respond to children's use of words they had heard but did not understand and introduce a new idea which they absorbed into their play and their understanding. Talk (in Chapter 10) about what can or can not represent the characteristics of a place on a map stick, like many other discussions in the book, may appear simple, but on reflection contains very sophisticated reasoning. It occurs spontaneously because the children are interested in a real problem in their 'adventure' play.

Continuity and progression

The title of this book is *Exploring Time and Place through Play: Foundation Stage–Key Stage 1*. However, although there are suggestions for extending the activities for older children, most of the case studies took place in Foundation Stage classes. This was an intentional bias. We hoped to show, first, that it is appropriate for Foundation Stage children to build on the considerable implicit understanding they already have about their own times and places and about more distant times and places. The case studies show how finding out about time and place links with all the areas of learning and in particular how it developed children's self-esteem, personal and social and communication skills. Secondly, we think that it is important that holistic approaches to teaching and learning, which are appropriate in the early years, with an emphasis on play and story, should be extended into Key Stage 1. Certainly Egan (see Chapter 5) argues that the mythic stage of development (in which children create other worlds alongside the real world) continues from the age of four-until eight-years-old (Egan 1983). Lesley Staggs, Director of the National Primary Strategy has said recently that, 'People must understand that an active, play-based curriculum doesn't have to get in the way of achievement – it supports achievement' (Staggs 2003). It is more fun for the adults too. In the same edition of this paper Alex Walker, Assistant Head of Avondale Park Primary School, Kensington, remembers one of her pupils. 'I think with affection of Michaela, who went through a phase of wearing a silver glitter wig and would only do what was asked of her if I addressed her as, "flying horse" ' (Walker 2003).

References

Egan, K. (1983) 'Children's path to reality from fantasy: contrary thoughts about curriculum foundations', *Journal of Curriculum Studies* **15**(5) 357–71.

Siraj-Blatchford, I., Sylva, K., Muttock, S., Gilden, R. and Bell, D. (2002) *Researching Effective Pedagogy in the Early Years*, (Research Report 356). Annersley: Department for Education and Skills. (http://www.dfes.gov.uk/research/data/).

Staggs, L. (2003) 'Roots of revolution', *Times Educational Supplement* 10 October: 24.

Walker, A. (2003) 'Pupils I'll never forget', *Times Educational Supplement* 10 October: 6.

Appendix: Drama plan for Bo Peep

Roles and props

Roles for children: Helpful people – the props/role signifiers

Roles for teacher: Farmer George or Jane – hat, dog bowl
                    Bo Peep – hat and stick

Other props: chairs for fence, pictures and map/model

Structure outline

Examples of direct speech by teacher in or out of role are given in italics.

Session one

1. Out of Role (OoR): *We are going to do a new story today, one with new people in it. You are in the story and I am going to be two different people in the story. Let's take a look at a picture that helps us think about where our story takes place.*

    Hold up a picture of farmer, sheep dog and sheep. Discuss what the children can see.

    In the story we are going to do you are going to meet a farmer like that one in the picture. Let's see what he is doing. I'm going to be him and you will know I am him when I am wearing this hat.

    Put on the hat and pick up the dog bowl.

2. Teacher in Role (TiR): Whistling, calling and putting the bowl down. *Here we are now, Fly. We'll have a rest. You've done really well this morning. Finding that lost ewe and rounding her up was excellent. I'll give you a drink. There you are. I bet you'll like that.*

    Stop the drama.

3. OoR: *Let's stop the story there. Who is that? What is he doing? Who is he talking to?* Discuss with them.

   I'll be him again and you can see if you're right.

   See if they talk to him and if not prompt them.

   Are you the people who have come to visit my farm today?

   Let me introduce you first. This is my sheep dog, Fly, one of the best. I'll even let you make friends and stroke her if you like, though she's a working dog and we don't normally pet her. You shouldn't go up to stroke a dog unless the owner says it is all right.

4. OoR: Negotiating into the 'as if' world. *How can you show you are stroking this pretend dog?*

   Get some of the children to demonstrate and let volunteers one at a time do it with care and authenticity. If more than one starts to come forward the TiR says, *Only one at a time; otherwise you might frighten Fly.*

5. TiR: *Well, let me show you my farm. I have a new map of my farm that a local person has made for me and I'm really pleased with it.*

   Do you like it? Can you see where all the places are?

   Produce the outline and show all the pictures.

   The task is for the children to recognise the pictures and compare them to the models on the map.

   Now that is where my sheep are at the moment up on the hill, in Oak Tree Field. My niece, Bo Peep, should be up there looking after them. I'd better go and check that she is up there and the sheep are safe. Let me show you how we have to get there on the map.

   Lay down footstep markers to show the route.

6. TiR: *You seem very helpful people. I've got a problem as one of my fences here in the farmyard is broken. Could you help me mend that so I can get up to the sheep? It would be much faster if you helped. I have to mend it before the sheep come down from the top field. One of the horses knocked into it. Could you help me? I'll leave you all the tools but I have to make sure where the sheep are. Are you OK to get on on your own?*

   OoR: *What did he want? What would you need to mend a wooden fence? How would you pretend to work on the fence so that it looked right?*

Occupational mime

Move into a space and set the children the task. Help them by having them all practise each type of movement together if necessary. Working with the class, get them to demonstrate sawing, hammering nails, using a screwdriver and measuring the wood.

7. From narrative to TiR: *The children were busy mending the fence; . . . was sawing the wood; . . . was hammering. They were all working very hard when someone new appeared.*

   OoR: *Let's look at who this new person is and what she is doing. Tell me how you think she is feeling when you have looked at her.*

   Pick up the straw hat and shepherd's crook (or equivalent) – TiR as Bo Peep. She is very worried. Talking to herself . . .

   I'm late. He'll be very angry if I don't look after the sheep. But I can't find the field. Is it this way, or is it down this other path? I can't remember where he said that field was. I'd better just run away and hide.

   Make as though to run away and freeze.

   OoR: Reflecting on what they have seen. *What is she doing? How is she feeling? Why? Is she right to run away? What are you going to do? Who do you think this is?*

   Discuss what they think and then . . .

   We'll see what you can do to help her with her problem next time.

Session two

8. OoR: Recap on what happened in the last session and who they met and what they did. *Who did you meet at the end of the last session and what was she doing?*

   TiR as Bo Peep: The children can talk to her to find out what is going on. They have to get her to explain what the problem is. Reluctant at first she then begins to tell. Depending on the questions she can answer like this:

   Uncle George said I have to mind the sheep up in Oak Tree Field and I can't find it. You see I am only visiting Uncle George's farm and I really don't know it very well. I know the field's somewhere on the farm. I think I have to pass the church and cross the river by the old bridge, but I can't even find the church.

   She gets to the point where she asks for their help.

   They can show her the map and take her through it. She has never seen it before.

   They take her immediately to the field.

9. Journey to Oak Tree Field. Do this as a walk round the room, the children escorting Bo Peep and telling her each place they pass (they can refer back to the map).

   When they get there, there are no sheep! They have disappeared.

10. TiR as Bo Peep: *Oh I can hear Farmer George coming. Please tell him it wasn't my fault.*

   She runs out. (Or she hides and asks them not to tell on her. This can be an interesting episode, but if you do it like this there can be a split between the children, some wanting to tell and some not and you have to go OoR to sort it out. Some teachers do not want to have episodes where children are tempted to lie even when it is to help a TiR child. If so have her run out and then there is not the same dilemma.)

TiR as Farmer George: *Have any of you seen Bo Peep? She was supposed to be here by now looking after the sheep and they have got out of the field and I don't know where they are.*

(Sounding quite angry) *I give her a simple job to do and she can't do it! She's not as reliable as you all are. If you see her tell her I am looking for her and I am not happy.*

He goes.

Children may explain what has happened to Farmer George but he is angry and insists Bo Peep must get the sheep back.

11. Bo Peep returns and the children explain to her what has happened. What are they going to do about the missing sheep?

   She listens and then takes her mobile phone from her pocket. She listens to it and then puts it away. She tells the children it is her mother phoning to say she has seen the sheep down by the church.

   TiR as Bo Peep: *How do I get down there?*

12. The children sort out the route from the map. This is the reverse journey part way.

   Bo Peep thanks them and says they have done so much, but could they help catch the sheep?

13. She explains that they have to catch them by forming a big circle holding hands and then surround the sheep, driving them back through a nearby gate, that one of the children 'opens'.

   Bo Peep thanks them very much and goes to tell the farmer.

14. Farmer George turns up and is very pleased and forgives Bo Peep and thanks the children.

   This is the resolution – the children winning.

Index

Care
early

This book provides a comprehensive and up-to-date review of key issues in the field of care and education in early childhood. The authors draw on their extensive expertise in the field to provide a book that is uniquely wide-ranging in its coverage.

In this timely and accessible text, students will find:

- an overview of the principles of effective practice;
- discussions on equal opportunities and equal rights;
- an examination of how children learn and the learning difficulties they may face;
- investigations into what working with parents really means;
- a consideration of the different early years systems in operation;
- summaries of key management issues and useful information on how to address them;
- a comparison with European perspectives on early years care and education.

The book covers the whole age range from zero to eight years with a special section on the zero-to-three-years age group. Each chapter is fully referenced to enable the reader to follow up on research or access new materials.

Informative and engaging, the book challenges the reader to think about how underlying theory may be reflected in practice. It is essential reading for all students of early years care and education, and early years practitioners will also find it extremely helpful.

Audrey Curtis is World President of OMEP, the World Organisation for Early Childhood Education, which works with early childhood educators in many parts of the world, and as a consultant to UNESCO and UNICEF. Prior to this, she was a Senior Lecturer at the Institute of Education, University of London.

Maureen O'Hagan MBE is Director of Quality Assurance at the Council for Awards in Children's Care and Education (CACHE). She is also President of the National Association of Early Years Practitioners and was awarded the MBE for Services to Education in the 2002 New Years Honours list.

Care and education in early childhood

A student's guide to theory and practice

Audrey Curtis and Maureen O'Hagan

RoutledgeFalmer
Taylor & Francis Group

LONDON AND NEW YORK

First published 2003
by RoutledgeFalmer
11 New Fetter Lane, London EC4P 4EE

Simultaneously published in the USA and Canada
by RoutledgeFalmer
29 West 35th Street, New York, NY 10001

RoutledgeFalmer is an imprint of the Taylor & Francis Group

© 2003 Audrey Curtis and Maureen O'Hagan

Typeset in Goudy by Wearset Ltd, Boldon, Tyne and Wear
Printed and bound in Great Britain by TJ International Ltd, Padstow, Cornwall

British Library Cataloguing in Publication Data
A catalogue record for this book is available from the British Library

Library of Congress Cataloging in Publication Data
A catalog record for this book has been requested

ISBN 0–415–22595–7

CONTENTS

INTRODUCTION

Early childhood care and education is the subject of considerable debate and interest among governments and politicians in all parts of the world. International organisations such as UNICEF and UNESCO are stressing the importance of providing quality early childhood education and care to all children, not only those from less-advantaged backgrounds. Their arguments are based upon the increasing research evidence that has shown the long-term benefits of offering young children quality care and education in the early years. During recent years in the UK, there have been numerous government initiatives relating to the care and education of young children. Some of these, such as Sure Start, have been very successful, whereas others have proved to be more complicated to implement and fund. Nevertheless, there is now a general consensus among politicians and administrators that quality early childhood care and education should be available to all children if their parents wish it. For children under the age of three this is mainly in the private sector; for older children it is predominantly within the state system.

This Level 4 textbook offers the reader a sound theoretical and practical basis for work or study in the field of early childhood care and education. It aims to cut through the changes and offer sound underpinning theory and practice needed by those who wish to work or are working with the zero-to-eight-years age group. Some chapters are academically based, whilst others link theory and practice, a result of the combined expertise of the authors.

The book opens with a chapter that examines the principles of effective practice. There is an emphasis on the importance of reflective practice and on the reflective practitioner who is able to link theory and practice in order to improve the quality of care and education he or she offers. The following chapter looks closely at Children's Rights and discusses current legislation in this field. Whilst issues relating to equal opportunities are explored fully in this chapter, the authors have attempted throughout the book to address issues in relation to sex, race, religion and gender.

Chapters 3 and 4, 'How children learn' and 'Communication and communication disorders', provide the reader with information about current research in these fields. In discussing how children learn, the authors have attempted to provide readers with knowledge that will enable them to support young children's learning in the most effective way. Consideration is given to the development of memory and concentration skills and the role they play in learning. Attention is also drawn to the role of emotional intelligence in learning and development. There are two parts to the chapter on communication and communication disorders. The first part deals with the development of verbal and non-verbal skills, highlighting the ways in which social and cultural factors affect language and language learning. There is also a discussion of the challenges of second-language learning and the ways in which the adult can meet the needs of second-language learners. The second part of the chapter introduces some of the main communication disorders that may be met in early childhood settings. Several pages are devoted to the problems associated with the 'dyslexia syndrome' and the way this disorder can affect children who suffer from it.

There has been considerable development in the field of work with under-three-year-olds and this has become an important part of the early years practitioner's role. Brain development before and after birth and how the adult is able to stimulate children's development during these early years is the subject of Chapter 5. At the time of going to press the Department for Education and Skills has set up a working party to look at a curriculum for under-three-year-olds. It would appear likely that this group will be favouring the High/Scope approach that has been successful in other parts of the world. Feelings and relationships are explored in Chapter 6 and some practical suggestions are given to help practitioners manage young children's feelings.

Working with parents is a very important aspect of the role of the early years practitioner. Chapter 7 explores what working with parents really means: particularly those issues relating to the differences between parental involvement and partnership with parents.

For many decades play has been recognised as a conduit for learning by early years practitioners. However, in society as a whole it appears that play is neither fully understood nor suitably implemented. The crucial role of play has been threatened by recent curriculum developments as we move from a process model of learning to one that is concerned with end-products. Chapter 8 aims to provide readers with firm evidence with which to argue the case for play in the early years curriculum.

With the rapid increase in the number of early years settings over the past few years, there is a need for practitioners to address the many management issues that arise. Chapter 9 identifies and reflects upon the major areas of concern and provides useful information for managers and would-be managers.

The next two chapters address curriculum issues for children from three to seven years. Chapter 10 offers the reader an account of the different types of early years education systems that are in operation, including the High/Scope and Montessori programmes, as well as an in-depth consideration of the Early Learning Goals and the Foundation Stage for children from three to six years. Chapter 11 investigates the core subjects of the National Curriculum at Key Stage 1.

There is a discussion of issues relating to the teaching of reading and mathematics and a consideration of the role of investigation and questioning in the education of young children.

The book ends with a chapter that examines the European perspectives of early years care and education. Information is drawn from both western and eastern Europe to highlight the chief differences and similarities that exist between the UK and its European counterparts.

The early years of education are of crucial importance to children and it is vital that all who work in or who are contemplating working in this field have an understanding of early childhood, theory and practice. This introduction is only able to offer a snapshot of the contents of the book; however, we hope that all those studying or working in the field of early years will find the book's approach, with its combination of theory and practice, useful.

CHAPTER 1

Principles of effective practice

One of the most important demands of the early years care and education worker is an ability to operate effectively within the job role. All underlying principles of practice should reflect the requirements of the Children Act 1989 as a minimum. In addition to this should be observed the basic rights for the child as laid down in the United Nations Convention on the Rights of the Child 1989 and the Human Rights Act 1998. Effective practice must be an underlying principle for all workers, not just the managers of the setting. It is only by ensuring that practice is effective can one be certain that the children are receiving the best quality of care possible. This chapter will examine the underlying principles of good practice and the reflective practice, which is needed if the child care and education worker is going to deliver a high-quality service. It is important that all practitioners reflect on their practice so that they can acknowledge how things have gone and whether there is room for improvement.

Underlying principles of practice

A good starting point is to examine the Statement of Underlying Principles, which is part of the National Standards in Early Years, Care and Education. These ten principles are intrinsically linked with all the National Standards in order to ensure that children and their families will receive a high quality of provision. It is necessary for all NVQ (National Vocational Qualification) candidates to demonstrate as part of their competency that their work practices are based on the ten principles. The ten principles are as follows:

1 The welfare of the child

The Children Act 1989 makes it very clear that the welfare of the child is paramount. Therefore children must come first. Children must be listened to and their opinions respected and treated seriously. In managing children's challenging behaviour the child care and education worker should emphasise the positive aspects of behaviour and physical punishment must never be used.

2 Working in partnership with parents/families

Early years care and education workers must respect a child's parents and family and work with them in planning the care for their child. It is to be remembered that the parents and family will know more about the child than anyone else and in addition to respecting opinions etc. from parents and carers they must also be given regular information about the child's development and progress. Child care workers must comply with parents' wishes for their child and family; cultural and religious values must be respected.

3 Children's learning and development

The first five years of a child's life is a period of rapid growth and learning. Therefore children need activities which will stimulate their social, physical, intellectual, linguistic, emotional and moral development. The early years curriculum should be linked with a child's stage of development, which can be ascertained by careful observation of the child and discussions with the parents and family. The child's progress should be monitored, recorded and shared with the parents.

4 Equality of opportunity

The individuality of each child must be recognised and each child should be treated according to its needs. Each child should have the same opportunities to play, learn and develop according to its potential. Every child should be treated with equal concern thus avoiding stereotyping and labelling on the basis of gender, religion, culture, race, class or disability.

5 Anti-discrimination

Early years care and education workers must not discriminate against any child, group/family. They must respect a child and its family, race, religion, gender, culture, class, language, disability etc. Expressions of prejudice by staff members, children or adults must be challenged and the victims should be supported. early-years care and education workers must work within the requirements of the laws, i.e. Children Act, Race Relations Act, Human Rights Act, and the policies of the setting.

6 Confidentiality

Policies in the setting relating to confidentiality must be adhered to. Information relating to a child and/or its parents or family must not be disclosed unless it is in the interests of child protection. In the latter circumstances any disclosure should only be to other professionals involved in the case. Confidentiality policies should also ensure that information about working colleagues is not disclosed without permission.

7 Keeping children safe

It is the responsibility of every child care and education worker to ensure that the setting is safe for the children and fellow workers. Daily work practices should ensure the prevention of accidents and the protection of health. Familiarity with emergency procedures and the recording of accidents must be adhered to. It is also part of the role of the child care and education worker to protect children from abuse.

8 Celebrating diversity

The UK is a pluralistic society and as such it is important that cultural diversity is appreciated and viewed positively; no one culture should be viewed as superior. Children should be helped to develop a sense of their own identity within their race, culture or social group. Children should be introduced to other cultures in a positive way and encouraged to sample food, art, stories and music from different cultures.

9 Working with other professionals

In order to ensure the best interests of the child, when appropriate, early child care and education workers should confer with colleagues and other professionals from outside the setting for support and advice. Respect for other professionals' opinions should be maintained and confidentiality observed at all times.

10 Reflective practitioner

Reflecting on their own practice is an important part of the role of early years care and education workers. Such reflection should result in the extension of their practice. Continuing professional development would be a part of this extension, as would be advice and support sought from colleagues or other professionals.

A number of the above ten principles are discussed in other chapters in this book; however, there are others that are worth expanding upon here.

Equality of opportunity is an expression that is used very frequently but is not always properly understood when it comes to integrating this into one's own practices. All early years settings are required to have an equal-opportunities policy but in many cases this sits in a folder on a shelf and is never monitored in terms of how it is being implemented. Equality of opportunity means that each child is given the opportunity to develop to its maximum potential. However, each child's potential will be different; therefore each child should be treated according to its own individual needs. Some children's needs may be greater than others' and may therefore require a greater input from the staff who are caring for them. In this context the word 'needs' does not refer to the special needs of a child but to any need that a child may have – for example the need for outdoor play of a child who lives in a high-rise flat. When a child is accepted into a day-care establishment the first thing that should happen is that its needs are assessed and a plan is drawn up to ensure ways of meeting those needs. All the staff who are caring for the child should have a copy of the assessment and the plan for addressing the areas where there may be needs. In this way the staff team will be working together in the best interests of the child. There should be frequent reviews of each individual child's needs and assessment done on a regular basis as needs will change over time.

Anti-discriminatory/anti-bias practice is an area that directly affects the delivery of care that a child is getting. As human beings we all have our own biases: that is, areas that we do not feel comfortable about and therefore hold prejudices against. However, whatever these are they must not be allowed to affect the way in which care or education is delivered to children. Staff must never voice or enact their prejudices when dealing with children, parents or other staff. Respect must be shown for all parents, even those whom staff may regard as abysmal. Most parents strive to do their best for their children in spite of very difficult circumstances and some of these parents may not have the knowledge and skills to distinguish what is the right thing to do in a particular circumstance. The last thing that these parents need is a lack of understanding from the people who are caring for their children. Situations such as poverty, homelessness, poor diet and so on may not be the fault of the parents, who may be the victims of society. These circumstances require the early years worker to have empathy and understanding so that a relationship can be formed that is beneficial to the child and the parent. In the same way, the early years worker must ensure that he or she is not behaving in a biased fashion towards children because of the parents' behaviour. After all, the child is not able to control its parents. An integral part of maintaining an anti-bias early years setting is taking action when incidents arise. Siraj-Blatchford (2000) offers the following short-term action strategies, which can be implemented as soon as the incident takes place:

- explaining to the person/child making the remarks that they are offensive and hurtful;

- explaining why the remarks are hurtful and trying to tease out the feelings of the person who made the remark and the receiver;
- explaining why the comment was wrong and correcting any misconceptions which the remark may convey;

and long-term action strategies, such as:

- working with parents whose children have made the remarks and ensuring they understand the setting's equal-opportunities policy;
- creating an ethos in the setting that promotes and values diversity;
- developing topics and reading stories which raise issues of similarities and differences in language, gender and ethnicity;
- encouraging children to talk about their feelings.

In their book *Anti-Bias Training Approaches in the Early Years*, Gaine and van Keulen (1997) offer a list of attitudes which early years workers need to develop. Students/workers will show through their practice that they:

- respect and value the individuality of children, their families and other members of staff;
- are willing and able to learn from others;
- are willing and able to think critically about child development theory and are able to recognise the bias of theorists;
- are willing and able to reflect on their own ethnic and cultural experiences;
- are committed to implementing a culturally relevant anti-bias approach;
- are actively engaged in resisting discrimination;
- are able to empathise, i.e. to put themselves in other people's shoes and feel them pinching;
- feel confident about their own ethnic and cultural identity.

MacNaughton (1999) states that staff should be aware of providing a wide range of opportunities for all children, regardless of social class, ability, gender or culture, and even challenging children to cross gender or cultural boundaries through play. Staff need to facilitate this play by encouraging children to join in with their peers and supporting the interactions without controlling them. In this advice MacNaughton is able, very succinctly, to offer an example of good practice that covers both equal opportunities and anti-bias practice. In her book *Combating Discrimination* (2001), Babette Brown offers ways in which early years practitioners are able to challenge children's hurtful remarks to other children through the use of 'persona dolls'. A persona doll is a tool that can be used to help a child empathise with another child or with what is happening to a child. Early years workers use the dolls as vehicles in order to facilitate powerful story-telling sessions. Children are able to talk about how the doll was feeling when a hurtful remark was made about it, such as when being called names by other children or being bullied. The children are able to empathise with the feelings of the doll and offer solutions for helping the doll feel better and gain its self-esteem. Thus persona dolls empower children to respect the feelings of others.

Following on from equal opportunities and anti-bias working, it would seem logical to go to the eighth principle, *Celebrating diversity*. This area is about children developing a feeling of worth and self-esteem within the setting regardless of their cultural background. This can be achieved by the staff presenting a variety of cultures in such a way that they are viewed by the children and adults as positive images, which are valued and integrated into the ethos of the setting. However, Siraj-Blatchford and Clarke (2000) do offer a warning about well-meaning but poorly informed practice in this area. They point out that token measures such as multilingual posters, black dolls, puzzles and books with positive gender role models are rarely the focus of attention. Misplaced are the energies of staff who provide a thematic approach such as 'Greek week' or 'Chinese New Year' without recognising that diversity should be reflected across the curriculum. If a setting is going to celebrate festivals then these should be part of an overall multi-faith/multicultural curriculum programme. What children learn about the real story of Easter from bunnies, chicks and chocolate eggs is debatable. In fact, these ideas probably stem from the Christian Church, when all eggs were used up on Shrove Tuesday (hence the pancakes) to enable the fasting period required through Lent; eggs then came back into circulation on Easter Sunday. However, I am unable to find any reference to how bunnies came into the picture! Celebrating festivals with children can be fun and may help them to learn something about other cultures but, as Brown (2001) points out, such festivals are unlikely to have much effect upon children's attitudes towards adults and children from these cultures. There is a need to examine why we celebrate particular festivals and a need to ensure co-operation of the parents, who may not wish the early years establishment to celebrate something that is usually confined to its own community. Bisson (1997) offers the following objectives in the celebration of festivals:

- to promote connections among children, families and practitioners;
- to learn about important events in the lives of all children and families;
- to support and validate the experiences of children, their families and practitioners;
- to reinforce connection to cultural roots;
- to celebrate both similarities and differences in children's lives;
- to stretch children's awareness and empathy.

(Bisson 1997: 36–7)

Confidentiality is an integral part of the work of the early years care and education practitioner. *The Oxford English Dictionary* offers the following definitions of confidential:

1 spoken or written in confidence;
2 entrusted with secrets.

Confidentiality therefore means being entrusted with information that the discloser does not wish to be passed on to anybody else.

Because of the nature of their work, early years practitioners will often find themselves in a position whereby a parent, family member or carer is disclosing information that needs to be kept confidential. Such disclosure may be given in order for the parent, family member or carer to ensure that those caring for the child are aware that there are particular circumstances that may affect the child's behaviour or emotions. The early years practitioner must then decide whether the disclosure is of such a level of seriousness that it needs to be passed on to a more senior member of staff. The benchmark for any judgement in this area must be the welfare of the child. Certain information may need to be passed on in order to protect the child. Once the practitioner has passed on the information, he or she has broken confidentiality with the person who disclosed the information. This is a common dilemma for many early years practitioners.

Most early years settings have a policy relating to confidentiality and this must be adhered to at all times. In the first instance, when the original disclosure is being made, if the practitioner judges that it is information that may have serious consequences then he or she should try to persuade the discloser to talk to a senior member of staff. The practitioner may also, gently but firmly, explain to the discloser that, as the practitioner, he or she will have to pass the information to a senior member of staff as this is the policy of the setting. This decision may be met with hostility from the discloser, who may need to be reminded that the child's welfare is paramount.

In addition to information relating to children, the practitioner may also be disclosed confidential information by members of staff. Once again, there may be information known that could affect the children in the care of the discloser and the practitioner must make a decision as to whether to pass this on. For example, what do you do if a fellow worker reveals to you that he or she has a drug addiction problem, or has forged cheques, or is having an affair with a parent of one of the children? Once again, the welfare of the child/children is paramount and it is always best if you can persuade the discloser to speak to a senior member of staff. If this suggestion is not met with agreement then you may have to explain to the discloser that you will have to reveal the information to a senior member of staff as it could affect the welfare of the children in the setting.

In addition to verbal disclosures of information, there are other ways in which practitioners can breech confidentiality. Child studies/observations, which may be placed in portfolios or dissertations, require the permission of the child's parents before they can be used outside the setting. It is also necessary to change the child's name and/or only use a first name for the child. Photographs in such studies are not a good idea (even with a parent's permission to take them) as they immediately identify the child to the reader of the study/observation, who may know the child. Particular care must be taken that a dissertation or child study ensures that the identity of the child is totally anonymous.

Another situation in which practitioners may break confidentiality is in talking about a child/family to another member of staff in a public place, such as on a bus, train, or in a bar. You never know when someone nearby is listening or is able to overhear the conversation, and this person may know the child or people you are talking about. It is not professional behaviour to discuss such matters in a place where you can be overheard. Discussing the matter in the first place may be a breech of confidentiality. In more recent years it has become a familiar sight to see people on trains or in other out-of-office locations working on laptop computers. There appears to be a myth that nobody else is able to read the screen of the laptop; however, sitting behind the operator puts someone in a perfect position to read what is on the screen. It is therefore not a wise move to decide to catch up on confidential documentation whilst working outside of the office. Many people also find it easy to read handwriting from a position upside-down to them. A breech in confidentiality, however it happened and whether it was intentional or accidental, is a serious lapse of professionalism.

The reflective practitioner

This is number ten on the list of underlying principles and is also an integral part of this chapter. One of the basic tenets of effective practice is the ability to reflect on one's own practice. Reflection is becoming a core skill in the profession of early years care and education and is found in unit EYD7 in the NVQ Level 4 National Standards, which is assessed in terms of the candidate producing a reflective account of his or her practice. Reflection on one's practice is one of the important differences between the professional child care and education worker and the non-professional, 'mum's army' worker. Professionals claim to contribute to social well-being, put the client's needs before their own and hold themselves accountable to standards of competence and morality. Professionals also claim a body of knowledge that shapes the profession; in Early Years Care and Education this has been legitimised by the National Framework of Qualifications, which offers the underpinning knowledge for the profession. Practitioners are frequently embroiled in conflicts of values, goals, purposes and interests. For example, teachers are faced with pressures for increased efficiency whilst at the same time they are expected to work within ever-decreasing budgets. Such dilemmas, which are out of the control of the teachers, make them disturbed, as they cannot account for the processes they have come to see as central to their professional competence.

The term 'reflective practitioner' was first coined by Donald Schön (1983) as a way for the professional to be able to resolve problems that did not just rely upon his or her professional knowledge. Schön refers to work by Edgar Schein that states that there is a gap between the application of knowledge – what he refers to as being 'convergent' – and practice – which he refers to as 'divergent'. Therefore, professionals in the areas of social work, teaching and so on need divergent thinking skills in order to resolve problems, as resolution cannot be solved by theory alone. Professionals have to analyse particular circumstances in order to assess how best to respond to them – what may be referred to as 'thinking on your feet' or 'keeping your wits about you'.

Schön maintains that a professional practitioner is a specialist who encounters certain types of situation over and over again and hence why the word 'case' is used by the practioner to describe units that go together to make up practice. Practitioners may reflect on practice whilst they are in the midst of it – what Schön calls 'reflection-in-action'. Reflection-in-action is central to the practitioner coping with divergent situations. This process of reflecting and analysing particular circumstances is what is referred to as reflective practice.

Megarry (2000) gives the following very good simple example of how using theory alone to analyse a problem can fail to take in all the variables and thus come to the wrong conclusions:

> A child consistently behaves badly when he comes to the childcare setting. There has recently been a new baby in the family and his mother tells you that she does not have time to give the child breakfast before he comes to the childcare setting. Using the knowledge of theory would tell you that children need a balanced breakfast before they start the day. Based on this theoretical knowledge the child's behaviour must be due to the fact that he is nutritionally deficient – hungry. So if you give the child breakfast his behaviour will improve.

Reflection-in-action would not draw this conclusion as it would enable the early years worker to take a holistic approach in order to consider all the variables: new baby; harassed parent; lack of attention to older child, and so on. Schön points out that in the real world problems do not present themselves as givens. They must be constructed from the materials of problematic situations that are puzzling, troubling and uncertain – what Schön refers to as 'problem-setting'. Problem-setting is a process in which we select what we will treat as the 'things' of the situation, set the boundaries of our attention to it and impose upon it a coherence that allows us to say what is wrong and in what directions the situation needs to be changed. In short, we define the problem, the end, and the means to the end.

According to Schön, to be an effective reflective practitioner it is necessary to be able to recognise:

- knowing-in-action;
- reflecting-in-action;
- reflecting-in-practice.

Knowing-in-action

This is the kind of knowing that is inherent in intelligent action; the know-how is in the action. Skilful action often involves knowing more than we can say. Schön gives the following properties of knowing:

- There are actions, recognitions and judgements, which we know how to carry out spontaneously; we do not have to think about them prior to or during their performance.
- We are often unaware of having learned to do these things; we simply find ourselves doing them.
- In some cases, we were once aware of the understandings, which were subsequently internalised in our feeling for the stuff of action. In other cases, we may never have been aware of them. In both cases, however, we are usually unable to describe the knowing which our action reveals.

Reflecting-in-action

Much of reflecting-in-action hinges on surprise. This is the 'thinking on your feet', 'keeping your wits about you' situation. It shows that we can think about something whilst we are doing it. (This seems to describe a very familiar situation for early years workers who are good at this type of thinking.)

Reflecting-in-practice

This involves reflecting on and questioning the above categories, on the way in which we acted and responded to different situations, and on our own role in the workplace.

A practitioner's reflection can serve as a corrective to over-learning. Through reflection, the practitioner can surface and criticise tacit understandings that have grown up around repetitive experiences of a specialised practice, and can make new sense of the situations of uncertainty or uniqueness that may be experienced. The practitioner needs to be open to his or her own practice and ready to see ways in which to improve on both knowing-in-action and reflecting-in-action.

Jill Rodd (1994) uses the term 'action research' to refer to a way of thinking that uses reflection and enquiry as a way of understanding the conditions that support or inhibit change. This is very different from Schön's thesis as it does not involve 'thinking on your feet' but is a six-point plan that is carried out as a team activity over a period of time. However, there does seem to be a valid place for both the Rodd and Schön theses within the early years care and education settings. Rodd points out that in action research the problem needs to be meaningful for the team and the team leader; it must be manageable within a realistic time-frame and appropriate to the research skills of the people involved. There also needs to be a healthy attitude within the team to problem solving and risk taking.

Rodd (citing Wadswoth (1984) and Kemmis and McTaggert (1988)) gives the following seven steps in the action-research-process cycle:

1 Identifying the problems of mutual concern – the present problems are brought into focus through the processes of observation and reflection by all members of the team.
2 Analysing problems and determining possible contributing factors – the ability to diagnose the determinants of a problem is required. The existing situation is monitored using recorded uncensored and uninterpreted observations from the members of the team.
3 Forming tentative working hypotheses or guesses to explain these factors – at this point, questionable assumptions are eliminated. Decisions are made about the form and method of the interpretation of the data which are to be collected.
4 Collecting and interpreting data from observations, interviews and relevant documents to clarify these hypotheses and to develop action hypotheses – accurate details of events need to be recorded in order to avoid erroneous or superficial influences.
5 Formulating plans for action and carrying them out – plans are experimental, prospective and forward-looking and may involve the acquisition of new skills or procedures in order to implement the plans.
6 Evaluating the results of the action – the processes of observation and reflection are used to critically assess the effects of the informed action and to make sense of the processes and issues that unfolded during the implementation phase. Collaborative reflection provides an opportunity to reconstruct meaning out of the situation and establishes a basis for a revised plan.
7 Introducing a revised cycle from step 1 to step 6.

In addition to the above there are the stages that go towards promoting reflection in general, as cited in Megarry (2000). These are outlined below.

Stage 1: Returning to experience

This is where the experience is revisited by recollecting what has taken place and replaying the experience in the mind's eye in order to observe the event as it happened and to notice exactly what occurred and one's reaction to it in all its elements.

This description provides the data for subsequent processes and can help to ensure that our reflections are on the basis of the actual events as we experienced them at the time rather than in terms of what we wished had happened.

The description should as far as possible:

- be clear of any judgements;
- observe the feelings evoked during the experience, both positive and negative.

Stage 2: Attending to feelings experienced

Emotions can be a signification source of learning as they can form barriers to learning, which need to be recognised and removed before the learning process can proceed.

Stage 3: Re-evaluating the experience

Elements of the whole process are:

- association – relating new data to that already known;
- integration – seeking relationships among the data;
- validation – determining the authenticity of the ideas and feelings that have resulted;
- appropriation – making knowledge one's own.

The outcomes of reflection may include:

- a new way of doing something;
- the clarification of an issue;
- the development of a skill;
- the resolution of a problem.

The changes and benefits of reflection may be small or large but unless they are linked to action they are worthless. Actions may not necessarily be observed or recognised by others but what is important is that the learner makes a commitment to action on the basis of his or her learning.

The ability to reflect on one's own practice or to promote action research within a team is one of the qualifications for leadership as put forward by Hodgkinson (1991), who states that leadership is:

- an art rather than a science;
- focused on policy rather than execution;
- concerned with values rather than facts;

- to do with generalism rather than specialism;
- the use of broad strategies rather than specific tactics;
- concerned with philosophy rather than action;
- reflective rather than active;
- concerned with human as opposed to material resources;
- focused on deliberation rather than detail.

The importance of reflective practice is recognised in the Level 4 National Standards in Early Years Care and Education in the form of an externally assessed unit within the core units. The unit is entitled 'Access and review and update your own knowledge of significant and emerging theory and practice', and the element titles are as follows:

D7.1 'Evaluate and update your own knowledge and practice';
D7.2 'Establish and implement procedures to review and update current knowledge and practice';
D7.3 'Integrate outcomes from review into own practice';
D7.4 'Apply underpinning equal opportunities and anti-discriminatory values and principles to own work'.

The assessment method for this unit is via an externally assessed piece of work, which draws together knowledge and performance evidence. A major self-reflective study is the required evidence for assessment of the unit, thus legitimising the fact that the reflective practitioner is a very important part of the role of early years care and education workers who wish to undertake leadership roles.

References

Bisson, J. (1997) *Celebrate: An Anti-bias Guide to Enjoying Holidays*, St Paul, Minn.: Redleaf Press.

Boud, D., Keogh, R. and Walker, D. (1985) *Promoting Reflection in Learning: Reflection: turning experience into learning*, London: Croom Helm.

Brown, B. (2001) *Combating Discrimination: Persona Dolls in Action*, Stoke on Trent: Trentham Books.

Council for Awards in Children's Care and Education (CACHE) (1998) *Candidate Handbook: NVQ in Early Years Care and Education*, Herts.: CACHE.

Derman-Sparks, L. (1989) *Anti-Bias Curriculum: Tools for Empowering Young Children*, Washington, DC: National Association for the Education of Young Children.

Gaine, B. and van Keulen, A. (1997) *Anti-Bias Training Approaches in the Early Years: A Guide for Trainers*, Utrecht/London: Agency MUTANT/EYTARN.

Hodgkinson, C. (1991) *Educational Leadership: The Moral Art*, Albany, NY: State University of New York Press. (Cited in Rodd 1994.)

MacNaughton, G. (1999), cited in Siraj-Blatchford and Clarke 2000: p. 80.

Megarry, B. (2000) *'Reflection' and the 'reflective practitioner'*, unpublished lecture notes, OMNA Early Years Training.

Rodd, J. (1994) *Leadership in Early Childhood: The Pathway to Professionalism*, Buckingham: Open University Press.

Schön, D. (1991) *The Reflective Practitioner: How Professionals Think in Action*, Aldershot: Ashgate Publishing.

Siraj-Blatchford, I. and Clarke, P. (2000) *Supporting Identity, Diversity and Language in the Early Years*, Buckingham: Open University Press.

CHAPTER 2

Children's rights

The idea that children have rights is a fairly new phenomenon in the UK and probably first appeared in 1924 when the League of Nations drafted the first Declaration of the Rights of the Child. However, it was not until sixty-five years later that we saw the rights of the child incorporated (in part) into UK law in the form of the Children Act 1989. Enabling children to exercise their rights empowers them and enables them to participate in the control of their lives. However, Saraga (1998) states that ' "rights" like "needs" is a highly contested concept particularly when applied to children'. Saraga goes on to say that children depend on the adults who care for them to assert their rights for them and that rights are limited by the child's vulnerability and dependency.

Gerison Lansdown (1996) points out that adults are confused about the issue of children's rights for a number of reasons: it is thought that children cannot have rights until they are capable of exercising responsibility; children are not competent to participate; rights for children threaten the stability of family life; the imposition of rights takes away children's opportunities for childhood. Lansdown would argue that the UK has a long way to go in order to meet the requirements of the Convention on the Rights of the Child. There is also the debate about how far such rights should be the child's entitlement and whether a child's rights should be considered at the expense of the rights of the adults. What cannot be disputed is that the Children Act 1989 clearly states that the 'Welfare of the child is paramount'. In the world of 'good practice' in child care and education, the rights of the child should always be considered when making decisions about a child, whether this is for social, developmental or other reasons.

As Phillipe Aries (1960) has pointed out, childhood has always been constructed by society rather than being defined by nature. There is no natural state defined as childhood. In modern sociological terms it is what Saraga describes as a social construct.

This chapter will look at specific situations and practical issues that may impinge upon children's rights, such as domestic violence, child abuse and family breakdown.

The United Nations Convention on the Rights of the Child 1989

As previously stated, the first Declaration of the Rights of the Child came about in 1924 at the instigation of Eglantyne Jebb, British founder of Save the Children. This version was superseded by the 1959 United Nations Declaration on the Rights of the Child. The Convention on the Rights of the Child was adopted by the United Nations general assembly in 1989 and came into force as part of international law in 1990. There are 191 countries that have ratified the Convention (the two countries that have not are the USA and Somalia), the UK having ratified it in December 1991. Once a country has ratified the Convention it is obliged to incorporate into its own laws the Articles within the Convention. Muscot (1999) points out that ratification creates an opportunity for public scrutiny of government performance. The United Nations has a Children's Rights Committee, which is responsible for monitoring how countries are complying with the convention. Each country that has ratified the Convention must produce a report after two years and then every five years. The report is presented to the Children's Rights Committee of the United Nations. The Convention points out the need for countries to work together co-operatively in order to implement the Articles to the maximum, with richer countries helping poorer countries. There are forty-five Articles altogether in the Convention, which cover many different areas of children's rights. A few examples are given in the box.

Some Articles from the Convention on the Rights of the Child

- Article 1 defines a child as every human being under eighteen years of age.
- Article 2 concerns discrimination.
- Article 3 concerns the best interests of the child.
- Article 8 concerns the preservation of identity.
- Article 9 concerns separation from parents.
- Article 12 concerns the child's opinions.
- Article 14 concerns freedom of thought, conscience and religion.
- Article 18 concerns parental responsibilities.
- Article 19 concerns protection from abuse.
- Article 23 concerns disabled children.
- Article 24 concerns health and health services.
- Article 32 concerns child labour.
- Article 34 concerns sexual exploitation.
- Article 38 concerns armed conflicts.
- Article 40 concerns the administration of Juvenile Justice.[1]

---

1 UNICEF has produced a booklet on the Convention Articles in which children have rewritten some of the Articles in their own easy-to-understand form.

In some countries, the implementation of the Convention has resulted in the appointment of a Children's Commissioner or Children's Ombudsman to oversee the rights of children. At about the same time as the 1989 Convention, the UK had amalgamated most of its laws relating to children into one comprehensive Children Act. This Act went a long way to incorporating a number of the Articles of the Convention; however, there are some areas that still remain unrecognised or neglected. For example, Article 31 deals with the child's right to play, leisure and recreation, yet this seems to be in conflict with certain political policies that advocate selling local playing fields for housing and retail development. Newell (1991) points out that a major obstacle to the implementation of the Convention in the UK is the lack of monitoring over the state of the UK's children. This results in there being a lack of information to enable researchers to draw conclusions on how well or how badly the Convention is being implemented. Whilst the UK would appear to be meeting many of the Articles contained in the convention, there are still issues over the numbers of children living in poverty, the way children can be excluded from school with no opportunity to defend themselves or express their views. In 1992 the UK set up the Children's Rights Development Unit (CRDU) to promote the implementation of the UN Convention. Major charitable trusts and child-welfare organisations funded this body. In 1994 the government submitted its first report to the UN Committee citing the Children Act 1989 as the evidence of its compliance. Lansdown and Newell (1994) point out that the CRDU described the report as complacent and stated that 'whether for reasons of poverty, ethnicity, disability, sexuality, immigration status or geography, many children are denied fundamental rights in the Convention'.

Whilst the Articles of the Convention go a long way towards stating what all the world's countries need to do in order to ensure a better lifestyle for their children, there is a necessity to monitor whether this is happening in reality. Like many other documents of this type, there are anomalies – not least in Article 38, which deals with the rights of children in situations of armed conflict. Whilst the Convention defines the age covered by 'childhood' as zero-to-eighteen years, in Article 38 it advocates not recruiting children under the age of fifteen years into the armed forces. In recent years we have seen a number of armed conflicts in which children, mostly boys, are recruited as fighters and taught how to use arms. In the UK, one can join the Armed Forces at the age of sixteen years and is legally able to carry arms at the age of seventeen years. It is surprising that in Article 38 the Convention did not recommend the age of eighteen years as the recruitment age in line with the recommendations in all the other Articles. There is a significant difference between a child (as defined by Article 1) and a child's development at the age of fifteen years and at the age of eighteen years, which does not seem to have been acknowledged.

The Articles could offer a set of underpinning values for those who work with children all over the world. In order to bring the Articles into context with the UK situation wherever possible and appropriate, the relevant Article will be quoted in full or summarised at the beginning of each section heading in the chapter.

The Children Act 1989

The Children Act 1989 was a major piece of legislation, which not only brought together existing pieces of legislation but also formulated them into a cohesive whole. The Act ensured that the welfare of the child was paramount and allowed children's opinions to be taken into account. Franklin (1995) sees the Children Act as placing a shift in the definition of children whereby they moved from objects of concern to people with rights, thus acknowledging that children have the ability to make decisions. When a child is very young it is assigned an independent guardian *ad litem*, who acts as an advocate for the child and who is responsible for ensuring that the welfare of the child comes first. Adults were not left out of the Act and some groups of adults, who in the past had had no laws to protect their interests in the child (for example, grandparents, fathers who were not married to the mother, or other family relatives who are part of the child's primary care network), are now able to apply for residency orders and suchlike in order to legitimise their positions.

The quality of children's care was taken into consideration by the Act as it brought in a registration and inspection regime for all settings in which children were looked after, apart from in their own homes (which made nannies exempt from registration). Local Social Services departments were made responsible for registering and inspecting care settings, for example childminders and family centres, and the Office for Standards in Education (OFSTED) was responsible for inspecting educational establishments. (Since 2001 OFSTED has been responsible for all inspections and for registration in all settings (Part X Registrations)).

On paper the Children Act gave hope that at last children's rights would be high on the agenda. In practice, however, that was not necessarily the case. One of the first disappointments was the case of a childminder who smacked a child in her care. The local authority, adhering to the Guidelines to the Children Act, which said that childminders must not use physical punishment on children in their care, removed the childminder's registration. The childminder then took the local authority to court for removing her registration, which in effect removed her livelihood. The childminder's lawyers argued that the parents had given their permission for the childminder to smack their child. The judge ruled that the Guidelines were not part of the Act and that only that which was written in the Act was legally binding. The Act did not say that physical punishment could not be used on children and therefore the Local Authority was obliged to reinstate the childminder's registration.

Saraga (1998) argues that the Children Act was more concerned with giving rights to parents than with the rights of children, citing the fact that there are no procedures in the Act to enable the child to complain about its parents or about any maltreatment it may receive from the system.

Human Rights Act 1998

Although this Act was passed in 1998, it was not actually implemented until 2 October 2000. Prior to this, Act litigants had to apply to the European Court of Human Rights in Strasbourg. In implementing the Human Rights Act 1998, judges and lawyers will need to refer to the precedents that have come from the European Court of Human Rights as a guide to their case law and decision making. The Human Rights Act has taken as its model Articles 2–12 and 14 of the European Court of Human Rights and Articles 1–3 of the First Protocol. It is too soon to know whether the Human Rights Act will be beneficial to the rights of children, although it has been reported that children who have been excluded from school may be able to bring a case under the heading of a 'right to education' (First Protocol, Article 2).

Child Protection

Article 19 Protection from abuse and neglect

States Parties shall take appropriate legislative, administrative, social and educational measures to protect the child from all forms of physical or mental violence, injury or abuse, neglect or negligent treatment, maltreatment or exploitation, including sexual abuse, while in the care of parent(s), legal guardian(s) or any other person who has the care of the child.

Such protective measures should, as appropriate, include effective procedures for the establishment of social programmes to provide necessary support for the child and for those who have the care of the child, as well as for other forms of prevention and for identification, reporting, referral, investigation, treatment and follow-up of instances of child maltreatment described heretofore, and, as appropriate, for judicial involvement.

Articles 33, 34, 35 and 36 deal with protecting children from drug abuse, sexual exploitation, selling and trafficking of children and other forms of exploitation.

Protecting children from abuse and neglect is a major responsibility for all societies. Child abuse is not a new phenomenon in our society; one only has to read the novels of Dickens to find out what was happening in the nineteenth century.

What is new is society's decision to take the maltreatment of children seriously and to legislate in order to protect children. In addition to this, the improvement in media communications has placed serious incidents of child abuse in the public domain, heightening people's awareness of and to a certain extent their anxiety over their own children's protection. In recent years a new global form of child abuse has appeared via the Internet whereby children are depicted in pornography. This is proving much more difficult to stop as it involves numerous people across a large number of countries.

The Children Act clearly states that local authorities have a clear duty to protect children who are at 'risk of harm' under the category of 'children in need'. The decision as to whether a child is 'at risk' and the course of action that should be taken to protect that child is a matter of complex professional judgement. However, there has been a number of cases that have been the subject of government enquiries, which have concluded that wrong or inappropriate judgements had been made, for example, The Maria Colwell case, the Kimberley Carlile case and the Cleveland case.

The Department of Health has produced definitions of child abuse and neglect, although individual local authorities are allowed to interpret these in order to fit in with their own child-protection policies. However, the categories of abuse used by the Department of Health and by local authorities remain the same: physical abuse, sexual abuse, emotional abuse, neglect and grave concern. Article 19 of the Convention does go further than the Children Act as it states that children must be protected from 'all forms of physical and mental violence'. It is interesting to note that the Department of Health definitions do not include other forms of abuse such as bullying and psychological abuse.

Emotional abuse is defined in the Department of Health document *Working Together* (1991) as 'the actual or likely adverse effects on the emotional development and behaviour of a child caused by persistent or severe emotional ill treatment or rejection. All abuse involves some emotional ill-treatment'. O'Hagan (1993) discusses the difficulties in defining emotional abuse and in proving that it has occurred because of the need for the evidence to show a lack of awareness, understanding and intentionality on the part of the carers in order for their behaviour to be considered abusive. Often emotional abusers are not aware that what they are doing is a form of abuse. Examples of such behaviour can include as ignoring the child, not interacting with the child verbally or non-verbally, being over-critical of the child, never giving praise for the child's accomplishments and using other members of the family as a threat, for example 'wait until your father gets home', as a form of control. Whilst any one of the above list may have been used by a carer or within the family in a 'one-off' situation, it is when such behaviour becomes part of the normal day-to-day treatment of the child that it would constitute abuse. O'Hagan states that emotional abuse is not perceived as creating a crisis in the same way as physical or sexual abuse is and therefore is given less attention by those who have a role in child protection.

Bullying is a form of emotional/psychological abuse and in recent years employees, organisations, teachers and others have become far more aware of the damage caused by bullying. Children are open to bullying by other children (older or in the same peer group), other family members and those who care for them. The child who is being bullied loses its self-esteem as it feels the shame of being called names or of always being the victim, unable to fight back. Eventually the child may reach a point of believing that the names it is being called are true and this can add to the child's suffering and feelings of humiliation and shame. Bullies often pick on the most vulnerable children, such as those with disabilities, those who look different in some way – for example, those who wear glasses or have a different skin colour – or those who are visibly poor or needy. Many schools now have anti-bullying policies but there is still an expectation that bullying is a school phenomenon and could not happen in the playgroup or nursery. As most early years workers know, children will often copy behaviour they have learnt from their parents, primary carer or older siblings and if this happens to be of a bullying nature then it is likely that the child will also take on a bullying role. If this happens it is important that the child care worker is aware of the situation and is able to deal with it in a positive way. To ignore bullying behaviour is to condone it and in doing this the welfare of the child who is being bullied is not being taken into consideration.

In November 1993 the Commission on Children and Violence was set up in the UK by the Gulbenkian Foundation. The aims of the Commission were to:

i   provide as accurate a picture as possible of the level of all kinds of violence to and by children and young people;
ii   propose ways of challenging social and legal endorsement of any form of inter-personal violence and policies and practices which tend to increase violence involving children and young people.

The Commission defined violence as 'behaviour by people against people liable to cause physical or psychological harm'.

Children themselves are not naturally violent; violence is a behaviour that is learned through parents, carers, older siblings or close others, or by exposure to inappropriate media via videos and television. The Commission's Report, Children and Violence 1995, states that children who themselves are violent are inextricably linked to having themselves been the victims of violence. The Report explores not only children as victims of violence but also children as violators. There is no doubt that it is a good idea to begin working towards a non-violent society from the moment children enter an early years setting. Children have the right to be looked after in a safe environment and this will require all staff to be vigilant and have procedures for dealing with physical violence, bullying, name calling and so on. Finch 2000 has produced a checklist for early years establishments to enable them to work towards a non-violent society.

Where domestic violence is concerned, the children in the family often suffer violence from the person who is abusing the parent. Domestic violence is usually the man physically abusing the woman and children; however, it is to be remembered that there is a small number of cases in which it is the woman who is the violent person. It was not until 1990 that the Home Office issued a circular to all police forces informing them that domestic violence was no less serious than any other type of civil assault. Police forces were asked to set up Domestic Violence Units and train staff in the correct ways of dealing with such cases. The Women's Aid Federation came into being to set up refuges for abused women and their children in order to remove them from the violent situation. Refuge workers supported the non-abusing parent in order to empower them to be in a position to promote the welfare and safety of themselves and their children. Tony Blair's government has declared a position of zero tolerance on domestic violence.

Refugee children

Article 22 Refugee children

States Parties shall take appropriate measures to ensure that a child who is seeking refugee status or who is considered a refugee in accordance with applicable international or domestic law and procedures shall, whether unaccompanied or accompanied by his or her parents or by any other person, receive appropriate protection and humanitarian assistance in the enjoyment of applicable rights set forth in the present convention and in other international human rights or humanitarian instruments to which the said States are Parties.

For this purpose, States Parties shall provide, as they consider appropriate, co-operation in any efforts by the United Nations and other competent intergovernmental organisations or non-governmental organisations operating with the United Nations to protect and assist such a child and to trace the parents or other members of the family of any refugee child in order to obtain information necessary for reunification with his or her family. In cases where no parents or other members of the family can be found, the child shall be accorded the same protection as any other child permanently or temporarily deprived of his or her family environment.

Other articles that can be used to promote the welfare and rights of refugee children include Article 2, Article 8, Article 9, Article 10 and Article 20.

The UK has numerous applications for refugee status each year (around 20,000 in 2002) from people arriving from countries such as Somalia, Uganda, Kosova and Afghanistan. Rutter and Hyder (1998) succinctly explain that the term 'refugee' has a legal meaning: 'a person must be judged to have left his or her own country or be unable to return to it "owing to a well-founded fear of being persecuted for reasons of race, religion, nationality, membership of a particular social group or political opinion" '. The term 'asylum seeker' is used to describe someone who has crossed an international border in search of safety and refugee status in another country. All children have refugee status or exceptional leave to remain and therefore have access to education and early years facilities. Asylum-seeking families with children under eighteen years of age are able to be supported by social services under Section 17 of the Children Act 1989. Asylum seekers and refugees tend to be the younger generation of a society and therefore are more likely to have young children. Many children and families seeking asylum or refugee status have experienced great trauma before reaching the UK and few will have a good command of the English language. The children and their families will be suffering from traumatic experiences, loss of the wider family and friends and the effects of change from having left their own country and the expectations of the new country. Because of the negative publicity in the UK media about asylum seekers, many families have been subject to racist discrimination from the local population where they are living. This only compounds their already traumatised state over the situations that made them leave their own country in the first place. Asylum seekers/refugee families are often moved around a great deal; in fact the government's white paper on *Asylum and Immigration* (Home Office 1998) advocates a policy of dispersal.

Research has shown that the uptake of early years provision by asylum seekers/refugees is very low. Rutter and Hyder (1998) offer the following reasons for this:

1 frequent moves of the families through a series of temporary accommodation;
2 lack of knowledge of the local social services;
3 unemployment and low income, meaning that some provision is beyond the means of the families;
4 cultural factors, such as viewing child care as an activity that takes place within the extended family or community;
5 inaccessibility of some services, such as places offered in nursery or playgroup that are too far away from where the family lives;
6 unwelcoming services, such as playgroups, One O'clock Clubs and such like that are used by a regular group of parents who do not welcome new members, particularly asylum seeker/refugees.

It is a sad indictment of society that the children who need the services most are not able to get them for a variety of reasons. In London there has been a small number of projects that have been targeted at children living in temporary accommodation. The voluntary sector has also proved to be responsive and has enabled community organisations to run playgroups and sessional nurseries. Examples of these include An Viet Foundation, Hackney; Armenian Community Playgroup, Acton; Minik Kardes Day Nursery, Hackney; Windmill Project for Refugee Women and Children.

Early years care and education establishments need to devise plans for helping asylum seekers/refugees to make better use of their facilities. This may be by undertaking outreach work, employing interpreters, producing information in a number of languages or offering facilities for the parents to have language support.

Non-discrimination

> ### Article 2 Non-Discrimination
>
> States Parties shall respect and ensure the rights set forth in the present Convention to each child within their jurisdiction without discrimination of any kind irrespective of the child's or his or her parents' or legal guardians' race, colour, sex, language, religion, political or other opinion, national, ethnic or social origin, property, disability, birth or other status.
>
> State Parties shall take all appropriate measures to ensure that the child is protected against all forms of discrimination or punishment on the basis of the status, activities, expressed opinions, or beliefs of the child's parents, legal guardians or family members.

The Children Act 1989 clearly states that 'child care provision must take into account the religious, racial, cultural and linguistic needs of the child'. This means that all early years workers must take into account these aspects of the child when planning meals and activities, and in their dealings with parents/carers. Not to do so would constitute discrimination against a particular family, child or group of children. The UK is a pluralistic society and as such its members should be aware of and respect each other regardless of differences in race, religion, culture, ability, class and other characteristics. Unfortunately, we are often aware that such tolerance and respect does not always exist in our society and there is bias among people and within institutions.

If early years workers are going to be strategically effective in combating discrimination in their work settings then they first have to examine and address their own biases. Everyone is biased against something; to err is to be human! However, it is important that every worker is aware of these biases and able to ensure that they do not influence decisions made about children and their parents. Bias is often based upon misinformation or unproven information, sometimes incited by the media. One must not condemn a whole group on the basis of the behaviour of one or two members of that group. For example, just because your dealings with the opposite sex may not always have been friendly and congenial, you cannot attribute the same behaviour to all members of that sex. To do so would be making stereotypical judgements, which are then transferred into the labelling of individuals. Sadly, much labelling can go on in staff-rooms of child-care establishments. For example: 'Beware of Ms Dodds the new parent; you know she is a cousin of Ms Harper, and you must all remember what she was like – the parent from hell!!' Poor Ms Dodds and her child probably stand little chance of proving that they are not just the same as their cousin. How did Ms Harper get such a reputation in the first place? Maybe nobody was listening to her and she became frustrated and tried to make herself understood using language that was not acceptable to the staff. Whatever happened, the actions of Ms Harper have now been attributed to the whole family, however distant the relationship. Research such as that by Rosenthal and Jacobson (1968) and in The Swann Report (1985) shows how teacher expectation reflects on how well a child will succeed within the education system. If teacher expectation is based upon discrimination and bias then certain children will stand very little chance of success.

Siraj-Blatchford and Clarke (2000) put forward four main conditions that need to be satisfied if a child is to learn:

- the child needs to be in a state of emotional well-being and be secure;
- the child needs a positive self-identity and self-esteem;
- the curriculum must be social/interactional and instructive;
- the child needs to be cognitively engaged.

These points need to be considered when planning the early years curriculum, particularly 'positive identity and self-esteem', as the foundations of these attributes are laid down very early in children. Milner (1983) found that children learned positive and negative feelings at a very early age and that by the age of three years they were able to demonstrate an awareness of racial feelings that mirrored the current practices of the adults around them.

The UK has a policy of inclusion for those children who have disabilities. Inclusion should be a very positive experience for these children but can easily turn into a negative model if the other children call them names, leave them out of games and generally marginalise them from the social interaction of the setting. It is important that the staff in early years settings are aware of what is happening in their setting and are trained in how to deal with incidents in a way that is sensitive to all the children involved.

Travellers' children are another group that suffers discrimination in the UK and elsewhere in Europe. Children from these families may be transient, moving from area to area and only attending the early years setting for a number of weeks before moving on. Some travellers live on permanent trailer sites and others live in houses. The children from these families will probably be regular attendees. Travellers' families are very close-knit, extended families sharing a rich culture, beliefs, values and history. Part of their history has been their survival under some of the most traumatic circumstances, not least of which being the holocaust, of which a large number of gypsies were victims. There is still a deep-rooted prejudice in our culture towards travellers; perhaps this is because we know so little about them, their history and their lifestyle.

Brown (1998) points out that those children who live in trailers may find the nursery or school a very daunting prospective. It may be the first time that they have been in such a large indoor space with running water, flushing toilets and a plethora of play materials and books. Brown suggests that setting up a trailer-home corner and using themes such as transport, working animals or homes can help these children feel more safe and secure in the nursery setting. Talking to the children and their parents can offer the best source of information for staff and other children.

It is important that if other children in the group come to school voicing their parents'/carers' prejudices against travellers this is dealt with by the staff in a positive way. Many local education authorities have specialist teachers who work with travellers' children and who may be able to offer ideas for constructive ways to enable these children to be accepted by the rest of the group.

On a positive note, Michael McDonagh (1996) (in Brown 1998), a traveller's child, writes:

> I like this school. I have lived in thirteen houses and a lot of sites, one in Dublin. I had two big dogs, Lassie and Wolf. My sisters go to school and my big sister goes to secondary school and her reading is good. I live in a house in Tottenham and I have been in this school for a year now. I have lots of friends, Jamil, Kelvin, Mattie, Michael and Daniel. They know I am a Traveller and they like me. I play football with them. I have a good teacher and a teacher for Travellers comes in to see me every week. A lady called Ivy helps me as well. I am better at reading and I have good writing. I can sound letters and make words. I like the computer. In my last school the children were not nice to me and I was fighting a lot. Here I have learned to get on better with other children. I like school.

International Decade for a Culture of Peace and Non-violence for the Children of the World: explanation and implementation

In November 2000 in Paris, the International Decade for a Culture of Peace and Non-violence for the Children of the World was launched by UNESCO and Living Values (an educational programme). The launch took the form of a conference on the theme of a Framework for Action on Values in Education in Early Childhood. Led by UNESCO and supported by the Living Values education programme, there was a commitment to involving as many countries as possible to sign up to and implement a culture of peace and non-violence for their children over the next ten years. Research has shown that there are 800 million children under the age of six years in the world and less than one third of these benefits from any form of early childhood education or intervention. There are five levels of action required in order to facilitate implementation of the Framework:

- personal level – adults need to learn to express feelings; children need to learn to listen, model, acknowledge diversity, to have time, to enjoy, to play, to feel;
- family level – parents need to be supported, helped, educated;
- school level – educators need to be trained to take into account emotional and affective attitudes;
- community level – communities need to have/create places/spaces where children can be welcomed and nurtured, including street children, AIDS children/orphans;
- state level – states have a responsibility to implement the Convention on the Rights of the Child and to provide education.

The guiding principles for action are based upon the fact that every child has the right to early childhood care and education and all programmes should be based upon the values of trust, respect, non-discrimination and the right of the child to grow in an environment of peace. The key organisations involved in using their networks to promote the Framework are UNESCO, UNICEF and Education International; however, in each country there will be additional organisations who will take up the implementation of the Framework at a local level. Each organisation will define its own level of participation. One concern of educating children for peace is that of how early years workers can get children to empathise with each other. Levin (1994) offers the following suggestions (adapted):

- the child care and education worker should be a role model and should show empathy and compassion;
- feelings of the child should be validated before correcting behaviour;
- emotions should be given a name;
- interpret emotions of others for the children;
- use visuals to teach children to recognise emotions;
- provide opportunities for children to demonstrate caring behaviours with others;
- notice and value acts of kindness;
- use 'us' puppets to role-play situations.

There is also a need for early years care and education workers to know how to deal with conflict when it does arise. As with adults, the best solution is to ask about the problem, talk to the people concerned and possibly also to others about what may be acceptable solutions to the problem, choose the best idea and put it into action. For young children a system of traffic lights can be used: Red – stop, what's the problem? Amber – what can we do? Green – Go ahead with the best plan for a resolution. It is not quite the same as the football penalty cards system but can certainly have the same positive effects!

References

Aries, P. (1960) *Centuries of Childhood*, Harmondsworth: Penguin Education.

Brown, B. (1998) *Unlearning Discrimination in the Early Years*, Stoke-on-Trent: Trentham Books.

Calouste Gulbenkian Foundation (1995) *Children and Violence: Report of the Commission on Children and Violence*, London: Calouste Gulbenkian Foundation.

Coppock, S. (1997) 'Families in Crisis', in P. Scratton (ed.), *Childhood in Crisis*, Berkeley, CA: UCL Press.

Department of Education and Science (1985) *Education for All: The Swann Report*, London: HMSO.

Finch, S. (2000) *Towards a Non-Violent Society: Checkpoints for the Early Years*, London: Forum on Children and Violence.

Franklin, B. (1995) 'The Case for Children's Rights: a progress report', in B. Franklin (ed.), *The Handbook of Children's Rights*, London: Routledge.

Lansdown, G. (1996) 'The United Nations Convention on the Rights of the Child – Progress in the United Kingdom', in Cathy Nutbrown (ed.), *Children's Rights and Early Education*, London: Paul Chapman Publishing.

Lansdown, G. and Newell, P. (1994) *UK Agenda for Children*, London: Children's Rights Development Unit.

Levin, D. E. (1994) 'Building a Peaceable Classroom: Helping young children feel safe in violent times', in *Childhood Education*, 70, 267–70.

McDonagh, M. (1996) 'Michael's Story', in *Stories from Travelling Children*, London: Haringey Traveller Education Service. (Cited in Brown 1998.)

Milner, D. (1983) *Children and Race: Ten Years On*, London: Ward Lock Educational.

Muscot, S. (ed.) (1999) *Children's Rights: Reality or Rhetoric*, London: The International Save the Children Alliance.

Newell, P. (1991) *The UN Convention and Children's Rights in the UK*, London: National Children's Bureau.

O'Hagan, K. (1993) *Emotional and Psychological Abuse of Children*, Buckingham: Open University Press.

Rosenthal, R. and Jacobson, L. (1968) *Pygmalion in the Classroom*, New York: Holt Rinehart & Winston.

Rutter, J. and Hyder, T. (1998) *Refugee Children in the Early Years: Issues for Policy Makers and Providers*, London: Refugee Council/Save the Children.

Saraga, E. (1998) 'Children's Needs: Who decides', in Mary Langan (ed.), *Welfare: Needs, Rights and Risks*, London: Routledge/OU.

Schwer, B. (2000) *A Guide to the Human Rights Act 1998*, London: Rowe and Maw.

Siraj-Blatchford, I. (1994) *The Early Years: Laying the Foundations for Racial Equality*, Stoke-on-Trent: Trentham Books.

Siraj-Blatchford, I. and Clarke, P. (2000) *Supporting Identity, Diversity and Language in the Early Years*, Buckingham: Open University Press.

UNICEF (1995) *The Convention on the Rights of the Child*, London: UNICEF UK Committee.

CHAPTER 3

How children learn

I hear and I forget;
I see and I remember;
I do and I understand.
(Ancient Chinese proverb)

From conception we all have a different set of experiences and interact with the environment in a unique manner. These affect the content of what we learn and the use to which we can put this knowledge. We also learn in different ways – some children and adults are highly curious and motivated and engage in active experimentation, whereas others are more reflective. The learning styles we develop emphasise some learning abilities over others; we all have some strong and some weak areas.

In this chapter we shall be looking at some of the theories that have been put forward to explain how we learn and how internal and external factors affect that learning.

What is learning?

The term 'learning' is one that everyone uses and understands, but how we learn has yet to be fully understood. The *Oxford English Dictionary* defines learning as 'knowledge got by study' a definition that does not cover all aspects of learning. In psychological terms learning is a process whereby a relatively permanent change of behaviour occurs as the result of prior experience. However, there are difficulties with this definition, as it does not cover such activities as learning to stand up. Although not completely comprehensive, a useful definition is that of Kolb (1984), who wrote that 'learning is the process whereby knowledge is created through the transformation of experience'.

What is development?

The other term that will be used a great deal during this chapter is 'development'. Development involves changes over time and is sometimes seen as a gradual, linear, continuous process that is affected by both experiences and physiological changes. Growth and maturation follow a fixed programme that may be either continuous or discontinuous.

One of the major issues relating to development is the relative contribution of nature and nurture to the changes that occur. How much can parents, teachers and others support a child's development and how much is dictated by genetic inheritance? Psychologists agree that development is influenced by the interaction of innate and environmental factors, but the relative importance of each is still being discussed.

Old versus new thinking about the brain

In the past decade there have been advances in our understanding of the brain and its functions and this research has implications for our understanding of how children learn. Until quite recently, neuroscientists believed that the genes we are born with determine the structure of our brains and that that fixed structure determines the way we develop and interact with the world. However, new investigations have shown that although heredity may determine the basic number of brain cells (neurons) that children are born with and their initial organisation, this is only a framework. The child's environment has enormous impact on how the circuits of the brain are 'wired'.

We know that the brain at birth is composed of trillions of neurons and synapses (connections between the brain cells), many more than we actually need. As the child has more and more experiences and learns more skills, the synapses grow and the existing connections are strengthened. In the early years the child's brain forms twice as many synapses as will eventually be needed. Those that are used are reinforced and become a permanent part of the brain. We also know that connections that are not used eventually fade away. Therefore, children's experiences during the first years of life are even more decisive than we had once believed. We now know that by the age of three, children's brains are twice as active as those of adults and that activity levels begin to drop during adolescence.

During the first three years in particular, brain connections develop quickly in response to outside stimulation. The child's experiences, good or bad, directly affect the ways in which the brain is wired and the connections in the nervous system.

Recent research by Gunnar (1996) has demonstrated how 'stress-sensitive' systems in the brain are shaped by outside experiences. For example, one particular stress-sensitive system is activated when children are faced with emotional or physical shock. The system produces a steroid hormone called cortisol, high levels of which cause the death of brain cells and a reduction in connections between the cells in certain areas of the brain. Research on adults who have experienced chronic or intense activation of the system that produces cortisol shows shrinkage of an area of the brain that is important in learning and memory. There appears to be a clear link between physical or emotional trauma and long-term impairment to learning and development. On the other hand, babies with strong emotional bonds to their caregivers show consistently lower levels of cortisol, which will have a positive effect upon their learning

Critical periods for learning

Are there 'critical periods' in young children's learning, and what happens if they do not gain the knowledge or skill at a specific time? Although the human brain has a remarkable capacity to change – the plasticity of the young child's brain is phenomenal – there seem to be 'prime times' when the brain will develop in specific areas and it will grow or strengthen connections most readily at these times. For example, visual and auditory stimuli promote synaptic development most quickly in the second and third months of infancy. Equally negative experiences or the absence of appropriate stimulation are more prone to serious and sustained effects at these times. Trauma, abuse, neglect and lack of stimulation or social exposure can all interfere with healthy brain development and therefore with learning. Such negative experiences can result in the creation of a brain prone to anxiety, depression and an inability to form social attachments.

Can the early childhood educator influence the brain's growth and learning?

Babies do not come into the world with 'clean slates' but with a number of behaviour patterns that help them to deal with how the world works, but their innate structures are transformed by their experiences with objects and other people. It was Vygotsky who made such a profound contribution to our understanding of human nature when he suggested that nurture, which is how others change us, is part of our nature. If we adopt this approach we can see that there is no real conflict between biology and culture. A unique feature of human learning is that we depend upon other people for learning.

There is no doubt that early care and education has a fundamental and long-lasting effect upon how people develop, their ability to learn and their capacity to regulate their own emotions. Not only should we be offering children emotional and social security but we should also be mindful that the brain is the greediest organ in the body for oxygen, as it uses some 20–25 per cent of the body's intake. Fresh air and physical exercise are as essential as a challenging environment for successful learning.

Factors affecting learning

Memory

Memory plays an important part in our learning and the use that we make of our experiences. Like other areas of brain research, research into memory and the way in which it develops has undergone a major rethink in recent times. A big shift has come in the past two decades with the emphasis on the importance of socio-cultural factors on our cognitive development.

Since the 1980s, cognitive and neuro-sciences have shown that the brain has multiple memory systems – two of these systems are explicit (or declarative) memory and implicit (or procedural) memory. Explicit memory relies on the conscious recollection of names, places, events and other information whereas implicit memory represents a variety of unconscious abilities, including the capacity for learning habits and skills. Declarative memory is characterised as fast and flexible whereas procedural memory is slow and results from gradual learning. We use both systems all the time.

As children grow older, from about seven years of age, they, like adults, learn to organise their memories. It appears that we organise memory for individual events (episodic memory) in chronological order, whereas memory for facts (semantic memory) seems to be organised by meaning.

An important change in both our thinking and the way in which we use our memory comes with the development of metamemory, that is, the knowledge that we have about our memory processes. Very young children have no idea about how their memory works and that they will not remember everything they are told, but from about five to six years of age, children come to have some understanding of metamemory. There will of course be individual differences in the age at which they develop this highly important skill. As humans we are good at knowing what we know and what we don't know.

As they develop metamemory, children begin to use memory strategies such as rehearsal, organisation or elaboration to help them remember in the same way as adults. Over-confident children often do poorly in memory tasks, as they do not see the necessity to use appropriate strategies. It seems that the more general knowledge children have in their long-term memory, the more readily they are able to absorb new information, since we know that familiar and meaningful information is more easily remembered than the unfamiliar. Retrieval processes can be difficult for children, particularly those with learning disorders. Adults often forget how long it takes young children to retrieve information, particularly when they have been asked a question, and become impatient if a response is not immediately forthcoming.

Memory can be divided into short and long-term memory. Short-term memory lasts only a minute or two while the brain sorts out how to store the information. Children's improvement in short-term memory as they grow older appears to result from the changes in strategy that they use rather than from an increase in the capacity of the memory store. This does not change much throughout childhood.

However, pre-schoolers are able to use their memory effectively in many situations. For example, if children have mislaid a toy in the playground, they are well able to retrace their steps to try to find it. They can remember where they last saw it and then are able to infer that this is the best place to start searching. If they are so good at this why then are they unable to carry out tasks such as carrying messages efficiently?

Basically it seems that memories that arise incidentally as a result of other activities are retained better than activities that require deliberate memorisation. There has been much research to show that when young children are asked to memorise as an end in itself they do not have the strategies to proceed whereas when the memorisation is part of an activity in which they are involved the young child is able to cope.

As educators it is important that we offer children strategies to help them develop. Although no one wants to reintroduce drills and rote learning, we should not ignore the role of rehearsal and repetition in learning.

Memory is a complex subject that links closely not only to areas of cognition, such as perception, language and representation, but also to our social experiences. Like us, children attend to, concentrate on, or memorise information most effectively if it is seen to be pertinent to their lives and interests.

Concentration and attention

Every educator is aware that there are some children who do not appear to be able to concentrate on a task and whose attention flits from one activity to another. However, many of these 'flitters' will focus on a task once they find one of interest and/or once there is an adult who is willing to support their learning. There is, though, a smaller group of children who have genuine attention deficits, and the difficulties of these children need to be recognised because the inability to concentrate has serious implications for children's learning. This will be discussed in greater detail in the next chapter.

Many educators are now using the two observation scales produced by the Effective Early Learning Project (EEL) to help them assess the level of concentration of the young children in their institutions. The Leuven Involvement Scale is designed to help the adult see whether or not the child is really involved deeply in an activity or whether the involvement is superficial. The second scale, the Adult–Child Engagement Scale, aims to help adults look at their involvement with the children. Are they providing appropriate materials to meet the needs of the children and helping them to become independent, autonomous learners? There may be a number of reasons for the child's behaviour and careful observation may help the educator solve or ameliorate the problem.

Cognitive styles

Just as some adults are more effective in the morning and others work better in the evening, so parents recognise early that their children have different biological rhythms. Children, as adults, also have different ways of tackling problems and dealing with challenging situations. It seems that some of us are more analytical in our approach whereas others take a more holistic view to tackling a problem. It has been argued that an extreme global style involves field dependence, intuitive and emotional thinking, which involves a simultaneous processing of many aspects of experience and a tendency towards impulsive behaviour. At the other end of the scale there is a total field independence style that involves the dispassionate noting of detailed objectives, critical and logical thinking and a focus on learning step by step, rather than taking a comprehensive overview. In most instances people do not adopt either extreme but rather use a balance of the two. It has been argued that these differences come about as a result of parenting strategies. However, modern research has realised that cognitive style is not a stable trait and that motivation is also an important factor to be taken into account.

Intelligence

The argument as to whether intelligence depends upon learning and experience (nurture) or is fixed because it is inherited (nature) has dominated the thinking of scholars until recent times.

During the first half of the twentieth century the nature/nurture dilemma was one of the most controversial topics in psychology. But it was not just an academic issue; there are deep political implications to the question of whether intelligence depends upon learning and experience or whether it is inherited and fixed. Educational policies were designed based on the belief that intelligence could be measured accurately and decisions about children's education were made dependent upon their scores in intelligence tests. IQ tests such as the Stanford–Binet or Merrill–Palmer scales were developed and widely used. These tests were developed by a white, male, middle-class group of psychologists, many of whom saw intelligence testing as a way of identifying the 'innate feeble minded' who in their eyes were the source of many of the social problems of the time. Terman, writing in 1916 in the introduction to the first version of the Stanford–Binet test, stated that:

In the future, intelligence tests will bring tens of thousands of these high grade effectives under the surveillance of society, this will ultimately result in curtailing the reproduction of feeble-mindedness and in the elimination of an enormous amount of crime, pauperism and industrial inefficiency.

(Terman 1916: 6–7)

In spite of the reservations of many psychologists concerning the validity and reliability of intelligence testing, the 1944 Education Act introduced verbal reasoning and other tests based on number and memory to decide whether children should go to grammar schools, technical schools or secondary modern schools at the age of eleven. Opportunities for higher education were effectively closed for any child who did not make 'grammar school'. It soon became very apparent that testing at the age of eleven favoured male, middle-class children. It also became very apparent that there were big discrepancies throughout England and Wales as to the number of grammar-school places available in different parts of the country.

Not only was there criticism that the intelligence tests favoured children from a white, middle-class culture, but also that they looked at intelligence from a very limited point of view and did not take into account abilities in music, creativity or interpersonal skills. The question that intelligence might consist of a number of different, independent skills (multiple intelligences) had already been raised.

By the 1960s, the writings of Piaget were becoming more generally known and his ideas about how children construct their view of the world helped to raise questions about the nature of intelligence and the importance of the environment to children's learning.

Piaget defined intelligence as a basic life function that helps the organism to adapt to its environment. He believed that:

- all children are active learners trying to make sense of their world;
- all children go through discrete stages of learning and development;
- children think differently from adults;
- children play a crucial role in their own development;
- children vary in the age at which they reach a particular stage;
- each stage rests firmly on the preceding one;
- no stage can be omitted;
- children can be at different levels of attainment within a stage at the same time;
- children use first-hand and prior experiences in order to learn.

Educators began to realise that a stimulating environment could increase intelligence. This led to wide-scale programmes of compensatory education in the UK and throughout the rest of the Western world as well as to major changes in secondary schooling.

Intelligence tests have a part to play in the assessment of children, particularly those with special educational needs, but they fail to provide a whole picture of the individual. Observations and other forms of assessment are also necessary before a full analysis of a child's needs can be made.

Gardner's theory of multiple intelligence also has implications for education. He proposed that within the brain there is a system of discrete information-processing operations that deal with the different kinds of information that humans encounter during their everyday lives. These modules include:

- linguistic intelligence, the ability to use language effectively either orally or in writing;
- logical/mathematical intelligence, the ability to use numbers correctly, to think inductively or deductively; to classify, generalise and categorise;
- musical intelligence, the ability to understand and use musical concepts; to develop an appreciation for music;
- spatial intelligence, the ability to represent spatial information effectively;
- bodily kinaesthetic intelligence, the ability to use physical means to represent ideas and feelings;
- interpersonal intelligence, the ability to relate to others;
- intrapersonal intelligence, the ability to be able to understand oneself and to have self discipline.

These processes are genetically pre-programmed but are subject to cultural influences. Therefore in his view, individuals may differ in the strength of their intelligences and therefore possess personal 'profiles of intelligence'. Gardner has suggested that children already enter school with distinctive 'profiles of intelligence' and that these need to be cultivated through suitable activity-centred curricula.

Writers since Piaget have argued that intelligence needs to be defined socially. Cross-cultural studies have shown that Western definitions of intelligence are at variance with those in other cultures. For example, the Baoulé argue that technological skills have to be integrated with social skills as the child's abilities are useless unless they are applied to the well-being of the social group.

Emotional intelligence

In recent years, writers such as Goleman (1996) have stressed the importance of children becoming what he termed 'emotionally literate' – a skill that he and others have considered vital for later learning and development.

The key components of emotional literacy are:

- emotional awareness (understanding the cause of feelings, being able to name and recognise emotions, recognising the difference between feelings and actions);

- managing emotions (the ability to manage anger, frustration and sadness, avoiding aggressive or self-destructive behaviour, monitoring self-criticism);
- communication (being able to talk about one's feelings effectively, being a good listener, being able to ask appropriate questions);
- personal decision making (examining your actions and understanding their consequences, distinguishing between thoughts and feelings when making decisions);
- empathy (being sensitive to others' feelings, having the ability to see things from another person's point of view);
- handling relationships (the ability to analyse, understand and solve problems in relationships, being considerate, being able to work as part of a group, share, co-operate, negotiate and solve conflicts).

Goleman and others have argued that emotionally intelligent people who can motivate themselves, know and manage their emotions and recognise emotions in others are more likely to be able to handle relationships effectively and use their cognitive abilities to the full. The evidence for emotional intelligence is impelling and has definite implications for how we support children's learning.

Theories of learning

In this section we shall consider some different approaches to learning and their effectiveness in helping our understanding of how children learn.

Behaviourist approaches

Classical conditioning

The founder of this school of thought was the Russian psychologist Pavlov, who based his learning principles upon the notion of conditioning. From his experiments with dogs, Pavlov developed a set of principles, three of which are of particular importance for educators.

- The principle of reinforcement – Pavlov demonstrated that the act of achieving success, or of getting a response right, means that it is more likely to be repeated.
- The principle of extinction – the response stops when there is no reinforcement.
- The principle of generalisation – Pavlov found that it is possible for both animals and humans to generalise their responses from one situation to a similar situation.

A number of behavioural programmes have been based upon these principles, particularly in relation to extinction and reinforcement. Educators are encouraged to ignore children when they are attention seeking as it is argued that if the behaviour is ignored, it will either fade or disappear entirely.

An instance of conditioning occurs in many schools in the morning when children first arrive in the playground. They will be playing or talking to each other when they see their teacher come into the playground. The children will immediately line up in front of their teacher ready to go in to school.

Operant conditioning

Skinner was a behaviourist who advocated a form of conditioning or learning, which he termed operant conditioning. He worked with rats and pigeons, rewarding them with food if they did what was required (positive reinforcement) and punishing them if they did not behave appropriately (negative reinforcement), thus extinguishing undesirable behaviour. Skinner argued that desirable behaviour can be shaped by his operant conditioning techniques as undesirable behaviour is ignored and desirable behaviour is reinforced.

Contribution of behaviourism

The major contribution to our understanding of learning by the behaviourists is that they carried out strict experiments to test behaviour and found that their theories worked. The principles of reinforcement and extinction are used in child-rearing practices, particularly in relation to discipline, but they have weaknesses in that they do not explain how all learning occurs or take into account motivation. Most of the early work was carried out on animals but a child's real life is rather more complex. It may also be argued that the behaviourists have too simplistic an approach to learning as they do not take into account situations such as when children are experimenting with sand and water for fun and enjoyment and do not receive any form of reinforcement. Skinner can explain how existing behaviour becomes repeated but does not adequately explain where new behaviour comes from. For example, learning to stand up is not the result of previous experience. Like learning to walk and talk, this is a skill that has to be practised before it is fully acquired.

Observational learning

Observational learning results from observing the behaviour of other people. Almost anything can be learned from watching (or listening to) others.

Social-learning theorists, of whom Bandura is one of the most important, accept that children learn a great deal from reinforcement and punishment, but argue that children acquire large parts of their behaviour by observing and imitating. Children model their behaviour upon those whom they hold in high esteem, such as parents, teachers, peers and famous people.

Bandura argues that there are two main ways in which this modelling takes place.

Modelling behaviour: children often copy new pieces of behaviour that they did not previously know. Children do not seem to need to practise this behaviour or learn it by trial and error. Bandura carried out a famous experiment whereby he showed children a film in which adults acted in a very aggressive manner. After seeing the film, the children quickly began to exhibit aggressive behaviour without any prompting or suggestion of any kind. Bandura argued that watching the behaviour of a role model can result in some children changing their usual way of behaving by either strengthening or inhibiting their usual responses. This is one of the ways in which children learn how 'far they can go' and find the levels of tolerance that other people will accept in particular situations. For example, if there is a new member of staff who allows children to carry out normally unacceptable behaviour, the children will produce a higher level of undesirable behaviour than they would with a more established member of staff. If the behaviour goes unchecked, then the children are more likely to repeat the deviant behaviour. Some would argue that if the deviant behaviour is ignored it will be extinguished.

Eliciting Effect: Behavioural changes can take place from what is termed the 'eliciting effect'. The behaviour can be initiated by cues given by the model. This behaviour is not inborn, but it is argued that the child merely copies the behaviour it sees in others with behaviour or actions that it already possesses but had previously suppressed. For example, a girl had refrained from hitting another child at school but came home and saw her father, her model, hitting her brother. Immediately she believes that this is acceptable behaviour and on a subsequent occasion will strike another child.

Role models can have a positive effect and help to make learning more efficient. They can also account for why some people are more influential than others are over what children learn and how their personalities develop.

However, criticisms can be made of this approach:

- children are all different and even if they see the same role model they may react differently;
- children do not always copy the behaviour of people who seem influential. Their behaviour may be the result of trial and error or have no apparent cause at all;
- it fails to take into account that children are active in their own learning;
- it fails to accept that children are capable of learning different things at different ages.

In the first half of the twentieth century this approach to learning had a powerful influence upon educators and education. Children were exposed to vast amounts of rote learning and intermittent schedules of reinforcement – irregular periods of practice. Lessons were all pre-planned and there was little or no scope for questioning or investigation by the children. Even reading was taught in this fashion.

Gradually it was realised that traditional learning theories, based upon principles of stimulus and response, could not account for all aspects of children's learning and other psychologists were putting forward the idea that the thinking of young children was qualitatively different from that of adults. It was not only lack of experience that produced such unexpected responses to adult questioning.

In spite of the criticisms, behaviour theories still play an important part in behaviour-modification programmes and the underlying principles are important in many aspects of early childhood education. Furthermore, there are early childhood programmes flourishing in various parts of the world that are based entirely upon these approaches to learning.

The next three theorists mentioned in this section all have a profound influence upon early childhood education today.

Constructivism

Jean Piaget

The writings of Piaget had a great impact upon educational thinking in many parts of the world during the second half of the twentieth century. He emphasised the link between cognitive/intellectual development and learning, believing that the child constructs its own understanding about things. However, unlike the two other theorists mentioned in this section, he did not emphasise the role of social relationships in learning.

Assimilation and accommodation

Piaget argued that as young children experience new activities or events, they try to make sense of them by assimilating this knowledge into existing schemas (organised patterns of thought or actions which we construct in order to interpret our experiences). This process, which he called assimilation, is balanced by accommodation. During accommodation children try to adapt their previous knowledge to the new experience. Learning takes place when a state of equilibrium (balance) has been reached.

Children are constantly adapting to new situations and in so doing move from a state of equilibrium to a state of disequilibrium. Piaget gives the term equilibration to the overall interaction between assimilation and accommodation.

For example, most children between the ages of four and six think that animals are the only living things. On hearing that plants are also alive the child may become confused and unsure about how one knows that something is alive. In Piagetian terms, the child is in a state of disequilibrium. Gradually the child begins to discover similarities between plants and animals in that they both need water and food. The new knowledge about plants and animals helps to achieve a state of equilibrium as the child now realises why it is said that both animals and plants are alive.

Early concepts

Children learn about the world around them through their senses and perceptions. The feedback from these senses helps babies to develop ideas about objects and people. Research has shown us that babies begin to develop concepts about themselves and the world around them at a very early age, gradually linking past experiences with present ones. Piaget termed these early concepts, schemas. These are linked patterns of behaviours from which the child can generalise and use in different situations.

Schema approach to learning

Athey (1990) carried out a research project over a five-year period from 1972 to 1977 to investigate the use of schema in children's learning. As a result of her observations she suggested that children possess patterns or schemas that grow in complexity and become co-ordinated with one another. Athey describes a schema as a pattern of repeatable and generalisable actions that can be applied to objects or events.

According to her research, the following schemas were found to be present in children's behaviour between the ages of three and five years:

- transporting, e.g. moving objects from one place to another;
- dynamic vertical, e.g. flying a kite;
- dynamic back and forth/side to side, e.g. moving on the climbing frame;
- dynamic circular, e.g. hopping round in circles;
- going over and under, e.g. taking cars over and under a bridge;
- going round a boundary, e.g. building a block boundary around toy cars, taking the cars around it;
- enveloping and containing space, e.g. wrapping a teddy bear in a blanket;
- going through a boundary, e.g. building a boundary around toy cars, taking the cars through it.

Schemas were also observed in one-to-one correspondence, ordering and connection.

Each schema was considered under four headings:

- *motor level* – senses and movements;
- *symbolic level* – graphic representation, action, and speech;
- *functional level* – cause and effect;
- *thought level* – anything that children can talk about without a reminder, in other words internal representation.

According to the researchers, the marks and actions relating to these descriptions of movements can be identified in young children's drawings, play and thinking. They argued that these schemas form the basis for later learning as they become incorporated into more complex concepts and can be related to Piaget's stages of cognitive development.

Stages of cognitive development

1 Sensori-motor stage: from birth to around eighteen months to two years. This is characterised by the child exploring its world through the child's own physical actions. The child recognises and explores objects with its senses. By the end of the first year most children understand object permanence, that is, that objects and people continue to exist even when they are no longer in sight. Children also develop some understanding of cause and effect. This stage comes to an end with the development of language and thought.

2 Pre-operational stage: from around eighteen months to seven years. This period begins when children begin to represent actions with symbols and we see the beginnings of pretend play and the use of props to symbolise other objects, for example a stick may represent a doll. It is also the time when children may begin to invent imaginary playmates. At this stage children are moving towards operational thinking but are still not able to link schemas in a logical way. There are inconsistencies in their reasoning as children at this stage have rather primitive concepts compared with older children and adults. One of these Piaget termed animism, that is, attributing life to inanimate objects. For example, a child may think the wind is angry because it blows so hard.

Another inconsistency he termed transductive reasoning, which means the child reasons from the particular to the particular. When any two events occur together the child will assume that the one has caused the other. For example, Piaget quoted his daughter who stated 'I haven't had a nap, so it isn't afternoon.' In this case the child had missed her normal lunch-time sleep and so could not understand that it could be the afternoon.

Another limitation to the child's thinking is associated with what Piaget terms egocentric thinking. The child sees the world from its own viewpoint and fails to take into account the perspectives of others.

Children of this age have a different perception of right and wrong. For example, a child who accidentally drops a glass when carrying it to the kitchen will be perceived as naughtier than a child who has deliberately taken a glass from the cupboard after being told not to touch, even though it has not been broken. For the young child, what is right or wrong is based on what happens rather than on the motive. Piaget called this moral realism.

Towards the end of this phase, children begin to show a decrease in egocentricity. Many children can now sort by shape, size and colour although they are still dominated by their perceptions and classify objects according to their perceptual attributes. This is referred to as the intuitive period because thinking is still centred on the way things appear, rather than on a rational thought process. Piaget uses the term centration to describe this inability to focus on more than one feature of a situation.

3 Concrete operational period: from approximately seven to eleven years. During this period the child becomes less egocentric and can take on the views of others. The child is able to classify and organise objects but is still dependent upon concrete experiences. Not only do children develop conservation of time, mass, number, volume, shape, size and area throughout these years but they also develop the concept of reversibility. This is the ability to mentally undo an action they have witnessed. For example, they can look at a ball of clay, watch it being made into a sausage shape and then see it turned into a round ball and appreciate that there is the same amount of clay. The development of reversibility is crucial in the child's cognitive development.

4 Formal operational stage: from approximately twelve years onwards. Thinking about abstract ideas and hypothetical issues becomes possible. In practice children no longer require concrete reality to understand and manipulate ideas and relationships between things. Abstract concepts like peace and justice can be understood and problems can be solved. This ability to handle abstract concepts and ideas is not necessarily reached by all adults and many people use both abstract and concrete thinking throughout their lives.

For Piaget development is sequential and each period is dependent upon the previous stage. However, he recognised that children may master certain tasks at different rates and therefore be at the concrete operational stage for one task while at the pre-operational stage for another. This is termed *décalage*.

Criticisms of Piaget

- Piaget used clinical interviews to gather his information and these have been criticised as they were seen as too subjective;
- Piaget relied heavily upon children's language and memory skills. Later research has shown that he underestimated the ability of children under five years;
- it was also argued that his model drew attention to what children could not do rather than what they could do;
- he argued that young children are egocentric and unable to see another person's point of view;
- Piaget failed to take account of the effects of the social context upon children's development.

Susan Isaacs was one of the first critics of Piaget. She argued that young children were not only less egocentric than he had suggested, but that they were capable of logical thought at a much earlier age. Many years later the research of

Margaret Donaldson and her colleagues led to a major shift in thinking about Piaget's stage theory. The main thrust of Donaldson's argument was that if children were asked to undertake activities or problems within a familiar context they would be able to think and reason at a higher level than that suggested by Piaget. She argued that some of the failure to respond came from children's lack of understanding of either the question or the reason for asking the question – neither of which suggested that the children did not understand the task.

Donaldson and her researchers decided to repeat some of Piaget's tasks with some changes in the methods of administration. She showed that if children were provided with tasks that made sense to them then they could draw upon their previous experience and be able to undertake more complex activities. Donaldson believed that the knowledge we bring with us to a particular learning task is of crucial importance, and suggested that the meaning of the activity is embedded in the actual situation. Donaldson, as had Isaacs, demonstrated that children were not as egocentric as Piaget had suggested and that they could certainly empathise with people, particularly younger children, which cast doubt upon the view that they were unable to take another person's point of view.

Piaget's views on object permanence have also been challenged as researchers have shown that babies achieve this understanding much earlier than he had recognised.

However, in spite of the criticisms that have been made of his work it appears that Piaget was largely right in his description of the ways in which children develop cognitively.

Social constructivists

Jerome Bruner

Bruner is a cognitive psychologist who has exercised considerable influence upon the early years curriculum in recent years. Like Piaget, Bruner believed that children are active learners and need first-hand experiences to help them develop their ideas. He suggests that we develop skills that enable us to represent the environment to ourselves in three main ways:

- enactive representation;
- iconic representation;
- symbolic representation.

ENACTIVE REPRESENTATION

By this term, Bruner suggests that the human represents many things through motor experiences and actions. He argues that such activities as riding a bicycle, driving a car or swimming become represented in our muscles. Automatic patterns of activity are built up and we can reproduce them as needed.

ICONIC REPRESENTATION

Iconic representation is a development from enactive representation and occurs when we are able to build up a series of mental pictures or images of things we have experienced. Usually these images are formed from a variety of similar experiences. Bruner argues that it is essential for us to have a great deal of motor skill before we can form an image to represent a sequence of acts. We have to have a lot of practice at riding a bicycle before the actions become automatic. He considers that it is difficult for an educator to distinguish between enactive and iconic representation, but stresses the importance of talking with children and discussing actions and events with them so that they have the words to build images.

SYMBOLIC REPRESENTATION

Symbolic representation occurs when children are able to translate their experiences into symbolic form. To help the child with this, the educator and child must continually be talking together, asking and answering questions and explaining the meanings of words and actions.

A radical difference between the two theorists is that whereas Piaget expected children to reach a particular stage of development before moving on to the next, Bruner believes that we should help the child move forward in its thinking, not wait for a particular stage. To support this view he made his now famous statement in his book the *Process of Education* (1960), writing 'any subject can be taught effectively in some intellectually honest form to any child at any stage of development'.

Bruner speaks of a 'spiral curriculum' where the child learns first through actions, then through images and pictures of the world and finally through the symbols of numbers or words. In his view, we use all three modes of representation throughout our lives as and when it is appropriate.

Bruner, like Vygotsky, suggests that the adult has a key role to play in supporting or 'scaffolding' the child's learning in a way that will enable the child to go beyond the immediate information or experience and reflect and produce new ideas and ways of looking at the world.

Scaffolding includes:

- gaining the attention and interest of the child;
- simplifying the number of responses the child needs to make;
- maintaining the child's interest by giving encouragement and feedback;
- identifying the key points of the task so the child knows what is needed;
- providing a model to the task, for example demonstrate how it might be done.

The most important aspect of Bruner's work has been to emphasise the importance of the adult in children's learning. Many early childhood education programmes have with good effect adopted the notion of the adult as a 'scaffold' for children's learning.

Lev Vygotsky

The Russian psychologist Vygotsky has also made a considerable contribution to the discussion on learning and of how young children learn. He focused on the effects of society on children's learning and development. He criticised Piaget for apparently ignoring the context of situations and the cultural and historical factors that he believed affected children's learning.

Whereas Piaget was convinced that children learn as individual learners striving to make sense of their world, Vygotsky argued that only through interaction with adults and peers can we extend our experience. Children do not grow up in isolation and therefore the social groups in which they mix have an important effect upon their knowledge and understanding of the world. Like Bruner, Vygotsky believed that children would be able to attempt more complex tasks if they had some support from others. In his view, when a child carried out a task independently, for example building with Lego bricks, it was performing at an 'actual level of development', but with the help of an older child or that of an adult, the child's ability could be stretched and a more sophisticated model would be constructed. This he termed the zone of proximal development (ZPD), or the next area of development, which could only be achieved with the help and support of others.

The ZPD is the gap between what the child can do alone and what it can do with the help of others. For Vygotsky, adult interactions and the quality of those interactions were crucial, and he therefore argued in favour of co-operative or supported learning. Vygotsky, unlike Piaget, highlighted what children could do rather than what they could not do, starting from their own knowledge and building on it. Wood (1988) has pointed out that co-operatively achieved success lies at the foundations of learning and development. Co-operative learning is very important in play situations and by playing together and trying out new ideas and combinations of skills, children are able to come to understand many of the skills and behaviours that are expected of them by the adult world.

Leading on from the work of Vygotsky and his colleagues, the newer approaches to learning stress the importance of looking at the role of society and culture in children's learning. We have moved away from the traditional theories that focus on the individual in a decontextualised way. In the social cultural approach, development and learning are assumed to take place through the child's participation with others in activities that constitute daily life within the child's cultural community. This stress on the importance of the family and community in young children's learning is having an impact on early childhood programmes throughout the world.

References

Athey, C. (1990) *Extending Thought in Young Children: A parent–teacher partnership*, London: Paul Chapman Publishing.

Bandura, A. (1977a) *Social Learning Theory*, Englewood Cliffs, NJ: Prentice Hall.

Bruner, J. (1956) *Studies in Cognitive Growth*, New York: Wiley.

Cowan, N. (ed.) (1997) *The Development of Memory in Childhood*, Hove: Psychology Press.

Donaldson, M. (1978) *Children's Minds*, London: Fontana/Collins.

Gardner, H. (1983) *Frames of Mind: Theory of Multiple Intelligences*, New York: Basic Books.

Goleman, D. (1995) *Emotional Intelligence*, New York: Bantam.

Gunnar, M. R., Broderson, L. and Rigatus, R. (1996) 'Dampening of behavioural and adrenocortical reactivity during early infancy: normative changes and individual differences', in *Child Development* 67 (3): 877–89.

Kağitçibaşi, C. (1996) *Family and Human Development across Cultures*, New Jersey: Lawrence Erlbaum Associates.

Kolb, D. (1984) *Experiential Learning*, Englewood Cliffs, NJ: Prentice Hall/London: Paul Chapman.

Nutbrown, C. (1994) *Threads of Learning*, London: Paul Chapman Publishing Co.

Piaget, J. (1962) *Play, Dreams and Imitation in Childhood*, London: Routledge, Kegan and Paul.

Piaget, J. and Inhelder, B. (1969) *The Psychology of the Child*, New York: Basic Books.

Shore, R. (1996) *Rethinking the Brain*, New York: Families and Work Institute.

Terman, L. M. (1916) *The Measurement of Intelligence*, Boston: Houghton Mifflin.

Vygotsky, L. S. (1978) *Mind in Society*, Cambridge, Mass.: Harvard University Press.

Wood, D. (1988) *How Children Think and Learn*, Oxford: Blackwell.

CHAPTER 4

Communication and communication disorders

The first part of this chapter deals with the ways in which young children develop non-verbal and verbal communication skills and the factors that affect development. As most children who have communication disorders are now in mainstream education, the second part of this chapter includes a discussion of some of the more common language disorders that early years educators may meet during the course of their work.

Communication is the process by which messages are imparted and exchanged. It can take many forms, such as speech, writing, hand gestures and even objects such as traffic lights. From birth, babies try to communicate with others, at first through crying and using various body movements that are often difficult to interpret. As children grow older, they, like adults, use facial expressions (a smile, frown or eye contact) and body language to convey feelings. The type of body movement and gesture will vary according to the culture. Many of our movements are regulators, for example nodding to imply 'yes' or 'no', and these are often culturally based. Children and adults from different cultures need to understand how to interpret these so that they do not misread the signals.

Besides gestures and facial expressions there is also 'voice communication'. The way we use our voices can convey many different messages, for instance a shout, a whisper, a particular emphasis on a word or sentence are all effective ways of stressing the message. The intonations and nuances are frequently cultural and children have to learn the meaning of these messages.

What is language?

The one truly remarkable achievement that sets humans apart from the rest of the animal kingdom is our ability to use language. There is considerable evidence to show that animals can communicate with one another with a limited number of sounds and calls, but the adult human being is able to produce from a small number of individually meaningless sounds a vast number of words and messages. Language is creative and everyone who knows our language will be able to understand our ideas as long as we stick to the rules and conventions of the language we are speaking.

Languages are highly complex and abstract and yet children from all cultures come to understand this intricate form of communication, some long before they are able to walk.

How can this occur? Are all infants biologically programmed to acquire language? What relationship is there between a child's cooing, babbling and gesturing and the later production of meaningful words? How do infants come to attach meaning to words? Do all children in all cultures pass through the same stages in order to acquire their native language? What is the role of the adult in developing these language skills?

First of all let us consider what children have to know and understand before they can use language effectively. They need to know that there are four components to language: knowledge of phonology, semantics, syntax and pragmatics.

Language is a small number of individually meaningless symbols (sounds, letters and gestures) that can be combined according to agreed rules to produce an infinite number of messages.

Language development involves both listening and speaking. Listening is a receptive system that involves:

- the physical aspect of hearing;
- the attention of the learner;
- the ability to process auditory information.

Speaking is an expressive language system that involves:

- the production of speech sounds (phonology);
- the ability to produce meaningful sentences and use grammar rules;
- the ability to use speech for a range of purposes.

Researchers are agreed that in order to develop linguistic proficiency, four kinds of knowledge are required: *phonology*; *semantics*; *syntax*; and *pragmatics*.

Phonology. This is the sound system of a language and the rules for combining these sounds to produce meaningful units of speech. *Phonemes* is the name given to the basic units of sound that are used in a spoken language.

Each language uses only a small proportion of the sounds that a human being is capable of making. For example, the English language uses forty-five phonemes and no language uses more than sixty. Each language has rules for combining these phonemes and for pronouncing these combinations. For example, an English speaker would understand that it is permissible to begin a word with *st* (*stop, study*) or *sk* (*skull*) but not *sb* or *sg*. In other languages there are other acceptable combinations. Each child has to learn to discriminate the sounds acceptable to its mother tongue.

Semantics refers to the meanings expressed in words and sentences. The most basic meaningful units of language are called *morphemes*; they include words and grammatical markers such as the suffix *-ed* to denote the past tense and *s* indicate the plural noun. There are many suffixes and prefixes, which children learn about over time. Later in this section when we look at children's development of the past tense we shall see how this occurs.

Syntax is the structure of a language, the rules specifying how words and grammatical markers are to be combined to produce meaningful sentences.

Consider the following sentences:

The dog bit John.
John bit the dog.
The dog John bit.

Even very young speakers of English would recognise that the last sentence violates the rules of English, although this word order would be acceptable in some other languages. The first and second sentences, however, are grammatical although they convey different meanings.

An understanding of *pragmatics* is also necessary. Pragmatics is the term given to the principles that underlie the effective and appropriate use of language in a social context. Even very young children have to learn the pragmatics of language if they are to communicate effectively. For example, six-year-old Emma is trying to explain to her two-year-old sister how she wants her to play a game, and already knows that she has to adjust her speech if she wants to be understood.

Pragmatics also involves sociolinguistic knowledge, that is, knowledge about how you use language in a particular social context. A three-year-old may not yet have learnt that the best way of getting a sweet from Grandma is to say 'May I have a sweet, Grandma, please' rather than 'I want a sweet', but in a very short time the child will have learnt the strategy.

Besides the enormous task of coming to understand the necessary knowledge about pragmatics, phonology, semantics and syntax, the young child has to learn about the non-verbal communication that plays such an important part in our conversations. Young children hear what is said to them but do not read the accompanying body language. For example, a parent may have grumbled at a child for some misdemeanour, but his or her facial expression is not that of a very angry person even though their voice sounded cross. An older child or an adult would have read all the signals and understood the true message, that although her mother was cross, her eyes showed that she was not as angry as she sounded.

The following two tables summarise the main factors that affect language acquisition and development.

Table 4.1 *Factors affecting language acquisition*

Factors affecting language input

1   An environment in which language is spoken by competent speakers in a variety of communicative situations
2   An ability to hear spoken language

Factors affecting language processing

3   An ability to process the language heard and the context in which it takes place in order to 'make sense' of the information

Factors affecting language output

4   The ability to form units of spoken language with the organs of speech so that they can be understood by others

Table 4.2 *Factors affecting language development*

Factors affecting input

1   Environmental factors
    a   social circumstances
    b   bilingualism.
2   Sensory deprivation
    a   hearing loss
    b   visual problems

Factors affecting language processing

1   General cognitive deficiencies
2   Specific affective deficiencies (autism)
3   Specific language deficiencies

Factors affecting language output

1   Disorders of oro-motor control
2   Structural abnormalities

The pre-linguistic period

The period of a child's language development for the first ten to thirteen months of life is often termed the pre-linguistic period as this occurs before the child speaks its first meaningful words. However, that is not to say that children do not communicate before that time. They are responsive to language from the time they are born. Research has shown that by three days of age an infant already recognises the parent's voice and clearly prefers it to the voice of a stranger (Crystal 1986). By one month it has been found that children are as capable as adults at discriminating the consonant sounds such as 'ba' and 'pa' or 'da' and 'ta', and by two months of age the baby can discriminate certain vowel sounds.

All normal healthy babies are capable of vocalising at birth and they communicate in a predictable sequence. Neonates cry to signal distress and by three to five weeks of age babies begin to coo; a few weeks later babbling commences (usually between four and six months). This involves the baby making vocal/consonant combinations such as 'dada' or 'mama'. These may sound like words but are not used meaningfully even though proud parents believe the child is saying something recognisable. Early babbling worldwide is very similar, which makes researchers believe that it is influenced by maturation of the brain. However, environmental factors soon come into effect as by six to nine months deaf infants do not continue babbling. By eight months hearing babies have the ability to listen carefully to the adults around them and match the pitch and intonation of their babbles to the language they hear. They actually begin to sound as if they are speaking a language. Although children are born with the ability to make every sound required for any language, by listening to the language of the adults around them they practice the sounds they hear and gradually the other sounds are dropped from their repertoire. As this occurs, so the 'language' of the future English-speaking child will become different from the 'language' of the future Chinese-speaking child.

Even at this stage babies know about language and communication. For instance, during the first six months babies often coo or babble while their caregivers are speaking, but by seven to eight months they are generally silent when their companion speaks and will wait to respond until their partner has finished talking. At a very early age they have learnt turn taking. The game of 'Peek-a-boo', a firm favourite with many children and their caregivers, is an example of the way in which children learn to take turns in conversation. Moreover, by nine months the child will make noises or gestures to encourage the adult to continue the exchange if the adult fails to respond. The importance of this kind of interaction between children and adults will be drawn upon later in the chapter.

By eight to ten months the child is using gestures and other non-verbal responses to communicate. These are mainly of two kinds; declarative gestures, in which the child points or touches objects, and imperative gestures, in which the child tries to persuade others to carry out its wishes. For example, a child will tug at the leg of the caregiver and put up its hands in the hope of being picked up. It is at this age that adults can be deceived into thinking that a child understands particular words, when in reality the child obeys commands by correctly interpreting the speaker's non-verbal gestures. In the same way the child appears to understand the meaning of the word 'no' when in fact it is the intonation that the child has understood.

By the beginning of the second year the child is able to understand a great deal more than it can say. Receptive language is ahead of expressive language.

A breakthrough in children's language development comes once the child understands that words can be used as labels. For example, a young child has seen the dog in the house but not until the child realises that the word 'dog' refers to an actual object and is not just a meaningless sound does it have meaningful speech. This awareness is called referencing. The first stage of meaningful speech has been termed the *holophrastic* phase. This is the phase when children use one word to convey a sentence of meaning. For example, the child may say 'Ball', but this will convey a variety of meanings according to the context of the situation. It may mean 'give me the ball' or 'I have a ball' or 'throw the ball'.

Between eighteen and twenty-four months the child's vocabulary increases rapidly, anything from ten to forty words a week, the typical two-year-old possibly now having a vocabulary of around eighty words and understanding a great many more.

What types of words do children of this age use? Nelson (1973) studied the first fifty words of eighteen children and found that 65 per cent of utterances were object words. Referring to unique objects like Mummy or Katy, or to classes of objects like 'doggie', 'car', 'man'. Action words like go, bye-bye and up were used 13 per cent of the time, while 9 per cent of the children's utterances referred to what she termed modifiers, that is words that refer to the property or quantity of things like 'mine', 'bit', 'hot'. Personal and social words like 'no', 'please' 'ta' accounted for 8 per cent of the language while the remaining language referred to function words, i.e. words that have a grammatical function like 'what', 'for' and 'where'.

Telegraphic speech

Around eighteen to twenty-four months children begin to combine words and produce simple sentences such as 'daddy go', 'mummy milk', 'no car'. These early sentences are called *telegraphic speech* because they contain only the critical content words – nouns, verbs and adjectives – and leave out the less-meaningful parts of speech, for example prepositions, pronouns, auxiliary verbs. Although it is not grammatical to say 'no wet', the meaning is clear. This development of spontaneous two-word utterances has been found to occur in other languages, such as German, Finnish and Samoan. However, it is not universal as researchers (De Villiers and De Villiers 1992) have found that Russian and Turkish children use short, reasonably grammatical sentences from the very beginning.

It is interesting that although these early sentences are incomplete, they are always in the correct word order of the language being learnt.

Some examples of two-word utterances are:

to locate or name	'there book'
to demand	'more milk'
to negate	'no go', 'no wet'
to indicate possession	'my shoe'
to modify/qualify	'big dog'
to question	'where ball'

Language development from two to five years

During the period between the ages of two-and-a-half to five years, children make enormous strides in language development. They not only increase their vocabulary at a rapid rate but they also master basic syntax. They develop the use of morphemes, modifiers that give more precise meaning to the sentence. It is these that indicate whether the word is singular ('book') or plural ('books') or whether the verb is in the present or the past tense ('help' or 'helped').

Acquisition of English morphemes

Morpheme	*Example*
Present possessive *-ing*	She is sitt*ing* down.
Preposition 'in'	The doll is *in* the box.
Preposition 'on'	The book is *on* the table.
Plural *-s*	The boys ran away.
Past irregular, e.g. 'went'	The girl *went* home.
Possessive *-s*	The girl'*s* trousers are blue.
Uncontractible copula 'be', e.g. 'are'/'was'	*Are* they houses?
	Was that daddy?
Articles 'the', 'a'	He has *a* toy
Past regular *-ed*	He jump*ed* the stream
Third person regular *-s*	She run*s* fast
Third person irregular, e.g. 'has', 'does'	*Does* she play?
Uncontractible copula 'be' e.g. 'is'/'were'	*Is* he running?
	Were they in the garden?
Contractible copula 'be' e.g. -'s, 're	That'*s* a man.
Contractible auxiliary 'be' e.g. -'s, 're	They'*re* running fast.

Overgeneralisations

Around the age of three years, many children begin to make apparent mistakes in their grammar as they overgeneralise. For example they have come to understand that one adds an '-ed' ending to make the regular past tense and may use this rule inappropriately: they may say 'I runned' or 'I goed' when a few months earlier they had been using the correct grammatical form. This is not a sign that they are regressing but rather evidence that they have learnt a new grammatical principle and are applying it creatively to their language. In the beginning they had imitated words correctly; now they are using their newly found knowledge. Children continue to make these 'mistakes' well into primary school and although the adult may model the correct form, the child will ignore the correction. It is interesting that a child who can read and understand that the past tense of the verb 'fight' is 'fought' will continue to use 'fighted' in general conversation.

Asking questions

There are two basic kinds of questions – yes/no questions and the *wh-* questions. The simpler yes/no questions are the first to develop. Initially the child indicates a question merely by a change in intonation. Sometimes *wh-* words are placed at the beginning of telegraphic sentences, such as 'Where Mummy?'

The second phase of question form is when the child asks 'What Daddy is eating?' Finally the child realises that it has to transform the words and ask 'What is Daddy eating?'

'What', 'where' and 'who' questions come long before 'why', 'when' and 'how'. This is probably because the first category involves referring to concrete things, whereas the second involves abstract concepts such as cause and effect, and time – concepts that are not normally used by children under the age of four to five years.

Negative sentences

Just as questions develop gradually, so do children's negative sentences. In the beginning children simply place the word 'no' in front of the word, for example 'no go' or 'no sock'. Gradually children begin to extend such sentences using phrases like 'I not wear mitten'. By the age of four most children can negate sentences in the same way as adults 'I am not wearing the shoes.'

Gradually children develop complex sentences, first by joining two simple sentences with 'and', and then producing embedded sentences with clauses. By the end of this period most children are using all the grammatical rules of their language and are speaking very much like adults. However, they still have difficulties in interpreting the passive tense. Here is an example of an active sentence followed by its passive form:

The girl hit the boy.
The boy was hit by the girl.

Most young children will understand the second sentence to mean that the boy hit the girl, not the girl hit the boy.

Conversational skills continue to develop and by the age of five most children are good communicators and spend the next few years refining their use of language and using it for more complex tasks like reading, writing and hypothesising. In the next two or three years children begin to develop metalinguistic awareness, that is, the ability to think about what they say. One way in which this ability manifests itself is when children begin to play with words and make up nonsense words for fun. Children come to realise that language can be used for purposes other than communicating. There is evidence to suggest that during communication they take into account the sociolinguistic understanding required to make the right kind of speech adjustments so that the message is clear for the listener. Children also become better listeners.

However, although many children reach a high level of language development by the time they enter school, there are many individual differences and a lot of children may still have immature speech and language development.

Speech acts

As children grow up they have to learn to 'read' the linguistic strategies that adults use in general conversation. So often we use expressions and language that we do not expect to be taken literally.

These utterances where we expect the listener to 'read between the lines' are termed speech acts. The child has to interpret the underlying meaning of the statement. For example, a child asks its parent for a sweet and instead of being told 'no', the parent replies that 'it is nearly tea time'. The child has to reconcile the question and response and realise the intent of its parent's answer.

An adult may say to a child, 'there are stains on the carpet'. The child replies 'yes' and is surprised then to be told, 'Don't just say yes, tell me how it happened.' The child had responded to the comment but had not taken on board the full implication of the statement.

Most children have been exposed to examples of this type of utterance from an early age and know how to respond, but for some children who have not been exposed to this form of dialogue at home, it can lead to genuine misunderstanding if they meet such statements or questions at school. This type of language presents particular difficulties for second-language learners who are not aware of the cultural implications of the statements.

Young children can also be confused by the different meanings of a word. Perhaps the most famous example is that quoted by Laurie Lee in *Cider with Rosie* where on his first day at school he is told by the teacher to 'wait there for the present'. The unhappy five-year-old went home and complained to his mother that the teacher had not given him the promised present.

All people who work with young children can recall instances in which their use of language has led to misunderstandings, and with second-language learners it is imperative that we use unambiguous language and express ourselves clearly.

Relationship between language and thought

The development of language and thought are closely linked but there has been a great deal of discussion among psychologists as to whether we can think without words. Piaget (1959) argued that language is only one of several possible ways in which children can represent their knowledge. For him thought is a precursor to language, it is a symbolic system that can be used to express our thoughts and experiences. This belief that thought precedes language led Piaget to the idea that the language that children use will reflect their cognitive development. However, other psychologists such as Vygotsky argued that although thinking and language occur together, they do not necessarily have the same origins. He argued that thinking is a cognitive activity that arises as children learn about their world. Language develops because infants hear it around them from their caregivers and other children and adults. Vygotsky believed that at around two years of age there is a crucial moment when the two areas of pre-linguistic thought and pre-intellectual language join together. For him, 'thought becomes verbal and speech rational' (Vygotsky 1962). From now on language has two different functions for the child, an internal function that directs internal thought and an external social function to do with communicating with other people.

For the adult, language has two different functions: inner speech, which we use to monitor our thinking, and the communicative function for speaking or writing. Vygotsky says that young children also use what he terms egocentric speech, when they express their thoughts and ideas out loud without any reference to a listener. Children talk to themselves to organise their thinking, express their feelings or regulate their behaviour. This egocentric speech normally fades as children grow older and they can internalise their thinking more effectively, although, as we know, adults talk to themselves on occasions.

Theories of language development

As we have seen, most children by the time they enter the reception class have an understanding of the grammatical structures of their native language without ever having had a grammar lesson. Psycholinguists and psychologists have raised the question of how this occurs. Is language learned or is it innate? This was one of the controversies of the twentieth century and the debate still continues.

Learning-theory approach

Imitation and reinforcement are the key factors in this approach to language development. The leading exponent of this approach is Skinner, who argued that children learn by imitating adults, who shape the child's language by selectively reinforcing the sounds that sound most like speech. During conversations with adults the baby's babble is expanded into words and the child then imitates the sounds it hears. The child is then praised for its efforts (reinforced) and so makes the sounds again. Other learning theorists, such as Bandura, also believed that children gain most of their linguistic knowledge by carefully listening to and imitating the speech of others.

There are problems with this approach. Imitation plays an important part in children's learning but, as research has indicated, if children are not ready to have their grammatical structures shaped then no amount of disapproval will have any effect. If a young child is telling you that he/she 'sawed a bird', no amount of correction will persuade the child to say 'saw a bird' until he/she has developed and internalised the appropriate linguistic rules. Furthermore, the majority of parents do not correct grammatical errors but will correct statements which involve falsehoods. For example: 'We sawed a bird this morning.' 'No, we saw a bird in the garden *yesterday* morning.' Skinner's approach may help to explain how children increase single words in their vocabulary but it does not explain the complex original sentences that children generate in such a short time.

Nativist approach

In 1965 Chomsky challenged the behaviourist view of language development and demonstrated that children can generate new sentences that they have definitely not heard before. He argued that children were born with an innate Language Acquisition Device (LAD) that enables them to structure their language. It provides what Aitchison (1996) terms a 'blueprint for language'. Children learn to talk partly because they are born with this device and partly through the people they meet. It is an innate ability, but requires humans to trigger the process. Researchers studied the errors made by children and found that these gave them important clues about the development of language. However, in 1986 Chomsky abandoned his earlier viewpoint, arguing that this did not account for how children acquired the full grammar of their language with such little information to work on. He now assumes that children are born with a two-tier system of language that is independent of other cognitive abilities. Children are born with a set of language principles and they learn to 'set switches' to the language to which they are exposed in order to acquire further aspects of language.

There is support for this theory as there seems to be a sensitive period during which children can learn language more easily. Studies with children deprived of human contact at an early age, for example the Wild Boy of Averyon and, more recently, the twins in America, show that there is a crucial time for language development. Support for the sensitive-period hypothesis, postulated by Lenneberg (1967), also comes from brain-injured children who were found to recover their language almost completely if the accident occurred before the onset of puberty. According to the nativists the sensitive period for language learning is a product of biological maturation.

Recent research has not borne out all the ideas of Chomsky but it seems that there is evidence to show that children seem to be equipped with some sort of innate linguistic device that helps them to extract language from the jumble of sounds around them. As Aitchison writes:

> They have relatively little knowledge about the actual *form* of the language, but seem instead to have a remarkable ability for processing linguistic data. We are still a long way from specifying exactly how the operating principles work. And we do not know how children backtrack in order to correct their wrong assumptions. This is still quite puzzling, since they seem to be impervious to corrections by other people.
>
> (Aitchison 1996: 265)

Therefore, the nativist approach alone does not seem to provide an adequate explanation of how children learn their language.

Social-interactionist approach

Neither learning theory nor the nativist approach is able to provide a complete answer to language development. In recent years cognitive theorists including Piaget, Vygotsky and Bruner have argued that biological factors, cognitive factors and the linguistic environment interact to affect the development of children's language. According to interactionist theory children all over the world may talk alike because they are members of the same species who share common experiences. Bates (1993) has suggested that what is innate is not a special language mechanism but a sophisticated brain that matures very slowly and predisposes children to develop similar ideas around the same age. They then express the ideas in their own speech.

Advocates of the interactionist approach place a general focus upon general cognitive development as well as the social and communicative factors that promote language learning. For advocates of this approach, other humans, older children as well as adults, contribute to children's understanding by the way in which they tailor the level of language to the child's needs.

Social factors affecting language

Although the vast majority of children develop language, some children enter school with a wider vocabulary, and speaking in more complex sentences, than others. Research by Bernstein in the UK and many others in the USA argued that children from working-class homes were disadvantaged because they used what has been termed a *restricted language code*, which held them back at school. By contrast, children from middle-class homes used what Bernstein termed an *elaborated code*, which enabled them to achieve more in school. However, as Labov (1969) and others showed, these children were not impoverished in their language; rather they used a non-standard English that was rich, varied and grammatical. To be fair to Bernstein, he did not say that the children from lower socio-economic groups had impoverished language, rather that children who did not speak standard English were likely to be disadvantaged in schools where standard English was required.

This view has been taken more recently by researchers who have realised that the problems are more likely to reflect the failure of the schools to recognise that staff may come from different cultures and backgrounds and therefore may not value and respect the language and culture of the children. Furthermore, research by Gordon Wells (1986) has shown that there is no evidence to support the assumption that there is 'verbal deprivation' in families of lower socio-economic status. He has shown that the problem lies in the fact that teachers do not have real everyday conversations with children, talking about what is of interest to the child. When they do, the teachers would find that many 'disadvantaged' children are able to produce a great deal of language. Children have substantially different sets of communication skills at home and at school.

Dialects

Children growing up in different areas of a country will speak differently from one another. Sometimes these differences are just in the way they pronounce words, the accent. For example, children in London will speak with a different accent from children in Glasgow or Liverpool. However, people throughout the country also speak with different dialects; in other words, not only is the pronunciation different, but the actual words and grammar are different. Many people in the south-east of England speak with a standard English dialect; this is the dialect used mostly on television and radio. However, in Scotland and parts of the north-east of England people may use different words. For example, the word 'bairn' is used rather than 'child'. This is not standard English, but it is not wrong.

It is important to realise that children who do not speak in a standard dialect do not have an incorrect or impoverished language. Yet one of the problems that these children may encounter in school is the prejudice of teachers who use only a standard dialect and view the children's grammar, in particular, as wrong.

Bilingualism/multilingualism

For the majority of the world's population the ability to speak two or more languages fluently is normal. Only in countries with a very powerful first language, such as English, French or Spanish, do people tend to be monolingual, that is, speak only one language.

Until the 1960s, linguists from monolingual societies considered that learning two languages rather than one hindered a child's language proficiency or slowed intellectual development. This research has been shown to be flawed. Contrary to popular belief, learning two or more languages rather than one neither hinders a child's language proficiencies nor retards a child's intellectual growth. Recent research shows that there are cognitive advantages to bilingualism.

Later research shows that children exposed to two languages before the age of three have little difficulty in becoming proficient in both. They occasionally mixed phonologies and sometimes applied the grammar and vocabulary of one language to the second language being acquired, but by the age of three they were aware that the two languages had independent systems and were used in different contexts and situations. By the age of four they displayed normal language proficiencies in the language of their community and solid to excellent linguistic skills in the second language, depending on how much they had been exposed to it. Research has also shown that children who do not acquire a second language until after the age of three, when they already have a first language, can often become near native speakers of the new language within a year.

There are many advantages to children of being bilingual/multilingual:

- they learn about the culture that is linked to the language;
- they can think in different ways about the same thing, for example in Arabic there are many more words for sand than in English, so children can think about sand in greater detail;
- they grow with an understanding of two or more cultures, which should help them to be more tolerant of others;
- they can think more divergently.

Role of the adult in children's language development

From birth, the adult has an important role in the child's language development. It is from the adult, or another child, that the baby hears the language of its environment. It is through hearing that language that the early babbles and coos become language specific and the baby practises the sounds that are part of its mother tongue.

As introduced earlier in the chapter, the caretaker will play games like 'Peek-a-boo' with the child, helping to develop an understanding of *turn taking* and its importance in conversation. In responding to the baby's cries and gestures, the adult is helping the baby to understand about communication.

Adults support the early language of children in a number of ways. One way is by *expansion of utterances*. When the baby utters a word such as 'milk' it is the adult who puts the statement into context and who responds by saying, for example, 'You want some milk?', 'Here is the milk' or 'You have finished your milk'. As the child progresses to two-word sentences, the adult will continue to expand and extend the language so that the child is exposed to new grammatical structures. At the same time, the language used by the adult tends to be simplified, slow and involve a lot of repetition. This has been termed *caretaker* language. Although it is used in many cultures, the approach is by no means universal as in some cultures the babies are rarely spoken to directly until they are able to respond. Even quite young children will modify their language to an even simpler form when they are talking to a baby.

Adults also help children in both their language and cognitive development when they accompany their language with actions. For example, the caretaker on lifting the baby out of the high chair, may always say 'up we go'. As children grow more competent in language they still need actions to accompany language as in this way they come to understand language more fully. Activities are often accompanied by a running commentary, such as 'Are we going to make those cakes? Are you going to help me put the mixture into the cake tin?' When adults respond to children they will use correct grammatical structures, although normally any correction of the child's language is factual, not grammatical. For example, if the child makes a factually incorrect statement the adult will probably correct it, whereas a grammatical error will not be corrected.

It is through language that we transmit our culture, values and mores. An important role of the adult is to read and tell children the stories and rhymes that reflect the values and customs of society. It is also important that children engage in conversations with adults and their peers, but adults need to remember to talk 'with' not 'at' the child. Bruner refers to the adult as providing the 'scaffolding' for the child. Adults teach children turn-taking skills but, sadly, as the children grow older, many adults seem to want an extended turn, forgetting that conversations should be two-way. Children are expected to listen and not given the opportunity to put forward their own points of view.

Some ways of fostering language development are to:

- give children something to talk about;
- be prepared to listen to the children;
- tell stories, rhymes and poems;
- help children to understand the world around them;
- engage in genuine dialogue;
- wait for a response – small children often take time to organise their responses;
- help children to express their feelings;
- help children to organise their ideas;
- help children to turn take.

Communication disorders

Any discussion on the concept of delayed language development depends upon an understanding of normal language development. We have already seen that the usual pattern of language acquisition is complete by the age of five years and those children who are late talkers usually catch up by that time if they are exposed to a lot of language. However, if this does not occur and other aspects of development are normal then something needs to be done.

Although it is not possible to provide detailed specialist knowledge in this chapter, listed below is some information about several of the syndromes associated with language impairment in childhood that practitioners working with children from birth to seven years may encounter.

Abuse and neglect

It has been suggested (Westcott and Cross 1996) that children with delayed speech and language development are more at risk of abuse and neglect than their speaking peers as their inability to communicate their experiences makes them more vulnerable to abuse. Frequently, these children also have learning disabilities and as a result may not realise that they are being abused. Lees and Urwin (1997) have argued that there is a cyclical relationship between abuse and communication impairment.

Angleman syndrome

This condition is sometimes described as the 'happy puppet syndrome', as children who suffer from it have marionette-like facial expressions and movements. These children do not develop normal language. There are relatively few children who suffer from this syndrome and although they should attend special schools, there is a possibility that they may be placed in a nursery school in the first instance.

Asperger's syndrome

First described by Asperger in 1943 as an 'autistic psychopathy', this syndrome is classified in the range of autistic disorders. Children who suffer from it are severely impaired in their social skills and generally develop an all-absorbing, narrow, repetitive interest that is carried on to the exclusion of all other activities. The child has very poor motor co-ordination, resulting in clumsiness as well as communication problems. Frequently the child will have developed single words by the age of two and communicative phrases by three; in other words, superficial normal language development. Experts disagree as to the amount of language these children will eventually acquire.

Autism

First described by Kanner in 1943, this disorder has been the subject of considerable research following discussion about its possible connection with the MMR injections.

Children with this syndrome manifest:

- impairment of social interaction – aloofness or indifference;
- impairment of imagination and inability to play imaginatively with objects or toys or with other children or adults;
- repetitive stereotyped activities, for example rocking, flicking to no purpose (also sometimes an insistence on lengthy routines and a fascination with certain topics);
- lack of understanding of language use – although they may acquire a good vocabulary;
- literal comprehension and difficulty with non-verbal communication, including gestures and facial expressions;
- impairment of social communication, sometimes also accompanied by immaturity of grammatical structures and abnormal features such as echolalia (echoing phrases);
- sometimes a total non-development of language.

Cerebral palsy

This is a disorder of movement and posture caused by a defect in the immature brain. This affects the ability to produce speech and, in severe cerebral palsy, there may be a significant gap between receptive and expressive language abilities, with comprehension being well developed but with little or no ability to produce speech because of severe motor difficulties.

Cleft palate

Clefts of the palate and lip are among the most common abnormalities and occur in approximately one in a thousand live births. Early surgery is normally carried out but even then speech production difficulties may persist. However, the prognosis for most children is good.

Down's syndrome

This is a chromosome disorder affecting approximately one in eight-hundred live births. It is a common cause of severe learning difficulties. Speech and language development is usually delayed to between two and four years for first words, the amount of further language development varying from child to child. Some children suffering from Down's syndrome may be able to function satisfactorily in the nursery and the lower end of the primary school.

Muscular dystrophy

This title is given to a group of disorders associated with progressive degeneration of muscles. Delayed language development can occur.

Otitis media

This condition, inflammation of the middle ear, is very common among children and is the most common cause of conductive hearing loss. Some children have frequent bouts of otitis media, which, if not dealt with promptly, can cause difficulties with expressive language. Auditory perception and comprehension skills are also affected and can present difficulties in learning to read.

Dyslexia

Dyslexia is probably the most common communication disorder. Every school will have children suffering from dyslexia in its classes every year, who will need specialised attention if they are not to experience later school failure. There has been a great deal of discussion about the topic and in spite of evidence there are still those who regard it as a middle-class syndrome and a useful cover-up for 'lazy children'. Watch a child who has this difficulty and you will soon appreciate that this is a child who is experiencing a learning disability. If not dealt with at an early stage, dyslexia can result in failure to gain competence in literacy, with the result that the child has a very real handicap in today's society.

What is dyslexia? The term dyslexia comes from the Greek and literally means 'difficulty with' (*dys*) 'words' (*lexis*). It refers to difficulties with words read, spelled, pronounced, written, and also to the association of meaning with words. Not every child experiences all these disorders and they will be found in varying degrees of difficulty, but it is a syndrome that cuts across class, age and intelligence. Children with this syndrome may also be referred to having a 'specific learning disability' or being 'learning disabled'.

Many teachers are loathe to identify children with these terms as they feel that by labelling a child they are drawing attention to the disability. On the other hand, speech and language experts argue that it helps these children to understand why they are not keeping up with their peers. Children need to understand that there are some things that we are good at and some things we have difficulty with and that dyslexic children like themselves simply have difficulties with reading and spelling. They need to understand that they can begin to get on top of the problem with help, *if* they work hard. Most teachers find that with hope and help, children are willing to work hard.

What are some of the characteristics of dyslexia and how do they affect learning?

Poor visual recall. Many children have poor visual memories and are unable to recall a word, even if they see it again and again on the same page. This is particularly disastrous if their introduction to reading is through the 'look and say' method instead of one that involves recognising the words that have to be decoded. Spelling also presents a challenge when there is little or no visual recall, particularly if accompanied by a lack of knowledge of phonics and language structure, as the children affected have no idea of what to write. Likewise, both handwriting and numeracy will be affected as without an image of the letters/numbers it is impossible to know how to form these letters or numbers.

Phonological difficulty. This is a difficulty with building up an awareness of speech sounds and linking them to the written word. This makes a phonic approach to reading inappropriate.

Sequencing. Some children suffering from dyslexia experience difficulties with sequencing, not only with letters and numbers, which they write in the wrong order (for example, string may be spelled as 'stirng', or the date 1476 may be copied as '1764'), but also with days of the week and months of the year. The ability to sequence verbal and symbolic material correctly is a crucial skill. Although many people may have minor problems with sequencing, for example knowing the difference between right and left when map reading, the difficulties of the dyslexic leaves them in great confusion, often resulting in a great deal of loss of self-confidence and self-esteem. Imagine the child who cannot sequence the days of the week. This child will not know which day of the week it is when waking up each morning. Children need good directional awareness and need to understand that in our culture we read from left to right; for those with sequencing problems these skills are difficult to acquire.

Orientation. Spatial relationships are particularly difficult, for two possible reasons. Language-based difficulties may lead to an inability to understand such words as 'left' and 'right' or 'further' and 'nearer' and, for a more severely affected group, it is possible to be totally confused in both time and space. Our sympathy and support is certainly needed for this small disadvantaged group of children.

Learning difficulties. These may well be aggravated by ear infections and high- and low-frequency hearing losses that make it difficult for a child to hear properly. Likewise, a child may have eye defects that can affect progress in reading. Visual defects can affect reading, writing and spelling. Eye and ear problems may be the cause of reading difficulties for non-dyslexic children, but they are additional factors with which the dyslexic child has to contend.

Poor visual and auditory memories. A dyslexic child may experience these as the result of an inability to form a mental image or retain a sequence of words or numbers. For the dyslexic child, learning must be multi-sensory and the programmes offered should use auditory, visual, olfactory and tactile senses.

Language processing. It is generally accepted that dyslexic children have a weakness in language processing. Many have difficulties in understanding simple questions such as 'What is this colour?', even though they can match and sort colours accurately. These children also have difficulties with understanding time and with verb tenses. For example, a seven- or eight-year-old child may say 'I have done it soon' or 'I will do it yesterday', long after its peers have sorted out issues of time and tense.

Dyslexic children may continue long after other children to take idioms and expressions literally. For example, a nine-year-old dyslexic child, when asked by a parent to 'give me a hand', will offer the parent an actual hand and not appreciate was really being asked.

There are two types of language-processing difficulties: those of expressive language and receptive language. Expressive language difficulty results in the individual having problems putting thought into words, while the person with a receptive language difficulty is unable to follow adequately the language of others. Some children and adults may have both an expressive and a receptive language difficulty.

It is not always recognised that speech and language processing are a problem for some children and adults, as often speech problems are only considered if articulation is poor. The more subtle difficulties of expressive and receptive speech and language are often overlooked, particularly as the child may have developed some early ability to read, even though there is little or no progress beyond this basic level.

For some children, dyslexia is associated *with Attention Deficit Disorder* (ADD) or *Attention Deficit Hyperactivity Disorder* (ADHD), the main characteristics of which are:

- inattention (poor concentration);
- impulsivity;
- hyperactivity (restlessness).

Speech and language specialists warn that it is important that before children are labelled ADD or ADHD, the symptoms are of at least six months' standing and have been evident since childhood. There must not be any evidence of any other significant disorder. There is evidence that a number of children grow out of these symptoms at puberty.

Again, as with the label of 'dyslexia', parents and teachers are often relieved that their child is not just being 'naughty' but that there is a recognisable difficulty. One of the problems that parents have to deal with is that although medication such as Ritalin can be given to children to increase concentration and decrease hyperactivity, this does nothing to remediate the learning difficulties or normalise behaviour. One of the most effective ways of helping these children is to ensure that affected children are given as few distractions as possible.

Dyspraxia is another form of communication difficulty that affects dyslexic children. Here the child has difficulty with the acquisition of patterns of movement. This can affect not only speech and language but also eye/hand co-ordination, especially handwriting and organisation. Such children do not necessarily have difficulties with reading and spelling, but with physical activities, including handwriting, and will probably be labelled 'clumsy'. Some research has indicated that the incidence of clumsiness occurs in as much as 5 per cent of the population.

Poor motor control will lead to poor handwriting and for these children when they are writing under stress it will deteriorate even more. The advent of the computer in the classroom was a boon for such children, as they can now produce a piece of work of which they can be proud.

Reading is part of the total language process so it is no surprise that a child who has difficulties with speech and language will also have trouble with learning to read, since reading involves:

- recognition and recall of the letter shapes;
- linkage of these shapes to sounds/words;
- understanding the meaning of these shapes and sounds.

These three areas are identified as potential hazards for children suffering from the dyslexic syndrome. However, most dyslexic children eventually learn to read but may require a very different multi-sensory approach rather than the traditional 'look and say' or phonic approaches. Teachers need to use any method that works. As a former teacher who worked with children with reading difficulties, I know that it is necessary to use any method that will support the affected child. It is probable that many dyslexics will need supporting throughout life with reading as they will always read slowly, even when they have mastered the basic level.

Spelling has always been given less prominence than reading although the National Curriculum is now placing a greater emphasis upon the subject. It is possible for some children to learn to read and yet be unable to spell as they lack the necessary ability to recall the words visually. For these children a multi-sensory approach to spelling may be helpful.

Research has suggested that about 40 per cent of dyslexic children have difficulties with mathematics, reading and spelling, and most of these children quickly learn to feel school failures. Many are highly intelligent and it requires a lot of skill and support from both parents and the school to ensure that these children develop a positive self-image and realise early that the problems they have are not due to laziness or stupidity.

The best prognosis for children suffering from dyslexia and/or ADD and dyspraxia is early intervention and the positive support and understanding of parents and teachers.

Language delay

Another group of children who will need specialist attention in the classroom are the hearing impaired. A child who has a hearing impairment may experience language delay, although talking and listening can be done through signs and the British Sign Language is now officially recognised as a language. Both British Sign Language and Makaton involve gestures and touch and agreed shared signs and finger spelling with computers and keyboards. Hearing-impaired children benefit from mixing with children and adults who can speak fluently so that they can hear and learn the appropriate patterns of language.

There are some children who through choice do not speak. Generally this is caused by emotional difficulties. Some will elect to be mute at school even though they talk at home; others do not speak in any situation. It is important for children who do not speak to be able to hear and understand the language around them. The educator needs to continue to talk to them as though nothing were amiss, and eventually most children will begin to talk in the classroom once they have overcome their emotional difficulties.

The ability to communicate effectively is a highly important skill. Without language, which is the basis of most of our communication, the child will find it very difficult to learn in school. In this chapter the development of language has been looked at in some detail in the hope that it will help educators to understand the processes involved in the acquisition of language so that they can identify early any difficulties in the young children in their care.

Appendix 1

Some useful addresses

Below are listed the names and addresses of various organisations concerned with children with specific educational needs. This information is accurate at time of going to press.

National Autistic Society
Willesden Lane
London NW2 5RB
Office 020 7833 2299
Website address: www.nas.org.uk

Association for Brain Damaged
    Children
Clifton House
3 St Paul's Road
Foleshill
Coventry CV6 5DE
024 7666 5450

Scope (Cerebral Palsy)
6 Market Road
London N7 9PW
Office 020 7619 7100
Helpline 0808 800 3333
Website address: www.scope.org.uk

National Deaf Children's Society
15 Dufferin Street
London EC1Y 8PD
Family Helpline 0808 800 8880
Website address: www.ndcs.org.uk

Down's Syndrome Association
153 Mitcham Road
London SW17 9PG
020 8682 4001
Website address:
www.downssyndrome.org.uk

British Dyslexia Association
98 London Road
Reading
Berkshire RG1 5AU
0118 966 8277
Helpline 0118 966 8271
Website address:
www.bda-dyslexia.org.uk

Dyspraxia Foundation
8 West Alley
Hitchin
Herts SG5 1EG
Helpline 01462 454986
Website address:
www.dyspraxiafoundation.org.uk

Royal Society for Mentally
 Handicapped Children and Adults
 (MENCAP)
National Centre
123 Golden Lane
London EC1Y 0RT
020 7454 0454
Website address: www.mencap.org.uk

Association for All Speech Impaired
 Children (AFASIC)
69 Old Street
London EC1
Helpline 020 7490 9410
Website address: www.afasic.org.uk

Professional organisations

The Royal College of Speech and
 Language Therapists
2 White Hart Yard
London SE1 1NX
020 7378 1200
Website address: www.rcslt.org

The Chartered Society of
 Physiotherapy
14 Bedford Row
London WC1R 4ED
020 7242 1941
website address: www.csp.org.uk

The National Portage Association
127 Monksdale
Yeovil
Somerset BA21 3JE
01935 471641
Website address: www.portage.org.uk

The Association of Educational
 Psychologists
26 The Avenue
Durham DH1 4ED
0191 3849512
Website address: www.aep.org.uk

British Association of Teachers of
 the Deaf
Paul A. Simpson
21 The Haystacks
High Wycombe
Bucks HP13 6PY
01494 464190
website address:
www.rmplc.co.uk/orgs/batod

References

Aitchison, J. (1996) *The Articulate Mammal*, third edition, London: Routledge.
Bates, E. (1993) *Nature, Nurture and Language*, New Orleans Society for Research in Child Development.
Bernstein, B. (1972) 'Social Class, Language and Socialisation', in P. P. Giglioli (ed.), *Language and Social Context*, Harmondsworth: Penguin.
Chomsky, N. (1965) *Aspects of the Theory of Syntax*, Cambridge, Mass.: MIT Press.

Chomsky, N. (1986) *Knowledge of Language in Nature, Origin and Use*, New York: Praeger.

Crystal, D. (1986) *Listen to Your Child*, Harmondsworth: Penguin.

de Villiers, J. G. and de Villiers, P. A. (1992) 'Language Development', in M. H. Bornstein and M. E. Lamb (eds), *Developmental Psychology: An advanced handbook*, Hillsdale, NJ: Erlbaum.

Kanner, L. (1943) 'Autistic disturbances of affective contact', in *The Nervous Child*, 2: 217–50.

Labov, W. (1969) 'The logic of non-standard English', reprinted in P. Giglioli (ed.), *Language and Social Context*, Harmondsworth: Penguin.

Lees, J. and Urwin, S. (1997) *Children With Language Disorders*, second edition, London: Whurr Publishers.

Lenneberg, E. H. (1967) *Biological Foundations of Language*, New York: Wiley.

Nelson, K. (1973) *Structure and Strategy in Learning to Talk*, monograph of Society for Research in Child Development 38.

Piaget, J. and Inhelder, B. (1969) *The Psychology of the Child*, London: Routledge & Kegan Paul.

Pinker, S. (2000) *The Language Instinct*, Harmondsworth: Penguin.

Vygotsky, L. S. (1962) *Thought and Language*, Cambridge, Mass.: MIT Press.

Wells, G. (1986) *The Meaning Makers: Children learning language and using language to learn*, London: Hodder and Stoughton

Westcott, H. and Cross, M. (1996) *This Far and No Further: Towards ending the abuse of disabled children*, Birmingham: Venture Press.

CHAPTER 5

Working with the under threes

The first three years of life is a time of rapid growth and development for young children and therefore proves to be exciting and challenging for the child care worker or carer. Gopnik, Meltzoff and Kuhl (1999) state that babies have the best technical support for learning as the adults around them are able to play a powerful role in their development. Therefore, anyone who is envisaging working with this age group needs to realise the importance of this role in the children's development.

The Carnegie Task Force Report (1994) highlights the first three years of life as being the foundation upon which other learning will be built. Goldschmeid and Jackson (1994) refer to 'people under three' in order to reinforce the concept that zero- to three-year-olds are not just 'empty vessels' waiting for adults to 'fill them' but are people in their own right.

Historically, this has not always been the case as babies were swaddled into inactivity and left to sleep and eat, stimulation and play not being viewed as part of a child's development. One of the most comprehensive accounts of how babies were viewed by society and treated over time can be found in Christine Hardyment's book *Dream Babies: child care from Locke to Spock* (1984). One of the most popular texts on babies that did not stem from the religious or medical world was Jean Jacques Rousseau's *Emile, ou L'Education* (1762). Rousseau followed the belief that children were born 'free, natural and innocent' and should not be swaddled but left free to move and play, whereas Locke was of the opinion that babies' minds were a 'blank sheet' (*tabula rasa*) and that it was the responsibility of the adult to 'write' upon this sheet.

Piaget (1952) thought that babies' minds assimilated information in the same way as their bodies assimilated milk, whereas Vygotsky viewed the adult influence on children's minds as part of human nature and stressed the role of language on this area of development. Modern technology such as the video has enabled developmental psychologists to study babies' non-verbal behaviour in order to analyse facial expressions, eye movements and other features. As a result of this there is much more research in the field of developmental psychology being carried out on babies and very young children, all in the hope that adults will have a greater understanding of how young children's minds develop.

Physiological development of the brain

As previously stated, babies are not born with a brain that is like an 'empty vessel' or a 'blank sheet' just waiting for the adult to 'fill it up' or 'write upon it'. The baby's brain, as other parts of the body, grows and develops through the nine months of pregnancy. Brain cells begin to form as early as three weeks after conception and multiply at a rapid rate, continuing up until one year after birth. A great deal of foetal development of the brain depends upon the genetic make-up of the child; however, a mother's health and emotional state during pregnancy can impact upon this development. If the mother has a problem with drugs, alcohol or living in a toxic atmosphere, for example, these factors can all have an effect upon the way the brain cells of the foetus develop. Studies carried out on pregnant women seem to suggest that if, during the pregnancy, the mother experiences fear, anger or job stress, this may result in the production of an irritable/bad-tempered infant (Healy 1994). Sadly, trauma during the actual birth process can destroy some brain cells, resulting in cerebral palsy or other related conditions.

Once babies are born their brains contain billions of nerve cells, which become organised into systems and networks we can recognise as thinking, talking, remembering and so on. Activities, environment, adults and other factors stimulate the nerve cells into action – what Healy (1994) refers to as the 'building of neural highways'. Each child's brain is unique and through this process 'each child weaves his own intellectual tapestry, the quality of which depends on active interest and involvement in a wide variety of stimuli' (Healy 1994).

By studying babies' eye movements scientists have found that within a few days of birth babies can recognise human faces and voices and discriminate between them. They also have a well-developed sense of smell that enables them to distinguish between different adults. Whilst it has long been known that new-born babies have a limited visual capacity (about 12 inches) in the early weeks of life, they are able to use hearing and smell to aid their limited sight in order to discriminate between adults and environments.

The brain is divided into four areas:

- the *occipital lobe*, which relates to vision;
- the *parietal lobe*, which relates to touch and spatial awareness;
- the *temporal lobe*, which relates to hearing and language;
- the *frontal lobes*, which are sub-divided into:
  - the *motor cortex*, which relates to body movements;
  - the *pre-frontal cortex*, which relates to reasoning, memory, attention, judgement, planning and self-control.

Each lobe/cortex has a right and left side (*hemisphere*) and in humans the right side of the brain dominates the left side of the body and vice versa. A dominant right side of the brain will result in the child being left-handed. This can also be seen in people who have strokes, where the paralysis left by the stroke will affect the side of the body that is opposite to the side of the brain in which the stroke has actually taken place.

At birth the brain is 25 per cent of its adult weight, whereas the baby's body is only 5 per cent of its adult weight. At six months of age the brain is nearly half its adult weight. So here we have this tiny baby, with a huge brain and the capacity to build up numerous pathways within the brain through the baby's ability to participate in complex thought patterns. As the baby lies in the cot, watching, listening and feeling, it builds up a picture of people and the world around it. It is therefore important that the child care worker is aware of this rapid development in the baby's brain and is able to stimulate the child visually and auditorily in order to encourage the 'neural highways' to develop. However, be guarded against over stimulation, which can be caused by persistent loud noises and a cacophony of sound.

Communication with and between babies

From work undertaken by a number of researchers using video film, we know that babies not only communicate with adults but also with each other. Using this technology, the National Children's Bureau was able to produce a training pack called 'Communication between babies in their first year' (1996), which contains very interesting video footage. Honig (1994) states that children respond appropriately to other children's inviting glances and gestures. Whaley and Rubenstein (1994) made videos of a number of children between the ages of twenty-two and thirty-six months, in day-care settings. They analysed the results and concluded that young children are capable of complex reciprocal relationships and that having such relationships helped to develop their self-esteem.

A baby's first communication is with the mother, whose voice and heartbeat they learn to recognise in the first days of life. Trevarthan (1995) maintains that infants can, from around four months of age, learn to join in musical games and body play providing that the adult is able to offer feedback to the baby's actions in the form of mirroring. Babies are then able to make sense of these interactive communications and over a period of time this is internalised and changes the way the baby thinks. Trevarthan maintains that the number of abilities possessed by babies and infants has long been unrecognised by psychologists. Only recently – and possibly video has aided this development – have psychologists studied and recorded the minutiae of babies interactions. Trevarthan states that, 'the developing social consciousness of a seven to eight month-old is manifested simultaneously in pretending or joking with "friends", and in sensitivity to incomprehension or ridicule by a stranger' (1995: 11). Trevarthan also refers to something called 'protolangauage', which combines vocalisations, gestures and facial expressions to communicate babies' interests to other babies and close adults. It is important that babies are able to socially interact with their carers, thus consistency in the relationship between parent and baby or carer and baby is an important aspect of the child's communication.

Bruner (1980) suggests that children learn better when adults support or 'scaffold' children's tasks so that the child's activities are extended. However, Trevarthan sees these activities as more complex than straightforward 'scaffolding', as they are recreated by the child out of the learning situation.

As children grow older they learn language that encodes their previous non-verbal communications. They are able to name objects in addition to understanding the properties of the object, many of which they have probably known long before they could verbalise them. An indication that children have a lot more knowledge than the language they have to express this knowledge is when the frustration in trying to communicate manifests itself as a temper tantrum. This usually begins around eighteen months to two years and abates as the child's language abilities develop. At one year of age a child may understand between forty and one hundred words but can only verbalise up to twenty words (Trevarthan 1995). By the time children have reached the age of three years they are able to communicate in a way that is understood by parents and carers. The development of children's language is well documented in numerous child psychology/child development textbooks. However, it must be remembered that the development of a child's language is dependent upon the interactions between the child and the adult.

Factors that may affect children's development

Each child is an individual and develops at its own unique pace. However, there are some external factors that may impinge upon the child's development, such as sex differences, social class and culture.

Since the introduction of ultrasound scanning, expectant parents are now able to get photographs of their child whilst it is still developing in the mother's womb. Another aspect of this is that the sex of the foetus can also be made known to the expectant parents. In some instances, such as when there is an illness that is carried on a sex-linked gene, it may be very important to know the sex of the foetus as soon as possible so that decisions can be made as to whether the pregnancy should be continued or terminated. Expectant parents are asked by the ultra-scan technician whether they wish to know the sex of the foetus. Some may wish to know in order to plan, whereas others may be happy to wait until the birth. It appears that the sex of a child makes little difference to the way the child will develop. Neither, does it appear, are boys more demanding than girls. What does affect development is when a child is encouraged to develop or prevented from developing in certain directions because of its sex. For instance, parents will often have boisterous play with their male offspring whereas they may treat their daughters in a gentler fashion. Expectations of a child's behaviour in relation to its gender may inhibit certain areas of development. For example, it is not uncommon to find that girls are poor map readers or do not feel confident dealing with mathematical or spatial concepts. Such distinctions can start at a very early age with the toys that are presented to children, soft cuddly things for girls; building blocks for boys. Society is becoming more aware of the effects of this type of gender-instigated selection and many parents are making decisive efforts to avoid this happening.

Social class can make a difference to a child's development in terms of environment and financial input. Poor families often live in poor housing in city areas that may be overcrowded and poorly serviced by public transport and amenities. It must not be forgotten that in rural areas the families of farm labourers may also suffer from similar deprivations in terms of poverty, public transport and amenities. In terms of child development, poverty is one factor that can inhibit a child's potential. Infants from poor families are more likely to be born with a low birth weight and the mothers may experience complications in pregnancy and delivery. However, Bee (1992) does point out that when one compares healthy babies from middle-class families with healthy babies from poor families in the early months of life, there are no differences in perceptual skills, motor development or learning. Poor diet can result in poor physical development or illness. There is reliance in our present society upon pre-prepared foods that are easily cooked in a microwave. This can mean that the quality of the food that children are receiving is not always healthy in terms of nutritional value. The number of cookery programmes on television also seems to indicate that there are very many people who have forgotten how to produce dishes from raw ingredients. Poverty can result in lack of stimulation of the child because of lack of space, few toys and living in an area that is poorly serviced for playgroups, nurseries, mother and toddler clubs and so on. In Western cultures there is a reliance on manufactured toys, whereas in many other cultures children get their stimulation from playing with natural materials found in the immediate environment. Children born into middle-class families do not suffer the effects of poverty but rather they could suffer the effects of too much money and high expectations. Many middle-class women have careers to which they want to or may have to return as quickly as possible after giving birth. The baby is then left in the care of a nanny or mother's help. The quality of care that the child will get is very dependent upon the qualifications of the carer. If the carer is not trained to a level whereby he or she is able to undertake sole charge posts then the child may not get the stimulation and developmental opportunities that it needs.

Middle-class parents have high expectations of their child's development. They would have read all the books and would know all the milestones and be aware of which toys the child should be given at which stage of development. However, what they often miss is the fact that children's development is an individual process and milestones will happen when the child is ready, not when the book says so. This sometimes leads to stress between the parent and child (and sometimes the nanny) when the child is not developing at a rate that meets the expectations of the parent.

Cultural differences in child development have not been investigated in great depth as there is a danger that misinterpretation of results could lead to racial prejudice. There was a great deal of controversy over the research that purported to have found differences in IQ between white and black Americans, particularly as the results mitigated against the black Americans. There are also dangers in how any such research findings may be used; for example, research undertaken on Jews in the 1930s was used to justify the holocaust. In her book on child development, Helen Bee does cite some studies that have investigated cross-cultural differences. Daniel Freedman (1979) observed newborn babies from four different cultures, Caucasian, Chinese, Navaho and Japanese. Of the four he found that the Caucasian babies were the most active and irritable and the hardest to console. Both the Chinese and Navaho infants were relatively placid, whilst the Japanese infants responded vigorously but were easier to quieten. Freedman's argument is that these were newborn children so their parents had not yet shaped them. However, as other research has shown, interaction between the parent and its newborn infant is very important. Perhaps this is a dimension that Freedman has not taken into account. Whilst these results are interesting, Freedman does extrapolate a conclusion that says that our idea of what is 'normal' behaviour in a child is strongly influenced by our own cultural expectations. I do not think that anybody would disagree with this conclusion. Certainly research in Africa has shown that black babies are more advanced than western babies in their gross motor skills from an early age. However, they are usually living in a spacious outdoor environment with lots of room to move about in and lots of stimulation from numerous adults and older children. An area that has been heavily researched is bilingualism. One of the most common questions asked is whether children will become confused if they are spoken to in two different languages. Siraj-Blatchford (2000) points out that learning a language is a complex task and that children need to learn the sounds of the language, the vocabulary, the grammar, the way sentences are put together and the rules of the language. As discussed in Chapter 4, it would appear that children cope perfectly well with being spoken to in two different languages from an early age. There are sometimes problems when a second language is introduced much later on. In some cultures a child may be exposed to three languages. For example, most Orthodox Jewish households speak Yiddish, Hebrew and English. Bee cites research into bilingualism by McLoughlin (1984), who states that what would confuse a child is if sentences consisted of more than one language, as this would prove much more difficult for the child to understand. In a number of cultures the extended family is the 'norm' and young children may bond with more than one person or just with their parents. Where you have people living in small villages that comprise a tribe or clan, the baby may bond with people who are not members of its direct family. This may also happen in Western societies when the mother returns to work very soon after the birth and the child is left with a childminder or with a key worker in a day-care setting. There do not seem to be any ill effects if a child bonds with a number of people, provided they are constant figures in the child's life.

Heuristic play

Heuristic play is a term used to describe how children learn by exploration and discovery. It is linked with the work of Elinor Goldschmeid, who developed the 'Treasure Basket' as a tool for heuristic play. The Treasure Basket does not contain toys or objects made from synthetic substances such as plastic. It uses everyday objects made of natural materials in order to stimulate children's senses of touch, sight, smell and hearing. The child explores the objects in the Treasure Basket and discovers the properties of the objects, for example their shape, form, size, rigidity, softness, temperature, flexibility and so on. Children get great pleasure from exploring the contents of the Treasure Basket from an age at which they are able to sit unaided.

Goldschmeid (1994) says that the objects put in a Treasure Basket should be able to offer the child the following experiences:

- touch – texture, shape, weight;
- smell – variety of scents;
- sound – ringing, tinkling, banging, scrunching;
- sight – colour, form, shininess, length.

She offers the folowing suggestions for objects to put in the Treasure Basket:

- natural objects – fir cones, large pebbles, shells, gourds, big feathers, walnuts, lemon;
- objects from natural materials – woollen balls, bone shoehorn, small raffia mat, wooden nailbrush, shaving brush;
- wooden objects – small boxes, small drum, clothes pegs, cubes, spoon, small bowl, coloured beads on a string;
- metal objects – spoons of various sizes, bunch of keys, small tins, whistle, bells, bicycle bell, lengths of chain, metal eggcup;
- objects in leather, rubber, textile, and fur – leather purse, leather bag, velvet powder-puff, fur ball, rubber tubing, rag doll, bean-bag;
- objects made from paper and card – notebook, tin foil, greaseproof paper, small cardboard boxes, cardboard roll from inside kitchen roll.

(Adapted from Goldschmeid and Jackson 1994)

A selection of things from each of these categories can be placed in a wicker basket (not less than 351 mm in diameter). It is *extremely important* to ensure that all the chosen objects are safe for the baby to be left alone with. The basket is placed near the child, who is able to reach out and take things from the basket and explore them. The adult's role in this activity is to organise the collection of the items for the Treasure Basket and keep them in good repair. The adult is not involved in the child's exploration but is able to observe the child and record/register what the child is learning from the experience. It is also possible to watch two babies exploring one Treasure Basket and note the interaction between the children.

Children over eighteen months of age can be introduced to what Gold-schmeid calls 'heuristic play with objects'. This is when a group of children is offered a large number of different kinds of objects for a defined period of time in a controlled environment. The children are able to play freely with these objects without adult intervention. The types of objects that can be used are empty tins, woollen pom-poms, table-tennis balls, small bags and boxes, old keys tied in a bunch, curtain rings, hair rollers, bottle corks, cockle or snail shells, rubber doorstops, cardboard cylinders and so on. The objects are placed in large cloth bags with a drawstring. There should be about fifty or sixty items in each bag and at least twenty bags for a group of eight children. Each bag should contain only one variety of items, and there should be at least fifteen varieties of items available for the children. Once again, the adult's role is one of facilitator making sure that the time limit for the activity is kept to and involving the children in the clearing up process.

Heuristic play is something that can be used with children as part of an activity programme drawn up over a week or a fortnight. It is not envisaged as a daily activity. Holland (1997) states that Hutt *et al.* (1989) put forward two different kinds of play behaviour.

Epistemic play behaviour:

- is concerned with acquisition of knowledge, skills and problem solving;
- gathers information;
- is exploratory;
- is productive;
- discovers;
- is invention-, task- or work-oriented;
- is relatively independent of mood state;
- has constraints that stem from the nature of the attention focus;
- needs adults to support, encourage, answer questions, supply information, be involved.

Ludic play behaviour:

- is playful;
- is fun;
- is lacking in specific focus;

- is highly mood-dependent;
- has constraints that (when they exist) are imposed by the child;
- does not need to involve adults;
- requires that adults are sensitive to children's needs;
- has the key features of enjoyment and fantasy;
- is unconstrained;
- is idiosyncratic;
- is repetitive;
- is innovative;
- is symbolic.

Heuristic play would come into the category of epistemic play although not all the characteristics of this type of play would apply.

Infants/young children in day care

During the 1950s, 1960s and part of the 1970s it was not the norm for mothers to go to work and leave their children in some type of day care. The attitude of society was one that discouraged women with children to work, and this was reinforced by psychologists such as John Bowlby. Bowlby (1951) argued that 'an infant and young child should experience a warm, intimate and continuous relationship with its mother'. This began the debate relating to bonding and maternal deprivation in young children. It left many mothers who were forced to return to the workforce for economic reasons feeling very guilty about what they may be doing to their child by placing it in a day-care situation. Around the same time, James and Joyce Robertson made a series of direct-observation films entitled *Children in Brief Separation*. These films showed children being separated from their mothers for a short period through hospitalisation, or being placed in a residential nursery whilst the mother gives birth to a second child, or other scenarios. The visual images of the Robertsons' films served to back up Bowlby's theories on maternal deprivation and attachment and loss. The debate went on through the 1960s and 1970s. Other researchers produced 'evidence' that upheld the Bowlby theory, not least of which being Harlow's experiments with baby rhesus monkeys who, when taken from their mothers at an early age, bonded with 'terry towelling' mothers that were placed in their cage.

In an attempt to counteract the maternal-deprivation theories a number of American studies were undertaken to compare attachments of children in day care with those who had remained at home, cared for by their mother. From these studies came two important factors: (1) the quality of the substitute care was of great importance; (2) the substitute relationship gave stability. British studies undertaken by Mayall and Petrie (1977) and Garland and White (1980) came to similar conclusions as the American studies. Thus a new look was taken on how the best day-care provision could provide consistent, high-quality substitute care. Small-scale day-care situations such as childminders and nannies came to be viewed as preferable for the care of very young children to larger institutions such as day nurseries and family centres. In order to address the issues of staff consistency of those working in baby and toddler rooms, the large institutions were encouraged to introduce a system of key workers. Key workers, usually two per child so that one was on duty at all times, were assigned to work with specific children so that they could offer these children continuity and stability of care.

By undertaking home visits, key workers were able to establish relationships with the child and the family before the child was admitted to the nursery. These visits enabled the key worker to understand the child's home environment, the child's preferences in toys, food and comfort objects, and the child's sleep patterns. Key workers were also able to establish the relationships with the other children and adults in the family with which the baby shared its home. When a child started at the nursery, the key worker represented a familiar person with which the child could identify and to which the family could relate.

Goldschmeid and Jackson (1994) point out that there are difficulties in implementing the key worker system. It is expensive in terms of staffing and is probably not a viable option unless each key worker is responsible for four children. Holidays and illness can result in a child's key worker being away and the child can then experience a sense of loss. One way of overcoming this is to have two key workers attached to each child, one who is the predominant carer and the other who is a secondary carer, familiar with the child but not taking the lead role in its care. Another problem is that staff may object to the key-worker system, as it requires them to form a close relationship with one or two children. Too close a relationship can result in the key worker experiencing loss and deprivation when the child becomes old enough to move to a different room in the nursery. Key workers may become upset if the child they care for appears to be neglected at weekends when it is with its parent. Relationships between the key worker and the parents can become strained if the child bonds with the key worker and not the parent. Parents may feel particularly guilty when this happens. A parent may become jealous of the key worker's relationship with the child. The parent may also feel that the key worker is judging his or her parenting skills and may report the outcome to social workers and others in authority.

However problematic the key-worker system appears to be to implement, it is imperative that centres persevere with it as it is preferable to the child being handled by multiple carers. Research has shown that within our society, multiple carers are detrimental to a young child's emotional and cognitive development.

In order to cope with the new demands that being a key worker entails, staff will need to be trained and, when necessary, have the opportunity to consult a counsellor about their own feelings in times of difficulty. Tony Blair's government places great emphasis on women with young children returning to the workforce and has produced a policy that it describes as 'wrap-around care' in order to enable mothers to return to work. However, there are very few instances in which this 'wrap-around care' can be offered in one establishment; in the majority of cases it may involve a combination of a childminder, a day-care centre and an out-of-school facility. For the two- to three-year-old this is not a good situation but for the under-two-year-old it can prove a disaster. For the very young child, a placement with a childminder could offer both high-quality care and stability. Childminding is now a profession in its own right. There are qualifications for childminders on the National Qualifications Framework produced by the Qualifications and Curriculum Authority (QCA), and all childminders are encouraged to take these in order to validate their professional status. Childminders must be registered with the local authority or OFSTED. A large number of people become childminders when their own children are small and many were previously teachers, nurses and child-care workers before having their own children.

Working in partnership with parents

It is imperative that those caring for children under three years of age work in partnership with parents or the primary carer of the child. In many inner-city areas there is a large selection of full day-care establishments that take children from zero to three years; however, individual establishments will have different methods of dealing with this age group. For very young children, surveys have suggested that the most popular choice of parents is to leave their child with a relative or a registered childminder. Childminding is able to bridge the gaps that other forms of day care may be unable to fulfil; for example, when mothers return to work after maternity leave, when parents work shifts or unsociable hours or when parents are studying at colleges that have no child-care facilities. The small-scale situation is able to offer consistency in terms of the numbers of people a child needs to relate to and much closer links between the carer and the child's parents.

Before admitting a young child to any form of full day care the parents need to be consulted on the child's normal routine such as sleep patterns, food preferences, favourite comforter and so on. This is best done via a home visit or a pre-entry interview with the parent or primary carer.

In recent years we have seen many more fathers choosing to stay at home to look after their children. In many cases the mother may earn a great deal more than the father and so sensible economics result in the father becoming the primary carer. On a recent radio programme that interviewed a number of these fathers it was sad to hear about the prejudices they were encountering. One father had been asked not to attend the mother-and-toddler clinic as the mothers objected to him being there when they were breast-feeding. The Health Visitor did visit him at home but, as he pointed out, he missed the opportunity to talk to the other parents and this left him very isolated. A number of the men had been viewed with suspicion over their underlying motives for wishing to be the primary carer of their child. Such prejudice came from all directions: other men, mothers and professionals. As paedophilia features more and more in the media, so the feelings against male primary carers becomes more widespread. The men interviewed in the programme expressed their sadness about this situation but were not deterred from continuing their role as primary carer.

There is more information on working with parents later in this book.

Recent government initiatives

Sure Start: an intervention initiative

A major aim of the Sure Start initiative is to prevent families spiralling into situations in which they are unable to cope. The government has invested £452 million into setting up 250 Sure Start programmes over a three-year period. In 1999 the first sixty Sure Start programmes were implemented and they were designated as the trail-blazers. Sure Start programmes must cover the physical, intellectual and social development of the zero- to four-years age group. Sure Start programmes are locally devised so that they answer the needs of a particular area or group of people. Any Sure Start bid must demonstrate an integrated delivery of services across the following areas:

- outreach services and home visiting;
- support for families and parents;
- services to support good-quality play, learning and childcare;
- primary and community health care;
- support for those with special needs.

Local programmes must ensure that stakeholders work together to improve the quality and accessibility of services for families. This includes parents, community volunteers, GPs, health visitors, midwives, education providers, child care professionals and others. Local programmes are able to provide services not already in the area, add value to existing services, provide new facilities, give parents clear information, train existing professionals and volunteers and improve joint working and co-ordination between existing service providers. Clear target objectives are laid down in order to evaluate local programmes.

In the initial stages there was some opposition from rural areas to the Sure Start initiative as the requirement to bring the services to the people in need was clearly impossible in these areas. Schemes whereby local authorities in these areas had provided transport to bring the people to the services did not appear to fit in with the Sure Start requirements and were in danger of being marginalised or lost altogether. Clearly, rural areas needed to be consulted as to the best practice available to them in order to ensure that the people in need got the services they required in the easiest and most cost-effective way.

Early Excellence Centres

These are centres that the government has designated as models of good practice in integrating early education and day care for children from birth. The first centres were launched in 1998 and it is expected that there will eventually be over twenty centres across England. The centres are expected to provide a fully integrated education and care programme by becoming a focus point for co-ordinating all local agencies. For example, the Pen Green Early Excellence Centre in Corby has two nurseries, an antenatal and baby clinic, an after-school club and youth club, an NVQ training centre for child care and a range of flexible education courses. All of these are on site. (Corby is also one of the Sure Start trail-blazer areas.)

Early Excellence Centres provide:

- high standards of integrated provision;
- commitment to multi-agency working;
- staff training and development, available to other providers;
- effective outreach and support for families;
- beacons of excellence for other sectors, including private and voluntary;
- well-established strategy for development of services;
- staffing and management arrangements that are clear and convincing;
- suitable plans for monitoring and evaluation;
- provision of parental involvement, education and training;
- one-stop-shop access to services, advice, information and counselling.

The first evaluation of Early Excellence Centres was carried out by Chris Pascal and Tony Bertram (Centre for Research in Early Childhood, University College, Worcester) on behalf of the DfEE. The report was published in 2000 and looks at the impact of these centres on the children and their families, the practitioners and the local community. The report also looks at the ways in which the local centres may have impacted upon the costs to the agencies involved. For example, although an outreach service had cost £30,355 it had actually saved £51,745 by its intervention, thus, avoiding involvement of other staff and agencies.

The above two major government interventions should, over the next few years, be showing other benefits to young children and their families.

References

Bee, H. (1992) *The Developing Child*, sixth edition, New York: HarperCollins.

Bowlby, J. (1951) *Maternal Care and Mental Health*, Geneva: World Health Organization.

Bowlby, J. (1979) *The Making and Breaking of Affectional Bonds*, London: Tavistock Publications.

Bruner, J. S. (1980) Under five in Britain, *Oxford Pre-school Research Project 1*, London: Grant McIntyre.

Carnegie Task Force Report (1994) *Starting Points: Meeting the needs of our youngest children*, New York: Carnegie Corporation.

DfEE (2000) *Early Excellence Centres: First findings Autumn 1999*, Suffolk: DfEE Publications.

DfEE (2000) 'Providing a wrap-around service in early years and childcare', in *Good Practice in Childcare*, No. 8, Suffolk: DfEE Publications.

Freedman D. (1979) in H. Bee (2000) ninth edn, 'The Developing Child', Needham Heights MA: Allyn and Bacon.

Goldschmeid, E. and Jackson, S. (1994) *People Under Three*, London: Routledge.

Goldschmeid, E. and Selleck, D. (1996) *Communication Between Babies in Their First Year of Life*, London: National Children's Bureau.

Gopnik, A., Meltzoff, A. and Kuhl, P. (1999) *How Babies Think*, London: Weidenfeld and Nicolson.

Healy, J. (1994) *Your Child's Growing Mind*, New York: Doubleday.

Holland, R. (1997) ' "What's it all about?": how introducing heuristic play has affected provision for the under-threes in one day nursery', in Lesley Abbot and Helen Moylett (eds), *Working With the Under-3s: Responding to children's needs*, Buckingham: Open University Press.

Honig, A. S. (1994) 'Helping toddlers with peer group entry skills', in *Zero to Three*, 14, 5.

Mayall, B. and Petrie, P. (1983) *Childminding and Day Nurseries: What kind of care?*, London: Heinemann.

Piaget, J. (1952) *The Origins of Intelligence in Children*, New York: International Universities Press.

Priya, J. V. (1992) *Birth Traditions and Modern Pregnancy Care*, Dorset: Element.

Rousseau, J. J. (1762) *Emile, ou L'Education*, London: T. Bechet (English version).

Siraj-Blatchford, I. and Clarke, P. (2000) *Supporting Identity, Diversity and Language in the Early Years*, Buckingham: Open University Press.

Trevarthan, C. (1995) 'The child's need to learn culture', in *Children and Society*, 9, 1: 5–19.

Whaley, K. L. and Rubenstein, T. S. (1994) 'How toddlers "do" friendship: a descriptive analysis of naturally occurring friendships in a group child cares setting', in *Journal of Social and Personal Relationships*, 11, 3: 383–400.

CHAPTER 6

Feelings and relationships

This chapter will explore the feelings and relationships between children and adults. First relationships are formed at birth within the family and slowly these are extended to encompass other adults and children. As we all know, not all relationships are happy ones, and throughout the chapter reference will be made to instances when things may go wrong and feelings may be hurt. An important aspect of feelings and relationships both for children and adults is the cultural dimension. Most people have heard of the English 'stiff upper lip', which is when it is not culturally acceptable for adults to show their emotions in public or to their children. Fortunately this attitude is changing but there are still large numbers of English people who find it difficult to express their emotions or who view the expression of emotions by their children as weakness. At the opposite end of the scale we have people from the Mediterranean area who are very open in expressing emotions in public and whose everyday conversations are smattered with dramatic hand gestures and facial expressions. We need to remember that different cultures have different ways of establishing relationships with children and, where appropriate, examples will be cited. In addition to the cultural aspects, some people have been trained, because of the nature of their jobs, not to express their emotions; for example, doctors, nurses, police officers, armed-services personnel. These people may find it difficult to override this training when it comes to expressing emotions and feelings in their personal life and this can be very hard for their children. Children are very good at reading non-verbal communication from adults via body language and facial expression and adults are not always aware of this. This chapter will also explore how children's behaviour can best be managed and how adults may interpret children's behaviour.

First relationships and feelings

John Bowlby put forward his theories on attachment and loss in 1969, whereby he claimed that infants have an inborn drive to form stable attachments (or 'bonding') to their primary carer. At the time that Bowlby's book was published, the primary caregiver was interpreted as being the mother of the child. This led to a great deal of publicity being given to the idea that mothers returning to work following the birth of their child could do that child long-term damage by leaving its care to somebody else. There were also beliefs that children who had failed to bond/make attachments would be more likely to become juvenile delinquents. However, the present-day interpretation of Bowlby's thesis, whilst not totally detracting from what he was advocating, makes it clear that the primary carer does not need to be the mother, though it does need to be somebody who is consistently available and responsive to the needs of the child. Such attachment or bonding is what makes the baby feel secure following birth. Studies have shown that an infant is able to have an attachment to more adults than just the mother, thus any consistent adult who deals with the child, answering its needs on a regular basis – for example, father, grandparent, older sibling – also become attachment figures in the baby's life. Research carried out in the kibbutzim (communal farms) in Israel found that the baby was equally attached to its mother, father and primary carer in the nursery. In agricultural societies, following the birth of a child the mother may return to the fields to work, leaving the baby with grandparents, aunts, older siblings or other close family members with no ill effects on the attachment relationship between mother and child.

A newborn baby is able to recognise the voice of its mother and the rhythm of her heartbeat. Later the baby will recognise the voices of other members of the family. The baby is able to identify those who are in regular contact with it by the way they hold it and touch it. From these early social interactions the child learns which behaviours will get which responses from the adult, for example crying usually results in the child being picked up and cuddled and talked to.

In recent years the role of the father has become more prominent in the attachment debate as more single-father families have come into existence, as have fathers who choose to stay at home to look after the children because the mother is the bigger income earner. Many fathers attend the birth of their child and are able to make attachments with the baby from the beginning. Sweden is a country that has encouraged the involvement of fathers since the 1960s, being one of the first European countries to legislate to allow paid paternity leave so that fathers could be with their child at the birth and in the weeks following the birth.

Bowlby's theory of maternal deprivation (attachment and loss) relied heavily upon the thesis that there was a 'critical period' during which attachment took place. However, many critics of Bowlby have carried out research that shows that bonding can take place much later than Bowlby's 'critical period'. This is illustrated by relationships between adoptive parents and their children and instances when a mother and baby are separated soon after birth because of illness of the mother or baby or prematurity of the baby. The present-day research would appear to discredit Bowlby's 'critical period' for attachment, particularly its link with juvenile delinquency and behaviour problems in children said to be caused by lack of bonding. Factors previously related to the consequences of lack of bonding and attachment are now linked to poor parenting skills, inconsistency of care and the breakdown of the family and changes in family values.

Once the mother's maternity-leave period is over the family will have to make decisions as to whether she will stay at home to look after her child or return to work and make alternative arrangements for the child's care. If that care is to pass to somebody other than a family member then it may involve hiring a nanny or finding a suitable day-care setting for the child. This will also require the child to make relationships beyond the home. For very young children a small-scale day-care setting such as a childminder may be viewed as preferable to the larger setting of a day nursery. A childminder is able to offer the consistency of the same person caring for the child every day. However, research has shown that providing the adult/child ratios are good, the care is of a high quality and there is low staff turnover, then there are likely to be no adverse effects in placing a young child in a nursery (Melhuish 1990). There appears to be no research that shows that placing a child with a childminder or in a day-care setting has any detrimental effects upon the child's attachment to its mother or other family members. Once in the day-care setting, the child interacts and forges relationships not only with its carers but also with other children. Research carried out by Goldschmeid and Selleck (1996) produced a video film showing babies in their first year interacting with each other. This offers evidence to show peer-group relationships developing.

For good relationships to be made with young children, whether this be in the early days of life or later, it is important that there is interaction between the adult and the child. Whilst responding to the child's needs is an important part of this action, there is also a need for the adult to have physical contact with the child, talk to the child and play with the child. The child needs to be shown affection as cold, clinically delivered care does not lead to the forming of attachments. Therefore, in any relationship there must be feelings that are positive and make the child feel loved and secure. Bruner (1983) said that 'Babies are born endowed to interact with others and their principal "tools" for achieving their ends are other human beings.'

Relationships between children

As stated above, communication between children starts at a very early age. However, it is some time later before children start to form relationships with other children. The first children that a new member of the family will make a relationship with are its siblings. As children differ in their relationships with adults, so this will be the case with siblings. About 80 per cent of children have siblings, although this statistic may be a lot lower in countries where there are more one-child families such as China and Germany. Judy Dunn (1993) points out: 'The striking differences between sibling pairs in their relationships are clear even to the most casual observer. Some brothers and sisters appear affectionate and concerned, real friends to one another. Others are constantly in conflict, even coming to blows.' Older siblings can be very caring and tolerant of younger siblings or they can be ambivalent and aggressive towards them. This latter reaction may be put down to sibling rivalry and, although researchers recognise this as an important dimension to the relationship, it is more complex than just straightforward rivalry. Dunn points out that some children are attached to each other very early on in the sibling relationship and for some children this is a major aspect of their security. A longitudinal study carried out by Dunn and Kendrick (1982) showed that by the age of around one year the younger sibling was imitating the older sibling and this continued for a number of years, sometimes into adulthood. However, it would appear that there has been little if any research carried out that looks at the gender differences or the age gap between siblings and how these may affect relationships. Changes in sibling relationships can occur when one sibling starts nursery or school and becomes more self-confident.

The child who has no siblings can sometimes be a very lonely child who spends more time with adults than with other children. What may appear as advantages over having siblings, such as them not having to compete for their parents' attention, not having to share or take turns, can in many ways prove to be disadvantages for the child when it is outside the home. Whilst these children may appear very confident in their dealings with adults, they may be socially inhibited when dealing with other children. Some of these children may appear mature for their age, enjoy being the centre of adult attention and can sometimes seem self-centred. It is very important that parents of only children recognise the need for them to spend time with other children. This should start at an early age and could be achieved by taking them to a mother-and-toddler club or attending a pre-school playgroup on a regular basis. In these situations they will learn to socialise with other children so that they gain an understanding of sharing, taking turns, working co-operatively and so on. The parents can also invite other children into the home to play on a regular basis so that their child is able to get used to sharing its own toys, sweets and other things.

Relationships with children from outside the family begin when a child meets with other children. Such meetings may start between two families who have children of a similar age. As previously mentioned, children in the first year of life will communicate (Goldschmeid and Selleck 1996) by touch and babbling. Between fourteen and eighteen months children may appear to be playing together but this is most likely to be parallel play, where the two are playing side by side. Around two and a half years, there may be more co-ordinated play between two children involving imitation and chasing games. At the age of three years children start to play more co-operatively with their peers and this is the first step in forming friendships. Such friendships make children sensitive to other children's feelings and enable them to develop social skills. Howes (1987) studied the friendships of pre-school children over a period of two years and found that these early relationships were not just passing occurrences but lasted for at least six months and many for much longer periods of time, such as a number of years. Other studies of pre-school friendships have found that the children who are friends are more tolerant, forgiving and supportive of each other and spend a lot of time interacting whereas those children who are not friends are not treated in the same way. As children get older, so their friendships get stronger and more complex, as can be seen from observing children in the imaginative play areas. They discuss situations, decide on roles, take turns and so on. Sometimes they are capable of being 'cruel' to those who are not part of the friendship circle and who may be less confident in their interactions. The 'outsiders' may be given less-interesting roles or the 'friends' may be very bossy towards them or not let them join in the play. Early years workers need to be alert to these situations, as they can be very damaging for the child who is constantly the 'outsider'. Children who lack confidence and social skills may have difficulty in becoming part of the friendship circles, which leaves the child who is timid, shy or awkward very lonely and vulnerable. Early years workers also need to be aware of the dominant child making friends with one of the more vulnerable children as this may be a bullying situation that will need to be dealt with. The nature of friendships can change and friends will argue and become competitive, the latter being more common in boys (Hartup 1989). At this point one friendship may cease and new friendships start.

Ramsey (1991) puts forward what he describes as crude descriptors of four categories of children's social behaviour, as described below.

- *Popular* children are usually very capable and more intellectually, socially and emotionally mature than their peers. It is also a sad but evident truth that popular children are often more physically attractive and this is particularly noticeable with girls.
- *Rejected* children may show aggressive or withdrawn behaviour. They may angrily retaliate against others or avoid other children.
- *Neglected* children appear to take little part in the social life of the group and are often content with their own company.
- *Controversial* children are described as having a major impact on the social group, are socially and intellectually talented, but are often in trouble for aggressive behaviour and rule breaking. Although children in this group are often group leaders, some other children regard them with caution.

Many children who are socially well adjusted may not fit into any of these groups.

Relationships with adults outside the family

Bee (2000) states that between six and sixteen months of age children have a fear of strangers and between nine and sixteen months they experience separation anxiety. Between these age groups children often become anxious, fearing strangers and crying and/or clinging to their mothers or primary carers when in the presence of strangers. Before they enter this stage of development they are quite happy to be picked up and cuddled by anyone and then suddenly they seem to develop a fear of strangers and separation anxiety. They become fearful to leave those they are familiar with. This type of behaviour begins to lessen around the age of two years. When children are going through the separation-anxiety phase it is not a good time to introduce them to new situations in which they will be left with people whom they do not know; people who appear to them as strangers. If the child has been looked after by a childminder or relative from an early age it will have formed attachments with this person and is likely to cling to him or her when strangers appear or experience separation anxiety if visiting unfamiliar places such as the mother-and-toddler club. Separation anxiety is very common when young children are first introduced to the pre-school playgroup or nursery setting around the age of two to two and a half years. It is important that the early years workers understand this and have a programme for phasing in a child's admission. This entails the mother/primary carer staying with the child and when leaving the child, this should be for a very short period of time in the first instance, gradually building up to longer periods of time spent away. The length of time the parent stays away from the child should be arranged in consultation with the staff who know how the child reacts when the parent leaves. With some children it can take a period of weeks before they are able to overcome their separation anxiety and settle down in the playgroup or nursery without signs of distress. It is important that in these early days of separation from the parent the staff in the setting give the child special attention and wherever possible assign one person to be the child's key worker. The child then only has one person to relate to and this can help encourage feelings of confidence and security. It can be too overwhelming for a young child in this situation to have to relate to lots of adults and children. For parents and children from diverse ethnic backgrounds the settling in period may be particularly stressful. Pre-school playgroups and nurseries may be a new concept for the parents and they may be very concerned about leaving their child with other people. There may be language difficulties: even if the parents speak English they may have spoken to the child only in their heritage language. The clothes the staff wear, the routine and the food may all be unfamiliar to the child, which may only add to its initial anxiety. Siraj-Blatchford and Clarke (2000) offer the following settling-in strategies for children from diverse backgrounds, although many of the points on the list would be good practice for dealing with any new child who is settling in:

- encourage parents to visit with their children on several occasions before leaving them for the first time;
- encourage parents to explain the events of the day to their child in their own language;
- try to understand the parents' perspective and concerns for leaving their children for the first time;

- suggest to parents that they make the first few occasions when the children are left short;
- suggest the parents say goodbye, tell the child where they are going and when they will return, for example, after sleep;
- encourage the parents to leave something of their own for the child to care for in their absence;
- provide bilingual support for the child;
- allocate a particular staff member to remain with the child;
- make sure the parents leave a phone number on which they can be contacted during the day;
- provide play materials that are familiar;
- find out the routines of the child.

Once children have settled into playgroup/nursery they very quickly learn the routine of the establishment and what is expected of them. Routines are important to a child as they offer security – as they do to many adults! Children also learn what is acceptable behaviour within the setting and what is not acceptable. They also learn the consequences of unacceptable behaviour. Much of this comes to the child as it becomes familiar with the setting; however, with older children their peer group may be the ones to inform them of the 'house rules'.

Communication between adults and children is a two-way process and it is important that adults listen to children and take what they are saying seriously. Adults have an important role in developing and enhancing children's language development. Communication is not just talking and listening as messages can be transferred via body language, gestures, eye contact and so on. Children are very good at picking up non-verbal communication signals and many adults do not appreciate this fact. So whilst telling a child it should 'eat its greens', be careful that your own expression does not convey your distaste for 'greens'. Children aged between two and four years will often use gestures to help you understand the message they are sending. It is very easy for adults in their communications with children to make the children feel insecure. This usually happens when adults consistently start conversations with negative statements. Adults must respect children and accept that, like adults, children are also capable of making mistakes and we all learn by our mistakes.

Managing children's behaviour

All adults need to understand how they should react to children. Children need to be praised, trusted, encouraged, communicated with and empathised with in order for them to feel confident and happy. Managing children's behaviour is not just about dealing with behaviour problems but also about recognising and acknowledging when the child has achieved something or made great efforts to achieve something, however small that achievement may be. We all like to be praised for our efforts and children are no different from adults in this respect, as self-esteem and self-image are very important parts of the human psyche. A child's self-esteem and self-image build up slowly as part of the developmental process.

There are a number of stages in a child's development of a concept of self (Bee 2000). The first stage is called the subjective self and occurs in the first year of life. During this period the baby is developing a sense of itself as an agent who can make things happen, and this is seen in the delight it gets from doing things such as moving a mobile, making a noise with a squeaky toy and communicating with adults. From this the child derives a sense of self. Piaget (1969) maintains that a critical element in the development of the subjective self is an understanding of object permanence that the child develops around nine to twelve months. As the child begins to understand that objects exist even when they are out of sight, so the child begins to understand that its parents exist and so does it exist.

The second stage in developing the concept of self (or objective self) comes when the child understands that it is an object in the world. As a toddler, the child discovers that just as the objects that surround it, so does it have a name, gender, size and personal qualities. A child of two-and-a-half to three years will know its own name, whether it is a boy or a girl, whether it is big or little and whether it has brothers and sisters, grandparents, aunts and other close relatives. Harter (1998) describes the pre-school child's self-concept as 'rather like a list: "I'm good at running"; "I don't like to play with dolls"; "I live in a big house"; "I have blue eyes".' Children's perceptions of themselves are at this age tied to specific settings and specific tasks.

As they get older, children will begin to compare themselves with other children in their peer group. From this the child is able to make a self-evaluation and judge its own strengths and weaknesses. The child's position in the family, the nursery or the class may reinforce its own evaluation of itself. By this time the child would also have mastered the different rules that govern its reactions and behaviour such as socio-cultural rules, moral rules and rules relating to expected behaviour in different settings. All of these things will be contributing towards the development of the child's personality. The following (adapted from Woolfson 1994) is a list of things that adults can do to improve a child's self-concept:

- take an interest in all the child does, the small things as well as the big things, and value what it does;
- respect the child for who it is not what it does;
- ensure the child has access to positive images that relate to its skin colour, gender, ability, disability and so on;
- emphasise with the child's strong points, especially if the child feels less capable than its peers;
- even when the child misbehaves, do not repeatedly remind the child of how bad it is;

- take the child's feelings and wishes into account when making decisions about what it is allowed to do;
- act as a positive role model for the child, which requires the adult to have a positive self-image;
- provide experiences for the child in which it is likely to be successful and avoid those that you know the child is bound to fail at;
- have realistic expectations of the child's abilities and achievements.

Children with a poor self-image do not relate well to other children and may be social loners. They have high anxiety levels and are very critical of anything they do, never accepting that what they do may be of normal standards. They often feel guilty and ashamed and find it difficult to have honest, trusting relationships with other children and adults. It is important for child-care workers to recognise these behaviours so that they can work with the child towards helping it have a more positive self-image.

At some time all children will present challenging behaviour to their parents, carers or teachers. This is a natural way for children to find out about the world around them. Their behaviour will usually have a goal but they may operate on a trial-and-error basis. Behaviours that enable the child to reach its goal will be repeated; those that do not will be discarded. The child may be testing the adults by trying to find the answers to questions such as 'How far can I go with that adult before I am stopped?'; 'If I do that again tomorrow do you think that adult will notice or will I get away with it?' The child may be trying to be recognised, to feel important or to belong. First behaviours are learned within the family and it is therefore important to involve the family when devising a way of dealing with children's challenging behaviour. In order to influence children's behaviour, the parents and the day-care/school staff need to work together. If children are persistently using challenging behaviour then the adults concerned with the child should be looking to see if there are deeper reasons for this than just the child going through a developmental stage. For example there may be problems within the family that are having a detrimental effect upon the child's development. In these cases the parents need to be consulted and, where necessary, outside help offered. Much of children's challenging behaviour is based on the goals of wanting to seek attention from adults or other children, and/or wanting power over adults or other children.

Attention seeking is by far the most common form of challenging behaviour in children and it is a form of behaviour used by many adults in order to get their own way. Attention seeking can involve behaviours such as being a nuisance, being a clown, being a 'smart Alec', always asking questions, embarrassing people, unpredictable actions and mischief making. Unfortunately, some of the previously mentioned traits are viewed favourably by adults, such as clowning or being a smart Alec. Whilst adults should not give a lot of attention to this behaviour, they cannot totally ignore it. They need to explain to the child what they do not like about this behaviour and ask the child to stop it. Sadly, some children may lack attention at home and so deliberately seek it when they are outside the family.

Other types of attention-seeking behaviour may be more passive and include shyness, fearfulness, anxiety, tearfulness, eating problems, always wanting help and laziness. With this type of behaviour the child is gaining attention by not doing things. These behaviours are often of lesser concern to adults because the children that use this type of behaviour are usually very nice and do not disrupt the other children. However, these children are not interested in independence, as they want to rely on the adults to do everything for them, thus getting the attention they seek. With these children self-reliance needs to be encouraged, with the adult explaining to the child that it is possible to do things for yourself. For example, if a child is refusing to eat for no particular reason then the adult should not feed it but encourage the child to feed itself. If the child does not co-operate then the food can be taken away and no snacks given between meals. In this way the child has not had the attention it would have got by being coaxed and fed by the adult.

When children want power over adults and other children they may exhibit behaviours such as being rebellious, being argumentative, being defiant, contra-dicting, being disobedient, bullying, lying, being bossy, having temper tantrums (long after the age when it is normal development to have these), refusing to co-operate or being stubborn and forgetful. These types of behaviours upset adults as they feel that their authority is being challenged. Most parents and adults want control over the children in their care and the instinctive reaction is to take on the challenge. However, adults entering the power struggle are just what the child wants. The best way to avoid this is to talk to the child, asking it to co-operate and encouraging it to participate with you in carrying out whatever is being asked, for example picking up toys. However, adults cannot make children do something they do not wish to do and they can only hope to be a role model that the child will follow.

There are other forms of challenging behaviour that would not be considered as part of a child's normal developmental experience. These behaviours are likely to alert adults that there is a far deeper underlying problem that the child is trying to find ways of dealing with. Examples of these are when a child is delib-erately cruel, inflicting pain on other children or animals, stealing, withdrawn, refusing to mix with other children, behaving in babyish ways or bedwetting. Children with special needs may exhibit difficult behaviour and they may be less receptive to the normal methods for dealing with that behaviour. Because of their disability these children may have low self-esteem and may not yet have learnt the social rules of behaviour. These children will need special attention, preferably through a key worker who can build a relationship with them as a secure base to work from.

Adults must look for positive ways to manage children's challenging behavi-our. There need to be consistent ground rules that all children and staff under-stand but these must be based upon positive statements that are realistic and achievable. When dealing with children the word 'realistic' means in relation to the child's understanding and developmental stage. If it is necessary to discipline children then physical punishment, such as smacking, must *never* be used. Neither should the adult use methods that threaten, humiliate or bribe children as these can damage a child's self-esteem and confidence and not result in any behaviour change. When a child does conform to a request from the adult then this should be acknowledged through praise or by giving the child a reward such as reading a favourite story or playing a favourite game. If children are angry or upset about something they should be given the opportunity to tell the adult how they feel. With very young children the adult may need to distract their attention away from the situation that is causing conflict and interest them in something else.

Most early years settings have a behaviour policy that has been written by the staff in conjunction with the parents. Such a policy enables staff and parents to understand what is acceptable and what is unacceptable behaviour in that setting. Behaviour policies should be regularly reviewed and always leave room for children to have choice within a defined framework. The policy should be written in positive terms and cover underlying principles such as not hurting others, not saying unkind things, not taking or damaging other people's property, not harming plants or animals. These underlying principles then need to be translated into a positive set of ground rules that the children understand, for example:

- we always try to be kind to others;
- we always try to speak kindly to each other;
- we look after our own and others' things;
- we put things back where they belong;
- we look after living things.

These positive statements will be understood by the children and form the basis of their behaviour management.

It is always difficult to know how to deal with the child who will not listen and who may present very challenging behaviour. The Save the Children website has a lot of useful information for parents on how to manage their child's behaviour. It offers the following advice for dealing with the child that will not listen:

- kneel or sit so that you are at the child's level;
- hold the child gently by the shoulders or hands while you make the request;
- look right into the eyes of the child;
- talk in a firm, clear, calm voice;
- look serious while you speak;
- make it clear you expect to be listened to as you would listen to the child;
- listen to the child's response and carefully consider its views;

- give children options wherever possible;
- try negotiation;
- give ample opportunity for children to complete the task;
- praise co-operation or explain the consequences of non-co-operation (without resorting to threats);
- give warnings and helpful reminders;
- encourage children's problem-solving skills.

As children get older they may repeat things that they have heard at home and this may lead to them making derogatory remarks about other children. Such remarks may be racist, sexist or refer to a child's disability and they always need to be challenged by the adult in a sensitive way. No name-calling may be one of the ground rules that have been established in the setting and this will need to be sensitively explained to the offending child. If the child is repeating what it has heard at home then it is important that the adult does not undermine the child's parents when dealing with the incident. The adult must explain that these remarks hurt and upset the child they are directed at and that they are not expressions that are used in the setting. The recent Persona Doll Project described in Chapter 1 has offered a very successful way of dealing with such incidents within the nursery. Persona dolls are able to give adults the opportunity to explore with young children issues that may otherwise be difficult such as racism, disability, being in a traveller family, being in a one-parent family, being fostered, and so on. Adults make persona dolls that represent children from these different backgrounds and tell the children the doll's story. Through the dolls the adults can explore with the children the feelings and concepts experienced by someone who may be different. However, an important aspect of persona dolls is that they come alive for the children and therefore need to be brought out at regular intervals and treated with care when not in use so that children do not worry about where they have gone. If they are not going to be used anymore then their story must involve them moving away to another town so the children are able to accept why they have gone. Persona dolls are now being used successfully in the USA, Australia, Denmark, the Netherlands and Britain, where training to use the dolls is now an integral part of some early years care and education courses.

References

Adler, A. (1957) *Understanding Human Behaviour*, New York: Fawcett.

Bee, H. (2000) *The Developing Child*, ninth edition, Needham Heights: Allyn & Bacon.

Brown, B. (2001) *Combating Discrimination: Persona dolls in action*, Stoke-on-Trent: Trentham Books.

Bruner, J. (1983) *Child's Talk*, New York: Norton.

Dowling, M. (2001) *Young Children's Personal, Social and Emotional Development*, London: Paul Chapman.

Dunn, J. (1993) *Young Children's Close Relationships: Beyond attachment*, London: Sage.

Dunn, J. and Kendrick, C. (1982) *Siblings: Love, envy and understanding*, Cambridge, Mass.: Harvard University Press.

Goldschmeid, E. and Selleck, D. (1996) *Communication Between Babies in Their First Year of Life*, London: National Children's Bureau.

Harter, S. (1998) 'The development of self-representations', in W. Damon (ed.), *Handbook of Child Psychology*, volume 3: 'Social, emotional and personality development', New York: Wiley.

Hartup, W.W. (1989) 'On relationships and development', in Hartup and Ruben (eds), *Relationship and Development*, New Jersey: Lawrence Erlbaum.

Hennessy, E., Martin, S., Moss, P. and Melhuish, E. (1992) *Children in Day Care: Lessons from the research*, London: Paul Chapman.

Howes, C. (1987) *Peer Interaction of Young Children*, Monographs of the Society for Research in Child Development, 217, 153, 1.

Melhuish, E. (1990) 'Research on day care for young children in the United Kingdom', in E. Melhuish and P. Moss (eds), *Day Care for Young Children International Perspectives*, London: Routledge.

Murray, L. and Andrews, L. (2000) *The Social Baby: Understanding babies' communication from birth*, Richmond, Surrey: CP Publishing.

Petrie, P. (1989) *Communicating with Children and Adults*, London: Edward Arnold (Hodder & Stoughton).

Piaget, J. and Inhelder, B. (1969) *The Psychology of the Child*, New York: Basic Books.

Ramsey, P. G. (1991) *Making Friends in School*, New York and London: Teachers College Press.

Save the Children website: http://www.savethechildren.org.uk/onlinepubs/workitout

Siraj-Blatchford, I. and Clarke, P. (2000) *Supporting Identity, Diversity and Language in the Early Years*, Buckingham: Open University Press.

Sonstegard, M., Shuck, A. and Beattie, N. (1979) *Living in Harmony With Our Children*, Luton: Millford Reprographics.

Thompson, M. and O'Neill, C. with Cohen, L. (2001) *Best Friends Worst Enemies: Children's friendships, popularity and social cruelty*, London: Michael Joseph.

Woolfson, R. (1994) *Understanding Children: A guide for parents and carers*, Glasgow: Caring Books.

CHAPTER 7

Working with parents

Parents[1] are the child's first carers and know their children; it is therefore imperative that early years workers establish good relationships with the parents of the children in their care. This chapter explores a number of concepts relating to working with parents, parental involvement and partnerships with parents. Whatever conclusions are drawn between these concepts, there is no doubt that parents have a right to know how their child is developing and be given explanations of the activities that the child is involved in at the early years setting. It is important that the staff in early years settings make decisions about the role of parents within the setting. This will ensure that harmonious relationships are forged that are beneficial to the children and the setting.

Involving parents is not a new concept but one that has been advocated for many years, one of the earliest references coming from Margaret McMillan (1860–1931), who argued that mothers had a right to participate in and manage the nursery schools that their children attended (further detail is given in Chapter 10). Another advocate was J. W. B. Douglas (1964), who found that variation in parental attitudes could account for more of the variation in children's school achievement than either the variation in home circumstances or in the schools. Following on from Douglas, the Plowden Report (1967) recommended that in order to achieve a closer partnership with parents there should be open evenings and reports that give more information to parents. The early 1960s saw the beginnings of the Pre-school Playgroup Association, an integral part of which required the involvement of the parents of the children in the group in order for the groups to operate. In 1988 the Education Act introduced parent-governors into the management of schools in the expectation that such involvement would encourage more parents to participate.

Definitions and terminology

In more recent years the term 'parental involvement' seems to have become synonymous with the term 'partnership with parents'. In many cases it would appear

[1]Parents in this chapter means anyone who is the primary carer of a child.

that the two terms are interchangeable, for example the Department for Education and Skills website (February 2002) has a page labelled 'Parental Involvement' and the article below this title is sub-titled 'Partnership with parents'. The distinction between partnership and involvement does not appear to be recognised by the user groups or higher authorities. Many textbooks have chapters entitled 'Partnership with parents', when the content of the chapter is actually on involvement of parents or parent participation. This confusion of terminology needs to be addressed, as it does not help the professionals or the parents to understand their roles.

Mittler and Mittler (1982) describe the elements of a partnership as 'mutual respect and recognition of the essential equality between parents and professionals; sharing information and skills; sharing of feelings; sharing the process of decision making and recognition of the individuality of families'. Likewise, Pugh and De'Ath (1989) define a partnership as 'a working relationship that is characterised by a shared interest of purpose, mutual respect and the willingness to negotiate. This implies a sharing of information, responsibility, skills, decision-making and accountability.' How different this is from the definition of parental involvement by Howe, Foot and Cheyne (1999), which offers three forms of involvement:

- involvement with daily activities;
- special events (fundraising, excursions, etc.);
- administration.

Smith (1980) has defined five categories of parental involvement: 'working with the children on educational activities, working in the group doing the chores, servicing the group but not actually working, involvement in management and the parent sharing in the child's experiences'.

Partnership with parents or parental involvement?

In 1990 the Department of Health published the document *Playgroups in a Changing World*. Part of this research into pre-school playgroups looked at the involvement of parents. The researchers found the word 'parents' misleading as involvement was predominantly that of mothers and in non-rural areas less than half of the parents were involved in the actual sessions with the children in the playgroup. When there was involvement it was usually on a rota basis whereby parents agreed to one or two sessions every few weeks. One of the most important areas of parental involvement was as a member of the management committee. Some parents helped with the cleaning and maintenance in the playgroup. None of the above roles could be described a partnership with parents as defined by Mittel and Mittel or Pugh and De'Ath.

Parents need clear statements to questions such as: 'Am I involved in my child's nursery or am I a partner? If I am involved in the nursery what is expected of me? If I am a partner in my child's education/care what is expected of me? If I am a partner and this is a true partnership am I able to participate in the decision-making process for my child or am I just here to wash the paint pots and be an extra adult on outings?'

Professionals also need to understand their own role and need answers to questions such as 'What am I able to share with Mrs Y about her child? Is it my role to discuss the behaviour of Mrs Y's child with her and together we work out a plan for dealing with the behaviour? Can I ask Mrs Y to accompany the group on outings and if she does come is she allowed to take responsibility for children other than her own?'

It could be questioned as to whether any parent whose own child is a member of a playgroup or other early years setting is able to work in that group or setting with all the children. This would require a level of professionalism whereby the parent is able to put aside its own child's needs in order to satisfy the needs of the other children in the group. Most professionals prefer not to have their own child as a member of the group for which they are responsible and some may prefer to work in a totally different establishment to that attended by their own child. Howe *et al.* (1999) draw attention to the tensions that can arise when parents are participating in early years settings. Such tensions range from the parents wishing to remain involved because they wish to meet other parents to criticisms about the lack of confidentiality over how some children in the setting behaved. Many staff would have felt happier if they were able to select which parents could be involved with the setting rather than operating an 'open house' invitation.

Parental involvement is linked at one level with socio-economic factors. A parent who is in employment is not always able to participate in a parental involvement scheme that requires attendance on a regular basis, although such a parent may be happy to take part in fund-raising activities. However, this may not preclude the parent being in partnership with the setting as this enables discussion of the child's progress and the sharing of information at the end of the session or at open evenings. Providing the setting respects that this is a working parent and makes the required arrangements, there is no reason why a successful partnership cannot exist. However, this parent would never be able to fulfil the roles required by involvement other than participating in the odd fundraising event such as buying raffle tickets and going to the summer fair.

Cultural factors may prevent a parent's involvement. A parent who has English as an additional language may not feel confident in being in a totally English-speaking environment. In some cultures, including some members of the white working-class culture, the tradition may be to deliver one's child to the school or playgroup and leave the rest to the professionals who work there. A home visit before the child joins the nursery or playgroup can help cement initial relationships with reluctant parents. A person feels most confident on home territory. However, the home visitor must be mindful not to draw stereotypes from a person's home and thus label the child and its family on the strength of a snapshot picture. Those embarking on home visiting should first undergo training so that they are aware of how these sensitive situations should be approached. A nursery or playgroup may find it useful to involve local projects, which could be based on their site, such as adult-education classes that enable the parents to visit on a regular basis in order to gain new skills. Many of the Early Years Centres of Excellence have adopted this idea and it has proved extremely successful in enabling parents to become more confident. As the parent's confidence grows so will the parent's involvement with the establishment grow, based on mutual respect and trust.

The Child Care Bureau of the United States Department of Health and Human Sciences has funded the Child Care Partnership Project. The project provides a series of technical assistant resources and materials to support the development and strengthening of partnerships with parents. The project offers the following tips for success:

- teach parents and partnership leaders how to work together;
- give parents meaningful roles;
- facilitate parent involvement;
- draw linkages between parents.

Cullingford and Morrison (1999) examined the complexities of involving parents in the school. They claim that official attitudes towards parents are ambiguous: for example, on the one hand parents are made accountable for the truancy of their children and on the other hand they are given greater power over schools. This ambiguity can lead to mistrust and recrimination on the parts of parents and the establishment.

As David (1999) points out, one of Tony Blair's government's major projects is to get more women, especially mothers, back into the workforce when their children start school, thus moving the balance away from parental involvement in school and into the workplace.

The DfEE publication *Good Practice in Childcare No. 12* (2000) devotes a whole chapter to children and parents. The opening paragraph, entitled 'Building a partnership with parents', states:

Parents need to be sure that while they are at work or studying, their children are safe, well looked after and enjoying themselves. When parents bring their children to your scheme, they are asking you to become closely involved with their family and will want to work in partnership with you. You need to be accessible to parents and should encourage and welcome their ideas. Parents can offer a lot of support to a scheme; help with fundraising, useful contacts, involvement on the management committee and so on.

This very much gives the impression of parents as consumers/customers. Martin and Vincent (1999) put forward a theory about consumerism and customer choice based on Hirschman's work *Exit, Voice and Loyalty* (1970). Voice is when the customer is able to make known its opinions and criticisms, which in turn leads the provider to become more accountable and change its practices and policies. This aspect of consumerism is applauded within the public sector as it promotes better services. Citizens' Charters were the early attempts to give the clients of the public sector a voice. The Citizens' Charter for Parents lays down the citizen's responsibilities in the form of parents' involvement in their children's education, in addition to their rights to receive certain standards of service. This led to more accountability on the part of the producers, publicised in the form of league tables for education, hospital death rates for health, and so on. These act as quasi prices; for example, where school league tables are poor or hospital death rates are high, consumers are expected to vote with their feet and go elsewhere (what Hirschman refers to as 'Exit'). However, the parents/clients are not in control of the league tables or hospital death rates and therefore in reality they are not able to exert their opinions on them; thus they do not really have a choice. Where would they go? The private sector is the only alternative and is beyond the means of the majority of families. Martin and Vincent do not explore the 'Exit' and 'Loyalty' aspects of Hirschman's theory.

There are ambiguities raised in extrapolating a consumerist theory and applying it to education, as Martin and Vincent point out. For instance, having the opportunity to choose a school for one's child does not necessarily lead to corresponding opportunities for a voice within that school. The school normally determines the home/school relationship on its own terms. Martin and Vincent researched six schools, three of which were primary schools and all of which were described as having high levels of parental involvement. One of the highest levels of parental involvement was in the area of what the authors term as 'Volunteerism', where the school involves the parents as active volunteers/parent helpers. In one school, despite its population being multicultural, the majority of mothers who volunteered were white, monolingual women who had time available.

Easen, Kendall and Shaw (1992) explored the views of parents working together with educators and found these were grounded in two main opinions:

- some parents ought to be worked with in order to compensate their lack of skills and inadequate lifestyles;
- all parents as taxpayers and consumers of education have a *right* to be worked with.

The main assumption of the first viewpoint is that parents will be able to bring up their children better if professional workers tell or show them how to do it. More recently this compensatory approach has been questioned and thinking about partnerships has become more refined. A more effective way for parents and educators working together to promote children's development may be possible when a shared relationship is established and information exchanged.

The partnership relationship is complex and is fraught with problems in practice. The 'equal but different' definition does not take into account the very real inequalities of power between professional workers and parents. There are also inequalities in what people think it is important for them to know as opposed to what other people think it is important to tell them. This argument is taken up by Frank Furedi (2001), who maintains that no parent can be an equal partner with the child-care expert as the terms of any such unequal 'partnership' will be set by the party that has the professional expertise. The parent has to listen and defer to outside opinion as to ignore such expertise is to risk the accusation of being an irresponsible parent. Parents are unlikely to have a strong sense of control if they constantly feel the need to prove themselves. Furedi views this solution as the disempowering of parents by undermining their confidence and promoting the authority of the professional. The writers and deliverers of parenting programmes and 'working together' philosophies appear to be insensitive to their potential in undermining and deskilling parents. Professionals are not concerned with the negative impact they may have on parental confidence as they believe that their crusade is far too important for them to worry about what upset they may cause to the odd mother or father. Furedi believes that the professionals have vastly inflated the complexity of the child-rearing task, thus viewing their own role as indispensable. According to Furedi, a responsible parent today is someone who is prepared to solicit the indispensable advice and support offered by the professional. However, Furedi points out that the very concept of a parenting 'skill' obscures the essence of a child–parent relationship. Children do not benefit from the erosion of their parents' authority. He does acknowledge that there is a need for professional support for families but says that that support should be unobtrusive and targeted towards the small minority of parents who have genuinely failed to establish their authority over their children.

From all of the above research there is one very clear message and that is that settings must be very clear about whether they are advocating parental involvement or partnership with parents. The two concepts are not the same or interchangeable. Having decided which of these positions the setting is going to take then clear definitions of roles and expectations for parents and professionals need to be drawn up. There also needs to be training for the professionals in order to bridge any gaps in their knowledge and skills associated with working with parents.

Empowering and engaging parents

Whilst there are references in the literature of the UK to empowering and engaging parents, the most detailed ideas and research appear in the literature of the USA. This is probably because the USA has been involved in implementing these concepts for a great deal longer, starting in the 1960s with Project Head Start.

Dean (1991) defines empowerment as a process through which people and communities move towards more equitable, respectful interrelationships with themselves and their environment. Dean advocates that for lasting change to occur, it needs to have both personal and policy components. In order for empowerment to happen the balance of power needs to change from 'power over' to 'power with'. Empowerment emphasises family members' strengths. Goldring and Hausman (1997) state that parental empowerment goes beyond simple involvement as it requires also the mind-set, attitude and beliefs of parents in their own abilities to be involved in education and to influence decisions. However, the researchers point out that the emphasis on power-sharing in the empowerment equation makes the professionals reluctant to empower parents as they do not wish to share their own power. Low-income parents have more difficulty accessing a power-sharing relationship than do affluent parents. Goldring and Hausman believe that empowerment comes as a result of the parents' motivation to want to change things. Empowered parents feel more ownership of their children's education whilst enlightened professionals view empowered parents as an asset to the setting. Parents are able to bring a valuable perspective to the setting, as they understand their children's needs and are aware of the community's perceptions, values and beliefs.

Once a setting has decided that it is going to implement a real partnership with parents, in which there will be changes in the balance of power, it needs to look at ways in which it can engage parents in order to encourage them to become involved. Swick (1991) puts forward the following ideas for engaging parents and professionals in joint learning activities:

- support each other in joint learning activities;
- support each other in the respective roles of parent and professional;
- carry out classroom- and school-improvement activities;
- conduct collaborative curriculum projects in the classroom;
- participate together in various decision-making activities;
- be advocates for children.

In addition to these Swick points out that an integral part of success in these areas is the various parent and teacher roles and behaviours that make for a successful partnership.

The DfES (2002) has drawn up the following points for consideration as the medium for engaging parents when producing a home–school agreement:

- Have you asked parents what they expect from the school?
- What do you expect from the parents?
- Have you asked parents what they think of the school?
- How do you involve parents?

- Why do some parents not get involved?
- What can you do to establish an effective working relationship with the 'missing' parents?
- What can you do to help parents help their child?
- What priority do teachers give to working parents?
- What does your school do to listen to the views of pupils?

The document then goes on to list practical methods that might underpin better and more effective relationships with parents. One of the ideas put forward relates to inter-agency collaboration with services that share an interest in parents and their children such as health workers, Travellers' Service, adult education, English as an Additional Language workers and voluntary-sector workers.

Research carried out by Rosado (1994) in the USA looked at ways of promoting partnership with minority parents. A number of findings from this research could be used to inform professionals in the UK when they are designing their implementation strategy for parental partnerships. Researchers worked with Hispanic parents, who are the second-largest ethnic minority and the largest linguistic minority in the USA. The results of the study suggested that cultural, socio-economic, linguistic and educational differences affected the participation of Hispanic parents in the education system. The Hispanic parents in general perceived the teachers as being distant and impersonal as they did not speak to these parents or give them equal attention with that given to other parents. Parents viewed a lack of respect for them from the school staff as a major barrier. Particularly for Hispanics, respect is seen as the foundation for any professional relationship. Once respect is lost it is virtually impossible to resume the interaction. Parents also cited language- and work-related problems as reasons for not being able to visit the school more frequently. The educational background of Hispanic parents also discouraged their participation in school activities (57 per cent of parents in the study had either never been to school themselves or had had less than five years of schooling). As a result of their own poor schooling, these parents found it difficult to be role models and to perform their educational duties as parents.

Settings need to ensure that their staff are behaving towards parents in a way that does not embarrass, humiliate or disrespect the parents. Where additional languages might present communication problems, the setting must ensure that there are interpreters available when the parents visit. It is not respectful to the parents to expect their children to act as interpreters, and it could also be embarrassing if the child is asked to interpret things about itself or confidential information about the family situation. Settings also need to give consideration to the difficulty that parents may have attending meetings and functions when they are in poorly paid jobs that only pay the worker for the hours spent at work. In these cases it means that a time slot convenient to the parents needs to be found in order to ensure that they can attend.

Finally, given below is a useful list of positive things that need to be remembered when setting out to establish effective partnerships with parents.

- All families have strengths.
- Parents can learn new techniques.
- Parents have important perspectives about their children.
- Most parents really care about their children.
- Cultural differences are both valid and valuable.
- Many family forms exist and are legitimate.

It is also important to remember that when forming relationships with parents, special skills are required on the part of the professional. These include good listening techniques, tact, kindness, consideration, empathy, enthusiasm and an understanding of parent–child relationships.

References

Central Advisory Council for Education (1967) *Children and Their Primary Schools* (Plowden Report), London: HMSO.

Cullingford, C. and Morrison, M. (1999) 'Relationships between parents and schools: a case study', in *Educational Review* 51, 3: 253–62.

David, M. (1999) 'Home, work, families and children: New Labour, new directions and new dilemmas', in *International Studies in Sociology of Education* 9, 2: 111–32.

Dean, C. (1991) 'Empowering partnerships with families', in *Innovations in Community and Rural Development*, Cornell Community and Rural Development Institute, Cornell University.

Department of Health (1990) *Playgroups in a Changing World*, London: HMSO.

DfEE (2000) 'The Childcare Start Up Guide', in *Good Practice in Childcare*, No. 12, Nottingham: DfEE Publications.

DfES (2002) 'Parental Involvement: partnership with parents' on the Standards website: http://www.standards.dfee.gov.uk/parentalinvolvement

Douglas, J. W. B. (1964) *The Home and School*, London: MacGibbon and Kee.

Easen, P., Kendal, P. and Shaw, J. (1992) 'Parents and educators: dialogue and development through partnership', in *Children and Society*, 6, 4: 282–96.

Furedi, F. (2001) *Paranoid Parenting*, London: Allen Lane, The Penguin Press.

Goldring, E. and Hausman, C. (1997) 'Empower parents for productive partnerships', in *The Education Digest*, 62, 6: 25–8.

Howe, C., Foot, H. and Cheyne, B. (1999) 'Moving towards real partnership', in *Research in Education*, 64, Spring 1999, Edinburgh: Scottish Council for Research in Education.

Martin, J. and Vincent, C. (1999) 'Parental voice: an exploration', in *International Studies in Sociology of Education*, 9, 2: 133–54.

Mittler, P. and Mittler, H. (1982) *Partnership with Parents*, London: National Council for Special Education.

Moss, P., Brophy, J. and Statham, J. (1992) 'Parental involvement in play-groups', in *Children and Society* 6, 4: 297–316.

Pugh, G. and De'Ath, E. (1989) *Working Towards Partnership in the Early Years*, London: National Children's Bureau.

Rosado, L. A. (1994) 'Promoting partnerships with minority parents: a revolution in today's restructuring efforts', in *The Journal of Educational Issues of Language Minority Students*, 14: 241–54.

Smith, T. (1980) *Parents and Preschool*, London: Grant McIntyre.

Swick, K. (1991) *Teacher–Parent Partnerships to Enhance School Success in Early Childhood Education*, Washington DC: National Education Association.

CHAPTER 8

Play

'ALL WORK AND NO PLAY MAKES JACK A DULL BOY'

From time immemorial children and adults have played. Early writings and paintings have described activities that are seen as the opposite of work, a form of time wasting when people were engaged in trifling activities as a break from their normal routines. However, the old adage recognises that play has some value and since the middle of the nineteenth century philosophers and psychologists have realised that 'play' has an important role in the lives of adults and children, and young children in particular.

But what is play? Many people have spent long hours debating the meaning of the activities that we term play. To date there has been little success in finding an exact definition, as it is a word that means different things to different people in different settings. The *Concise Oxford Dictionary* has twenty-four definitions of the verb 'to play' and ten interpretations of the noun. The first definition of the verb is 'to move about in a lively or capricious manner'. However, when we think about some situations in which the word is used it is apparent that play does not always involve 'moving about in a lively manner'.

Let us consider the following very ordinary settings in which the verb is used.

1 The baby is lying in the pram, playing with her fingers.
2 Two adults are sitting at a table, with intent expressions, playing a game of chess.
3 The girls are building a castle. They have been playing with the Lego for hours.
4 The teacher told the children at the back of the class to stop playing around and get on with their work.
5 The organist was playing a difficult piece of music.

Does play mean the same thing in each of those situations? I suspect that most readers would think that playing the organ or a game of chess were different from the baby playing with her fingers or the children being disruptive in class. It is not surprising that there are numerous definitions of play when the word is used in such a wide range of settings. Furthermore, as Sutton-Smith (1995) has pointed out, any definition reflects the discipline, ideology and cultural preferences of the author.

Even if scholars cannot agree over a definition, it is universally agreed that we engage in playful activities throughout life, although play is mainly associated with childhood and early childhood in particular, from birth to eight years. Throughout the world whenever we observe children in natural settings we see that play is the unique, single central activity of childhood. All children unless they are sick or severely mentally disturbed will play if given the opportunity, as it is through play that they learn to make sense of their world and to come to terms with their environment. However, social and cultural preferences affect the development of play and will also affect whether or not it is acceptable to play in certain settings. For example, children soon learn that in some societies it is unacceptable to play in the presence of elders.

Characteristics of play

Although we cannot define play precisely, authors agree that there are certain characteristics associated with play and playful activities. The most generally accepted are those described by Garvey (1997), Rubin, Fein and Vandenberg (1983) and Fromberg (1997), who argue that play can be defined in terms of dispositions and characteristics.

For them play is:

- *Symbolic* in that it represents an 'as if' and 'what if' attitude. 'As if' behaviour involves the play itself, which enables children to experience particular feelings and attributes, whereas 'what if' behaviour is the activity of the mind that promotes further thinking of ideas through play.
- *Meaningful* in that it connects or relates experiences.
- *Active* because individuals are doing things. The playing of children is always an active process and it is also essential for adult thinking.
- *Pleasurable* even when the activity is serious, for example playing a game of chess.
- *Voluntary and intrinsically motivating*. The motive may be curiosity, or mastery.
- *Rule-governed*, whether implicitly of explicitly expressed. Children's play is often highly rule-governed although the child usually imposes the rules.
- *Episodic* in that there is evidence of emerging and shifting goals that develop through experience. As children play, their goals alter and develop in various ways.
- *Flexible*. For Garvey, flexibility is a hallmark of play.

I think readers will see that if play is defined in terms of these dispositions and characteristics then it will cover all the situations described earlier.

Tina Bruce (1991) has argued that these characteristics and dispositions are not sufficient to describe the play of children and has focused on what she terms free-flow play. She developed a view of play derived from the principles of Gleick's (1988) Chaos theory. This theory is based on the view that the relationship between the process and the product in all systems is non-linear. In play situations the observer is never entirely sure how the child is involved and what the child is getting out of it. As a result there is chaos and controversy inherent in the adults' interpretation of the play and its value. According to Bruce, free-flow play helps the child to integrate, adapt and apply its knowledge and understanding in a play environment without adult direction.

Bruce characterised free-flow play under twelve headings, many of which have much in common with the dispositions of Rubin *et al.* (1983).

For Bruce free-flow play:

1 is an active process without a product;
2 is intrinsically motivated;
3 exerts no eternal pressure to conform to rules, pressures, goals, tasks or definite direction;
4 is about possible alternative worlds, which involve supposing and 'as if'. This involves being imaginative, creative, original and innovative;
5 is about participants wallowing in ideas, feelings and relationships and involves reflecting upon and becoming aware of what we know, or metacognition;
6 uses previous first-hand experience, including struggle, manipulation, exploration discovery and practice;
7 is sustained and, when in full flow, helps us to function in advance of what we can actually do in our real lives;
8 during free-flow play, we use the technical prowess, mastery and competence we have previously developed and so can be in control;
9 can be initiated by a child or an adult, but if by an adult he/she must pay attention to features 3, 5 and 11;
10 can be solitary;
11 can be in partnerships or groups of adults and/or children who will be sensitive to each other;
12 is an integrating mechanism, which brings together everything we learn, know, feel and understand.

Bruce summarises the twelve features by stating that:

Free-flow play = wallowing in ideas, feelings and relationships + application of developed competence.

(Bruce 1991: 59–60)

Theories of play

In this section we shall look at some of the major play theorists and consider their contribution to the argument that play has a crucial role in children's learning.

Friedrich Froebel

Froebel, whose influence was widespread in both Europe and England, postulated his views on play in *The Education of Man*, which was published posthumously in 1896. In this he wrote that 'play truly recognised and rightly fostered, unites the germinating life of the child attentively with the ripe life of experiences of the adult and thus fosters the one through the other'. Froebel believed that play is developed from within the child, but that the presence of the adult and the provision of appropriate materials nurture it. He produced a set of structured toys and playthings, materials which, although not used today, were at the turn of the twentieth century seen as an important part of education for play. He wrote 'at this age play is never trivial, it is serious and deeply significant' (para. 30). Froebel is discussed in more detail in Chapter 10.

Herbert Spencer

Spencer put forward a surplus-energy theory. He believed that the higher animals, including humans, often had periods of excess energy, and play is an acceptable way to use up this excess energy. For him play had no value other than this and it is totally separated from work. In his book *The Principles of Psychology* (1898) he argued that play is carried out 'for the sake of the immediate gratifications involved, without reference to ulterior benefits'. The origins of the surplus-energy theory can be traced back to the writings of the eighteenth-century philosopher Schiller.

Karl Groos

Karl Groos published two important books, *The Play of Animals* (1898) and *The Play of Man* (1901), in which he criticised Spencer's theory arguing that surplus energy may provide a favourable condition for play but was not essential. He argued that play was the means of helping children prepare for life as it provided opportunities for the practice of skills and the possibility of exploring and learning what they will need to know as adults. This is a view that is held by some modern theorists, such as Bruner, whose ideas are discussed later in the chapter.

G. Stanley Hall

Stanley Hall disagreed with the views of Karl Groos, whom he said saw play simply as practice and in its place he proposed the recapitulation theory of play. Stanley Hall argued that through play the child acts out all the human being's primitive behaviours of our evolutionary past. For example, rough-and-tumble play is reminiscent of the wrestling and fighting of the past.

Freudian theorists

Most Freudian theorists have referred to play but I have selected those whom I believe have had some impact upon our understanding of play with young children.

Sigmund Freud

Although Freud did not write a great deal about play, it has nevertheless become an important part of psychoanalytic theory. Freud believed that play was a cathartic experience for children. According to psychoanalytic theory, play takes the form of wish fulfilment and enables the child to master traumatic experiences. Freud (1958) wrote that 'every child at play behaves like an imaginative writer, in that he ... creates a world of his own or, more truly, he arranges the things of this world and orders it in a new way that pleases him better' (page 45). Play enables children to express themselves completely, without reservation or reprisal, because children at play feel safe. Children will use toys and other materials to express the feelings and ideas that they are unable to verbalise. Likewise, during play they will do things that they know they would be reprimanded for doing. For example, the arrival of a new baby in the family may produce anti-social behaviour in the older child as it comes to terms with the existence of a sibling. The child is perfectly aware that it must not hurt the baby, but there is nothing to stop the child giving vent to feelings of jealousy and hatred by drowning its doll. Another way for the child to express its distress could be to engage in an imaginary play situation and walk around sucking a fantasy bottle in an attempt to draw attention to its own need to be fussed over.

Eric Erikson

Erikson also refers to the importance of play, calling his third stage of development, from four to six years, the 'play age'. During this period children need to engage in both solitary and co-operative play as it helps them to develop their initiative and deal with their disappointments and failures. Like Freud, Erikson sees 'as if play' to be important during childhood.

Donald Winicott

Winicott stressed the importance of the transitional object in the development of play. For him play allows children the possibility of suspending reality and exploring potentially threatening experiences in the 'safe' environment of their fantasy world.

Susan Isaacs

Susan Isaacs advocated the importance of play in both the emotional and cognitive growth of children. As a psychoanalyst she believed in the emotional benefits of play, arguing that play has a positive effect upon children's social and cognitive development. She wrote, 'play is indeed the child's work, and the means whereby he grows and develops. Active play can be looked upon as a sign of mental health; and its absence, an indication of either some inborn defect, or of mental illness' (1929). For her, it was through play that children can tell us about their emotional states and we can begin to understand their personalities and behaviours. Susan Isaacs derived her ideas from the many observations she made of children at the Malting House School at Cambridge. Isaacs' influences on the early education curriculum are described in detail in Chapter 10.

Cognitive theorists

Jean Piaget

Piaget based his theory on observations of his own and other children in schools in Geneva. He argued that children are active learners and that two activities, play and imitation, are important for the development of infants and young children. Piaget considered that play was a product of assimilation, whereas imitation resulted from accommodation. During play, children act out their already established behaviours and adapt reality to fit them in an enjoyable manner. During imitation, by contrast, children are trying to copy other people's actions in order to understand the world around them.

Piaget argued (1962) that children's play evolves in three stages, which could be linked to his four stages of intellectual development. There are three different forms of cognitive play that emerge during the early years: 'practice games or mastery play, symbolic games, and games with rules'. The mastery stage is predominantly associated with his sensori-motor stage of cognitive development, while the symbolic stage is closely linked to the pre-operational stage of behaviour. For him it is not until the phase of concrete operations that children are able to engage in games with rules. Piaget argued that the symbolic-play stage was crucial for the development of symbolic representation, which he believed is necessary before children can engage in co-operative play. True co-operative play is impossible until children can develop social perspective taking skills, which are a pre-requisite to playing games with rules. Piaget has argued that at the pre-operational stage children's thinking is egocentric and therefore they cannot engage in true game play. More recently theorists have argued that children are capable of playing co-operatively at an earlier age and have disputed the point of view that children are unable to see another person's point of view. (See Chapter 3, on 'How children learn'.)

Jerome Bruner

Bruner sees play as beneficial to cognitive development as for him it is a preparation for the 'technical social life that constitutes human culture'. He argues that play serves both as practice for mastery in skills and as an opportunity to try out new combinations of behaviour in a safe setting. Exploratory play, in which children experiment with materials, and social play, which encourages children to acquire the rules and rituals of the society in which they live, are beneficial to the child. Bruner believes that all play has rules, but unlike Piaget he does not think they come with increasing age, rather that the rules are there from the start. In his now-famous Peek-a-Boo experiment he demonstrated that even a very young child understands the rules of turn taking that are the basis of this game. However, Bruner does not see all play as being of equal value. For example, he sees rough-and-tumble play as less intellectually challenging than 'high yield' activities such as construction or drawing activities, which are more goal-orientated (Sylva, Roy and Painter 1980).

Lev Vygotsky

Although his ideas were known in Russia earlier, Vygotsky's views on play did not become well known in the West until the second half of the twentieth century. For Vygotsky play is a vehicle for social interaction and is the leading source of development in the pre-school years. He argues that a 'zone of proximal development' is created by play, and therefore in play children are learning how to function beyond their present capabilities. Like Piaget, Vygotsky sees play developing into games with rules but, for him, just as the imaginary situation has to contain rules of behaviour, so every game with rules contains an imaginary situation. For example, when children are playing at 'hospitals', each child within the group will have taken on a role and be acting it out according to his or her own interpretation. Each child will be governed by the rules laid down by the group. Vygotsky, as Bruner and Piaget, believes that from about eight years of age games with rules are more important than free-flow play.

Play develops symbolic thinking by facilitating the separation of thought from objects and actions. A special feature of the Vygotskian approach to play is his belief that in play the child is not truly free, as the play situation actually sets the limits on behaviour. Through language and symbolic thought, play involves self-regulatory behaviour that involves children developing the ability to plan, monitor and reflect upon their own behaviour. Vygotsky argues that children who are unable to practise these skills in their play will be unable to use these processes when they are engaged in other non-play activities.

Maria Montessori

By contrast with some of the more recent theorists and early childhood educators who advocate the value of play in children's learning, Maria Montessori considered that children learn through real-life activities. For her, play 'in the life of the child … is perhaps something of little importance which he undertakes for the lack of something better to do' (Montessori 1956). Montessori is discussed in depth in Chapter 10.

What are the functions of play and how does it contribute to young children's learning?

Since the end of the nineteenth century, the writings of Rousseau and Froebel have been influential in promoting a tradition in western Europe and the USA that regarded play as essential to learning and development. One of the leading early childhood educators of the time, Susan Isaacs (1929), wrote that 'play indeed is the child's work and the means by which he or she develops'. This point of view is still held today by many early childhood educators who aim to provide young children with ample opportunity to practice and develop skills and competencies in play settings.

Before we consider the contribution of play to children's learning it is important that we look at the various stages of play and how they develop throughout childhood. One of the earliest studies to look at the development of children's play is that of Mildred Parten (1933), who observed children between the ages of two and five years playing in nursery school without any adult intervention. Parten identified four categories of social participation among these children.

1 *Solitary independent play* – the child plays alone independently and with its own toys, without reference to others.
2 *Parallel activity* – the child plays independently but the chosen activity encourages the child to play beside others, although not influenced by the activities of the other children. The child plays *beside* rather than *with* other children.
3 *Associative play* – the child plays with other children. There is a sharing and borrowing of materials but the play is not organised; each child behaves according to its own wishes, without reference to a group.
4 *Co-operative play* – generally around four to five years of age the child plays in a group that is organised for a purpose. For example, socio-dramatic play, or playing a formal game.

Although the younger children normally prefer solitary or parallel play, there are also occasions when older children choose to play alone. The level of solitary play may be lower when engaged in by the youngest children but, as Rubin has pointed out, when older children are involved in solitary play, it can be cognitively very complex, for example when an older child is playing with construction material.

Sarah Smilansky (1990) researched into children's play behaviours and has shown how play develops as a complex adaptive system as children grow older. She argues that there are five basic forms of play.

1 *Functional or exploratory play* – the child uses sensory motor abilities to learn about its surroundings; much of the motor and object play in the early years is at this level.
2 *Constructive play* – the child combines objects or articles, such as blocks.
3 *Dramatic play* – the child pretends to be someone else, imitating a person's actions and speech, role taking and using either real or imaginary props.
4 *Socio-dramatic play* – this involves co-operation between at least two children around a theme that evolves over a period of time.
5 *Games with rules* – these include co-operative players, often winners and losers. The rules are normally child-controlled rules and are therefore different from the competitive games or sports that have adult-regulated rules.

Socio-dramatic play is the most complex, combining as it does elements or combinations of other types of play. It is this form of play that is valued most highly by early childhood educators as they believe that in these play bouts children learn a great deal about the world in which they live.

Fantasy/socio-dramatic play

Piaget saw fantasy play in terms of assimilation and accommodation, arguing that during fantasy play children create pretend new situations and they assimilate the fantasy elements into existing schema. In this way they come to make sense of their world. Several writers have emphasised the importance of fantasy play in children's learning. Erikson (1965) stressed the importance of the life-rehearsal element in fantasy play, suggesting that it helps children come to terms with social issues such as loneliness, failure and disappointment. Bruner, on the other hand, saw fantasy play as the precursor of social rules. Cognitive, social-interactionist and psychoanalytical theorists all appear to agree that fantasy play has value for children's development. Singer and Singer (1990: 152) wrote: 'Imaginative play is fun, but in the midst of the joys of making believe, children may also be preparing for the reality of more effective lives.'

Pretend play becomes evident around twelve months of age, as children use a brush or comb on their hair or a cup to pretend to drink. However, this early pretending is a solitary activity and it is not until around two years of age that such activities as taking a baby doll for a walk in parallel with another toddler occur. Even though two two-year-old children play together at going shopping, they are not yet aware of the social roles involved. By the time the children are three or older they can engage in complicated dramatic play sequences, which become more and more involved with increasing age. Role-play develops and it is not uncommon for children to take on a whole range of characters, both real and fictional. Socio-dramatic play involves high levels of both verbal and physical interaction with other children.

What do we mean by socio-dramatic play or fantasy play? Smilansky and Shefataya (1990: 22) believe the following elements should be present:

- imitative role-play – the child undertakes a make-believe role and expresses it in imitative action and/or verbalisation;
- make-believe with regard to toys – movements or verbal declarations and/or materials or toys that are not replicas of the object itself are substituted for actions or situations;
- verbal make-believe with regard to actions and situations – verbal descriptions or declarations are substituted for actions or situations;
- persistence in role-play – the child continues within a role or play theme for a period of at least ten minutes;
- interaction – at least two players interact within the context of the play episode;
- verbal communication – there is some verbal interaction related to the play episode.

The first four of these relate to fantasy play, but to be defined as socio-dramatic play there must be all six elements.

Smilansky observed three- to five-year-old children at play and proposed a number of ways in which she thought socio-dramatic play was beneficial in the development of the creativity, intellectual and social skills of children.

In socio-dramatic play, children can be seen carrying out some or all of the following:

1 creating new combinations out of experiences;
2 selectivity and intellectual discipline;
3 discrimination of the central features of a role sequence;
4 heightened concentration;
5 enhanced self-awareness and self-control;
6 self-discipline within the role context (for example, the child within a game might inhibit shouting out because it was not in keeping with the behaviour of the character);
7 the acquisition of flexibility and empathy towards others;
8 the development of an intrinsic set of standards;

9 acquisition of a sense of creativity and empathy towards others;
10 development of co-operative skills since make-believe games in groups require effective give and take;
11 awareness of the potential use of the environment for planning and other play situations;
12 increased sensitivity to alternative possibilities so that the notion of father need not be one's own father but may include many kinds of behaviour associated within the broader concept of fathering;
13 increased capacity for the development of abstract thought through learning first to substitute the image for the overt action and then later a verbal coding for both the action and the image;
14 heightened capacity for generalisations;
15 a set towards vicarious learning and a greater use of modelling.

(Smilansky in Singer 1973: 224)

Other writers, for example Johnson (1990), have argued that it is during socio-dramatic play, when children formulate their own goals and engage in co-operation and reciprocity, that they develop the ability to build the conceptual frameworks necessary to help them understand and integrate different areas and levels of experience.

Case study: a group of four children aged four years

The following is a description of a socio-dramatic play episode that took place in a nursery after two of the children had visited local dentists.

The teacher, who was aware that the children had recently visited the dentist, had arranged the Home Corner as a dental surgery. A group of four children wandered into the area and spontaneously decided to 'play at dentists'. One girl took on the role of the dentist and two boys were patient and dental nurse respectively, while the youngest child was given the role of the receptionist.

During the play, which lasted for more than twenty minutes, the children acted out their roles with a considerable degree of accuracy, using the language and behaviours of the adults they were imitating. The play was complex and as the children acted out their roles they recalled their previous experiences at the dentist, showing clearly that they had an understanding of the various adult roles. One of the liveliest language exchanges took place when the two children who had been seen in two different surgeries discussed the 'differences' between the two practices. As the play progressed, so the children moved away from the rules that govern 'dentist play' and adopted another theme, which had been triggered by their discussions. All the time they were reformulating and elaborating their plans and renegotiating their roles. To the onlooker it was apparent that the new theme was as absorbing as the original one.

Throughout the play bout all the children had displayed a high level of social and emotional competence and had demonstrated their ability to transform past experiences into new settings. Both perceptual and motor skills were used as they acted out their interpretation of the roles of dentist, patient, nurse and receptionist. To the adult onlooker during this particular play episode there was evidence to uphold Smilansky's thesis on the value of socio-dramatic play in the developing of intellectual and social skills.

What other evidence is there to suggest that children learn through play? One of the few controlled studies to test this was carried out by Hutt (1966). She suggested that there are two forms of play: exploratory and ludic. During exploratory play children are involved in a range of activities that are conducive to learning, as opposed to ludic play, which she considered to be trivial and purposeless.

Hutt set out to see how a group of children reacted to a novel object (a toy box that had flashing lights and made different noises) and whether the exploratory behaviour changed as they became more familiar with the toy. From her observations of thirty children aged from three to five years, Hutt argued that children explored first and then played. In the beginning, when the children explored the toy box 'to find out what it could do', their behaviour was serious and focused. Once they had satisfied their curiosity their behaviour became more relaxed and play changed to 'what can I do with this object?' In 1972, Hutt and Bhavnani followed up the children who had been involved in the original study. They found that those children who had played in many imaginative ways with the toy after a thorough exploration scored significantly higher on tests of creativity than those who had not played much with the novel object.

More recently a study of children with learning difficulties has linked physical play to learning and in a study carried out in a Frankfurt kindergarten it was found that 'increased accidents in the playground were directly linked to lack of movement and body control' (Blythe 2001).

Value of play in children's emotional development

Children possess the capacity for experiencing deep emotions. When the child hurts, it hurts all over. You have only to observe a three-year-old child who has momentarily lost its mother to see the intensity of feeling as the child calls out 'Mummy, Mummy' and sobs and sobs, its whole body shaking. Equally, when children are happy they are intensively happy. Their mood swings are rapid and to the adult unpredictable. At this early age children are unable to manage their emotions, and the feelings of frustration, anger and sadness they experience can be very frightening. Young children do not possess the verbal language to express the depth or range of their feelings; for them the most natural language of communication is through play. Play is a form of self-expression and symbolic play in particular is an important vehicle for expressing feelings. When children are offered a safe and non-threatening environment they will communicate the depth of their feelings through play. Children do not talk about their concerns and problems, they play them out.

Bettelheim suggests that during play, 'objects such as dolls and toy animals are used to embody various aspects of the child's personality which are too complex, unacceptable, and contradictory for him to handle. This permits the child's ego to gain some mastery over these elements, which he cannot do when asked or forced by circumstances to recognize these as projections of his own inner processes' (1978: 55).

As discussed in Chapter 3, more recent writers, such as Goleman (1996), have argued the case for 'emotional literacy' as an essential part of children's later learning and development. See the list on pages 37–8 for a reminder of the key components of emotional literacy.

All the skills and competencies of emotional literacy can be learned most effectively in play settings. Socio-dramatic play is especially valuable for helping children to develop emotional literacy, as during their play children can have feelings of power over the environment, emotional awareness and sensitivity. Above all, in many role-play situations young children can develop emotional strength and stability, humour and positive feelings about themselves.

Empathy and understanding of the feelings of others develops from an early age. One has only to see the concern on the face of the two/three-year-old when another child falls over and cuts its knee to realise that children are certainly not totally egocentric. During role-play in pre-school and primary-school settings, children are able to interact through language. As they interact with assumed roles, children are able to experience emotional responses to each role and can decide whether to continue in that role, swap roles or select an entirely different role. This type of activity is not only supporting children's emotional development but also helps in problem-solving situations.

Strong emotions such as aggression, frustration and fear can all be controlled during play sessions. Susan Isaacs believed that it was crucial for educators to understand the inner world of the child, a world that adults did not necessarily share. She realised that early capacities for emotional expression and recognition are the foundation of social learning and communication.

A study by Kelly-Bryne (1989) showed how one child's play revealed themes of fear, aggression and violence as she played out battles of good and evil, beauty and ugliness, sense and stupidity. The little girl was displaying powerful feelings and behaviours that some children can only learn to control and understand in prosocial ways if they are given the opportunity to articulate these feelings in a supportive context. The result may be behavioural problems that lead further into a negative cycle of difficulties that then impact upon peers and adults alike.

It is through their subjective, emotional world that young children learn to make sense of their relationships and eventually their place in the wider world. All this can be learned in play situations.

Cultural and gender differences in children's play

In a review of play in different cultures, Curtis (1994) found that play was the dominant activity of children in all cultures. Although writers such as Brazelton (1977) have argued that among some cultures in which swaddling is practised infants are not able to play because they are on their mothers' backs all day, others have observed these children finding opportunities for playing with objects, even if it is only the jewellery worn by their mothers. Imaginative play is another area in which writers have observed differences between the cultures. Feitelson (1977) argued that children from some traditional cultures are deficient in imaginative play abilities, but I and others would argue that if children are observed for long enough it is possible to see the emergence of imaginative play even when there is a paucity of toys and equipment. I have watched young children in South America playing with tins and stones and although I could not understand what they were saying it was very obvious that some form of imaginative play was taking place.

There are interesting cultural differences in the value placed on toys. In most Western societies adults value toys that are designed to teach skills and develop cognitive understanding, whereas in most traditional African societies, parents give their children toys just to play with; the learning comes later. Children not only need time and space to play, but they also need adults to help them develop their skills. Parental attitudes towards their children's play varies across cultures, but the evidence suggests that where the attitudes are positive, children are likely to become involved in high levels of imaginative and creative play.

There are few studies that look in detail at children's play in different cultural settings and, as has been pointed out by Roopnarine et al. (1998), these have been mainly with North American or European families and may be culturally biased. From the review of the literature, they found that when traditional and non-traditional families were compared, the following differences could be noted:

- children's play is more likely to reflect rituals and customs in traditional societies;
- one-to-one play occurs more often in non-traditional families;
- gender differentiation has been observed in child–parent play in non-traditional families but not consistently observed in traditional societies;
- variations in games such as Peek-a-Boo and Pat-a-Cake between adult and child occurs in both types of societies;
- group participation, interdependence and community values are transmitted through play in traditional cultures whereas self-reliance, independence and competition are encouraged by non-traditional cultures.

(Roopnarine et al. in Sayeed and Guerin 2000: 20)

There has been a great deal of discussion about whether there are gender differences in children's play. Until about three years of age children of both sexes play in a similar way, but by the age of three it seems that play preferences emerge. Some researchers suggest that by the time girls are three they will focus upon play with dolls and household items, art activities and dressing up, while boys will play with cars, blocks and engage in more large-group and aggressive play. It has been suggested that during fantasy play boys will tend to act out fighting and more aggressive activities while girls will act out real-life situations based on their immediate culture. As early as 1933 Parten had found that during free play children elected to play with same-sex playmates, a finding that is supported by many early years workers of today.

In a review of the literature of children under school age, Nepply and Murray (1997) looked at sex-stereotypical behaviour and found that imaginative play tended to occur most frequently when children were in same-sex pairs. They found that boys are more likely to engage in large-group aggressive play whereas girls play in smaller, quiet groups. Interestingly, Thorne (1993) also found that the play of girls was generally more collaborative as opposed to the hierarchical nature of the play of boys. Serbin *et al.* (1982) found that girls, possibly because of their greater linguistic ability, were more likely to use polite requests and persuasion to get their own way, whereas boys were more likely to use force and aggressive comments. Whether this is true of the play of all children is questionable and it may reflect the approach of both the parents and the school as well as the personality of the child.

A cross-cultural study carried out by Lindsey *et al.* (1997) suggests that parents may contribute to children's gender-specific styles of play by treating their daughters and sons differently. They found that:

• girls were more likely to engage in pretend play;
• boys engaged more in physical play;
• fathers of boys engaged in physical play more with their children than mother or fathers of girls;
• mothers' presence encouraged both sexes to engage in pretend play.

In a recent study in Tower Hamlets, Sayeed and Guerin (1997) found that although teachers found few differences in children's play across cultures, there were distinctly identifiable gender differences.

Even though parents believe that they are providing their children with equal opportunities within the play setting, many are horrified when they realise that their children still adopt sex-stereotypical behaviours that they cannot believe they have learnt from home. Dixon (1990) has argued strongly that toys and play materials are important in shaping the outlook of young children. Television and the media have been criticised for the gender images they convey, but more recently research has suggested that children are not just passive consumers who accept the stereotypes shown, but do, in fact, work out for themselves what is appropriate. Hislam (1996) has pointed out that there are powerful influences upon children to behave in socially sexually appropriate ways and that by exploring the roles in their socio-dramatic play, children come to terms with 'who they are' and see themselves as individuals.

Role of other children in play

During the early years of life both adults and other children act as play partners, each providing different kinds of play experiences. Many would argue that the prime reason for sending children to early childhood settings is to help them to socialise and learn to play with others. There has been a great deal of research on the role of siblings and peers supporting development, which is discussed in Chapter 3, but overall it appears that during play, siblings and peers provide opportunities for children to:

- learn about different cultural and family backgrounds;
- broaden their experiences with a diversity of peers;
- develop friendships and other peer relationships;
- develop individuality apart from siblings and family;
- engage in different social roles in various play activities.

Role of the adult in children's play

There is no doubt that children can learn a great deal during free-play activities but, as most of the theorists have suggested, adults have an important influence upon children's play, both directly and indirectly. The adult may provide the stimulus by structuring the environment as in our example of the 'dental practice corner', or by taking children on an outing such as a visit to the shops. Vygotsky believed that the adult is needed to model and show the child how to play with materials and how to take turns. It is the adult who leads the child through the zone of proximal development and helps the child progress to higher levels of play. Bruner has a similar approach, arguing that the adult provides the scaffold for the child. This does not necessarily mean that the adult should be involved in the play, but should make the suggestions or organise the activities so that more mature behaviour occurs.

Smilansky (1968), working with disadvantaged children, believed that they seldom engaged in complex socio-dramatic play compared with children from more advantaged backgrounds. She suggested that educators work with these children to initiate role-play and help them to sustain and develop their roles. In her programme early years workers were trained to engage in 'play tutoring', using four main approaches.

1 *Modelling* – the teacher participates in the play and acts out a role, demonstrating how it can be carried out.

2 *Verbal guidance* – the teacher does not necessarily join in but comments and offers suggestions to the children on how to develop the role.
3 *Thematic-fantasy training* – the children are encouraged to act out familiar story dramas. This type of more structured approach is often found in nurseries in eastern Europe.
4 *Imaginative play training* – The teacher encourages the children to use finger puppets and to practise making facial expressions to represent different emotions.

From her studies, Smilansky and others argued that as a result of play tutoring children from socially disadvantaged backgrounds engaged in more sophisticated play and used more language. Smith carried out a similar experiment in nursery settings with children mainly from economically disadvantaged backgrounds and found that after play tutoring the children engaged in greater fantasy play. His sample was small but it is one of the few controlled studies in this country that points to the value of play tutoring.

Not everyone agrees that adults should intervene in children's play, particularly imaginative play, as it can have an adverse effect upon the children. There is no doubt that intervention must be sensitive and unobtrusive, otherwise that particular play bout will end abruptly. Most educators and parents can remember occasions when they have offered what they thought was a useful resource only to find it rejected by the children, who immediately ceased playing. Educators need to be skilled in knowing when and how to intervene and the strategies required to empower children as learners. Jones and Reynolds (1992) looked at the role of the educator in children's play and found that teachers used a variety of strategies to support and promote quality play. They acted as planner, stage manager, scribe, mediator, role model, player, assessor and communicator. In each of these situations the adult was helping the children to find their own solutions but at the same time accepting the ideas and interests of the children.

Conclusion

Article 31 of the United Nations Convention on the Rights of the Child states:

> Parties recognise the right of the child to rest and leisure, to engage in play and recreational activities appropriate to the age of the child and to participate freely in cultural life and the arts.

The importance of this right is recognised by most adults but many still consider play as a time-wasting activity and not as an activity that is the main vehicle for learning in the early years of life. Throughout this chapter we have seen evidence that play, and socio-dramatic play in particular, is of value in promoting children's social, and emotional development. However, there is little hard evidence to show that free play is essential for cognitive growth. Most early childhood educators will accept that there are certain skills and competencies that cannot be learned during free-play settings; for example, learning to cut with scissors. Nevertheless, they would argue that children are more likely to be successful in cognitive tasks in school if they have had the opportunity to explore and try out varying strategies in play settings before being presented with formal instruction. If play is to be seen as a process that will promote learning and development, it must be of high quality. Educators should not only provide an environment that offers high-quality resources but should also guide children so that they can develop their confidence as successful players and learners. No one would argue that play is the only way children learn, but the child who has been given ample opportunities for quality play of all types – physical, social and cognitive – is more likely to be an eager, enthusiastic and successful learner.

References

Bettelheim, B. (1978) *The Uses of Enchantment*, Harmondsworth: Penguin Books.

Blythe, C. (2001) *Play time not optional*, TES, 12 January 2001.

Brazelton, T. (1977) 'Implications of infant development among Mayan Indians of Mexico', in P. Leiderman, S. R. Tulkin and E. Rosenfeld (eds), *Culture and Infancy: Variations in the human experience*, New York: Academic Press.

Bretherton, I. (ed.) (1984) *Symbolic Play: The development of social understanding*, New York: Academic Press.

Bruce, T. (1991) *Time to Play in Early Childhood Education*, London: Hodder & Stoughton.

Bruner, J. (1971) *The Relevance of Education*, New York: Norton.

Bruner, J. (1972) 'Nature and Uses of Immaturity', in *American Psychologist* 27, 8: 687–708.

Curtis, A. (1994) 'Play in different cultures and different childhoods', in J. Moyles (ed.), *The Excellence of Play*, Buckingham: Open University Press.

Dixon, B. (1990) *Playing Them False: A study of children's toys, games and puzzles*, Stoke on Trent: Trentham Books.

Erikson, E. (1965) *Childhood and Society*, London: Routledge & Kegan Paul.

Fein, G. G. (1981) 'Pretend play in childhood: An integrative review', in *Child Development*, 52: 1095–118.

Feitelson, N. (1977) 'Developing imaginative play in pre-school children as a possible approach to fostering creativity', in *Early Child Development and Care*, 1: 181–95.

Fogel, A. (1979) 'Peers vs mother-directed behaviour in 1–3 month old infants', in *Infant Behaviour and Development*, 2: 215–26.

Freud, A. (1958) *Normality and Pathology in Childhood: Assessments of development*, New York: International.

Froebel, F. W. (1896) *The Education of Man*, New York: Appleton.

Fromberg, D. (1997) 'A review of research on play', in C. Seefeldt (ed.), *The Early Childhood Curriculum*, second edition, New York: Teachers' College Press.

Garvey, C. (1977) *Play*, first edition, London: Fontana Press.

Gleick (1988) *Chaology*, London and New York: Heinemann.

Goleman, D. (1995) *Emotional Intelligence*, New York: Bantam.

Groos, K. (1898) *The Play of Animals*, New York: Appleton.

Groos, K. (1901) *The Play of Man*, New York: Heinemann.

Hislam, J. (1996) 'Sex-differentiated play and children's choices', in J. Moyles (ed.), *The Excellence of Play*, Buckingham: Open University Press.

Howes, C. and Matheson, C. C. (1992) 'Sequences in the development of competent play with peers: social and pretend play', in *Developmental Psychology*, 28: 961–74.

Hutt, C. (1966) 'Exploration and play in young children', *Symposia of the Zoological Society of London*, 18: 61–87.

Hutt, C. and Bhavnani (1972) 'Predictions from Play', in *Nature*, 237: 171–2.

Isaacs, S. (1929) *The Nursery Years*, London: Routledge and Kegan Paul.

Johnson, J. E. (1990) 'The role of play in children's cognitive development', in E. Klugman and S. Smilansky (eds), *Children's Play and Learning: Perspectives and policy implications*, New York: Teachers' College Press.

Jones, E. and Reynolds, G. (1992) *The Play's the Thing: Teachers' roles in children's play*, New York: Teachers' College Press.

Kelly-Bryne, D. (1989) *A Child's Play Life: An ethnographic study*, New York: Teachers' College Press.

Klugman, E. and Smilansky, S. (1969) *Children's Play and Learning: Perspectives and policy implications*, New York: Teachers' College Press.

Lindsey, E., Mize, J. and Gregory, S. (1997) 'Differential play patterns of mothers and fathers of sons and daughters: implications for children's gender role development', in *Sex Roles: A journal of research*, 37 (9–10): 643–62.

Montessori, M. (1956) *The Child in the Family*, New York: Avon. (First published 1936.)

Nepply, T. and Murray, A. (1997) 'Social dominance and play patterns among pre-schoolers: gender comparisons', in *Sex Roles: A journal of research*, 36: (5–6).

O'Connor, E. (1991) *The Play Therapy Primer*, New York: John Wiley.

Parten, M. (1933) 'Social play amongst pre-school children', in *Journal of Abnormal and Social Psychology*, 28: 136–47.

Piaget, J. (1952) *The Origins of Intelligence in Children*, New York: Norton.

Piaget, J. (1962) *Play, Dreams and Imitation in Childhood*, New York: Norton.

Roopnarine, S., Lasker, J., Sacks, M. and Stores, M. (1998) 'The cultural contexts and children's play', in O. Saracho and B. Spodek (eds), *Multiple Perspectives on Play in Early Childhood Education*, Albany, NY: Steele University/New York Press.

Rubin, K., Fein, G. and Vandenberg, B. (1983) 'Play', in P. Mussen (ed.), *Manual of Child Psychology*, 4: 693–774, New York: Wiley.

Sayeed, Z. and Guerin, E. (1997) 'Play, assessment and culture', in S. Wolfendale (ed.), *Meeting Special Needs in the Early Years*, London: David Fulton Publishers.

Schwartzmann, H. B. (1978) *Transformations: The anthropology of children's play*, New York: Plenum.

Serbin, L., Spratkin, A., Elmin, M. and Doyle, M. (1982) 'The early development of sex-differentiated patterns of social influence', *Canadian Journal of Social Science*, 14: 350–63.

Singer, J. L. (ed.) (1973) *The child's world of make believe: Experimental studies of imaginative play*, New York: Academic Press.

Singer, J. and Singer, D. (1990) *The House of Make Believe: Children's play and developing imagination*, Cambridge, Mass.: Harvard University Press.

Smilansky, S. (1968) *Effects of Socio-dramatic Play on Disadvantaged Pre-school Children*, New York: John Wiley.

Smilansky, S. (1990) 'Socio-dramatic play: its relevance to behaviour and achievement in school', in E. Klugman and S. Smilansky (eds), *Children's Play and Learning: Perspectives and policy implications*, New York: Teachers' College Press.

Smilansky, S. and Shefataya, L. (1990) *Facilitating Play: A medium for promoting cognitive, socio-emotional and academic development in young children*, Gaitherrsburg, MD: Psychological and Educational Publications.

Smith, P., Cowie, H. and Blades, M. (1998) *Understanding Children's Development*, third edition, Oxford: Blackwell.

Spencer, H. (1898) *The Principles of Psychology*, New York: Appleton.

Sutton-Smith, B. (1995) 'The persuasive rhetorics of play', in A. Pellegrini (ed.), *The Future of Play Theory: Essays in honor of Brian Sutton-Smith*, Albany: State University of New York Press.

Sylva, K., Roy, C. and Painter, M. (1980) 'Child-watching at playgroup and nursery school', *Oxford Pre-school Research Project*, Oxford: Grant McIntyre.

Thorne, B. (1993) *Gender Play: Boys and girls in school*, Milton Keynes: Open University Press.

Vygotsky, L. S. (1967) 'Play and its role in the mental development of the child', in *Soviet Psychology*, 12, 6: 62–76.

CHAPTER 9

Management issues in the early years

Recent years have seen the publication of books on management that are specific to early years settings, thus acknowledging that not only is this an important topic but that it probably is quite different from other management situations. Managing an early years setting requires effective communication skills with parents, children and staff. It also necessitates communicating with a variety of outside agencies such as social services, psychologists, play therapists, health visitors, doctors, social workers, medical consultants and the police, to name but a few. It is rare that any non-early years manager is likely to have to liaise with so many different professionals in the day-to-day management of a company/department/section. It is the acknowledgement of this that has instigated people to write textbooks on nursery management and, in turn, that this area has been legitimised by the introduction of the Early Years Care and Education National Vocational Qualification (NVQ) Level 4 Management strand. The performance criteria for the NVQ Level 4 clarify what the management role entails and what the requirements are in order to be an effective manager of an early years setting.

Sadek and Sadek (1996) say that the role of the manager is to:

- ensure that the children are given a quality of service of care;
- support and supervise staff who deliver this service;
- consult and respect wishes of the children's parents/carers;
- provide adequate resources in the nursery to enable the service to function;
- set up a rich and stimulating environment in which the service can be delivered;
- undertake external liaison and fulfil an ambassadorial function;
- be a role model for the staff and children.

This chapter will look at specific aspects of management and the issues involved.

Managing the establishment

When we talk about managing children we quite often look at the effectiveness of ensuring that there are parameters laid down within which the children can function. Such parameters offer the child a secure environment in which to explore and learn. It is no different for adults, who, like children, want to know the boundaries within which they can safely operate. In managing a nursery these boundaries are defined by a mission statement and a number of policies and procedures within which staff have to work.

The idea of a mission statement originated in the USA amongst the big corporations and quickly spread to smaller establishments such as schools and welfare services. The UK has happily adopted the mission-statement concept and it has now become an integral part of most establishments' day-to-day working. A mission statement is best drawn up by all the staff so that there is a feeling of ownership and commitment to its aims. It is important that all workers, from the cleaners to senior managers, are in agreement with the philosophy of the setting as laid down in the mission statement. Sadek and Sadek (1996) state that an effective mission statement will:

- state clearly the purpose or intention of the organisation;
- indicate an underlying value system;
- be written in good plain English;
- be no less than 30 and no more than 100 words;
- be translated into the first language of all the users.

In addition to the mission statement there is a series of policy and procedure documents that the setting needs to have in place. Some of these will be required by law, for example the Health and Safety Policy, some may be required by the Children Act 1989 registration regulations, for example the Child Protection Policy and others may be there in order to ensure good practice, for example a policy on Financial Procedures.

Examples of policies required are as follows:

- Equal Opportunities Policy;
- Behaviour Management Policy;
- Health and Safety Policy;
- Inclusion of Children with Special Needs/Disabilities Policy.

Examples of procedures required are as follows:

- Complaints Procedures;
- Accident Procedures;
- Financial Procedures.

Whilst it might appear overly prescriptive to have such a large number of policies and procedures, it does add to the security of the staff as they know that if something untoward happens then there is a definite way in which it should be dealt with. Policies and procedures prevent haphazard thinking in times of stress and enable staff to feel reassured that by following the policy/procedure, they have taken the correct action in a moment of crisis. In terms of equal opportunities, policies/procedures ensure that all incidents are dealt with in exactly the same way regardless of who is involved.

Parents are also reassured by policies/procedures, as they know that the setting has thought through what it is doing and how situations will be handled in the event of their child being badly behaved or having an accident.

Sadek and Sadek (1996) put forward the following list of roles a manager needs to assume in order to manage staff:

- manager as leader;
- manager as motivator;
- manager as support;
- manager as empowerer;
- manager as controller.

However, as Adirondack (1998) points out, no one person can be good at all aspects of management; however, people can use their own strengths and skills to the best advantage in order to become a 'good enough manager'.

Managing people (human-resources management)

All nursery establishments have a range of staff such as qualified child-care workers, teachers, unqualified child care assistants, cook, laundress, caretaker, kitchen staff, gardener, and so on. Each occupational area will have its own conditions of service, pay scales, working hours and trade union or professional association. The person in charge of human resources and/or delivery of the service in the setting will need to be aware of the situation as it affects each occupational area and will need to work within these in order to get the best quality of service. For example, it is important to ensure that the staff are trained and are appropriately qualified to a standard that enables them to provide the establishment with the best possible service. Some staff may require additional training in order to achieve the establishment's mission-statement aims.

According to Adirondack, being a human-resources manager involves:

- ensuring the organisation has clear appropriate and workable policies and procedures for all aspects of employment;
- ensuring all staff, whether paid or voluntary, are properly recruited, inducted, supervised, trained and supported;
- ensuring all workers are valued and feel they are part of a team and the organisation;
- involving workers in discussions and decisions that affect their work or working environment;

- ensuring workers know what they are supposed to be doing, how to do it and how it fits into the organisation's overall work;
- helping workers plan their work and assess priorities;
- setting deadlines and informing workers about them;
- setting standards of performance and monitoring them and dealing with poor performance;
- dealing with workers' concerns and grievances.

(Adapted from Adirondack 1998)

Managing quality-of-service delivery

There are a number of steps to ensuring quality-of-service delivery within early years settings. First, there is the need to identify the customers' requirements: what do parents want/expect from your setting? Susan Hay (1997) suggests a list of questions that parents focus on when they first visit the setting. These questions fall into four headings: first impressions; what about the staff?; day-to-day operations; and hygiene and safety. Below is an example of typical thoughts that may go through a parent's mind on a first visit.

1 *First impressions* – am I and is my child made to feel welcome?; do the children look happy?; do the children talk with the adults?
2 *What about staff?* – are there enough adults working with the children?; are they trained for the job?; do they seem to enjoy being with the children?
3 *Day-to-day* – do the activities take into account my child's age, cultural background, special needs?; are both boys and girls encouraged to use the equipment?; is the food good and varied?
4 *Hygiene and safety* – Are the premises clean, maintained and safe?; are gates and fences secure?; are there adequate fire appliances?

Only when an establishment has ascertained what the customer wants and expects can it then move towards providing quality service delivery.

It is essential that the establishment has a method for researching and identifying parents' needs and expectations on an ongoing basis. The results of the research then need to be analysed and evaluated. Following the evaluation there may be a need to change methods of delivery or ensure that all staff are aware of the establishment's quality indicators.

In the field of early years care and education there is also a second group of customers, who are the direct recipients of most of the services offered: these are the children. One difficulty in viewing children as customers is that it is hard to get feedback on what they think of the service if they are very young. However, there are mechanisms for ensuring that the interests of the children are satisfied and these come via the inspections and registration carried out by OFSTED (Office for Standards in Education). In order for a setting to be operating within the law it must be registered with OFSTED under Part X of the Children Act

1989. The OFSTED Registered Inspectors will not just look at the premises and health-and-safety issues but also at the early years curriculum to ensure that the Early Learning Goals are being met. In 2002, the government is finalising the National Standards for the Regulation of Day Care and Childminding in England. The fourteen standards put forward are defined according to five settings: childminding; crèches; full day care; out of school care; and sessional care. The fourteen standards list the following subjects for consideration:

- suitable person;
- organisation;
- care and learning;
- physical environment;
- equipment;
- safety;
- health;
- food and drink;
- equal opportunities;
- special needs (including special educational needs and disabilities);
- behaviour management;
- working in partnership with parents and carers;
- child protection;
- documentation.

These standards will form the baseline on which establishments will be measured in order to gain registration under the Children Act 1989 Part X regulations. Many establishments may wish to enhance these baseline standards so that they can offer parents and children a 'value-added' quality of service.

Management styles

Styles of management result from the dynamics between the culture of the organisation and each individual's approach to management issues. The majority of managers adopt a different style of management, depending upon the task. Below are listed definitions of well-known styles of management, as cited in numerous management textbooks.

Authoritative. This is when decisions are made at the 'top' of an organisation and passed down to the workers to implement. Such decisions may be made by a board of management, by the most senior manager or by the senior management team. This form of management is necessary when the senior management is responsible for implementing decisions that have been made by a board of trustees, local councillors sub-committee or other outside body with a management role for the establishment. Authoritive management is more likely to be seen in voluntary-sector early years establishments such as playgroups or voluntary-body family centres, although it could apply to any setting.

Participative. This is when decisions are made based upon consultation with experts, advisers or those who will be affected by the decision. It is a useful way of working, although the final decision is likely to rest with the senior manager or board of management.

Democratic. This form of decision making involves everyone in the establishment and can result in a vote or a consensus of opinion. It is a useful way of making decisions as it means that everyone is 'signed up' to the outcome and therefore has a responsibility for implementation of the decision.

Authoritarian. Note that this is not the same as authoritative management. Authoritarian management is repressive, dominating and requires staff to obey orders without question. It is a management style that can produce rebellion or poor working output from staff. It does not result in a happy establishment and can therefore lead to a high staff turnover.

Individualistic. This style of management may lead to managers making decisions that they do not have the authority to make. This may happen when nobody appears to be managing or making decisions, which leaves the field open to others to take individual action.

Laissez faire. This is when the senior manager or senior management team choose to ignore issues that require decisions. Instead they adopt the 'ostrich position' of burying their heads in the sand. This can lead to those who shout the loudest becoming the decision makers.

Chaotic. This is where there is a lack of consistency in management decisions and workers not sure who is responsible. There is a lack of authority and so ordinary decisions are not made and situations develop into crises. So often we read about crisis management when something has gone dreadfully wrong and is featured in the media. A solution to the crisis may come from an authoritarian person stepping into the management role.

A manager needs to balance all the arguments and decide which is the best style of management to adopt in order to ensure that all the staff are behind decisions. However, at the end of the day it is the manager that is accountable as that is where the lines of accountability stop (as they say, 'the buck stops here'). There are also lines of accountability to outside bodies such as the Charities Commission and the Registrar of Companies. In early years establishments additional accountability comes in the form of parents, the local authority social services department, the Children's Act 1989 and OFSTED.

As a manager, it is useful also to know something about yourself. Jung (1971) came up with what is referred to as the four functions:

1 *Thinker* – enjoys tackling problems with logic, is strong on analysis but weak on implementation solutions, is a methodical worker, is sceptical of projects unless backed up with sound, rational arguments. At work the Thinker is good with facts and figures, researching, systems analysis, accounting, the financial side of business.

2 *Sensor* – is good at getting things done, often impatient with the planning

stage, feels at home with routine work, has a lot of common sense and is practical, works hard and is usually well organised, is energetic and single-minded. At work the Sensor is good at initiating projects, setting up deals, negotiating, troubleshooting and converting ideas into action.

3 *Intuitor* – enjoys playing with ideas and theories, is good at seeing the overview but misses the detail, is creative and has strong imaginative sense, will often get hunches about things that turn out correctly. At work the Intuitor is good at long-term planning, creative writing, lateral thinking and brainstorming.

4 *Feeler* – Enjoys human company, assesses on personal values not technical merit, is warm and sympathetic, is perceptive about peoples' moods, feelings and reactions, may overlook blatant facts in favour of gut feelings. At work the Feeler is good at cementing team relationships, counselling, arbitrating, public relations, will talk as easily with clerk as with executive.

Belbin (1981) carried out a long study on what was the best mix of characteristics in a management team. His first finding was that a team made up of the brightest people did not turn out as the best working team. From his work Belbin came up with the following eight roles needed for an effective management team:

1 *Chairman* – the team co-ordinator who is disciplined, focused and balanced. Talks and listens well, is a good judge of people and things and works through others.

2 *Shaper* – this is the task leader, who in the absence of the Chairman would leap into the role even though perhaps not doing it well! Strengths lie in the Shaper's drive and passion for the task, but this person can be over sensitive, irritable and impatient. The Shaper is needed to spur the team into action.

3 *Plant* – this person is the source of original ideas and proposals and is often the most intelligent and imaginative member of the team. The Plant may be careless in details and may resent criticism.

4 *Monitor-Evaluator* – this team member is analytical and has the ability to dissect ideas and see the flaws in arguments. Often less involved with other team members but a good quality checker.

5 *Resource-Investigator* – this is a popular team member, being extrovert, sociable and relaxed. Able to bring in new contacts, ideas and developments, the Resource-Investigator is the salesperson, diplomat or liaison officer.

6 *Company Worker* – this member is the practical organiser who turns ideas into manageable tasks. Methodical, trustworthy and efficient, schedules and charts are the Company Worker's thing.

7 *Team Worker* – this member holds the team together by being supportive to others, listening and encouraging. The Team Worker is likeable and uncompetitive.

8 *Finisher* – without the Finisher the team may never meet its deadlines. This is the person who checks detail, worries about schedules and chivvies the others with a sense of urgency.

(Adapted from Belbin 1981)

A management team needs a balance of all the above and in small team situations one person may have to adopt more than one role. As Adirondack points out, the best use of Belbin's categories in a small organisation is to identify and build upon the strengths of the individuals involved and fill gaps by bringing in new people or by developing those strengths within the existing staff.

Leadership

Jillian Rodd (1994) has devoted a whole book to examining leadership in early childhood settings. She begins by looking at the differences between leadership and management, using Hodgkinson's (1991) definitions of leadership (given in pages 12–13). Rodd states that successful leaders are more than just efficient managers. However, it could be argued that in order to be a good leader you do also need some management skills, the two roles not being divorced. A leader is good at delegating tasks to the people who are most able to carry them out. This requires the leader to have a good knowledge of the staff and to understand their strengths, weaknesses and the targets that they have been set at their appraisal. Sergiovanni (1990) defines these essential tasks of an efficient leader as empowerment, enablement and enhancement. Neugebauer (1985) offers four types of leadership:

1 *Task Master* – places heavy emphasis on the task or the results and little emphasis on relationships or morale.
2 *Comrade* – places heavy emphasis on relationships and morale but little emphasis on the task or results.
3 *Motivator* – places strong emphasis on both the task and relationships.
4 *Unleader* – places little emphasis on either results or relationships

From this list it would appear that the Motivator style of leadership would best suit early years establishments as it is a mixture of the Task Master and the Comrade, neither of which, on its own, is likely to fulfil Sergiovanni's definition of a good leader. Also, one of the main driving forces of early years workers is the need to motivate the children in their care to develop and learn; it therefore may seem appropriate that the Motivator style of leadership could have the same effect upon the staff.

Leadership involves influencing the behaviour of others, supervision of staff, planning and implementing change and administering the day-to-day service of the establishment. In carrying out these leadership tasks there is a need to remember the other aspects required of the leadership role so that all the staff are motivated to complete the tasks at hand. Although leadership and management complement each other, it is leadership that is responsible for inspiring staff and initiating change.

Rodd (1994) draws attention to the differences between women as leaders and men as leaders. There has been a great deal of research that shows that even when men and women perform the same leadership tasks there is a marked difference in their approaches. Men's leadership styles are generally concerned with authority and power whereas women seem to act more as facilitators. Women need to understand the male approach to leadership and ensure that they are able to cope with this by developing assertion and communication skills to give them confidence in a variety of situations. Whilst there are at present few men in early years management it is not uncommon for child-care and education workers to find themselves with men from other disciplines such as social work, medicine and policing working alongside them as members of a multi-agency team.

Assertion and communication skills

Alberti and Emmons (1970) describe assertiveness as a straightforward statement that conveys opinions, beliefs and feelings in a way that does not impact on the self-esteem of the other person. Assertiveness is not aggression, which is demanding, blaming, threatening, interrupting, attacking, putting others down. Assertiveness is stating clearly what you want, making brief but to-the-point statements, saying 'no' when you want to, making decisions, standing up for yourself, acknowledging another person's standpoint. Assertion is the position of balance between avoiding conflict and winning at all costs. In addition to behaving in an assertive manner it is also useful to think assertively. Thinking assertively ensures that your own and others' needs are met and individual rights are maintained. In order to act assertively you have to believe that you have the right to do so. There are nine rights that refer to the work situation:

- to know what is expected of me;
- to have regular feedback on performance;
- to make mistakes sometimes without having constantly to be blamed for them;
- to be consulted about decisions that affect me;
- to take decisions that are within my area of work;
- to refuse unreasonable requests;
- to expect a certain standard of work from my staff;
- to ask for information when I need it;
- to be able, when appropriate, to criticise constructively the performance of my staff.

However, as Rodd (1994) states, most people have some difficulty in communicating assertively in certain situations or with certain people. Few people have the level of confidence and skill to be consistently assertive. Being assertive is one aspect of good communications within the work place. An effective communication system is based upon the following, which are discussed beneath:

- knowing your purpose, strategy and message;
- identifying your target audience;
- overcoming the physical and psychological barriers;
- selecting the appropriate type and style of communication;
- transmitting the message;
- obtaining feedback.

Knowing your purpose, strategy and message. Before communicating anything it is important that you are aware of what you want to achieve. You can then decide first on the outcome you hope to obtain and then on what is the best way to word the message.

Identifying your target audience. This is the need to consider who you are speaking to and what language is best suited to the delivery of the message. How will the message be received by the target audience? There is a need to know the culture and values of the people you will be delivering the message to.

Overcoming the physical and psychological barriers. Physical conditions that may prove to be a barrier could include the temperature of the room, the comfort/discomfort of the seating, and the time of day that the meeting is taking place. The psychological barriers may include the gender of the audience, the age of the audience, and the cultural/religious/social values of the audience. The status of the speaker in relation to the audience may also be a barrier.

Selecting the appropriate type and style of communication. Is the message best communicated face to face, in a written form, via an email, or in some other way?

Transmitting the message. This is the most important part of the communication process and all the previously thought-out strategies may need to be abandoned in favour of another strategy if the message is not being received.

Obtaining feedback. This is the process whereby the communicator checks that the message has been received in the form that was planned. It is very easy for those receiving a message to get muddled, misinterpret the message or get a wrong message. Feedback is an important way to avoid this.

Communication may be verbal or non-verbal. Non-verbal communication usually refers to body language but at work we now have an additional mode of non-verbal communication in the form of email. A person's body language may be giving a message totally opposite to the verbal message they are transmitting. There are times when people wish to hide their feelings for reasons best known to themselves. Some people are very good at this, for example actors, politicians and salespersons. By and large most people are not good at this and so a situation occurs whereby a person is verbally giving one answer whilst giving out body signals that offer another answer. There is an important rider to consider when interpreting a person's body language and this is the cultural aspect associated with the way people behave. We live in a pluralistic society and a person's cultural values may lead to behaviour that is easily misinterpreted by the viewer. For example, many Asian women do not make eye contact with strangers for reasons of modesty rather than dishonesty. In some cultures it is accepted that it is not polite to have too great a physical distance between yourself and the person you are communicating with. This is the opposite to the Anglicised version of events, where invasion of personal space is not welcomed and where others are best kept at 'arm's length'. It is therefore a dangerous exercise to base interpretations upon body language alone.

Facial expression is a common way that true feelings may be revealed. A raised eyebrow might denote scepticism at what is being said, whilst wearing a continuous smile can belie anger and annoyance. Eye contact is another telling signal. When a person refuses to make eye contact there can be value judgements made; for example that the person is not telling the truth or does not like the other person. Physical proximity is another area that can send out conflicting messages. Moving too close to a person may indicate intimidation or admiration. However, it could also indicate that the person cannot hear very well. There are lots of human-resources textbooks that explore the different areas of non-verbal communication in depth.

Email is a modern method of communication between people in which words are transferred without the receiver being able to see the sender. It is used as a tool for improving and speeding up communications within companies as well as enabling easy contact with colleagues outside the company. Problems have resulted when people have not made themselves clear in an email and the recipient has become angry or upset. Emails are often dashed off as a quick response mechanism and little thought may have gone into the reply. Email may not leave any room for negotiation in the same way that a face-to-face meeting will be able to do. The language used in email can be interpreted as bullying/intimidating and can start a complicated situation within the work place. Whilst email has a place in modern society and is a quick mechanism for transferring important messages and files around a company or outside a company, it is not a useful medium for resolving conflict, motivating people or enabling people to be part of a greater whole. Most early years establishments are very small and so there is no necessity for introducing internal email to improve communication.

Managing conflict and dealing with difficult people

Conflict may arise within the team or from outside the team. In some situations managers may find that conflict arises from outside the early years setting, for instance from parents, social services departments or inspectors. Taylor (1999) gives the following three definitions of conflict:

- Conflict occurs when two or more parties believe that what each wants is incompatible with what the other wants.
- Conflict arises when differences cannot be satisfactorily dealt with.
- Chinese characters for conflict are Opportunity–Danger (this covers the idea of positive as well as negative potentials of conflict).

Handy 1993 puts forward the following causes of conflict:

- formal objectives diverge;
- role definitions diverge;
- the contractual relationship is unclear;
- roles are simultaneous;
- there are concealed objectives.

Handy's work directly relates to large companies but there is no reason to suppose that the information cannot be extrapolated in order to fit a small-scale setting. It is interesting that Handy refers more to the control of conflict than to the resolution. In a small-scale setting a speedy resolution to conflict is important as the consequences of a conflict that continues will affect everyone very quickly. According to Taylor, the main aspects of conflict resolution lie within each individual's personal response to the conflict and this person's skills in handling it, any external environmental or organisational factors that might be contributing and a manager's responsibility for providing a framework for handling team conflicts. In addition to these factors, how people react in difficult situations also depends on their personality, past history, and other individual characteristics. Conflict may arise out of personal differences, factors within a team situation, factors within the organisation or as a result of the management culture. As mentioned earlier, management styles are important and certain styles of management may lead to conflict, particularly those that come across to others as intimidating. The senior-management styles will often define the culture of an organisation, which may lead to conflict arising out of blame culture.

There are various types of behaviour that can lead to conflict or are used in response to conflict.

Aggression can be active or passive, the latter often being overlooked or not viewed as aggression. A passive-aggressive person will usually agree to undertake a request but rarely carry it out on time or at all. These are the people who agree to meeting dates and times but are then late or don't turn up at all, or who agree to do a certain piece of work but forget or overlook doing it. This is one of the most difficult types of people to deal with. Active aggressors are often hostile (but not always), dominating, antagonistic, arrogant and want to steamroller through their ideas or resolutions. They use tactics that terrorise or humiliate the other members of their team.

Defeatists and pessimists are those people who respond to every suggestion with a negative response and believe that only luck can produce a good outcome. These people have a destructive influence on the other team members and/or staff, as negative attitudes can become contagious. People who stay silent or offer only a mumbled acknowledgement fall into this category. These people can be soul destroying, particularly if you have put a great deal of effort into a project you are discussing with them or if you want the opinions of all the members of your team. Sometimes their silence is a form of self-protection; they may be naturally shy or unable to indulge in small talk. In other situations their silence may appear as rejection, silence being used to denote resentment. Silence can also indicate suppression, a prolonged silent period occurring whilst a person is trying to control true feelings of anger or other emotions (what in the past may have been referred to as 'gritting their teeth and bearing it'). Finally, silence may denote boredom, either with the topic being discussed or with the other people involved. Sometimes people just do not have anything to say or do not understand what is being discussed but do not wish to have matters clarified.

Dealing with each of the above personality types can prove challenging and may not always be successful as some of these personality traits may be too entrenched for one to expect any noticeable changes. However, in order to resolve conflict it is important to understand people's behaviour. Handy (1993) sees conflict as being a normal part of team development and gives the following definitions of the stages of a group growth cycle.

- *Forming* – the group is not yet a group but a set of individuals. This stage involves defining the purpose of the group, its composition and leadership pattern.
- *Storming* – most groups go through a conflict stage when a lot of personal agendas are revealed and a certain amount of inter-personal hostility is generated. This is an important stage for testing norms in the group.
- *Norming* – the group needs to establish norms and practices, when and how it should work, how it should take decisions, what type of behaviour, what degree of openness, and so on. At this stage there will be a lot of experimentation to test the level of commitment of the members.
- *Performing* – this is the final stage, at which the group reaches maturity and is able to be productive.

Once a conflict has arisen the manager must take steps to resolve the situation. First it is necessary to find out what has happened and what are the reasons for the conflict. The reasons for the differences may be related to roles, information or a person's perceptions or values. In additon to these other factors may be involved, such as personality, attitude, communication style or culture. If the differences involve bullying, harassment, prejudice or equal-opportunity issues then the manager may have to implement the disciplinary process or the victim may choose to use the company's grievance procedure. If necessary, the manager can arrange for the services of a neutral mediator from within the company or an outside facilitator. The manager may need to negotiate with the people concerned or alternatively attempt to solve the problem that is causing the conflict. Negotiation requires all parties involved to have a positive action towards resolving the issues. If taking the problem-solving route, the manager will need to ascertain what the real issues are, gather the evidence, evaluate and decide on alternatives/solutions. If the solutions are not acceptable to the persons involved in the conflict then more stringent action may need to be taken.

Quality-management systems

In recent years early years establishments have been working towards/ achieving recognised quality-management systems awards. A number of these awards are not specifically aimed at early years settings but can be applied for by any small business. Others, such as the governments' Early Excellence Centres and the National Day Nursery Association's Kitemark, are specifically aimed at early years settings. Tony Blair's government is also suggesting a star rating for early years establishments but in 2002 has not yet released details on this.

There are three major business quality awards which are commonly used:

- *BS EN ISO 9000* (formerly BS 5750) – this system is used by a large number of businesses. It requires the company to develop clear definitions of the organisation, along with appropriate measures and controls to ensure that services and products are of a certain standard when they reach the customer. A criticism of this system has been that it represents a paper exercise and that it is possible to achieve the outcome on documentation alone.
- *UK Quality Award/European Quality Award* – the criteria for both of these awards are the same. They measure the performance of the company as a whole and cover all aspects of the company's operations. There are nine criteria for this award, based upon leadership, people management, policy and strategy, resources, processes, people satisfaction, customer satisfaction, impact on society and business results.
- *Investors in People (IIP)* – this is a national-standard award and is popular with small businesses. In fact, a number of early years centres have achieved the IPP. The key purpose of the award is to achieve objectives and continuously improve performance by investing in people. It has four principles: commitment, planning, action and evaluation. This award has been promoted to small businesses as the one award that small-scale settings find possible to achieve. It is an award that promotes training for all staff with some government subsidy for this training, a point that appeals to early years settings.

With the rise in the numbers of private day-care centres and the local authorities' day care being managed by private companies, parents are keen to have some indication of the quality of the establishment to which they will be sending their child. Whilst the above three awards are not specific indicators of the quality of care that a child will receive, they do indicate to parents that there is an infrastructure in the setting that is committed to quality. In terms of quality of care the kitemark system, which is offered by the National Day Nurseries Association, is able to offer an indication that an early years setting is offering a value-added service. All settings must be registered with and inspected by OFSTED in order to operate legally. However, many parents are looking for indicators over and above those in the OFSTED inspections. The government has introduced the concept of Early Excellence Centres, which are designated as such because they are able to offer all-round care to their users and the local community. These centres are awarded this designation on the basis of the variety of services they are able to offer, not necessarily on the quality of those services.

Suffice to say, working towards an award brings all the staff together with a common goal, which, once achieved, will enhance the status of the early years establishment.

References

Adirondack, S. (1998) *Just About Managing? Effective Management for Voluntary Organisations and Community Groups*, London Voluntary Service Council.

Alberti, R. E. and Emmons, M. I. (1970) *Your Perfect Right: A guide to assertive behaviour*, Impact San Luis: Obispo.

Belbin, R. M. (1981) *Management Teams: Why they succeed or fail*, Guildford: Butterworth-Heinemann.

Berne, E. (1964) *The Games People Play*, Harmondsworth, Penguin.

Boutall, T. (1996) *The Good Quality Managers Guide*, London: Management Charter Initiative.

Denny, R. (1997) *Succeed For Yourself*, London: Kogan Page.

DfEE (2000) *National Standards for the Regulation of Day Care and Childminding in England (Consultation Document)*, London: DfEE.

Dickson, A. (1984) *A Woman in Your Own Right: Assertiveness and you*, London: Quartet Books.

Handy, C. (1993) *Understanding Organizations*, Harmondsworth: Penguin.

Hay, S. (1997) *Essential Nursery Management*, London: Bailliere Tindall.

Hodgkinson, C. (1991) *Educational Leadership: The Moral Art*, Albany, NY: State University of New York Press. (Cited in Rodd 1994.)

Jung, C. G. (1971) *Psychological Types*, London: Routledge.

Neugebauer, R. (1985) 'Are you an effective leader?', in *Child Care Information Exchange*, 46: 18–26.

Peters, T. (1987) *Thriving on Chaos*, London: Pan Books.

Peters, T. and Waterman, R. (1982) *In Search of Excellence*, New York: Harper and Row.

Rodd, J. (1994) *Leadership in Early Childhood*, Buckingham: Open University Press.

Sadek, E. and Sadek, J. (1996) *Good Practice in Nursery Management*, Cheltenham: Stanley Thornes.

Sergiovanni, T. J. (1990) *Value-added Leadership: How to get extraordinary performance in schools*, Florida: Harcourt Brace and Jovanovitch.

Smith, A. and Langston, A. (1999) *Managing Staff in Early Years Settings*, London: Routledge.

Taylor, G. (1999) *Managing Conflict*, London: Directory of Social Change.

CHAPTER 10

Early years education

There is an increasing amount of national and international evidence to show that quality early childhood education has a positive long-term effect upon children's later development. Governments, worldwide, have at last begun to recognise that early childhood education matters. However, successful quality early education is more than providing children with a few facts or cognitive skills, it is about empowering children and providing them with the opportunity to 'learn how to learn'. It is also about providing children with the resources to deal with challenges and failure and to help them understand that achievement is as much about persistence and motivation as it is about intelligence.

This chapter will look at the education of children between the ages of three to six years. In England this covers the Foundation Stage, which includes the first year of primary education, but in most of Europe this period is regarded as nursery or kindergarten education. We shall consider the principles of good practice for this stage of children's development and discuss some current approaches to the curriculum, both in the UK and overseas. The chapter will also look at aspects of evaluation from both the children's and the programme's point of view.

Early influences on the curriculum

Early childhood education has a long history in the UK and much of what is termed 'good practice' today can be found in the writings of the pioneers of the nineteenth and early twentieth century.

Friedrich Froebel (1782–1852)

One of the first theorists to influence the early years curriculum in the UK was Friedrich Froebel whose ideas on childhood pioneered a new approach to our understanding of children's activities and ways of learning. He saw children's development as a whole and argued that children need to develop and integrate all their activities through play. Froebel was the first to introduce play as a major medium for instruction in the school curriculum. However, he did not believe that play should be unstructured as it was too important to be left to chance. Froebel wrote:

> Just because he learns through play, a child learns willingly and he learns much. So play, like learning and activity, has its own definite period of time and it must not be left out of the elementary curriculum. The educator must not only guide the play, since it is very important, but he must also teach this sort of play in the first instance.
>
> (Lilley 1967: 167)

Froebel believed that children should have real experiences that involved them being physically active both indoors and outdoors. In his kindergartens children were introduced to a carefully sequenced set of materials known as 'Gifts', six sets of playthings that formed a sequence, beginning with a number of soft balls and leading on to wooden spheres, cubes and cylinders. He also expected children to carry out a set of creative activities such as drawing and modelling that he termed 'Occupations'. The Gifts and Occupations, together with singing, games, stories and talk, made up the curriculum. Froebel believed that teachers should maintain a flow of talk in the classroom by coaching, prompting, making suggestions and by asking questions. His emphasis on the importance of the teacher–child relationship has continued to be an important part of the philosophy of early childhood education to this day.

One of Froebel's many legacies to young children was his notion of treating the school day as a complete unit in which activities continue for varying lengths of time according to the needs and interests of the children. This practice, which exists today in the majority of nurseries, was in complete contrast to the infant schools of the time, in which all the children sat in rows and everything was governed by the bell.

Maria Montessori (1870–1952)

Maria Montessori was an Italian doctor who worked among the socially and intellectually handicapped children in Rome at the beginning of the twentieth century. From close observation of the children in her Children's House (the name she gave to her nursery schools), she concluded that children pass through sensitive periods of development when certain skills and competencies are learned more easily. This is supported by research referred to in Chapter 3. Montessori's stages covered the ages from zero to six years, six to twelve years and twelve to eighteen years. For her, the purpose of education was to aid young children to develop their fullest potential through their own efforts. The young child learns through observation, movement and exploration and for this reason must not be educated in the same way as the older child. Montessori also believed that children have an intrinsic love of order and expected each one to take responsibility for taking and replacing materials and equipment in good order.

Montessori's didactic materials are highly structured and designed to move from the simple to the complex. The child must always wait to be shown how to use new equipment correctly by the teacher and, if unable to use it properly, it is taken away and produced again later when the time is felt to be appropriate. Montessori believed that the child needs love, security and affection and a protected environment. The teacher, whom Montessori called a directress, is not there to direct the child but, where possible, the direction and correction for the young child should be inherent in the structure of the self-correcting exercises and apparatus. The role of the directress is:

- to prepare herself (or himself);
- to prepare the environment and provide a stimulating and challenging environment that will help children by creating a spontaneous learning situation;
- to act as a link between the child and the materials. This is done by demonstration and example;
- to observe each child and note its interests and how the child works. These observations are used to decide what next should be represented to the child, how it is presented and when.

For Montessori, the prepared environment is both in and out of doors, and includes the organisation of space and resources. The Montessori classroom is organised into areas of learning and, on the shelves, which are all low enough for children to access easily whatever material they require, is equipment to help develop all the senses of the children. Everything the child requires for a particular activity is to be found in one particular area of the classroom, and this is always in the same space in order to provide security for the children.

The curriculum has been developed based on Montessori's beliefs that the child has two 'creative sensibilities': an 'absorbent mind' and 'sensitive periods', which are aids to help the child adapt to the environment. In 'The Montessori Method' Montessori refers to freedom within a structured environment, but that does not mean a licence to do whatever one wants. Montessori argues that we cannot be absolutely free or we would not be able to live in society.

Montessori believed that the child needs freedom to explore and interact with the environment and so construct a cognitive understanding of the world around it. The child makes choices from a variety of materials, appropriate to its stage of development, that will lead to greater understanding. However, it is the directress who controls and limits the freedom of the child within the educational environment.

Unlike Froebel, Maria Montessori did not stress the importance of relationships or of being part of the community, but stressed that children must work alone as in this way they become independent learners. It has often been said that Montessori did not agree with play. In reality she did not ban play but believed that children should work through the learning sequences before being allowed free choice of creative activities. In this respect her philosophy is very different from that of her fellow educationalists in the first half of the twentieth century who believed that children learned about materials by playing with them, whereas Montessori only allowed children to experiment with materials after they had learnt to use them appropriately.

There is an increasing number of Montessori nursery schools in the private sector as many parents believe that their children will learn better in a structured environment and are impressed by the calm atmosphere and sense of order that almost always prevails in a Montessori nursery setting.

Rudolph Steiner (1861–1925)

Steiner based his view of education upon a specific view of child development. He believed that children go through three stages: the will, zero to seven years; the heart, seven to fourteen years; and the head, from fourteen years upwards, and that the education offered must be appropriate to these stages. Steiner was concerned primarily with the development of the whole child and believed that through understanding the nature of children their individuality will come to fruition. The child who is offered a creative and balanced curriculum will grow into a flexible and creative adult. The curriculum aims to provide children with balanced experiences of the arts and sciences as well as opportunities to develop processes of thinking, feeling and willing. Steiner believed that it is essential to provide children with open rather than limited options.

The organisation of the day is important. The teacher organises a routine for each morning with singing and circle games that provide plenty of opportunity for movement before the children are guided, sometimes through a story, into their play. The children may play alone or with others. They can play, draw or sew. The teacher is always ready to help them if required but the children are not offered any instructional material and no attempt is made to introduce them to numerical or reading skills. In Steiner's approach, during the period from zero to seven years children should be allowed to develop the full play of their imagination at an age when imaginative play is so important in their lives.

The teacher personally greets each child on arrival at school. The teacher's role is to help children learn to do things as well as possible. An important feature of the environment is the design of the classroom, which is a room painted in a warm colour with soft materials and few hard rectangular corners. The materials in the room are natural and always at the child's own level. All materials are stored in aesthetic containers such as wooden baskets that can be incorporated into the children's play. There are no plastic toys, but there are wooden blocks of every dimension and texture as well as natural materials.

There are small felt dolls and puppets and a workbench is available with minia-ture but real tools, where children can make their own toys. The home corner is filled with cots and home-made soft dolls, and there are simple cookers and ironing boards for children to use in their play. Everything that is in the room is multi-purpose and encourages children's play and imagination.

Outside, play equipment is minimal, but there are plenty of natural play-things: for example, trunks and logs for children to scramble over. It is argued that the lack of equipment encourages children to become more creative and imaginative.

At the end of the morning the teacher gathers the children together in a special part of the nursery where there are seasonal decorations. A child is asked to light the 'story candle' and the children wait quietly for the teacher to tell them a story. The story is always told, never read, as it is felt that books come between the children and the storyteller; also the children will be better able to imagine the situation and not have pictures in a book to destroy their own images. The morning closes with a farewell song before the children leave.

The influence of Steiner is not strong in the UK but I have visited a number of Waldorf kindergartens in Hungary and other Eastern European countries.

Margaret McMillan (1860–1931)

Margaret McMillan was a pioneer educator who believed in the importance of first-hand experiences and active learning. Like her sister, Rachel McMillan, she was concerned with both the health and home conditions of the children with whom she worked, arguing that children who are sick and undernourished cannot learn. In order to help these children and their families, McMillan set up medical centres to help improve their general health and provided baths and washing facilities for children that needed them. She also provided meals for all the children before the introduction of the School Meals Service.

McMillan saw her nursery schools as extensions of the home and encouraged her teachers to forge close links with parents as she believed that the family played an important role in the education of children. Aware that many of the mothers had received little or no education, Margaret McMillan encouraged mothers to come into the nursery and learn alongside their children.

She was a firm believer in the value of play and ensured that there was ample material available to stimulate children's imagination. During play children were able to develop feelings and relationships as well as physical and cognitive skills, and through story, rhyme, talk and song, children were encouraged to develop their language abilities and musical appreciation. McMillan's nursery schools had gardens in which children could find plenty of fresh air. They were encour-aged to play freely outside as it was here, she argued, that children learned the rudiments of science and geography. Both inside and outside, Margaret McMillan provided an environment in which learning was inevitable.

Her views on nursery education, to be found in *The Nursery School* (1919), had a profound influence upon nursery education in the UK for several decades. In 1937, P. Ballard, a nursery inspector, wrote that 'the modern nursery school is the product of Miss McMillan's genius'. Her views on the need for the nursery school to be part of the community and to work closely with parents are still valid and are characteristic of many of our nursery schools and current centres of excellence.

Susan Isaacs (1885–1948)

As mentioned in Chapter 8, Susan Isaacs contributed a great deal to our understanding of the social and intellectual development of children. At a time when very little was understood about the inner feelings of young children, Susan Isaacs, influenced by the psychoanalytic theories of Melanie Klein, made every effort to ensure that children had freedom of action and expression. At Malting House School in Cambridge, children were encouraged to express openly their feelings of hostility, anger, fear and aggression, as Isaacs believed that their suppression would be harmful to the child.

Susan Isaacs valued play and in particular make-believe play, which she thought gave children the freedom to think and reason and to relate to others. She also advocated that children should be free to move about as much as they needed and disliked classrooms that were very restrictive. Isaacs believed that young children could solve problems and disagreed with Piaget's view that young children were egocentric and unable to reason. Her detailed observations of the children at Malting House School demonstrate clearly that children can understand complex ideas if they fully understand the language used and are working with adults who pose meaningful and challenging questions. Like Margaret McMillan, Susan Isaacs valued the role of parents in their children's education and saw the nursery school as an extension of the home. Her links with parents were maintained through contributing regularly in a magazine for parents under the pseudonym Ursula Wyse, in which she wrote numerous articles including ones on the 'normal fears and anxieties of children'.

Probably her greatest contribution to early childhood education were the detailed observations she kept over a number of years and used in her in-service training courses for teachers at the London Institute of Education. Her books *Social Development in Young Children* and *Intellectual Growth in Young Children* are full of astute observations that are as relevant today as they were at the time they were written.

Through her lectures, Isaacs was to have a powerful influence upon nursery and primary education in the post-war years, particularly in creating an awareness of the need to appreciate the social and emotional inner life of children.

Early childhood curriculum

Every society has its own expectations of its children, and the curriculum, both in content and method of delivery, reflects these expectations. In some societies children are seen as 'empty vessels' that need to be filled with facts and figures. This seems a deficit model in which emphasis is placed upon what the child cannot do rather than what the child is able to do, the implication being that only the educator/adult can supply the knowledge and skills required for a child to become a competent person. The child is expected to be a passive recipient of knowledge and there is no recognition of the role played by the child itself. In other societies the approach is very different. Children are seen as active learners and it is accepted that they enter school with certain knowledge and abilities, the role of the educator being to build upon these strengths. A society that really respects children is one in which there is true communication between children and adults. The voice of the child is heard and listened to, and the child is involved in decision making from an early age.

Among early years educators in the UK the term 'curriculum' is associated with the image of the 'whole child', who is an active learner and who brings skills and competencies into the school. Learning cannot be compartmentalised. The cognitive, emotional, social and physical domains are integrated and learning in any of these areas must necessarily involve all the others. However, it is necessary for the educator to plan all the content areas of the curriculum to ensure that children receive as broad a set of learning experiences as possible.

What is a curriculum?

There are many definitions of the term 'curriculum', which traditionally has been interpreted as a 'course of study'. Readers may find the following definitions of interest.

The curriculum for young children includes:

- all the activities and experiences provided for them by adults;
- all the activities they devise for themselves;
- the language that adults use to them and that they use to each other;
- all that they see and hear in the environment around them.

(Drummond et al. 1989)

- The concepts, knowledge, understanding, attitudes and skills that a child needs to develop.

(DES 1990)

- A curriculum is an organised framework that delineates the content that children are to learn, the processes through which children achieve curricular goals, what teachers do to help teachers achieve these goals and the context in which teaching and learning occurs.

(National Association for the Education of Young Children 1991)

- In its broadest form, the curriculum involves a consideration of the process of learning (how a child learns), the learning progression (when a child learns) and the learning context (where and why a child learns).

(Ball 1994)

- The curriculum is everything that affects the child in the learning environment, overt and covert. It covers not only the activities, both indoors and outdoors, offered to young children, but also the attitudes of the staff towards not only the children but to each other, to parents and anyone who visits the setting.

(Curtis 1998)

- The term curriculum is used to describe everything children do, see hear or feel in their setting, both planned and unplanned.

(DfEE 2000)

The last definition is the one given in the Curriculum Guidance for the Foundation Stage of Education.

What are the principles for early childhood education?

The same principles should underpin early childhood education, in whatever setting (state, private or voluntary sectors).

Early childhood educators recognise that:

- children come into school with knowledge and skills – they have been learning from birth;
- quality care and quality education are inseparable;
- every child develops at its own pace; the role of the adult is to stimulate and encourage learning;
- learning is holistic and cannot be compartmentalised into separate subjects;
- trust, motivation, and positive attitudes and dispositions are important – each child should feel valued and secure;
- children learn best through play, talk and first-hand experiences;
- no child should be excluded or disadvantaged;
- what children can do rather than what they cannot do should be the starting point for the programme;
- parents and teachers should work together in the best interests of the child;
- the early years curriculum should be carefully structured to provide a balance

of appropriate activities – some planned by adults, others child planned or initiated;

- cultural and physical diversity should be respected and valued;
- quality care and education requires well-trained educators and ongoing professional training;
- skilled and careful observations are crucial to fostering children's learning.

(Adapted from DfEE 2000)

Principles into practice

These principles have to be put into practice by early childhood educators. Children need to be offered an appropriate curriculum in a secure and stimulating setting and in order to do this educators must have a sound understanding of how children develop and learn. Each child is different and will bring into school its previous experiences and expectations. Meeting the diverse needs of children means more than being aware of their previous experiences, interests, skills and knowledge. It also involves being aware of the requirements of equal opportunities that cover race, gender, and disability as well as the Code of Practice relating to the identification and assessment of children with special educational needs.

Children with special educational needs include the more able, children from diverse linguistic backgrounds, those with disabilities and children from different ethnic and cultural groups including travellers, refugees and asylum seekers. Each of these groups of children will need to be offered planned opportunities that build on and extend their existing knowledge.

Providing a differentiated curriculum to meet the needs of individual children who learn at different rates and in different ways requires much skill and knowledge from the educator. In planning the daily programme a wide range of teaching strategies will be necessary that involve individual, and large and small group activities. Not only should the provision offer children opportunities for a wide range of creative and imaginative play activities, but there should be sufficient time and space to allow children to develop and extend their play, sometimes alone and sometimes in the company of other children or an adult.

Children with special educational needs

Children with special needs may require individual learning programmes for part of the session, but it is important for their development and that of the other children in the nursery that they participate as fully as possible in the normal classroom routines. However, some children with disabilities will need extra guidance and support from an adult to gain from the normal learning opportunities that occur throughout the day. It may be appropriate to adapt the environment or an activity for a particular child.

Children with behavioural difficulties are a challenge to most educators and they require a well-structured programme to help them learn how to work effectively either alone or in a group. Strategies such as setting reasonable expectations in discussion with the child and its parents, establishing clear boundaries and giving positive feedback are all useful in helping the children to manage their own behaviour.

Children with English as an additional language

In many parts of the UK there are children for whom English is an additional language. Many of these children are bilingual from birth but there are others who come into the nursery from households in which there is no knowledge of English.

These children will have developed concepts, vocabulary and linguistic skills in the language of the home and can communicate their needs and interests. It is important that we do not ignore this prior knowledge. The educator needs to be particularly sensitive to this as many parents from non-English-speaking backgrounds are anxious about the possible distress that their children will experience when they enter the early childhood institution, especially since they themselves are probably facing difficulties in the community.

Children will learn English just as they learned their first language, through hearing it, and being encouraged to use it, in situations that are meaningful to them. Many children who are new to English will use gestures to communicate, point to things they want, and/or lead staff by the hand to show them. This period of non-verbal communication is frequently accompanied by the 'silent period', when the child does not speak at all. Although a normal part of second-language learning, it can be most perplexing for both adults and other children. During this period the children are acquiring knowledge of English and will begin to speak when they are ready. The role of the educator is to continue talking even when there is no response, in the same way as we hold conversations with very young children, as there is understanding long before there is talk. Children need to hear English and it is important that adults speak clearly and precisely to them as it is only in this way that children can learn the stress and intonation of our language.

As children begin to speak English they use spontaneous expressions that they hear, generally from other children, such as 'hello', 'It's mine', 'my go'. These phrases help to maintain a conversation and enable them to join in with their peers. Naturally the children make mistakes but gradually they become confident as users of English and are able to participate in all the nursery activities.

Having children in a nursery who are non-English speakers can be quite daunting to educators and where possible bilingual support should be available.

Children should be given opportunities to see books and hear their home language as well as English. Naturally if there are several children in the nursery who have the same mother tongue they will use that language, particularly during imaginative play bouts. However, normally as children begin to develop some facility in English they will also begin to play with native English speakers. Workers in nursery settings in which there is a large number of children with English as an additional language are always amazed at the speed with which these children learn a second language when given the appropriate support.

The role of the adult

The adult has an important role to play in supporting children's learning. Both Bruner and Vygotsky place emphasis upon the importance of the adult in facilitating children's learning. In this country the Effective Early Learning Project, led by Pascal and Bertram, has identified three main ways in which adults can help support children to learn. They termed this the 'Engagement Scale'. It considers:

- how the adult encourages the child to achieve independence;
- the sensitivity of the adult to the child;
- how the adult offers stimulating and challenging experiences.

Although a didactic approach is inappropriate in most instances, there are occasions when direct teaching is necessary, for example when a child is making a model and is having difficulties in joining two materials together. Adult intervention at that time is highly appropriate and will help the child to succeed and so feel in control of its own learning. This is a very different situation from a child being told to sit at a table and stick tissue paper onto a prepared shape or draw round templates. Over the years I have heard many reasons why these sorts of activity are of value to children, but no one can convince me that they have any intrinsic value. There are other more effective ways of encouraging the development of fine motor skills.

There is an increasing body of research to show that children can learn from each other as well as from adults, particularly when the children are of mixed ages. This type of grouping, which is a characteristic of our nurseries, is a legacy from our early childhood educators who were well aware of the value of child–child learning.

An important principle of early childhood education relates to the observation and assessment of children's progress. Through careful observation, early childhood educators can plan the curriculum and decide how best they can extend the children's learning and so help them progress to the next stage of development. Close and careful observation of children is the main way that adults can assess the young child's strengths and weaknesses and evaluate the learning opportunities offered.

Partnership with parents is an essential part of early childhood education. All the research has indicated that where parents are actively involved in their children's education the children will benefit most from their time in the nursery. Where the partnership with parents is built on mutual trust and respect, children feel secure and safe within the early childhood setting. Parental co-operation is particularly important at times of stress for the child, for example during the transition from home to school or from nursery to primary school.

Foundation Stage: three to five years

In 1996, the highly controversial document *Desirable Outcomes for Children's Learning on Entering Compulsory Education* was introduced in England. This document was designed to ensure that all four-year-olds, whether in the private, voluntary or public sector, should receive minimal curriculum requirements for personal and social development, numeracy, literacy, knowledge and understanding of the world, physical and creative development. Critics of the document argued that most nursery schools and classes go beyond these requirements in the provision that is offered but in the hands of the many untrained or poorly qualified staff it could result in four-year-old children being given an inappropriate formal curriculum.

The Curriculum and Assessment authority for Wales (Awdurdod Cwricwlwm AC Asesu Cymru) introduced a Welsh version of the *Desirable Outcomes for Children's Learning* that relates much more closely to the current thinking on the development and learning of young children and was based on a more holistic view of early child education. The areas covered are language, literacy and communication skills, personal and social development, mathematics, knowledge and understanding of the world, physical and creative development. The document stressed the role of play in children's learning and encouraged the use of the Welsh language. It also emphasised the importance of observation in planning a curriculum and evaluating a child's progress.

In May 2000, the Qualifications and Curriculum Authority introduced the Curriculum Guidance for the Foundation Stage that was now designed for all children from the age of three in every pre-school setting. It was to take effect from September 2001 in all English early childhood institutions receiving nursery-education grant funding and in reception classes in primary schools. For the first time there were national guidelines that covered the transition from nursery to kindergarten in communication, language and literacy and mathematical development.

The early goals have been modified since 1996 and practitioners are expected to provide a curriculum 'to meet the diverse needs of all children so that most will achieve and some, where appropriate, will go beyond the early learning goals by the end of the foundation stage' (DfEE 2000: 6).

Early learning goals

The goals are for:

- personal, social and emotional development;
- communication, language and literacy;
- mathematical development;
- knowledge and understanding of the world;
- physical development;
- creative development.

In the guidance, 'stepping stones' have been identified to help educators plan the knowledge, skills and attitudes that children need to learn in order to reach the early learning goals. The stepping stones are colour coded, but not age-related. However, it is assumed that the final stepping stone will describe the abilities of the older children. Children will progress from stage to stage at differing speeds and although some will go beyond the goals, others will not necessarily reach the final destination by the age of six.

Throughout the document, emphasis is upon meeting the diverse needs of children:

> Practitioners should plan to meet the needs of both boys and girls, children with special educational needs, children who are more able, children with disabilities, children from all social, cultural and religious backgrounds, children of different ethnic groups including Travellers, refugees and asylum seekers, and children from diverse linguistic backgrounds.

The curriculum content must vary according to the cultural needs of the children.

The guidance stresses that the early learning goals are not in themselves a curriculum, but provide a basis for appropriate planning. The guidance on 'communication, language and literacy' and 'mathematical development' is designed to cover from age three until the end of the reception year. The early learning goals in these areas are closely linked to the objectives of the National Literacy and National Numeracy Strategy and the reception-class teachers are expected to plan their programmes so that there is a smooth transition to the literacy and numeracy hours in Year 1.

Although the guidelines stress the value of well-planned play, both indoors and outdoors, this aspect appears to be overlooked, particularly for children who enter reception classes when they are only just four years of age. These children are frequently expected to sit at tables for long stretches of the day. Research from Sylva (2001) has shown that children who are encouraged to learn through play are likely to achieve better exam results than those who receive a formal nursery education. She has warned the government of the possible detrimental effects of placing too great an emphasis upon more disciplined forms of early education.

Personal, social and emotional development

Early childhood educators all over the world stress the importance of children's social and emotional development during the early years of education. Unless children learn to establish positive relationships with other children and with adults, they are unlikely to achieve their full potential in later life. The learning goals in this area of development focus on helping children to become independent and autonomous. Young children are naturally curious and it is important to ensure that they have a positive approach to new experiences.

Throughout the Foundation Stage educators help children to develop self-confidence and self-esteem. They also become aware that people have different needs, views, cultures and beliefs. This is a natural process for children growing up in a multicultural classroom but more difficult for those whose environment is less culturally mixed, although in every group of people there will always be differences of opinion and belief. Understanding about 'right and wrong' and being responsible for the consequences of one's actions is something that many children find difficult and may take a long time to appreciate. Nevertheless, self-discipline and self-control are crucial aspects of being able to deal with one's feelings and relationships with others.

Practitioners are well aware of the importance of supporting children in their personal, social and emotional development but it is often an area of the programme that is less well planned than others. Although much of this learning is incidental and occurs during play and other activities, there are times when planned intervention can be highly effective.

Communication, language and literacy

One of the main aims of this goal is to encourage children to have the confidence to speak and listen in different situations. Talk is an important part of our lives and learning how to engage in dialogue is a gradual process. Children need to have opportunities to speak and listen to others and to use language to represent their ideas, thoughts and feelings. For some children when they enter the nursery, for example those for whom English is a second language, their communication may be mainly non-verbal, with gestures, eye contact and facial expressions taking the place of words. Shy, non-confident children may also use non-verbal communication when they start but, as their confidence grows, language will come, first as a whisper, and then as an audible voice for all to hear. Even though children have the confidence to engage in conversations with others, few will initiate conversations with adults unless they have something meaningful to say and feel very secure in the company of the adult. When children and adults engage in conversation it is essential that the adult listens to the child and responds appropriately. Adult–child conversation is often dominated by questions and answers, with the adult asking a lot of 'closed questions' – those that have definite answers. Discussion needs to be open-ended and structured so that the child can respond in a variety of ways.

By the end of the Foundation Stage it is expected that children's language skills will have developed so that they can interact with others and negotiate activities and plans with other children. Children will also be learning how to use language to organise their thinking and express their feelings and ideas. The curriculum guidance for this stage gives educators some useful ideas on extending children's skills in this area.

The literacy content of this early learning goal involves talking about and listening to stories, poems and nursery rhymes. Some children have shared books and stories with adults from an early age and are already aware that the 'marks' on the paper can be deciphered into words. Others may enter the nursery with no knowledge of stories or nursery rhymes and may not even know how to turn the page of a book. Reading begins with listening to stories and as the children listen they extend their vocabulary and gradually come to understand that written language is different from spoken language. Children need to hear stories told as well as seeing them in books with pictures and written text.

During this period some children will be developing an awareness of sounds and the letters of the alphabet; others may have started to read. At the same time that children are developing as readers, so they are beginning to emerge as writers. Their first scribble patterns will gradually turn into recognisable letter shapes and finally into words. By the end of the Foundation Stage most children will be able to use a pencil and hold it correctly but they should not be pressurised into 'writing' at too early a stage.

In the next chapter we shall be looking at the emergence of literacy in greater detail and the role of the adult in that development.

Mathematical development

In a world in which so many adults are 'frightened' of anything to do with mathematics, it is imperative that children become confident in learning the skills associated with this area of the curriculum. Young children enjoy using and experimenting with numbers, particularly large ones, in their play and much early mathematical understanding is developed through imaginative play, stories, rhymes and games. This area of learning includes counting, sorting, matching, recognising shapes and patterns, understanding relationships and working with numbers, space, shapes and measures. Mathematics is about making connections and solving problems and there are many practical activities in the nursery that can help develop these abilities.

As children begin to learn to use numbers in appropriate ways they not only need practice in counting, but they also have to learn the language of mathematics – 'more' and 'less', 'addition' and 'subtraction' – before they can begin to understand the concepts.

During this stage children learn about topological concepts such as on/off; over/under; up/down; across; in/out. To understand these properly, children need lots of practical experiences so that they can feel their bodies going 'over' or 'under' the chair or 'across' the room. These mathematical concepts are constantly being reinforced during physical activities. Children will also be learning about shape and size. Some shapes will be geometrical ones, such as square, circle and triangle; others will be more amorphous and children will need to use their imagination to describe what they see.

Talking about objects of different sizes requires knowing the relevant adjectives for size and shape and comparisons such as 'bigger than' and 'smaller than'. These expressions have to be learned in context.

Cookery sessions offer endless opportunities for children to estimate and predict what will happen. They will be weighing and measuring using scales and balances, but it is also useful if the adult asks them to guess whether one amount is heavier than or lighter than the other. Children need to become familiar with terms such as 'the same as', 'more than', 'less than', 'full' and 'empty' as they are fundamental to their later understanding of mathematics. The language of mathematics cuts across all areas of learning and for children to use it accurately it is essential that they have as much practice as possible.

Many of the mathematical concepts that children develop during the foundation years will arise during a variety of activities. The educator can develop these by talking 'mathematically' with children during their play and other activities.

Knowledge and understanding of the world

Children are striving to make sense of the world from a very early age and will have brought to the nursery a vast range of experiences and knowledge. Young children are constantly exploring, observing, problem solving and making decisions about what they see, hear, feel, touch and taste. The nursery will continue to provide activities that extend this knowledge and understanding. This area of learning will lay the foundation for later work in science, design and technology, history, geography and information and communication technology.

Children need a wide variety of practical activities, mainly using the basic provision in the outdoor and indoor areas available in every nursery. There are endless opportunities for educators to introduce science to children in the Foundation Stage. For example, children like to experiment with sand and water – how and why does the material change? Experiments with water, magnets, pulleys and torches are common activities in many nurseries. Cooking is an activity that can help in learning about temperature, transforming materials from one state to another, as well as helping with mathematical concepts.

In the natural world of plants, trees and animals there are many opportunities for extending children's understanding and knowledge. Where possible, take children out to see real-life examples – even in a dense urban area there is usually some vegetation nearby. Books can be used to follow up and extend the experience.

Children learn skills through the use of a wide range of tools, for example scissors, rulers, computers, magnifiers and gardening tools. However, most of the skills we need in science come from observation, exploration, prediction and forming hypotheses. Children enjoy the challenge of being asked questions such as 'What will happen if . . . ?' or 'Which do you think will go the fastest?' It is the role of the adult to encourage children to ask 'what', 'why', 'when', 'where' and 'how' questions and to help them think logically. Children need help also to extend their vocabulary so that they have the language to be able to make predictions and hypothesise.

Both boys and girls are interested in finding out how things work and rapidly learn how to perform simple programmes on the computer. By the time they reach the end of this stage most children can use CD-Roms, videos, tapes and other media competently.

The foundations of history are laid down as children begin to develop a concept of time and to think about past and present events in their families and their own lives. At this stage children become interested in absent members of the family and what has happened to them. For example, if a grandparent has died before the child was born, questions are asked about that person.

During this period children become more interested in the environment and the role of those around them. They begin to develop a sense of place and will ask about their own cultures and beliefs and those of other people. Open discussions and stories and songs from cultures and languages help encourage positive attitudes towards others, irrespective of race, religion, gender or disability. There is evidence that many children enter school with negative stereotypes about certain groups of people and this area of the curriculum is designed to help overcome this. Much of this learning will take place through well-structured play, but even more will occur as a result of positive adult involvement.

Physical development

Young children need to move about and to get as much fresh air as possible. The importance of fresh air to our brain development has already been mentioned earlier in the book. This is a period when children are learning many large and fine motor skills and they require the time and space to practise them repeatedly before they are perfected. Young children are naturally curious and this leads them to be constantly on the move, much to the chagrin of many adults. Many educators feel that as the children come to the end of the nursery years they should be sitting at a table and carrying out paper and pencil tasks – 'getting ready for proper school'. The result is frequently a group of bored, inattentive children, who sit and stare or, more often, get up and walk around and may become generally disruptive. Educators complain that these children lack the ability to concentrate. This may be so but it is more likely that the task is inappropriate. If the children are involved in an activity of their own choice they are much more likely to display good attention skills.

The opportunity to move around freely and explore enables children to gain control and confidence in the use of their bodies. As they move around the classroom or the outdoor areas they are developing an awareness of space, of themselves and of others.

It is to be regretted, but once most children enter primary school there are limited opportunities for physical exercise during the school hours. Furthermore, changes in society means that children are less likely to play in the streets after school but will probably go home to sit in front of the small screen. There is official awareness of this problem and, with luck, changes may be made in the school curriculum in the future. In the meantime it is essential that children at the Foundation Stage get as many opportunities as possible for physical exercise as it is vital for their later academic development.

Creative development

For children to develop creative and aesthetic awareness, as many opportunities as possible should be made available to explore and experiment with a wide variety of materials and tools and to try out ideas alone or with others. This requires time and space.

Children should be exposed to both two-dimensional and three-dimensional activities and learn to explore colour, texture, shape and form in both dimensions. The guidelines point out that children must be able to express themselves freely and that the role of the adult is to support them where necessary.

Music is an important part of the early years curriculum and children should be encouraged not only to sing traditional songs from different cultures but also to listen to and make music for themselves. Children of this age will often break into spontaneous dance or act out a song to music. In European nurseries a large part of the curriculum is devoted to music and dance and I am always impressed by the high standards achieved by children as young as three or four years of age.

By the end of the foundation period it is hoped that most children will be able to use their imagination in art, design, music, dance, stories and imaginative play. Many children will enjoy seeing and talking about pictures and beautiful shapes and objects. Discussions with an adult or other children will help to foster language development and encourage children to express their feelings about what they see, hear, smell and taste.

Although this is the last learning goal, it is nevertheless fundamental to learning. Imaginative play and role-play are extremely important in learning as during their play, children cross the boundaries of various areas of learning. Earlier in the book the value of imaginative play was discussed and it is crucial that this aspect of the life of the child is not sacrificed in favour of a programme dominated by endless worksheets. It may be more difficult to assess the child's progress on learning targets during play but good observations by a skilled observer will reveal a wealth of learning across several areas of the curriculum.

These guidelines have some excellent suggestions for practitioners to follow. However, it is to be hoped that they will be used as 'stepping stones' and that parents and educators will accept that all children are different and develop at different rates, some needing longer on the beginning stones while others crossing with greater rapidity.

Some international examples of curriculum for children from three to six years

High Scope Curriculum

The High Scope Curriculum, originally called the Pre-school Perry Project, a programme for disadvantaged children in Ypsilanti in the 1960s, has been subjected to careful evaluation over a period of thirty years. Its consistently positive results have been used by many to support the argument for the cost-effectiveness of nursery education and the programme has been introduced in many countries worldwide, including the UK. Interested readers can find the details of this research in Schweinhart and Weikart (1993).

The programme sees children as active learners, encouraging them to become independent problem solvers and decision makers. It is not a rigid programme but provides a framework for children's learning. Although it has much in common with traditional nursery practice, the authors consider that it places greater responsibility upon children for planning and executing their own activities.

Working on a philosophy of *plan*, *do* and *review*, the environment is arranged so that it optimises children's learning, using key experiences to observe and plan for the individual needs of children, for example adult–child communication strategies, partnership with parents, observation and record keeping.

The key experiences implicit in the High Scope concept of active learning are:

- using language – describing objects, events and relationships;
- active learning – manipulating, transforming and combining materials;
- representing ideas and experiences – role playing, pretending;
- developing logical reasoning – learning to label, match and sort objects;
- understanding time and space – recalling and anticipating events, learning to find things in the classroom.

These key experiences not only provide the framework for planning and evaluating activities but also enable the staff to guide children from one learning experience to another. They suggest questions to put to the children and enable staff to assess children's development and provide a basis for discussion with the parents.

The daily routine provides adults and children with a consistent framework in which to work. It is planned to accomplish three main goals:

1 A sequence of plan/do/review. This process allows children to explore, design and carry out activities and make decisions in their learning.
2 Providing for many types of interaction. For example, small- and large-group work, adult to child, child to child, and times for both adult-initiated and child-initiated activities.
3 Providing the opportunities/time to work in a variety of environments, both indoors and outdoors.

The High Scope Curriculum is dependent upon careful planning and staff discuss the needs of both individual children and the group as a whole before a decision is taken on which aspect of the curriculum they must emphasise first. This consultation is termed 'team teaching' and is a feature of the High Scope classroom. Strange as it may seem to early childhood educators in the UK, in many parts of the world this is a new concept as co-operation among early years staff is not the norm.

Although the authors of this approach have been influenced by the work of Piaget, the conversations that children engage in with adults during the plan/do/review cycle embody the principles of Vygotsky's effective instruction within the zone of proximal development. The adult challenges children's thinking and helps them extend their ideas further. The High Scope Curriculum encourages children to develop mastery orientation and persistence in the face of failure. If a plan did not materialise as the child had hoped, then the feedback from an adult should help to increase the likelihood of a more successful outcome on the following day.

Developmentally appropriate curriculum

According to Kelly (1994), the term 'developmentally appropriate practice' indicates that the focus of the early childhood curriculum must be on the child and its development rather than on subjects and knowledge.

A developmentally appropriate curriculum must be based upon active forms of learning, on enquiry and discovery. It places emphasis on the process rather than the product. This approach is not new as it is similar to that advocated by the Hadow Report (1933), which put forward the view that the curriculum needs to be framed in terms of activity and experience rather than knowledge to be acquired and facts to be stored. In the USA, the developmentally appropriate approach was supported by the National Association for the Education of Young Children, who published curriculum guidelines based on this philosophy (Bredekamp 1987).

Developmentally appropriate practice is based on universal and predictable sequences of growth and change. It advocates that the teacher should take account of the age of the child and of its individuality in terms of growth pattern, personality, learning style and family background, and that children learn best through play that is:

- self initiated;
- self directed;
- self chosen.

The teacher's role is to:

- provide a rich variety of activities and materials;
- support the children's play;
- talk with the children about play.

This view of the curriculum is based upon a specific understanding of children's learning and development and upon a child-centred philosophy steeped in the deep-rooted beliefs and ideals widely shared among Western-educated specialists, and is based entirely upon Western psychological theory.

Since the 1980s psychologists and educators have challenged this type of programme, arguing that what is 'appropriate' in one setting may be 'inappropriate' in another cultural context. It has been argued that this approach is insensitive to the cultural diversity in children's family experiences and parenting practices and it risks, according to Woodhead (1996), resurrecting discredited judgements about deprived environments and the need for compensation. Criticism from a growing number of sources led the National Association for the Education of Young Children (NAEYC) to look again at its earlier document and it has now been revised by Bredekamp and Copple (1997). The new document incorporates greater attention to the role of families and culture in children's development. It also highlights the role of the teacher as decision maker and curriculum developer. However, there are critics who still point out that it refers to 'developmentally appropriate practice' without defining 'appropriate' or 'inappropriate'. The American research has also pointed out that although many teachers subscribe to the child-centred philosophy, they frequently take a didactic approach to teaching and learning.

Research into the value of this approach has indicated that where children are in programmes that are developmentally appropriate they are less likely to develop signs of stress and anxiety in test situations. Equally there have been a number of studies that have looked at motivation and achievement and these have found that young children in developmentally appropriate programmes were more likely to have higher expectations of their own success than those in academic programmes (Stipek *et al.* 1995).

Te Whariki: the New Zealand early childhood curriculum

New Zealand is one of the increasing numbers of countries that is carrying out longitudinal research into the effects of early childhood programmes. A current study carried out by the New Zealand Council for Educational Research is still showing positive results as the children move into secondary schooling.

In 1996, the government published a national early childhood curriculum that incorporated the Maori curriculum and was designed to form the basis for a bicultural education programme in that country. It has drawn upon the different philosophies available worldwide and recognises the diversity of early childhood education in New Zealand. The curriculum emphasises the critical role of socially and mediated learning and recognises the importance of responsive relationships for children with people, places and things. In the introduction it is written that 'children learn through collaboration with adults and peers, through guided participation and observation of others, as well as through individual exploration and reflection' (Te Whariki 1996).

There are four main principles at the heart of the early childhood curriculum: empowerment; holistic development; family and community; and relationships. Five strands and goals arise from these principles, which together form the framework for the curriculum. Each strand has associated goals with specific learning outcomes.

STRAND 1: WELL-BEING

Children experience an environment in which:

- their health is promoted;
- their emotional well-being is nurtured;
- they are kept safe from harm.

STRAND 2: BELONGING

Children and their families experience an environment in which:

- connecting links with the family and the wider world are affirmed and extended;
- they know that they have a place;
- they feel comfortable with the routines, customs and regular events;
- they know the limits and boundaries of acceptable behaviour.

STRAND 3: CONTRIBUTION

Children experience an environment in which:

- there are equitable opportunities for learning, irrespective of gender, ability, age, ethnicity or background;

- they are affirmed as individuals;
- they are encouraged to learn with and alongside others.

STRAND 4: COMMUNICATION

Children experience an environment in which:

- they develop non-verbal communication skills for a range of purposes;
- they develop verbal communication skills for a range of purposes;
- they experience the stories and symbols of their own and other cultures;
- they discover and develop different ways to be creative and expressive.

STRAND 5: EXPLORATION

Children experience an environment in which:

- their play is valued as meaningful learning and the importance of spontaneous play is recognised;
- they gain confidence in and control of their bodies;
- they learn strategies for active exploration, thinking and reasoning;
- they develop working theories for making sense of the physical, natural, social and material worlds.

The guidelines apply to all children in whatever educational setting and include children with special educational needs. Where appropriate an Individual Development Plan (IDP) is developed for children who require special resources. The programme has given rise to considerable interest among early childhood educators worldwide.

Evaluating children's progress

Educators need to monitor children's progress all the time in order to plan for the next stage of development and to identify any area of concern so that they can take action to provide support and seek additional help if necessary either within the nursery or from other agencies.

Practitioners also want to know whether the teaching programme is effective in helping children to achieve the desired learning outcomes. What benefits are there to children from attending the programme? If the benefits have not been as great as was hoped for, what must be done to amend the programme so that the learning goals can be achieved?

Another reason for assessing children's performance is to find out whether a particular teaching strategy has been more effective than others. The reflective practitioner may devise a variety of teaching approaches to support the children's learning and needs to know which is the most successful. For example, the practitioner may decide to change from a structured approach to one in which the children are allowed the freedom to select their own activities and wish to know whether this change has been beneficial.

Early years practitioners have traditionally based their assessment of children upon detailed observations supported by examples of the 'children's work' to provide evidence of progress over time. Since September 1998, when statutory baseline assessment was introduced into primary schools, teachers have been required to assess each child within seven weeks of entry into school and to submit the results to their local education authority. There are ninety accredited assessment schemes from which the school may select, although schools are required to consider the scheme nominated by their LEA when making their choice.

The purpose of the assessments is to provide diagnostic information about each child in order to help plan future teaching and learning. Parents are provided with the opportunity to discuss the outcomes of the assessments. Many practitioners in early childhood institutions have seen these assessments as a challenge to the quality of the education that they have been offering young children. As a result, they have been placing too great an emphasis upon the teaching the literacy and numeracy learning goals.

With the introduction of the Foundation Stage and accompanying curriculum guidance it was decided to revise the arrangements for baseline assessments. After consultation the government has decided to abolish baseline assessment and to introduce a profile scheme at the end of the Foundation Stage – that is, at the end of the reception year. The new scheme will involve ongoing observation and assessment of each child's progress towards all six of the early learning goals.

This national approach to assessment places emphasis upon observation, the traditional form of assessment in the early years of education, and the introduction of a standard scheme will provide the consistency that was lacking earlier. As with all assessment schemes for young children, there is a danger that it will be interpreted as a test to be passed rather than an assessment of children's progress to help teachers plan appropriately to support their learning. Parents are naturally anxious about their children's progress and, as a result, this could lead to unwelcome pressures on children unless the scheme is adequately explained. There is also the possibility that some early years practitioners will see the assessments as a test of their teaching during the Foundation Stage and they too will place too great an emphasis upon formal learning.

The introduction of this new approach is initially in England only, with Scotland, Wales and Northern Ireland still under consideration in 2002.

Quality in early childhood education

Much has been written about the need to ensure that we provide quality education for our young children and there is general agreement that a quality setting will involve the child, the family and the community. Many people subscribe to this view but few really analyse the meaning of the word 'quality' in this context. Quality is a relative-value-based concept that is totally subjective, but any definition we use must be as inclusive as possible. Different interest groups, for example parents, early childhood educators, stakeholders and even children themselves, will have a different view on what they call good-quality early childhood programmes. It is probably impossible to share a common definition of quality and therefore we must move towards a common understanding of what each person means by the term.

What are the key indicators that we should be looking for in a quality early childhood education programme? A great deal has been spoken and written about quality programmes and the need for high-quality care and education for young children to be provided for by well-qualified trainers/educators. Let us consider some of the possible indicators of quality in the context of early childhood education programmes.

Global Guidelines

For a number of years, early childhood educators both in the UK and elsewhere have been seeking common indicators of good quality. In 1999 two international organisations concerned with early childhood, OMEP (the World Organisation for Early Childhood Education) and ACEI (American Childhood Education International), gathered together a group of specialists from all five continents for four days to discuss these issues. Each delegate was a specialist in the field of early childhood education in his or her country and the resulting set of guidelines will, I believe, be of interest to all concerned with quality in the work place.

These guidelines, which can be downloaded from the website www.ecec21.org, highlight the areas that it was felt must be considered if we are to provide a comprehensive network of services that offer learning and care for children. The areas are:

- Environment and Physical Space Settings for Children;
- Curriculum Content and Pedagogy;
- Early Childhood Educators and Caregivers;
- Partnership with Families and Communities;
- Services for Young Children with Special Needs;
- Accountability, Supervision and Management of Programmes for Children.

Within each area, special attention must be directed towards:

- services with equal attention to all children;
- linkages among programmes and services for optimal effectiveness and utilisation of resources;

- recognition of the value of those who care for and teach young children, including working conditions and appropriate remuneration;
- intergenerational approaches whenever feasible;
- empowerment of communities, families and children;
- a mechanism for adequate and uninterrupted funding;
- cost analysis, monitoring and evaluation of programme quality.
                    (Early Childhood Education and Care in the 21st Century 1999)

The seven working groups produced extensive documentation that demonstrated how international are our concerns for young children and their families.

Indicators of quality

The European Commission Network on Childcare produced a comprehensive discussion document on indicators of quality in 1992. The following suggested indicators of quality have been based on this discussion paper.

The presence of the following in any setting (nursery school or class, playgroup, private nurseries or childminders) would be considered indicators of quality:

- a comprehensive range of activities available for the children to develop basic mathematical, scientific and biological concepts;
- opportunities for the development of linguistic skills;
- the encouraging of children to use their mother tongue, and opportunities to develop bilingual skills where appropriate;
- ample opportunity for children to develop artistic and creative skills through a variety of media;
- an opportunity for children to express themselves through play, puppetry and drama;
- help for children to understand basic concepts of health and hygiene;
- links for children with the local community;
- at least some control by children over the structure and pace of their activities;
- varied opportunities for children to develop their physical skills.

ENVIRONMENT

A basic physical environment should be one in which:

- the surroundings inside and outside should be safe;
- there is protection against obvious hazards and dangers;
- there are good health practices, safe and nutritious food, basic sanitation and potable water;
- children can contribute to the environment;
- there is an atmosphere of calm, well-being and freedom from fear;

- materials are easily accessible to the child;
- surroundings are aesthetically pleasing;
- there are opportunities for parents/caregivers to be involved on a regular basis.

ASSESSMENT OF CHILDREN AND LEARNING OUTCOMES

Many will argue that the most important aspect of any evaluation programme is whether the learning outcomes have been achieved. However, it is also important to discover the extent to which specific problems or talents are recognised or accommodated. To this end, indicators of good practice should include consideration of:

- whether the children are observed regularly;
- whether the assessments are carried out on an individual basis and monitored and recorded;
- whether assessments are discussed with parents;
- evidence that provision is made to support those children who have specific needs – both strengths and weaknesses.

Children learn a great deal from the adults around them, not only from the planned learning opportunities but also from the rituals and routines of daily living. The attitudes of the adults and other children and the social relationships that are formed are as crucial to children's development as the activities in which they are engaged. Our society expects children to learn to read, to be numerate and to communicate effectively and to learn all the things that it values, but it also expects children to learn to participate in a community of learners and to contribute to the quality of that community. In the early years the curriculum should be encouraging children to develop those skills and understandings that are essential to their future participation in society. This requires adults and children to learn together. It also requires educators and parents to show mutual trust and respect for the best interests of children.

References

ACEI and OMEP (1999) *Global Guidelines for Good Practice in Early Childhood Education*, www.ecec21.org

Ball, C. (1994) *Start Right*, London: Royal Society of Arts.

Bredekamp, S. and Copple, S. (eds) (1997) *Developmentally Appropriate Practice in Early Childhood Programs* (revised edition), Washington DC: National Association for the Education of Young Children.

Bredekamp, S. (ed.) (1987) *Developmentally Appropriate Practice in Early Childhood Programs Serving Children from Birth Through Age 8*, Washington DC: National Association for the Education of Young Children.

Bruner, J. (1956) *Studies in Cognitive Growth*, New York: Wiley.

Consultative Committee (Hadow) (1933) *Report on Infant and Nursery Schools*, London: HMSO.

Curtis, A. (1998) *Curriculum for the Pre-school Child*, second edition, London and New York: Routledge.

Curtis, A. (1999) *Evaluating Early Childhood Programmes: Are we asking the right questions?* Paper presented at Early Childhood Conference, Santiago, March 1999.

DfEE (2000) *Curriculum Guidance for the Foundation Stage*, London: QCA.

Drummond, M. J, Lally, M. and Pugh, G. (1989) *Working with Children: Developing a curriculum for the early years*, London: National Children's Bureau.

Edwards, C., Gandini, L. and Forman, G. (eds) (1998) *The Hundred Languages of Children*, second edition, London: Ablex Publishing Corporation.

Isaacs, S. (1930) *Intellectual Growth in Young Children*, London: Routledge.

Isaacs, S. (1933) *Social Development in Young Children*, London: Routledge.

Kelly, A. V. (1994) 'Beyond the rhetoric and discourse', in G. Blenkin and A. V. Kelly, *The National Curriculum and Early Learning*, London: Paul Chapman.

Lilley, I. (1967) *Friedrich Froebel: A selection from his writings*, Cambridge: CUP.

Malaguzzi, L. (trans L. Gandini) (1993) 'For an education based on relationships', in *Young Children*, 9, 1: 10.

McMillan, M. (1919) *The Nursery School*, London: Dent.

Ministry of Education (1996) *Te Whariki: Early childhood curriculum*, Wellington, New Zealand: Learning Media.

National Association for the Education of Young Children (1991) 'Guidelines for appropriate curriculum content and assessment in programmes serving children ages 3 through 8 years', in *Young Children*, 46, 3: 21–38.

Pascall, C. and Bertram, T. (eds) (1997) *Effective Early Learning*, London: Hodder and Stoughton.

Schweinhart, L. J. and Weikart, D. (1993) *A Summary of Significant Benefits: The High Scope Perry Pre-school Study through age 27*, Ypsilanti: High Scope.

Stipek, D., Feller, R., Daniels, D. and Milburn, S. (1995) 'The effects of different instructional approaches on young children's achievement and motivation', in *Child Development* 66: 209–23.

Sylva, K. (2001) Summary of Research Evidence on the Age of Starting School, DfES brief No. 17–01 (September).

Vygotsky, L. S. (1962) *Thought and Language*, Cambridge, Mass.: MIT Press.

Woodhead, M. (1996) *In Search of the Rainbow*, Netherlands: Van Leer Foundation.

CHAPTER 11

Core subjects in the National Curriculum at Key Stage 1

In July 1988 the Education Reform Act became law, sixty-two years after the control of the curriculum had been lifted. Two generations of primary-school teachers had devised their own educational programmes based on a child-centred approach and many were much affected by the introduction of the National Curriculum and its accompanying programmes of study that introduced a subject-based curriculum for children from five to sixteen years.

The National Curriculum applies to all pupils of compulsory school age in maintained schools, including grant-maintained schools, and is organised on the basis of four Key Stages (KS). The primary school covers KS1 and KS2, while KS3 and KS4 involve children from eleven to sixteen.

Since the introduction of the Curriculum Guidance for the Foundation Stage for children between the ages of three and six years, children in the reception class have not officially been involved in the National Curriculum until the end of the summer term, when the teachers begin to implement the National Literacy and Numeracy Strategies.

The school curriculum has two main aims. These are reflected in section 351 of the Education Act 1996, which requires all maintained schools to offer a 'balanced and broadly based curriculum'. The aims are:

1 the school curriculum should aim to provide opportunities for all pupils to learn and to achieve;
2 the school curriculum should aim to promote pupils' spiritual, moral, social and cultural development and prepare all pupils for the opportunities, responsibilities and experiences of life.

(DfEE 1999)

The curriculum provides a framework that is designed to enable all schools to respond effectively to national and local priorities, to meet the individual learning needs of all children and to develop a distinctive character and ethos rooted in their local communities.

The National Curriculum has four main purposes:

1 to establish an entitlement for all children, irrespective of their social background, culture, race, gender, differences in ability;
2 to establish national standards for the performance of all pupils in the subjects it includes;
3 to promote continuity and coherence so that it facilitates the transitions of pupils between schools and phases of learning and provides a foundation for life-long learning;
4 to promote public understanding of, and confidence in, the work of the schools and in the learning and achievements resulting from compulsory education.

Core and foundation subjects

At KS1 there are three core subjects, English, mathematics and science, and in each of these areas the children are assessed during Year 2, although since 1993 science is no longer assessed in the same way as mathematics and English. Other areas of the curriculum include design and technology, information and communication technology, history, geography, art and design, music and physical education.

There is a programme of study for each area of the curriculum that provides the basis for planning schemes of work. For numeracy and literacy detailed programmes are available, the National Literacy Strategy and the National Numeracy Strategy.

Although the programmes of study are given as specific subjects it is anticipated that teachers will deliver the curriculum in a cross-curricular manner as it is recognised that for young children learning is not compartmentalised and that they learn in a variety of ways.

Key skills

The National Curriculum describes six key skill areas that help the children in their learning, and these skills are embedded in the national curriculum:

- communication that includes skills in speaking, listening, reading and writing;
- application of number, which includes the ability to use a range of calculation skills and apply them within a variety of settings;
- information technology, including the ability to use a range of information sources and tools to find, analyse, interpret and evaluate and present information for a variety of purposes;
- working with others, including the skills of contributing to small and large group discussions;
- improving own learning and performance, which involves pupils reflecting and critically evaluating their own work and identifying ways of improving them;

• problem solving, which develops the skills and strategies that pupils need to solve problems in learning both at school and in later life.

Inclusion

One of the main tenets of the National Curriculum is that of entitlement. All schools have a responsibility to provide a broad and balanced curriculum for all pupils and that includes meeting the specific needs of individuals and groups of children. Teachers are required to offer effective learning opportunities for all pupils and three principles are set out as essential for developing an inclusive curriculum:

1 setting suitable learning challenges;
2 responding to children's diverse learning needs;
3 overcoming potential barriers to learning and assessment for individual and groups of children.

The hope is that by adhering to these principles, as few children as possible will be excluded from the National Curriculum.

The National Curriculum document (DfEE 1999: 31–7) details the ways in which these three principles can be implemented and how the diverse needs of children can be met within its framework. In many schools support will be available to enable children to function effectively but it is stressed that it is the role of the teacher to create an environment in which all children are valued and are helped to feel secure. Important issues relating to equal opportunities and second-language learning are also raised in this section of the document and have been addressed in this book in earlier chapters.

In this chapter we shall be looking at the core subjects in the National Curriculum (English, mathematics and science) and considering how they relate to the early learning goals of the Foundation Stage. One of the difficulties in working with such clear guidelines for the development of these subject areas, in particular literacy and numeracy, is that teachers could be tempted to deliver the curriculum without taking into account the knowledge that we have about how children learn and develop during the early years of schooling.

English: literacy and oracy

Probably the subject that causes most worry for parents is English, and reading in particular. Ask a random sample of parents anywhere in the country and you will find that their greatest concern is that their children should learn to read and write – to become literate members of our society. This concern begins almost from birth and although we want to see children 'bathed' in books from an early age, I am horrified at the amount of pressure that is currently being placed on practitioners in the nurseries and playgroups to 'get the children reading and writing'. So many of our three-year-olds seem to be spending a great deal of time completing worksheets and copying letters and shapes. Every time I return from my visits to early years institutions in other parts of the world I ask myself, is this really the best way to support children's literacy?

What is literacy? According to the National Literacy Strategy framework:

> Literacy unites the important skills of reading and writing. It also involves speaking and listening skills ... Good oral work enhances pupils' understanding of language in both oral and written forms and of the way language can be used to communicate. It is also an important part of the process through which pupils read and compose texts.
>
> (DfEE 1998: 3)

Literacy is an essential competence for success in school, and the Effectiveness Provision of Pre-school Education Project (EPPE) study, being carried out in 2002 at the Institute of Education in London, has shown that pre-school children who have access to books in the home perform better throughout KS1 regardless of their parents' education. Learning to turn the pages of a book and talk about the pictures helps to develop a child's literacy and oracy. However, we need to consider seriously the work of Locke and Ginsburg (2002), who have found that over-emphasis upon early literacy is delaying oracy. Putting children onto a reading scheme as soon as possible and pushing them into formal writing and reading exercises may damage the development of both literacy and oracy.

The National Literacy Strategy (NLS), based on the recommendations of the National Literacy Project, is designed to provide a framework for teaching from reception class through to Year 6.

According to the Framework for Teaching (DfEE 1998), literate primary pupils should:

- read and write with confidence, fluency and understanding;
- be able to orchestrate a full range of reading cues to monitor their reading and correct their own mistakes;
- understand the sound and spelling system and use this to spell and read accurately;
- have fluent and legible handwriting;
- have an interest in words and their meanings and a growing vocabulary;
- know, understand and be able to write in a range of genres in fiction and poetry;
- understand and be able to write a range of non-fiction texts;
- plan and edit their own writing;
- have suitable technical vocabulary through which to understand and discuss their reading and writing;
- be interested in books, read with enjoyment and evaluate and justify their preferences;

- through reading and writing, develop their powers of imagination, inventiveness and critical awareness.

These are obviously the anticipated outcomes for children at the end of the primary-school years, but readers taking a close look at this document will realise that many of these skills and competencies are introduced during the Foundation Stage and at KS1. These were discussed earlier in relation to the early learning goals for communication, language and literacy. Although it is recommended that aspects of the literacy strategy are taught in the reception classes, both the National Literacy Strategy (NLS) and OFSTED's framework suggest that the whole literacy hour is not introduced until the summer term. However, it appears that some inspectors and head teachers have been insisting on the NLS being introduced as a formal literacy hour, even in reception classes, in spite of the comments from government advisors. Research by Clark (2002) shows that there is a growing tendency towards formality and teacher-led didactic approaches in the early years classrooms that can be attributed to the National Literacy Strategy. It is hoped that with the universal implementation of the Foundation Stage, reception-class teachers will heed the official advice and not expect four-year-old children, of whom there are many in most schools, to be involved in the formal work of the literacy hour on entry into school.

In Western society children are born into a literate society and from the moment they can focus upon print they become aware of written language as part of daily life. Even children who come from homes without access to books are exposed to the printed word through advertisements, junk mail, shops, buses, and the labels on food and packaging.

Although the vast majority of children enter school with the ability to communicate and use language effectively, each child will enter school with a very particular and personal understanding of the purpose of reading and writing. Literacy is part of the social and cultural practices for which it is used and therefore each child's experience of literacy will be closely linked to its family and community. The studies of Brice-Heath (1983), Schieffelin and Cochran-Smith (1984) and Minns (1990) all point to the ways in which children learn about literacy from their family life.

Schools, early childhood classrooms and families are all dynamic cultural environments with unique views about literacy. Family views of literacy are dependent upon a range of factors including socio-economic levels, ethnicity, educational history, family stability and health. Hannon (1995) has pointed out that the literacy values and practices of families shape the course of children's literacy in terms of opportunities, recognition and models available to them. There is a great diversity of literacy practice among families and the failure of educators to acknowledge anything other than the 'mainstream' approach to literacy may, albeit unwittingly, contribute to academic failure (Makin *et al.* 1999).

Literacy, reading and writing finds its foundations in communication and talk. Enjoying books and understanding that the marks (such as letters, and numbers) carry messages is a crucial step in children's reading development. Literacy is generally embedded in many activities although frequently it is centred on story reading and discussion using the language of the dominant groups. Teachers are expected to provide a curriculum that offers equal opportunities for all children and that necessitates offering literature and discussions appropriate to minority groups. Otherwise, it could be argued, teachers perpetuate social inequalities by determining what is read and ways of being literate. We have long been aware of the importance of parental involvement in children's education and there is substantial evidence to show that the most academically successful children are those whose family literacy practices are most congruent with those of the school. Clay (1993) pointed out the importance of the degree of match between literacy practices of family and services, especially in the period of zero to six years. This knowledge makes it even more important that children coming from homes with different family literacy values and practices are not marginalised and do not develop into 'academic failures'.

As children learn to communicate with others, so they come to make meaning of the world around them. Psycholinguists such as Goodman (1967) and Smith (1988) have demonstrated that children's experience of learning to talk is fundamental to their development as readers and writers. Children appear to use similar strategies to make sense of written language as they did when learning to talk. Researchers such as Bissex (1980) Ferreiro and Teberosky (1982) and Minns (1990) have shown how children learn from opportunities to see written language in real contexts.

Hearing narratives and stories also plays an important part in helping children to make sense of reading and writing. Fox (1993) has shown that access to narrative writing helps children to gain sensitivity to the distinctive forms of grammar, for example the use of the past tense, as well as giving them introduction to more complex forms of language. Children are often helped to take on abstract ideas from stories and poetry.

One of the first ways in which children have an understanding of the written language is when they learn to recognise their names and those of their friends and family. Names mean something to children as they relate to real people, and Minns (1990) has argued that by seeing their names in print, young children begin to develop an awareness of the value and use of the written word. However, although they begin to understand about the nature of written language from reading and writing, the underlying processes involved in encoding meaning as a writer are different from those involved in decoding meaning as a reader.

Reading and writing are mutually supportive activities although they make very different demands upon children. We no longer consider it necessary for children to learn to read before they can be taught to write.

Writing

The foundations of writing are to be found in the scribble patterns of the toddler. Vygotsky (1978) has pointed out that drawing assumes particular importance as children come to realise that they can draw speech as well as objects. This understanding presents an enormous intellectual leap for young children. However, they also need to understand the difference between spoken and written language if they are to understand the power and purpose of writing.

When we are talking about writing it is important to remember to differentiate between composition – the expression of ideas and transcription – and the secretarial aspects of writing. Young children's compositional skills are far in advance of their motor writing skills, which is why teachers need to act as scribes for very young children or encourage them to write independently to free them from the pressures of 'getting it right'. The first compositions of children include symbols they recognise such as numerals, letters from their names and invented letter-like shapes. It is important that parents realise that this is normal development and that the child has really composed a piece of writing, even though it may be indecipherable to the adult. Parents have to be helped to understand that if disproportionate attention is given to presentation skills, children will think of writing as another motor skill, not as the composing of a text.

The National Literacy Strategy draws attention to the need for children to be able to spell correctly and includes high-frequency word lists for the children to learn. However, in the early stages of writing the younger children will develop ways of coping with the complexities of spelling by looking for regularities and patterns in exactly the same way as they looked for patterns when they were younger in dealing with the past tense (see Chapter 4). Bissex's work provides excellent examples of a young child's search for pattern.

Reading

By the end of the Foundation Stage children are expected to be able to 'read a range of familiar and common words and simple sentences independently'. These are very high expectations of young children after such a short time in school. As a result many nurseries are now expecting children to carry out formal work on letters and words so that they are 'not falling behind' when they enter the reception class. In a recent piece of research, David *et al.* (2002) asked a group of early years educators their views about literacy. They found that there was almost a 50:50 split, with half believing that children should not be involved in literacy activities until after the age of five and the other half believing that children were surrounded by print from birth and that most of them would be learning about it anyway.

The observations of these researchers were that those who advocated play as a vehicle for learning about literacy in reality called children away from their play activities singly or in small groups to carry out a task that was totally unrelated to what they had been doing throughout the session.

In the framework for the National Literacy Strategy children are expected to be able to carry out the following by the end of KS1:

- read simple texts with understanding and general accuracy;
- express opinions about events or ideas in stories, poems and non-fiction;
- use more than one strategy, such as phonic, graphic, syntactic and contextual, in reading unfamiliar words and establishing meanings.

It is intended that these aims will be achieved by offering children structured guidance and direction mainly during the literacy hour, although reading and writing skills will be developed throughout the school day.

The literacy hour is divided into four parts. For the first fifteen minutes teachers working with children at KS1 focus on whole-class instruction – looking at shared-text work, aimed to give a balance between reading and writing. The second fifteen minutes are geared towards focused word work with the whole class. Next comes a twenty-minute period spent on group or independent work, during which the teacher works with at least two ability groups on guided text work while the remainder of the class carries out independent reading or writing tasks. The final ten minutes are spent on reviewing and reflecting upon the work covered during the preceding fifty minutes.

How do children learn to read? Reading is a process that begins as soon as children can focus on print. The first print to which children are exposed is environmental print and many would argue that it plays as large a part in learning to read as the reading of books they are given at the early stages of reading. At home children will look at cereal packets and other packaging and point to the logos that identify them. At this stage children are dealing with the pattern of the whole word; decoding comes later. As children become more aware of the printed word they show an interest in detail and will start looking at and commenting on letters of the alphabet. Frequently the first one is the initial letter of their name. Around the same time many children start to notice the rhymes in songs or nursery rhymes.

The value of rhyming language is stressed by many as it has been found that texts that incorporate rhyme and recurrent tunes and contain language that is rhythmic and memorable make it easier for children to predict and anticipate the rest of the verse. Goswani and Byrant (1990) drew attention to the importance of offering young children opportunities for engaging in songs, rhymes and alliteration. They found that chanting and singing and playing with language gave children a sensitivity to rhyme that provided the basis for the development of phonological awareness and was strongly related to later success in reading.

Methods of teaching reading

There are three main methods of teaching reading that are used in primary schools today, although many use a mixture of methods appropriate to the needs of the child. Current commercial reading schemes, used in the majority of schools, offer children the opportunity to learn the necessary strategies to become fluent readers.

LOOK AND SAY METHOD

This method relies on children learning to recognise individual words, which they are expected to learn before they are given their first book. Proponents of this approach argue that children will meet with instant success as they will already know the vocabulary of the book.

Difficulties with the approach are that:

- children with poor visual memories find this method difficult;
- repetition can be boring;
- books with very limited vocabulary can sound very dull;
- children are not being helped to develop strategies to deal with words they have not met.

PHONIC METHOD

This method concentrates on sounds and letters. Children are introduced to single sounds at the beginning of words, for example *p*, *t*, *s*; to blends, for example *br*, *sl*, *pr*; to clusters, for example *spr*, *str*; to digraphs, for example *ch*, *th*, *sh*; to the last letters in words. These are practised in a variety of ways.

Difficulties with the approach are that:

- relationship between sounds and letters is not always straightforward;
- our ability to distinguish between sounds develops at different times;
- children with poor auditory discrimination find this method difficult;
- children with nasal or ear infections may have difficulties;
- regional variations can lead to confusion, such as 'fick' for 'thick'.

APPRENTICESHIP METHOD

This method builds on the child's experience of print and on the knowledge of stories, language that children bring with them to school. The emphasis is upon enjoying books and discussing them with the teacher. The children regularly read a book alongside the teacher until they feel ready to take over on their own. Critics of the method say that it is totally unstructured and does not guide the children appropriately. In reality the schools that use this method rather than reading schemes have a planned programme that ensures that children are exposed to the full range of strategies required for learning to read.

There is considerable disagreement between those who believe that reading can be simplified for children if it is broken down into constituent hierarchical skills and those who argue that using adult logic to simplify a complex process actually makes reading more difficult for children. Advocates of the whole-word approach argue that reading involves the complex integration of skills, all of which must be present at the start.

Those who favour this latter approach suggest that reading is an active transactional process between the reader and the text. Therefore it is important that children are offered texts that are meaningful and provide a satisfying experience. Books should also have high-quality illustrations that both support and clarify the text. Whichever approach is used, it must be remembered that reading should be a pleasurable experience and not a competition to see who can get through the various stages of the reading scheme the fastest.

Children need many opportunities to practise reading, which is where the shared and guided reading practices recommended in the National Literacy Strategy are effective, as part of the literacy hour should be spent with the teacher reading to the children and the children reading to each other. For the child who already has a grasp on reading, silent reading is an important next step.

What are some of the factors that contribute to successful reading?

A summary of the literature reveals that the following have an effect upon children's reading success.

Family literacy practices:

- story book reading at home;
- environmental print experiences;
- home–school links/mutual respect between home and school;
- opportunities for talk and discussion.

Classroom-based literacy practices:

- social context of classroom literacy experience;
- teachers fostering a desire to read;
- opportunities for challenge;
- opportunities for choice;
- opportunities for collaboration;
- story book reading in the classroom, including examples of good literature;
- shared reading in the classroom – reading to and by the teacher;
- literacy (reading and writing) integrated across the curriculum.

We no longer believe that children are not 'reading ready' until the age of six. Children are individuals who have different strengths and weaknesses and whose interest in learning to read will vary. Nevertheless, most learn to read and write conventionally within the first years of school. Schickedanz (1999) argues that these achievements represent the end result of years of literacy learning that begin the moment the very young child is able to focus on print.

Mathematics

Sparrow (1998) argues that mathematics is not just a collection of skills, it is a way of thinking. It lies at the core of scientific understanding, and of rational and logical argument.

Mathematics is not just about computation, traditional word problems and numerical algorithms but it is about how children develop their mathematical understanding. The mathematics curriculum builds on the early learning goals that have required children to:

- count and use numbers to at least 10 in familiar contexts;
- recognise numerals from 1 to 9;
- talk about and create simple patterns;
- begin to understand addition as combining two groups of objects and subtraction as 'taking away';
- describe the shape and size of solid and flat shapes;
- use everyday words to describe position;
- use early mathematical ideas to solve practical problems.

The curriculum for children in KS1 focuses on:

1 the use and application of number, the number system, calculations, using both mental methods and symbols, problem solving and representing and interpreting data;
2 the use and application of shape, space and measures. Pupils are to be taught to use and apply shape, space and measures to solve problems and understand the patterns and properties of shape, position and movement as well as to understand measures.

The poor performance of British children compared with children in other countries led to the setting up of the National Numeracy Project, whose initial concerns were:

1 the level of children's arithmetic skills;
2 the dominance of published schemes in schools, reducing teacher to scheme manager;
3 over-emphasis on standard written algorithms introduced too early.

From its findings, this group suggested that there should be:

- dedicated mathematics lessons every day;
- direct teaching and interactive oral work with the whole class and with groups;
- an emphasis on mental calculation;

- controlled differentiation, with all pupils engaged in mathematics related to a common theme.

These recommendations have now been incorporated into classroom practice in KS1 classrooms as the 'numeracy hour', although the National Curriculum does not require five hours of teaching mathematics each week.

The National Curriculum is heavily weighted towards number with mental methods for calculation in the first years of schooling. Use of calculators is restricted to Years 5 and 6, and then only for calculations and not for concept development and problem solving. Rousham and Rowland (1996) argue that it is surprising that the government was so adamant about the use of calculators and making them the scapegoat for disappointing mathematical performance when there is ample evidence to show that calculators in the hands of children with competent and imaginative teachers can promote the learning of mathematical concepts and stimulate mental calculation (Shuard *et al.* 1991). Is this a message about the competence of teachers?

The mathematics curriculum requires early childhood educators to include specific content in their planning and teaching and to ensure that children have the necessary knowledge, understanding and mastery of skills. However, in order to help children develop this knowledge and understanding teachers need to be very aware of how children develop their mathematical thinking. Recent research has highlighted some of the important factors that need to be considered (Steffe and Wood 1990; Nunes 1998).

Children enter the education system with a wealth of mathematical experiences and knowledge that they have gained from home and their environment. It is not always recognised as mathematical knowledge when a two-year-old complains that her brother has more sweets than she does. Unfortunately so many adults still see mathematics as separated from everyday life and as something that is carried out by mathematicians in their ivory towers. Although children can function mathematically from an early age they do not intuitively understand mathematical ideas in an abstract formal way; nor do they appreciate that what they are doing or saying is mathematics. They may not be able to count accurately or recognise conventional symbols but, as Hughes (1986) has pointed out, they are able to add and subtract even though they cannot represent these operations on paper in a recognisable form.

Part of the task of the early years educator is to introduce young children to the conventions of mathematics, particularly number. The Cockcroft Report pointed out, as long ago as 1982, that one of the important roles of the early years teachers is to 'open the doors of mathematical discovery' to the children in their care.

Aubrey (1997) has shown that reception-class children bring into school a rich informal knowledge of counting, recognition of numerals, skills in simple addition and subtraction and social sharing, but there is very little evidence that teachers build on this knowledge in the classroom.

Mathematics involves children being active investigators, 'doing' mathematics rather than just learning about it. Young children are constantly forming a sense of pattern and order and refining their abilities to think logically and compare, contrast and match what they know with the challenges of their environment. The role of the educator is to build on these developing strengths and help children to become actively involved in the learning process so that they can make meaningful connections within their existing frameworks and also make changes in their frameworks. One task of the teacher is to develop in the children the skills associated with knowledge about and the manipulation of our number system. However, there is a danger that too great an emphasis on number fails to take into account the wealth of mathematical knowledge that children bring into school. Calling the mathematics aspect of the National Curriculum the 'numeracy hour' reinforces this approach.

From the nursery to the first years of schooling we introduce learning to young children by the use of practical activities and materials, but we need to ask ourselves what the child makes of the representations we offer. Does a line of ten bricks really help children to understand 10, or are we simply offering a concrete example of an abstract idea that remains abstract however many concrete representations we make? Children will bring their own interpretation to any concrete representation and that can sometimes result in more complexities rather than conclusions, as every teacher knows well.

Piaget put forward an activity-based model of learning that has been extended by researchers such as Donaldson (1978) and Hughes (1986), who have pointed out that more effective learning takes place when it is presented to children within a context that is both familiar and meaningful. As we have seen, Bruner has criticised Piaget's model of development arguing that the teacher must set challenges for the child. He proposed a spiral curriculum, maintaining that any topic can be taught to a child at any age in an intellectually respectable form.

Vygotsky, like Bruner, was an interventionist, who stressed the importance of the adult taking an active part in children's learning. His identification of the 'zone of proximal development' has helped to focus attention upon the importance of open questioning in facilitating children's learning.

Number

'She knows her numbers and can count up to 100', is the sort of statement that many reception-class teachers hear from parents when their child enters primary school. Indeed children come into school having made some attempt to come to terms with our number system. As Ginsberg (1977) has pointed out, children struggle to understand the apparent arbitrary nature of numbers in our culture. We say 'one, two, three', not 'three, one, two'. The child sees learning to count as a song that has no end, as a new part is always being introduced and there is always one number larger than the one before. Counting is endless.

For the young child this task must seem overwhelming and yet children do learn to count, some even before they enter the nursery. Ginsberg (1977) has identified two important strategies necessary to succeed in this task: looking for order and pattern; and coping with a little of the task at a time. For example, children manage 'one, two, three' before they attempt 'four, five, six'. The search for pattern takes longer as our counting numbers do not reflect any pattern until we pass twelve and then twenty. There is an identifiable rhythm in the tens: twenty, thirty, forty, and so on, and within the tens, but there is usually a need for prompting when the child reaches twenty-nine to go on to thirty, although the child can then go on easily from thirty to thirty-nine. These problems are ones of our culture, as in some societies, such as China or Korea, the number symbols have a clear regularity, as do the number names. Fuson and Kwon (1992) reported that speakers of some Asian languages do not seem to have the same difficulties and are able to cope with the conceptual structures earlier than their English-speaking cohort. In our multicultural society the different counting systems of other cultures should all be used to help support children's mathematical development. The Swann Report (1985) was the first official report to make teachers aware of the need to introduce a multicultural approach to mathematics in the classroom. The use of the Rangoli and Islamic patterns will add another dimension when making children aware of symmetry and tessellation.

Children need to make the transition from counting by ones to counting by tens, hundreds, thousands and so on in order to develop effective problem-solving strategies and meaning for place value. Successful manipulation of the symbols within computational problems does not imply this transition, as many researchers have found that children can compute accurately without understanding (Kamii 1989; Kamii and Joseph 1988).

There is strong evidence to show that although most children have little problem with reading and writing numbers from zero to nine, the higher numbers, which involve an understanding of place values, can be more difficult. A common error is for children to write the number two-hundred-and-sixty-one as '200601' until they have a real understanding of place value.

However, learning to count involves more than learning number names and symbols. Gelman and Gallistel (1978) in a classic experiment identified five criteria that must be fulfilled before it can be said that counting has been successfully achieved.

- *One-to-one principle* – each and every item is given one, and only one, number name.
- *Abstraction principle* – what the objects are is irrelevant, what matters is that they all belong to the collection being counted.
- *Stable-order principle* – the number names are used in an unvarying order, for example one, two, three, four, etc. not two, three, four, one.
- *Cardinality principle* – the final number name denotes the number in the collection. For example, if there are five in a set, when the number five is reached, this gives the number in the set.

- *Order-irrelevance principle* – it does not matter in which order the items are counted as long as all the other criteria are met.

Through this exercise, Gelman and Gallistel have shown that what is a simple exercise to an adult is in fact a complex task for the young child.

Children use numbers in a variety of ways besides counting. For example: 'I live at number 89'; 'I have four buttons on my blouse', but teachers are most concerned with the aspect that deals with 'one and one equals two'. It is this use of number that ought to lead to the child's understanding of number in the abstract world of mathematics. Hughes (1986) argued that there is a gap between children's abstract understanding of number and their ability to represent this understanding in the formal language of mathematics. He urges that teachers must make links between the knowledge based on concrete experiences that the child is sure of and the abstract nature of the language or arithmetic. Piaget has argued that children need to attain the concept of conservation of number before they can see number as a property of a set. However, it may be that children need to be able to make a connection between their experiences of number and the representation of number in the world of concrete objects in order to deal with abstract mathematical ideas effectively.

There has been considerable research to show that the meaning of addition and subtraction and multiplication and division is complex and that children can only be said to understand these operations when they fully understand all the various interpretations. Experience with concrete objects is essential before children can make sense of the symbolic representations, although it is essential for teachers to listen carefully to the explanations children give so that they can understand the child's meaning. As has been said earlier, manipulation of concrete objects does not necessarily imply understanding.

Space, shape and size

If mathematics is perceived as the search for order, pattern and relationships to characterise ideas and experiences then spatial concepts are central topics in children's understanding of mathematics. They are also important for the science and IT programmes of study. Constructivist theories of learning have a fundamental tenet that children learn through their interaction with the environment. The development of spatial concepts is a gradual process and, according to Piaget, children have little understanding until they are around seven years of age. However, Donaldson's findings showed that when the children were placed in a context that was meaningful to them they had greater understanding. This research has highlighted the importance of providing the appropriate tools in the classroom to enable children to explore and develop the concept of space. One of the most appropriate ways is during structured play sessions, where the availability of open-ended situations in a meaningful setting will help children to develop this understanding.

Measurement

Measurement has many different aspects and is difficult for children to understand as we measure in different standard units, each one having been arbitrarily determined. We use linear measurement for some situations, measurements of capacity for others, and so on. Piaget's investigations led him to argue that the principle of invariance is associated with conservation and transitivity. According to Piaget, children at KS1 have not reached the stage of conservation of weight, time, mass and volume, although most will have achieved the concept of length at around six or seven years. Although there has been criticism that Piaget may not have been entirely correct, there is no doubt that young children cannot handle concept of measurement effectively until further up the school. However, the varied experiences that they are offered in the Foundation Years and in KS1 will provide the basis for the development of understanding these concepts.

A dictionary definition describes the verb 'measure' as 'to ascertain the extent or quantity of x by comparison with a standard or fixed unit or object of known size'.

This includes three important ideas, each of which needs to be considered when discussing measurement with young children:

- extent or quantity;
- comparison;
- fixed unit or object of known size.

The first idea relates to the purpose of measuring – how long, how thick, how heavy, how much is contained? When children are engaged in any form of measuring they will be required to make connections between shape and size, size and number (of units), number and order and ordering and shape.

By making these connections children begin to see the relationships within mathematics and between mathematics and other areas of knowledge. So ascertaining extent and quantity is not a simple operation for a child.

The second idea relates to comparison. This is an important notion and it is crucial for children to understand that it is an inexact one. For example, we may use two different weighing machines and find that they measure different amounts. From discussions on comparison children can then be encouraged to think about the ideas of estimation and approximation and to making judgements about appropriateness and efficiency. In the early stages of measuring, non-standard units may be used and in this way children can quickly come to understand the need for a fixed unit of measurement. It is soon realised that two of the teacher's hand spans measures more than two of a six-year-old. Children also need to realise that any unit of measurement is purely a social convenience.

Language and mathematics

Perhaps the most important part of the early mathematics curriculum is that children understand the language of mathematics and that they are engaged in problem solving, discussion and questioning with their teachers. The young child's first mathematical experiences are centred around oral language, both listening and speaking. We know that young children search for patterns and order among their experiences and often find confusion in the language of mathematics. For example, when we ask a child 'What is an odd number?' we are referring to something specific and do not mean the same as when we say, 'I saw something odd today'. Likewise, the word 'different' causes difficulties for many children. The term difference in 'What is the difference between a monkey and an elephant?' is not the same as in 'What is the difference between eight and five?' Children also become confused with the ambiguity of words in English. For example, a child is asked by the teacher to make its model 'twice as big' – Does this mean in all directions or only in height, length, or width, or two of these dimensions?

Talking with children involves the adult using precise, accurate language if we are not to increase their confusion. Some examples of this were given in Chapter 4, 'Communication and communication disorders'.

Value of problem solving

In looking at children's mathematical development, we must consider it in the context of the child's development as a whole. Mathematics is not just for the numeracy hour. Hughes *et al.* (2000) have found that there was not sufficient emphasis placed on problem solving and creative thinking at KS1 because of the favoured emphasis on number knowledge and calculation skills in the National Numeracy Strategy. Many opportunities for problem solving and creative thinking arise during play. We should not underestimate the value of play in children's mathematical development, although the inspectors have pointed out that many schools fail to make good use of the opportunities for the development and extension of mathematical understanding that arise during play situations.

When children are given the opportunity to solve problems, frequently they construct strategies within the social construct of the classroom as they share their ideas and invent strategies with other children. This is not just discovery learning as the teacher must pose questions and tasks that stimulate appropriate conceptual reorganisation by the children. This requires the teacher to understand the expected developmental sequence of mathematical understanding as well as the current levels of mathematical understanding held by the children.

Many argue that place value can not be learned by the use of concrete materials, but there is growing evidence to support the view that when arithmetic concepts and procedures are approached as problem solving, children's invented strategies foster number sense and understanding of multiple-digit addition and subtraction (Carpenter *et al.* 1998). When children are given problems to solve they should be presented with a variety of ways and with a variety of mathematical language. There is evidence that when the problem is set in a meaningful context for children, they can often solve problems mentally before they can use the written symbols correctly.

When talking with children, educators should:

- use open-ended and challenging questions;
- provide a focal point for discussion;
- allow children time to develop their own ideas;
- encourage children to develop their own ideas;
- encourage children to share and compare ideas;
- keep the children involved;
- ask questions to assess understanding;
- ask helpful questions to aid progress.

Children often learn numbers in everyday life but schools have the role of getting them to think about different sorts of numbers. As Nunes (1998) puts it:

> Numeracy is not just about learning, numbers and computations, it is first and foremost a matter of understanding the framework for thinking that mathematicians have developed over time. It is more likely that we understand these frameworks for thinking when we use them to solve problems.

Will the national numeracy strategy work in the long run? Only time will tell, but at least it has addressed some issues such as the neglect of mental mathematics and the use of the Vertical Arithmetic Syndrome (VAS), which had caused such problems for many children. It has challenged teachers in classroom mathematical thinking and teaching, but many would argue that there is still a high dependence on textbooks that favour the VAS as they are seen as surrogate teachers. A real challenge to policy makers is to ensure that during the Foundation Stage, as well as KS1, written work is postponed for as long as is appropriate. Parents may want to see worksheets covered in numbers and 'sums', but educators must convince them that it is in the best interests of the child to learn to problem solve mentally.

Science

An awareness of the poor level of science teaching in primary schools resulted in a number of government initiatives in the 1980s designed to raise standards and support the teachers, many of whom had little knowledge of the subject themselves. By 1989 the HMI reported considerable improvements in primary science teaching, although it was still a weak area in many infant classrooms where few teachers had any scientific knowledge of the physical sciences.

When the National Curriculum was introduced science was designated one of the core subjects, although less time is devoted to it than to mathematics and English. The recommendation is that science should be taught for approximately one and a half hours per week at KS1, compared with three and a half hours of mathematics and five hours of English.

At KS1, the programme of study aims to provide the children with knowledge, skills and understanding in four main areas.

Scientific enquiry

This is to include:

- ideas and evidence in science – where children learn how to collect evidence by making observations and measurements when trying to answer a question;
- investigative skills – encouraging children to learn how to plan, obtain, present, consider and evaluate evidence.

Life processes and living things

Life processes

The children are to be taught:

- the difference between things that are living and things that have never been alive;
- that animals, including humans, move, feed, grow, use their senses and reproduce;
- to relate life processes to animals and plants found in the local environment.

Humans and other animals

The children are to be taught:

- to recognise and compare the main external parts of the bodies of humans and other animals;
- that humans and other animals need food and water to stay alive;
- that taking exercise and eating the right types of food help to keep humans healthy;
- about the role of drugs as medicines;

- how to treat animals with care and sensitivity;
- that humans and other animals produce offspring and that these grow into adults;
- about the senses that enable humans and other animals to be aware of the world around them.

Green plants

The children are to be taught:

- to recognise that plants need light and water to grow;
- to recognise and name the leaf, flower, stem and root of flowering plants;
- that seeds grow into flowering plants.

Variation and classification

The children are to be taught:

- to recognise similarities and differences between themselves and others;
- to treat others with sensitivity;
- to group living things according to observable differences and similarities.

Living things in their environment

The children are to be taught:

- to find out about the different kinds of plants and animals in the local environment;
- to identify similarities and differences between local environments and ways in which these affect animals and plants that are found there;
- to care for the environment.

Materials and their properties

Grouping materials

The children are to be taught:

- to use their senses to explore and recognise the similarities and differences between materials;
- to sort objects into groups on the basis of simple material properties;
- to recognise and name common types of materials and understand that some of them occur naturally;
- to find out about the uses of materials and how they are chosen for specific uses on the basis of their simple properties.

Changing materials

The children are to be taught:

- to find out how the shapes of objects made from some materials can be changed by some processes;
- to explore and describe the way some everyday materials change when they are heated or cooked.

Physical processes

Electricity

The children are to be taught:

- about everyday appliances that use electricity;
- about simple circuits involving batteries, wires, bulbs and other components;
- how a switch can be used to break a circuit.

Forces and motion

The children are to be taught:

- how to find out about and describe the movement of familiar things;
- that both pushes and pulls are examples of forces;
- to recognise that when things speed up, slow down or change direction there is a cause.

Light and sound

LIGHT AND DARK

The children are to be taught:

- to identify different light sources, including the sun;
- that darkness is the absence of light.

MAKING AND DETECTING SOUNDS

The children are to be taught:

- that there are many kinds and sources of sound;
- that sounds travel away from sources, getting fainter as they do so, and that they are heard when they enter the ear.

(DfEE 1999: 78–81, adapted)

Throughout the document it is recommended that cross-curricular links are made, particularly with mathematics and IT. Teachers are also required to consider health and safety aspects and to encourage children to use simple scientific language to communicate and describe ideas.

Science is an exciting subject that interests and stimulates young children. From a very young age children are enthralled by many of the ongoing activities in the world around them. One has only to observe a young child watching a bee collect pollen from a flower to realise how much we take for granted. Children will have been introduced to many of the ideas encapsulated in the programme of study during the Foundation Stage as the early learning goals related to knowledge and understanding of the world make an excellent basis for the science curriculum at KS1. For example, cooking, which is a fundamental part of the nursery curriculum, will have provided opportunities for children to discuss with an adult the effects of the properties of heat on some materials. Naturally the understanding of the seven-year-old will be much greater than that of the three-year-old, but the seeds of scientific understanding will have been sown.

Although the concepts that are needed to understand most scientific activities are not fully developed in children at KS1, nevertheless the skills of observing, questioning and evaluating can be fostered during these early years. Some have argued that by defining the specific scientific content in the programme we are preventing children from 'learning through discovery'. However, it has been pointed out that sometimes children need to be helped to make their discoveries. Children can learn to carry out simple experiments that will help them to understand their world, but their limited conceptual understanding may prevent them from making scientific judgements without the help of an adult to 'scaffold' the situation.

When educators are helping children to investigate and explore they are inculcating them into a scientific way of thinking that can be used on many other occasions. By encouraging the development of scientific skills such as observing, questioning, communicating, measuring, classifying and recognising patterns, educators are helping to foster scientific attitudes and scientific concepts. Children need to talk with an adult and with other children and these discussions help them to find out about their surroundings and to make sense of the environment.

The core subjects of the National Curriculum all involve educators in talk, questioning and investigation and the good practitioner will offer the appropriate resources and materials so that children can gain knowledge about the everyday world around them at their own pace and according to their own interest. Pre-school and primary-school classrooms should be places in which each child's thinking is valued and in which it is expected that each child will be fully involved. There should be sufficient time for investigations and discussion is the accepted norm. In such classrooms there is the opportunity for every child to learn the necessary skills for life in the twenty-first century.

References

Aubrey, C. (1997) *Mathematics Teaching in the Early Years: An investigation of teachers' subject knowledge*, London: Falmer Press.

Bissex, G. L. (1980) *GYNS AT WRK: A child learns to write*, London: Harvard University Press.

Bryce-Heath, S. (1983) *Ways with Words: Language, life and work in communities and classrooms*, Cambridge: Cambridge University Press.

Carpenter, T. P., Franks, M. L., Jacobs, V. R., Fennema, E. and Empson, S. B. (1998) 'A longitudinal study of invention and understanding in children's multidigit addition and subtraction', in *Journal for Research in Mathematics Education*, 29: 3–20.

Clark, L. (2002) 'Lessons from the nursery: children as writers in early education', in *Reading 34*, 2: 69–74.

Clay, M. (1993) *An Observation Survey of Early Literacy Achievement*, Auckland, New Zealand: Heineman.

David, T. *et al.* (2002) *Making Sense of Literacy*, Warwick: Trentham Books.

DES (1982) *Mathematics Counts*, London: HMSO (Cockcroft Report).

DfEE (1998) *The National Literacy Strategy*, London: DfEE.

DfEE (1999) *The National Curriculum*, London: DfEE/QCA.

DfEE (1999) *The National Numeracy Strategy*, London: DfEE.

Donaldson, M. (1978) *Children's Minds*, Glasgow: Fontana/Collins.

Ferreiro, E. and Teberosky, A. (1982) *Literacy Before Schooling*, Exeter, New Hampshire: Heinemann Educational.

Fox, C. (1993) *At the Very Edge of the Forest: The influence of literature on story and narrative by children*, London: Cassell.

Fuson, K. C. and Kwon, Y. (1992) 'Learning addition and subtraction: effects of number words and other cultural tools', in J. Bideaud, C. Meljac and J. P. Fischer (eds), *Pathways to Number*, Hillsdale, New Jersey: Elrbaum Associates.

Gelman, R. and Gallistel, C. R. (1978) *The Child's Understanding of Number*, Cambridge, MA.: Harvard University Press.

Ginsburg, H. (1977) *Children's Arithmetic: How they learn it and how you reach it*, Austin, TX: PRO-ED.

Goodman, K. S. (1967) 'Reading: a psycholinguistic guessing game', in *Elementary English 42*: 639–43.

Goswani, U. and Bryant, P. E. (1990) *Phonological Skills and Learning to Read*, Hove: Lawrence Erlbaum.

Hannon, P. (1995) *Literacy, Home and School: Research and practice in teaching literacy with parents*, London: Falmer Press.

Hughes, M. (1986) *Children and Number: Difficulties in learning mathematics*, Oxford: Blackwell.

Hughes, M., Desforges, C. and Mitchell, C. L. (2000) *Numeracy and Beyond*, Buckingham: Open University Press.

Kamii, C. (1989) *Young Children Continue to Reinvent Arithmetic*, New York: Teachers College Press.

Kamii, C. and Joseph, L. (1988) 'Teaching place value and double column addition', in *Arithmetic Teacher* 35, 6: 48–52.

Locke, A. and Ginsberg, J. (2002) Report in *Nursery World*, 10 January 2002.

Makin, L., Hayden, J., Holland, A., Arthur, L., Beecher, B., Jones-Diaz, C. and McNaught, M. (1999) *Mapping Literacy Practices in Early Childhood Services*, second edition, DET and DOCS.

Minns, H. (1990) *Read it to Me Now: Learning at home and at school*, London: Virago.

Nunes, T. (1998) *Developing Children's Minds Through Literacy and Mumeracy*, London: Institute of Education.

Nunes, T. and Bryant, P. (1996) *Children Doing Mathematics*, Oxford: Blackwell.

Nutbrown, C. (1997) *Recognising Early Literacy Development: Assessing children's achievements*, London: Paul Chapman.

QCA (1999) *Early Learning Goals*, London: QCA/DfEE.

Richards, R., Collis, M. and Kincaid, D. (1986) *Early Start to Science*, London: Macmillan Educational.

Rousham, L. and Rowland, T. (1996) 'Numeracy and calculators', in R. Mertens (ed.), *Teaching Numeracy*, Leamington: Scholastic Press.

Schickedanz, J. (1999) *Much More Than the ABCs*, Washington DC: NAEYC.

Schieffelin, B. and Cochran-Smith, M. (1984) 'Learning to read culturally', in H. Goelmann, A. Oberg and F. Smith, *Awakening to Literacy*, Portsmouth, NH: Heinemann.

Shuard, H., Walsh, A., Goodwin, J. and Worcester, V. (1991) *Calculators, Children and Mathematics*, London: Simon and Schuster.

Smith, F. (1988) *Understanding Reading: A psycholinguistic analysis of reading and learning to read*, fourth edition, Hillsdale, NJ: Lawrence Erlbaum Associates.

Sparrow, C. (1998), quote from National Curriculum: 61.

Steffe, L. P. and Wood, T. (eds) (1990) *Transforming Children's Mathematics Education*, Hillsdale, NJ: Lawrence Erlbaum Associates.

Vygotsky, L. S. (1978) *Mind in Society*, Cambridge, MA.: Harvard University Press.

CHAPTER 12

European perspectives

Early childhood education and care has been a focus of attention for policy makers and educators in Europe for the past decade. Governments in almost every country have issued directives concerning the quality and quantity of educational provision for children under compulsory school age. The European Commission Network on Childcare has highlighted issues related to young children and their families throughout the European Union, particularly those concerning the inequalities that exist in the quality and quantity of provision available. Much of their work has looked at the services available to working parents, pinpointing the wide discrepancies in provision for children under compulsory school age.

Within Europe there have been many international meetings in which educators have discussed early childhood programmes and the most appropriate ways to support young children and their families. As the UK forms closer links with European countries, both within and outside the European Union, it is important to look at the ways in which the various countries educate and care for their youngest children. In what ways are their approaches similar to those of the UK and in what ways are they different?

Any discussion of early childhood care and education in Europe faces the problem of terminology and equivalence of institution. For instance, what is understood by 'childminding' in the UK is termed 'family day care' in several other countries. Similar difficulties arise when trying to make accurate comparisons between the content of the courses and level of competence achieved in the training of early years workers. For example, there is no exact equivalent of the UK's Diploma in Child Care and Education or of the qualification held by Danish social pedagogues. However, we are in an age of high job mobility and early childhood practitioners, like other workers, are finding employment throughout Europe. It is therefore crucial that we have some understanding of developments and programmes beyond our shores.

In this chapter, although there is some factual information about provision in most of the European countries, the focus will be upon using information from selected countries to highlight the issues under discussion. Throughout this chapter the word 'kindergarten' refers to pre-school provision for children from three to six/seven years and 'crèche' to provision for children from birth to three years. All early childhood educators are referred to as teachers or educators, even though their qualifications may be different.

Changes in Eastern Europe

Throughout Europe early childhood education and care is undergoing changes, but nowhere are the changes more revolutionary than in Eastern and Central Europe. The break up of the USSR and the decentralisation of the education system within the former Soviet bloc has had an enormous effect upon the early childhood institutions. In many countries changing economic circumstances have led to high unemployment among families and to a decrease in the number of children attending kindergartens. As a result, in some areas the kindergartens have been forced to close.

In those eastern bloc countries where there had been a strict enforcement of the centralised early childhood curriculum programme, the changes during the past decade have been momentous. It is always difficult for early childhood educators from the UK to conceive of a situation where every kindergarten in the land carried out the same programme, at the same time each day, with almost identical equipment. This was the situation in Bulgaria, the former German Democratic Republic and the USSR, and occurred to a lesser degree in the other countries.

Each of the newly independent countries has now developed national curriculum guidelines to meet the needs of its children, but their implementation has been left either to local authorities or to individual schools. These guidelines, drawn up by educators, many of whom had maintained contact with early childhood educational systems outside the communist bloc, promote a child-centred approach to early childhood education, providing children with the opportunity to make choices and to engage in spontaneous play. The class teaching that involved everyone working on the same task at the same time has disappeared. In Bulgaria, for instance, where there had been a rigid adherence to the policy of centralisation, there is now a wide variety of teaching methods used to help children develop the attitudes and skills they need to function successfully in a more open society.

But the introduction of these changes has been difficult and is often resisted by the teachers, who had been brought up in an authoritarian tradition. Many of the new programmes include involving parents in their children's education, an approach that has been a challenge to both teachers and parents. For almost half a century, parents had been used to leaving their children at the entrance to the kindergarten early in the morning and collecting them eight or ten hours later without any real contact with the teachers. The programme innovators soon realised that parents and teachers did not know how to talk to each other. In-service training and courses were needed to help educators cope with the changes, as well as the introduction of modifications to the initial training courses.

Teachers had been trained to see their role as transmitters of knowledge, not as facilitators of children's learning. Therefore when innovators suggested transforming classrooms into centres of learning in which children's needs, interests and strengths are paramount, teachers were required to adopt a new way of thinking. In place of a national curriculum handbook with its detailed programme and activities there were only guidelines. Teachers now had to reflect upon the needs of the children and then plan an appropriate programme of activities.

In Lithuania and Estonia, for example, where there have been some very exciting curriculum developments, the local authorities and the training institutions have held many in-service courses to help their teachers understand how to implement the changes. Support to the teachers has been forthcoming in all the countries in the region but the extent of this support has often been hampered by lack of finance.

Baduriková (2000), writing about the Slovak Republic, stressed the implications of the economic changes, which have brought large-scale unemployment and a decrease in the family income; in addition, more and more fathers are working either abroad or a distance away from home. Kindergartens are not free for children under five years of age but in spite of the unemployment levels there is still an insufficient number of kindergarten places. Perhaps, most importantly for early childhood education, an increasing number of qualified teachers are leaving the profession in search of better paid jobs.

On the positive side there is now diversification, with both public and private kindergartens as well as those affiliated to the churches. This is a country that has made a number of curriculum innovations and is offering its teachers the opportunity to enrol in university-level pre-school courses. As in most of Eastern Europe, the new initiatives are mainly regional.

The Czech Republic, which has recently been part of the OECD Thematic review of early childhood care and education, is one of the new countries that appears to be financially more able to sustain changes and, like Hungary, had maintained close contact with the German Federal Republic (West Germany) for many years before the dissolution of the USSR.

The current policy in the Czech Republic is to ensure that there exists a wide range of pre-school educational programmes in both the public and private sectors. Schools are now encouraged to make use of educational programmes such as Montessori, Waldorf and Christian pedagogy, and parents are encouraged to participate in their children's schooling. However, the vast majority of children attending kindergarten classes are in the state sector, although there is still a long way to go before 100 per cent coverage can be offered for children from three to six years.

Many of these countries have a long tradition of pre-school education and had established kindergartens by the beginning of the twentieth century or earlier. At that time much of their philosophy reflected the writings of Comenius, who stressed the importance of family education. So the trend towards working with families and valuing the contribution of parents has a historic precedence.

Ministerial responsibility for provision

Throughout Europe there is a clear division between the care and education of children from birth to three years and from three until the commencement of compulsory schooling. Ministerial responsibility for children from birth to three is in the hands of the Ministries of Social Welfare or Health and Welfare, although the locus of policy making may be national or local, or both. The exceptions are Spain and Sweden, where it is the responsibility of the Ministry of Education. Both these countries have passed laws, Sweden in 1997 and Spain in 1990, bringing the responsibility of all care and education under the aegis of the Education Departments. In Iceland all the provision for children is under the Ministry of Education, with the exception of childminders.

To many, this is seen as commitment by the respective governments to acknowledging the importance of both care and education in the development of young children. However, throughout Europe there is a scarcity of provision for children from birth to three years and much of it is in the hands of inadequately or non-trained staff in spite of regulations requiring all staff to be professionally trained. The poor salary and career structure, with the increasing demand for places by mothers wishing to return to work, has resulted in poorly trained staff being appointed.

Legal entitlement to a place in child care provision for children under three exists only in Sweden and Finland. In Sweden this is from eighteen months and in Finland it is from birth. Both countries have addressed the issue of training. In Finland, for example, all children up to the age of seven attend day-care centres, organised around the concept of parental and community educare, but the staff are differentiated within the institution. Those working with the children under three are paramedically trained, whereas those working with the older children are trained as pre-school teachers.

Responsibility for children from three until compulsory school age varies. Where the children are in full-time, home (childminders) or centre provision they are the responsibility of health and social welfare departments, as in Denmark, Finland and some parts of Germany.

Kindergarten education is mainly the responsibility of education departments, although in Norway the Barnhage (kindergarten) come under the Ministry of Child and Family Affairs.

Table 12.1 shows the wide differences that exist throughout Europe.

From my visits to kindergartens in most of the European countries it is apparent that the type of provision made for children varies according to the ministry

Table 12.1 *Terms and organisation of European provision*

Country	Compulsory school age	Ministry responsible 0–3	Ministry responsible 3–6/7
Austria	6	Regional Health/Welfare	
Belgium	6	Social Welfare	Education
Bulgaria	7	Health/Welfare	Education
Czech republic	6	Health/Welfare	Education
Denmark	7	Social Welfare	Education (5/6–7)
Estonia	7	Social Welfare	Education
Finland	7	Social Welfare	Education (6/7)
France	6	Social Affairs	Education
Germany	6	Social Affairs	Social Affairs*
Greece	6	Social Affairs	Education
Hungary	6	Health	Education
Iceland	7	Education**	Education
Ireland	6	Health	Education
Italy	6	Health/Welfare	Education
Luxembourg	6	Family Affairs	Education (4–6)
Netherlands	5	Social Welfare	Education (4+)
Norway	6	Children and Family Affairs	
Poland	7	Health/Welfare	Education
Portugal	6	Social Welfare	Education/Welfare
Rumania	7	Social Welfare	Education
Russia	7	Social Welfare	Education
Slovak Republic	6	Health	Education (2–6)
Spain	6	Education	
Sweden	7	Education	
Switzerland	6	Varies+	Education+
Turkey	6	Health/Welfare	Education

Key
*In Bavaria the ministry of Education is responsible for classes for some five-year-olds.
** Childminders are the responsibility of Ministry of Social Affairs.
+ Responsibility varies according to the Cantons.

responsible. In countries such as Belgium and France where there is almost 100 per cent provision for children from two and a half years until six, the emphasis on education and learning is very different from the emphasis on socialisation and play that is encountered in the Danish *Børnehaver*. In both France and Germany children from three to six years have a legal entitlement to kindergarten education but, whereas the provision is educationally based in France, a more community-orientated approach is taken in Germany.

Diversity of Provision

In most countries there is now public and private provision both in kindergartens and crèches. For example, in France there is a rapid growth of the *crèches parentales*, the parent-run co-operative nurseries as an alternative to the state-run crèches. It has been argued that diversity of provision allows for parental choice and the possibility of meeting the needs of every child. On the other hand, there are those who argue that diversity of provision can lead to lack of co-ordination of services and to a greater possibility that some of the children in greatest need will be overlooked. Certainly it can be argued that diversity often exists from political expediency in some countries.

In all the former eastern bloc countries, the governments are promoting diversity of provision to allow parents greater choice. By allowing choice and flexibility of hours of attendance, governments are encouraging early childhood institutions to introduce experimental programmes such as Step by Step and projects based on the Reggio Emilio approach.

The importance of a common policy framework in providing quality and accessible services to children and their families from birth until school age has been highlighted in the latest report from the OECD (2001), which has looked at early childhood education and care across twelve countries. This report has called for a systematic and integrated approach to policy development and implementation and argues that this requires a lead ministry that works in co-operation with other departments and sectors.

Age of school entry

Compared with most other countries in Europe, children in the UK start primary school at least one year, if not two, earlier than their European counterparts. The current trend for children to be admitted into reception classes at the beginning of their fifth year is unique to the UK, although in Luxembourg there is compulsory pre-primary schooling from four to six years. In the Netherlands compulsory education starts at five and there is provision for four-year-olds in the primary schools, and in Hungary all children must attend one full year of kindergarten education in the year before they commence primary schooling. However, as Table 12.1 shows, in most European countries children do not enter primary schooling until six or seven years of age.

As you can see from Table 12.1, only the Netherlands admits children at five years of age but not until the term after their fifth birthday. The UK alone feels that full-time primary education should commence at the beginning of the academic year in which the child will be five, even though statutory school age does not begin until the term after the child's fifth birthday. European children are still in pre-school settings or at home for two or more years than those in the UK.

During the past decade the early admission of UK children into primary classes led to heated debates in the Scandinavian countries, resulting in the reduction of the school admission age to six years in Norway. In Denmark the school admission age was not reduced but 98 per cent of the children attend kindergarten classes under the Ministry of Education, and in the Netherlands almost all children attend pre-primary classes at four years of age under the Ministry of Education. Under the 1997 Kindergarten Law in Hungary attendance in kindergarten is compulsory for all children from the age of five. Greece is one country that has moved against the trend as after a short period of lowered entry age to five and a half years, the limit has once again been raised to six.

What effect does the later start to school have on parents, children and the curriculum? Most European countries believe it is beneficial for entry into primary education to be deferred until at least six although, as we shall see later, many of them offer special 'educational' classes in the last one or two years of the kindergarten. Early entry is not regarded as a viable alternative to quality early childhood care and education.

Transition from kindergarten to primary school

Links between pre-school and primary school have been the subject of discussion within the Europen Union for several decades. Early childhood educators realised that for many children, the transition from pre-school to primary school may be a stressful experience as there were big differences in both content and approach between the two types of institutions. As a result, most countries have now introduced policies to co-ordinate the transition. The introduction of the Foundation Stage in the UK is one such move. One of the main reasons for the introduction of compulsory pre-school education in Luxembourg in 1992 from the age of four was to ensure that the large group of ethnic-minority children received some form of support before entering primary school.

In France and French-speaking Belgium, 'cycles of learning' have been introduced into the *école maternelle* to help smooth the transition. The first cycle covers the period from two to four years and includes social, emotional and cognitive skills; the second, from four to eight years, covers the last two years of the *école maternelle* and the first two years of the primary school and concentrates on numeracy and literacy. Like our Foundation Stage it takes place in two different educational institutions. In Finland, learning modules for five- and six-year-old children have been introduced into the day care centres and pre-school classes attached to primary schools. In the Netherlands the link became stronger when in 1985 pre-school education was integrated into the primary-school system.

In Denmark, since 1989 there has been an attempt to introduce a 'co-ordinated school start' for six-year-old children. These classes began first in Copenhagen. A large number of Danish primary schools now have a pre-school class attached that co-operates closely with the first two classes of primary school, often carrying out joint projects and visits. However, the children attend for only four hours a day and spend the rest of the time with staff from the *Børnehaver* (Centre). Currently Sweden is looking at issues relating to the transition between institutions.

In Eastern Europe, for example Poland and the Czech Republic, educators are looking closely at the organisation and curriculum of both the pre-school and primary school to consider how best they can be adjusted to help children make the transfer as effectively as possible. In the Baltic States some kindergartens arrange for children to visit the primary schools during their last term in the kindergarten in the same way as the UK.

One major difference among European kindergartens is the length of time that the children are in the institution. Where children attend for periods up to ten hours a day there is a compulsory period of rest for at least two hours after lunch. The change from this practice to primary-school hours must be a cause for concern.

Staff:child ratios

It is generally accepted that the staff:child ratio is important when considering quality education for young children. Where there is an established system for the care of children under three, as in Scandinavia, the ratios are 3:1 in Denmark, 4:1 in Finland, 7:1 in Norway and 6:1 in Sweden. The ratio is higher in Portugal where it is 10:1, and in Greece it is 8:1. It is difficult to assess the true ratios as statistics vary. Staff ratios are generally calculated in terms of the total number of children divided by the number of staff, even though there are times during the day when some of the staff are missing from the classroom. For example, during sleep time there is often only one member of staff in charge of thirty children.

There is an even larger range of permitted national staff ratios within the age range of three to six years, from 6:1 in Sweden and Denmark to 20–28:1 in Italy and similar numbers in France. In Ireland the average number of children in the pre-primary infant classes (for four- and five-year-old children) is 35 with one qualified teacher. In the UK children of four and five years can be in reception classes with a ratio of 30:1, although most classes are smaller and most reception-class teachers have a teaching assistant.

It seems that countries that have a real commitment to quality care and education for their children during the pre-school years are prepared to spend the money necessary to provide adequate numbers of staff to support children's learning.

Legislation regarding the amount of space required by each child varies, with the result that in some countries kindergartens, particularly those in the private sector, are limited for space. Children are in confined spaces both indoors and outdoors. On the other hand, in Eastern Europe and the Baltic States the kindergartens are much larger than our nursery schools, with ample space for the children and specialist rooms for music and physical education and occasionally for art. There is also a dining hall, as well as a hall designed for drama and other activities. The kindergartens are large; they may have as many as 250–300 pupils and each classroom will have a dormitory attached where the children sleep.

Emphasis is placed upon the health and welfare of the children and there is a resident nurse and psychologist on the staff as well as the educators and kitchen and cleaning staff.

Normally there is also a separate staff dining room and a special room set aside for entertaining visitors. Outdoor areas are generally large and have all the standard equipment, for example climbing frames, swings and bars. The large amount of space provided for the children is regarded as essential as they live in very cramped accommodation at home.

In much of Europe kindergarten classes are arranged chronologically, although the staff:child ratios for the children are the same. In Scandinavia the children in the centres are in mixed aged groups from three to seven, or even wider groupings in some instances.

Curriculum

Programmes for children below three years focus mainly upon aspects of care and health and in many countries the level of stimulation offered is low, mainly because of the poor level of training provided for the staff. However, in more and more countries educators are addressing the challenge of meeting the needs of the youngest children. Practitioners are being encouraged to reflect upon their needs, to talk more to the children and to provide opportunities for them to explore their world.

The type of curriculum offered to children from two and a half to six or seven years will depend upon whether the culture of the country sees early childhood education as a preparation for school or a phase in its own right. In many countries it is seen as a setting in which children develop social skills and learn about the cultural values and traditions of the country. In others this is only a part of the programme, as preparation for school is also high on the agenda. Kindergarten education in some countries may also be seen as a way of preventing later school failure. Where children attend full time, for eight to ten hours a day, the role of the day care/kindergarten is also to provide a place for children while their parents are at work.

Throughout Europe, early childhood educators firmly believe in the value of play in children's learning and the programmes are designed to ensure that children have as many opportunities for play as possible. However, the word 'play' is interpreted differently in different societies.

My first visits to kindergartens in Eastern Europe were a culture shock as, for example, socio-dramatic play was not at all as I had anticipated, but was what I would term a drama lesson. On this particular occasion the children were acting out a version of *Three Men in a Boat*, the parts being allocated by the teacher, and although not scripted, the children were given very clear guidance as to what they should say. Over the years I have seen a number of such episodes termed socio-dramatic play.

In this part of Europe the term 'games' is used to describe activities designed to develop fine and gross motor skills, and to take into account the holistic development of children. There are opportunities for children to foster and develop their aesthetic and creative abilities, although much of these activities is teacher directed. In some countries, specialist art, music and physical-exercise teachers are employed and the children have specialist lessons on a weekly or twice-weekly basis. The goals of the pre-school are to lead the child from game to school learning, thus ensuring a link to primary education. The current changes in the pre-school curriculum aim to take account of the biological, psychological, interpersonal, socio-cultural and environmental needs of the child, each area being clearly defined with specific aims and objectives.

Music and dance have an important place in the curriculum of kindergarten children in many European countries and I have always been impressed by the high standards achieved by children of four and five years of age. Traditional stories and rhymes also play a significant part in transmitting the culture and norms of society. This is part of a strong oral tradition and teachers are highly skilled at story-telling and the use of puppetry. Financial constraints have meant that schools cannot afford to buy a lot of commercial materials and excellent use is made of natural resources from the local environment. As a result, many of the kindergartens are aesthetically very pleasing as educators use their skills to decorate their classrooms and to demonstrate to children the importance of nature.

Even though teaching methods are less formal and there is freedom to implement the programme according to the needs of the children and their families, teachers are still expected to follow a fairly structured regime. Decentralisation has allowed kindergartens the freedom to introduce curriculum innovations to meet the needs of the area, for example programmes involving parents in the education of their children. In the Baltic States, where there have been close links with Sweden and Finland over the past decade, one can see the influence of the Scandinavian educational philosophies in the new programmes.

By contrast, the curriculum in Scandinavia, and Denmark in particular, is very different. Early childhood education programmes in both the crèches and educational institutions are based on the ideas of Froebel. Although in recent years there has been some pressure from groups stressing the formal learning aspects of kindergarten education, the majority stress the importance of play and the child's social and all-round development. There is no specific curriculum for children under compulsory school age as parents and teachers work together to set the goals for their children's education. However, as Lund (1998) tells us, in all kindergartens:

> the daily educational activities include musical activities such as drama, singing and music, rhythmics, gathering/collecting, outdoor play, excursions, and various activities with such materials as clay, wood, textiles, paper, etc. The activities are linked together in themes or subjects that spring from the children's every day lives or immediate community or nature itself.

Similar programmes with emphasis upon free play are to be found in most Scandinavian kindergartens. In 1998 Sweden introduced a National Curriculum for Pre-school, making pre-school the first step in the education system. The child is seen as a competent learner, capable of formulating its own ideas about the world. The new curriculum is based on the long-standing pedagogical tradition of:

- seeing the child's development and learning as continuous and taking place in close co-operation with the environment;
- play- and theme-oriented ways of working. Play is of fundamental importance for children and is the basis of all pre-school activity;
- linking to the child's own experiences and knowledge;
- the pedagogical importance of care through which children get to know themselves and the surrounding world;
- encouraging development in groups. Children need to experience the joy of working and learning together. Children need other children as well as adults or toys.

The curriculum is seen as playing an important role in developing quality in the pedagogical work of the pre-school.

Another country that has a highly established system of early childhood education is France. Here there is universal provision for children from three years until the commencement of statutory schooling, and in many parts of the country there is a large number of children who attend an *école maternelle* from two and a half years of age.

Education for this age range has three main objectives:

- *scolariser* – to turn the children into pupils;
- *socialiser* – to socialise and enrich the children's social relations;
- *faire apprendre et exercer* – to promote learning and allow time for practice and develop all the children's capacities.

(David 1993)

These objectives are met by offering children a curriculum based on physical activities, communication activities, oral and written expression, artistic and aesthetic activities and scientific and technological activities.

In the *école maternelle*, the day is divided into two sessions and children spend the first half-hour of each session in outdoor play, when they can choose from different items of gross motor equipment such as tricycles, skates or playing on the climbing frames. The teachers are free to decide how the rest of the morning or afternoon sessions are to be organised. However, they plan, evaluate and reflect upon their work in the same way as teachers in the primary school and know in detail what they will be teaching in the next week or month.

There are three age bands in the *école maternelle*. The youngest children (from two and a half years to four years) will be offered free choice of play from activities such as PE, music and movement or dance, language activities, singing, counting and rhymes, fine motor and perceptual activities, puppetry, picture and story books. Activities to stimulate the imagination and foster representation and expression are also encouraged. In the middle band (5 years) children are engaged in pedagogical activities, games of perception, sorting and classification and drawing. They also begin to read picture books and engage in gardening and cooking activities. The programme for the eldest children carries on into the primary school, and includes building on their existing knowledge and concepts and developing their verbal and literary skills by recording events and journeys. They are also involved in dramatic productions and a wider range of physical activities.

To read or not to read?

Unlike many other European countries where there are few story books available for children to pick up and 'read' for themselves, teachers in the *école maternelle* are expected to ensure that children have an understanding of the written and spoken language. Children are given worksheets and group instruction methods are used to introduce children to language concepts. Barrière (2000) has pointed out that the assumptions of the teachers, the activities they organise and the French school curriculum seem to be based on the notion of *Entré dans l'écrit* (penetrating/entering literacy) compared with our concept of emergent literacy. This approach is felt to be the most effective way to ensure that children have the prerequisite skills for later reading and writing.

Most European countries have adopted the emergent literacy and numeracy approach, where children learn about reading and writing and number through play and their day-to-day involvement in activities. Very few countries in Europe expect their children to begin reading at an early age and in some instances only the educators have access to books as they are stored either high up on shelves in the classroom or in the head teacher's office. Although many countries are unable to finance large quantities of books for children to handle or take home as happens in the UK, others believe that pre-school is too early to introduce children to the printed word. Children are, however, given worksheets to colour in or trace over letters.

In Italian kindergartens children are introduced to both oral and written language and literacy in an informal way, and in many nurseries there is a strong emphasis upon communication as well as mathematical and scientific experiences. Those who are familiar with the Reggio Emilia project will be aware of the importance that is placed upon the development of language and communication skills for children. In other parts of Italy there are many excellent kindergartens that provide children with a wide range of educational experiences using language and literacy.

Are other countries moving towards the concept of emergent literacy? seems that most countries are adopting this approach with some formal learni taking place in the year before compulsory schooling. In Iceland, which for many years had a tradition that children should not learn to read or be introduced to letters before the age of six, two teachers carried out an interesting project called 'Play and Print'. The objectives of the project were to expose children to a greater amount of the printed word, and to reinforce the role of play by offering a clearer picture of the relationship between role-play and the written language. Book corners, writing areas and role-play activities that involved writing were set up throughout the nursery and children were taken for label trips, which involved labels, signs, recipes and other written language in the environment being explained to them. Parents were involved in writing letters to be posted in the school post-box and these were read out to the children every day. The post-box was a particularly useful tool for increasing communication with parents.

The children were assessed four times over the school year and all were found to have shown a great improvement in language maturity. The majority of the older children (five to six) knew their letters and were able to read and write simple sentences and words.

As a result of the project, staff and parents began 'to understand that reading and writing are intertwined factors in the development of children's speech, and that children learn about reading and writing in play'. (Sigurdardottir and Birgisdottir 1998). I understand that a number of pre-school institutions are now using similar play activities.

Although most countries are exposing children to print and encouraging literacy and numeracy through play activities, none appears to have the specific learning goals that we are expecting children to achieve by the end of the reception year.

Social inclusion

Children with special educational needs

Throughout Europe there is legislation to ensure that there are equal opportunities for all children, irrespective of gender, religion or ethnic group. The integration of children with special educational needs has been most successful in those countries in which few special nursery schools had existed since there were no places to close or modify, or staff to transfer to other institutions. For example, in Italy, which had relatively few special educational institutions, all children, even those with severe learning difficulties, have been integrated into pre-primary schools since the late 1970s. In some countries, for example Belgium, there is a strong commitment from government towards policies relating to social exclusion and priority education programmes, and in Norway, where there is not yet 100 per cent availability in kindergartens, children with special educational needs have priority access.

In the former communist bloc there had been a wide range of special educational provision available and although there may be legislation to include all children into mainstream kindergartens, the reality is a little slower. For example, in the Czech Republic although there is a growing movement towards social inclusion for children with learning disabilities there are still many special kindergartens and schools in existence, even for those with relatively minor handicaps.

Children from minority ethnic, linguistic and cultural groups

Another issue that challenges many countries in Europe is how to promote ethnic, linguistic and cultural diversity. Early childhood educators are particularly concerned that children from linguistic minority groups who are not able to attend any form of pre-school provision may be at a disadvantage when they commence primary schooling. Many of these children, often from the poorest economic backgrounds, are unable to take advantage of pre-school education where provision is not free. However, most countries now offer means-tested financial support to enable the children to attend pre-school.

Language immersion and teaching in the national language seems to be the preferred approach throughout Europe in kindergartens as all countries use the national language in the primary school. As in the UK, bilingual classroom assistants are employed in Denmark, Norway and Sweden in the kindergartens to help children gain proficiency in the host language and further develop their mother tongue. The OECD Report (2001) recommended that early childhood care and education centres should provide appropriate services and additional resources, for instance materials in different languages, interpretation services and greater multicultural and anti-bias approaches to the curriculum. Long-term language support for both children and their parents is another important recommendation. In Scandinavia and the Netherlands there has been a number of pilot programmes that aim to build links between the culture of the minority group and the host group. For example, in the Netherlands the government is providing financial support for playgroups for two- and three-year-old children from ethnic minority groups.

In large parts of Central and Eastern Europe, the Roma children present an enormous challenge. In the Czech Republic, since 1993 pilot projects have been carried out to help these children and there are preparatory classes for socially or culturally disadvantaged children of six to seven years, for whom entry into compulsory education has been delayed.

At the First Central and Eastern European Meeting on Child Care and Development in 1999, several countries in the region mentioned the challenges of meeting the needs of the Roma children and it seems that an increasing number are now attending kindergarten. In Bulgaria and the Slovak Republic a number of innovative projects have been developed to support Roma children and their families. Sadly, at that meeting the Romanian delegates reported that an increasing number of Roma children were in institutions as their families considered that the institutions offered better conditions for children's development than their own families. Perhaps the major problem facing Roma children and their families is the prejudice that they encounter from the majority population.

Throughout Europe mainstreaming is accepted as the most appropriate system for children with special educational needs, whether they be due to physical, intellectual or sensory difficulties or to cultural, linguistic or socio-economic factors, provided it is deemed to be in the best interests of the child. However, for the policy of social inclusion to be effective so that every child can actively participate in the life of the community, finances need to be provided for both human and material resources. Improved initial and in-service training is essential in most countries so that every pre-school institution, whether in the public or the private sector, has at least some members of staff qualified to support these children and their families.

Training

The division between day-care and pre-school education applies to training as well. France, like Belgium, Italy, Luxembourg, the Netherlands, Portugal, Greece, Ireland and the majority of Eastern European countries, has separate systems. In most instances those working with children under three have a lower entry qualification and level of training than those working with the older age range.

In many countries the kindergarten teacher is a graduate with at least three or four years of training and in France and Poland (for the advanced teacher) a five year course has been taken. As in the UK, the teachers in the *école maternelle* and the advanced teachers in Poland are also qualified to teach in primary school.

Throughout Europe there are training programmes that prepare young people for working with children below the age of two and a half to three years and to work alongside the teachers in kindergartens. The level and extent of training ranges from short courses to four-year courses in countries where the student can commence training at fifteen years, for example Turkey and the Slovak Republic. The majority of courses are two years long but in most countries there are still unqualified workers in this field.

Denmark has a unified approach to training with highly trained personnel for all age groups from six months. Termed Social Pedagogues, these educators have a broad-based training that equips them to work in either pre-school centres or out-of-school and leisure-time facilities, as well as with children and adults with special needs. They have a very different career path from school teachers and a very different self-image.

Just as there are changes in curriculum content throughout Europe, so there are also changes within the training programmes. In Spain the Education Reform Act of 1990 (LOGSE) provided a new framework for education and the early childhood education now extends from birth to six years even though the period is subdivided from birth to three years and from three to six years. The new law takes a holistic approach to the education of children from birth to six years and aims to abolish the traditional division between education and care. There is also provision made for the upgrading of training, with a view to the profession becoming all graduate in the future. At present there are regular in-service training courses, which are certificated and carry salary increases but are not compulsory.

In Germany proposals have been put forward to improve the quality of the professionalism of the Social Pedagogues (senior workers in the kindergartens). At present the formal level of training of both the pedagogues and the kindergarten teachers is lower than in other countries within the European Union, with the exception of Austria. Although there are strengths to the existing course, for example it is one of the few courses in which the entire third year of training is spent in a work placement, many feel that it should be amended to offer a training that takes into account the more culturally and linguistically diverse society that exists in Germany today.

Currently the trend is towards longer and higher levels of initial training, with emphasis upon supporting educators to become more reflective in their practice. When national and regional governments embrace policies such as social inclusion and working with families and the community, it becomes essential that training institutions adapt their courses so that both practising and student teachers feel confident to work in these new ways. Such issues as the content of the courses, the balance between theory and practice and the impact of transferring early childhood education courses into the university sector have to be addressed.

Projects

In this section four projects are highlighted as examples of some of the innovative activities that are currently being carried out in Europe.

Step by step project

In January 1994, the Children's Resources International began to co-operate with the Soros Foundation Projects in Eastern and Central Europe and the former USSR to develop and introduce an educational programme called 'Step by Step'. According to the executive director, the programme is designed for young children from birth to eight years and their families, and supports open societies in emerging democracies while drawing on the 'best cultural traditions' in the participant countries. The programme is operating in most of the eastern and central countries and aims to give children, parents and teachers opportunities to learn to work together and promote learning in an open society.

It has been amended to meet the needs of each country but the general principles of the curriculum are to provide:

- an individual approach to every child;
- integration of games and activities into education and care;
- thematic and project planning;
- observation;
- activity centres in classes;
- active role of parents.

The project believes that some of the most important issues to be addressed in the classroom are those of:

- promoting equality;
- achieving the child-centred classroom;
- promoting skills, talents and creativity;
- communicating with parents;
- promoting positive behaviour;
- developing healthy habits;
- making the transition to primary school.

The success of this project can be measured by the extent to which government ministries are now accepting it as an alternative methodology, while pedagogical institutes and universities are giving training to teachers in the methods used. Emphasis is placed on the needs:

- for professional development for teachers;
- to work with and in the community;
- to encourage teamwork among teachers and schools;
- to encourage multicultural education without prejudice;
- to include children with special needs in the classroom.

In this project parents are encouraged to have access to the classrooms so that they can see their children at work. Probably the greatest impact of the programme on participating teachers is the way in which they were trained in the project methods. They came to the training sessions with the intention of listening to lectures and going away with handouts, but were met with a group of trainers who expected them to fully participate in role play, small group discussions and problem-solving activities and videos. Once the teachers became convinced of the value of active learning it was relatively easy for the project trainers to persuade them to use these interactive methods with the children.

The Averroès Foundation and the European Training Centre

As in many countries in Europe, the Netherlands has a large population of immigrants from Surinam, Morocco, Turkey and the Antilles who do not speak Dutch. The Averroès Foundation has worked closely with UNESCO to provide a number of programmes to support parents and children and to assist with the transition from home to school.

Instapje (First steps)

This is a programme designed to provide the first steps in stimulating communication between parents and children between the ages of one and two. Designed to improve the quality of the interaction between parents and children, it focuses on four dimensions of parental behaviour:

1 emotional support;
2 respecting the child's autonomy;
3 providing structure and setting limits on the child's behaviour;
4 providing information and explaining situations or tasks.

It is an intensive programme with a professional visiting the home on a weekly basis. During each visit the professional demonstrates the range of play materials and shows the parent how to adapt to the child's play. The programme is divided into four modules, each lasting for several weeks and focusing upon one of the four dimensions above.

Parents are encouraged to reflect upon the themes and the advice given within the framework of their own cultural beliefs and values. The evaluation of this project has shown that the programme has a positive impact on the children.

Klimrek (Climbing frame)

This programme is the Dutch version of the American Mother–Child Program developed by Phyllis Levenstein. Designed for children aged between two and four years and their parents, it lasts over a period of two years. It aims at stimulating verbal interaction between parents and child and making them aware that they are the first educators of their child. A toy demonstrator visits the family for two half-hour sessions per week, in each session acting as a role model for the parents by using the materials provided. These materials include coloured pictures, books and toys, which the family is allowed to keep. The methods and materials used have be found to be of value not only for traditional families from different cultural and ethnic groups, but also for travelling families.

Opstapje (Leg-up)

This is a project aimed at facilitating the transition from home to school for children from disadvantaged backgrounds. It is a two-year, primarily home-based programme for two- to four-year-old children and their parents. The parents are encouraged to interact and play with their children and in the second year they are given further information to help prepare the children for school. The home visits are carried out by paraprofessionals who support the parents in the home. There are also fortnightly group meetings led by a project co-ordinator during which the parents are given talks on various aspects of child development, education and child rearing. At these sessions the parents are also given information about neighbourhood facilities and services such as playgroups, schools and toy and book libraries. There is a continuation programme to this, Opstap Opnieuw (Leg-up, level 11), which is designed for children aged four to six years from disadvantaged backgrounds. This offers an extra-curricular programme to provide children with the knowledge and skills they require for successful learning in the Dutch education system.

There are also other programmes that involve the collaboration of parents, teachers and children in the early stages of learning to read, which in some instances develop into a peer-tutoring reading programme. Altogether there are nine programmes designed to support the communities either at home or in school.

All the programmes are culturally relevant, community-based and include parents. They are non-formal in approach and focus upon the 'whole child'. The programmers are constantly evaluating and re-evaluating the programmes and in each area, although the underlying principles are the same, the approach may be different. Just as Home Start and other projects in the UK may recruit their home visitors from people who have originally been clients, so the Averroès Foundation employs parents to act as paraprofessionals once their children have gone to school.

The principles upon which these programmes are based are now being adopted in various parts of the world.

The Reggio Emilia approach

Reggio Emilia in northern Italy has been the scene of an innovative programme for early childhood education for over thirty years. The *scuole dell infanzia*, for children aged from three to six years, and the *asili nido*, for children from three months to three years, were established in close collaboration with parents and aim to offer children a comprehensive education in which the rights of the child are paramount. The pre-schools in this affluent region have been visited by many thousands of interested early years educators from all over the world and the method has been copied and adapted in many countries. Many others have seen 'The Hundred Languages of Children', the travelling exhibition that has visited a number of countries. The main feature of the approach is that it advocates communication between adults and children and considers that early childhood education involves children, teachers, parents and the community.

Loris Malaguzzi, the educator behind this idea, postulated a theory of early education based on social relationships. He wrote:

> Our image of children no longer considers them as isolated and egocentric, does not only see them engaged in action with objects, does not emphasise only the cognitive aspects, does not belittle feelings or what is not logical, and does not consider with ambiguity the role of the affective domain. Instead our image of the child is rich in potential, strong, powerful, competent and most of all, connected to adults and other children.
>
> (1993: 10)

Malaguzzi stressed repeatedly the notion of the child as part of a community of adults, who lives and learns as part of the wider community:

> We must know that children, although naturally inclined, do not acquire the art of becoming friends or teachers of one another by finding models in heaven or manuals, rather children extract and interpret models from adults, when the adults know how to work together, discuss, think, research and live together.
>
> (1993: 3)

This is a society that believes that it is possible to combine education and social services for the community. It is a kind of education that focuses on the child in relationship with the family, the teacher, the other children and the broader cultural context of society. For the educators in Reggio Emilia, early childhood institutions are places of dialogue, places of participation and places of education in a process that involves children, teachers and families. In Reggio Emilia there is a social constructivist view of education, which consider that children have the right to be 'connected to others'.

Supporters of the Reggio Emilia philosophy have an image of the child as a person who experiences the world, and feels part of the world from birth. The child is full of curiosity, desire to explore, and has the ability to communicate from birth. In this respect the approach is not unique as it is one that is fully accepted by a number of other societies. In any community, institution or family, it is not only the adults who effect changes in the child, but the presence of the child also effects changes in the family, school and the wider society. We are all aware that some children have greater impact upon their environment than others – some are troublesome, some are less demanding, but each and every one in its own way leaves a mark upon home, school and community.

There are six stated principles of the Emilio Reggio approach:

1 the study of child development as central to practice;
2 the importance of the teacher–child relationship;
3 the need for children's experiences to be taken into account when building the curriculum;
4 the importance of a rich environment in developing children's learning;
5 the importance of ongoing professional development for teachers;
6 the importance of the role of parents in the life of the school.

The centres are of a high aesthetic quality and reflect the culture of the region. Children are provided with a wide range of materials and tools that help them develop their skills and abilities. Great value is placed on the role of the environment as a motivating force. Although it is a project-oriented curriculum, which I personally felt was too teacher-directed for the youngest children, there is a great deal of time and space to allow children to carry out their own ideas. Malaguzzi speaks of the need for the child to be away from the ever-watchful eye of the adult – and certainly in some of the nurseries there are many areas where the child can play away from the adult.

Each institution has an *artelierista*, a specialist art teacher, and a cook, as well as the regular educators and a *pedagogista* who may work with several institutions.

The children are grouped chronologically with twenty-five children in a class and two teachers. The children stay with the same staff members over the three years but have regular sessions with the *artelierista*, who is heavily involved with all the projects. During their last term in the *scuola dell infanzia* the school leavers prepare a booklet for the new intake of children about their school and the activities they carry out. Thus the sense of connectedness and communication is passed on to the new children about to enter the school.

Throughout the school year, teachers, parents and members of the larger community meet to discuss any problems associated with the programme. At these meetings the 'pedagogical documentation' produced by the teachers is used to inform discussions. This documentation is more than teacher observations but includes children's work and drawings, and photos and videos of the various projects that have been carried out.

The documentation not only records the final outcomes of the project but also incorporates the ideas of the children, their experiences and their observations of the teachers. The documentation serves three main functions:

1 to provide the children with a permanent record of what they have said and done and to help them to understand what they have achieved;

2 to provide educators with an insight into the children's behaviour and learning, thus enabling them to reflect upon and support later learning;
3 to provide parents and the community with detailed information about what happens in the school and to encourage better relationships between home and school.

There is no prescribed programme or curriculum, but *pedagogistas* use this pedagogical documentation to discuss, analyse and reflect with the staff on the practice in the institution. In this way the quality of the educational environment is maintained. The *pedagogistas* have time allocated within their working week for analysis and reflection.

The work of Loris Malaguzzi has been both a stimulus and a challenge to early childhood educators in many parts of the world. Currently educators in Estonia are working to introduce his ideas into their early childhood institutions and I have seen the Reggio Emilia approach in various countries in all parts of the world.

However, the uniqueness of this approach and the fact that there is no prescribed programme or curriculum means that there could be difficulties in transferring this type of practice to other cultures. Merely copying a project or using some of the ideas is not the same as adopting the philosophy. Adopting the approach means accepting *and* understanding the underlying principles and philosophy in the light of one's own culture.

The Stockholm Project

Since the Reggio exhibition was first invited to Stockholm in 1981, Swedish pedagogues and academics have been interested in the work being carried out in the early childhood institutions in Reggio Emilia. In 1993 the Stockholm Project was set up in conjunction with Reggio Emilia and Stockholm. It was entitled 'Early Childhood Pedagogy in a Changing World'.

The project, which is fully explained in Dahlberg *et al.* (1999), had the following work objectives.

1 To work on thematic and project work. This approach has a long tradition in Sweden but a re-evaluation of it was agreed in the light of the experiences of Reggio.
2 To work on the observation and pedagogical documentation. In Sweden these terms had been understood in relation to child-development theories and it was decided to look at them now in relation to the interpretations given to them in Reggio.
3 To create space for reflection.
4 To promote changes in the environment of the early childhood institutions.
5 To examine divisions of responsibility and use of time by the pedagogues.

6 To provide support for the pedagogues along the lines of the pedagogistas of Reggio Emilia.
7 To employ an *atelierista* consultant.
8 To work closely with parents.
9 To co-operate with the early childhood institutions.
10 To work with a specific local authority.

There were no set plans laid down in advance and the project evolved over the next four years. Seven institutions were selected but there has been continuous dialect with politicians and other institutions and the work has spread to other parts of Sweden. Dahlberg, who was the scientific leader of the project, has pointed out that this is not a replica of Reggio Emilia but 'a construction in which we have built an understanding of their practice in relation to our own Swedish traditions and culture' (Dahlberg *et al.* 1999: 130).

The project has challenged the pedagogy of Swedish early childhood education and encouraged educators to try to establish a 'co-constructive learning culture' by enhancing self-reflection through dialogue, pedagogical documentation and relationships between all concerned. Practitioners are encouraged to listen to the children and learn from what they do and say. However, this does not mean that children should not be challenged by adults.

Conclusion

Throughout Europe educators face many common challenges. At the level of the youngest children, the issue of poor and inadequate provision is of concern in most countries, as few governments are providing quality experiences for children from birth to three years. Furthermore, staff working in these settings are frequently poorly paid and have low social status.

Issues relating to social inclusion, and in particular to the support for the children and families from ethnic and linguistic minorities, need to be addressed by almost every country. As the European population becomes more heterogeneous, so there is an increasing need to provide teachers with training and resources to work with these groups.

It appears to be generally recognised that the most effective early education programmes are those that work with both parents and the community. Here again training is an important issue, as so many educators are being forced to re-evaluate their previous practice and to make major adjustments to meet these new challenges. Quality early childhood education is recognised as an important item on the programmes of most European governments; let us hope that sufficient finance is made available to ensure that within the next few years there will be adequate provision and support for all young children.

References

Baduriková, Z. (2000) 'Provision in the Slovak Republic', in *Early Childhood and Care in Eastern Europe*, UNESCO Education Sector Monograph, No. 113/2000.

Barrière, I. (2000) *Early Literacy in France: Entitlement and citizenship*. Paper presented at 10th EECERA Conference, London, September 2000.

Cordus, J. and van Oudenhoven, N. (1997) *Early Intervention: Examples of practice Averroès programmes for children – an experience to be shared*, UNESCO Education Sector Monograph, No. 8/1997.

Coughlin, L. (1996) 'Child-centred early childhood education in Eastern Europe: the step by step approach', in *Childhood Education*, 72, 6: 337–40.

Curtis, A. (1995) *Training for Work with Young Children in Europe: A comparative study of 22 European countries*, OMEP.

Dahlberg, D., Moss, P. and Pence, A. (1999) *Beyond Quality in Early Childhood Education and Care*, London: Falmer Press.

David, T. (ed.) (1993) *Educational Provision for our Youngest Children*, London: Paul Chapman Publishing.

Edwards, C. P., Gandini, L. and Forman, G. (eds) (1993) *The Hundred Languages of Children: The Reggio Emilia approach to early childhood education*, Norwood: J. Ablex.

Filippini, T. (ed.) (2000) *The Hundred Languages of Children: Narrative of the possibilities*, Reggio Emilia: Reggio Children.

Korintus, M. (ed.) (2000) *Early Childhood in Central and Eastern Europe*, UNESCO Education Sector Monograph, No. 113/2000.

Lund, S. (1998) 'Education in the Nordic countries: Denmark', in *International Journal of Early Childhood*, 30, 1: 1–7.

Malaguzzi, L. (translated by L. Gandini) (1993) 'For an education based on relationhsips', in *Young Children*, 9, 1: 10.

Oberhuemer, P. and Ulich, M. (1997) *Working with Young Children in Europe*, London: Paul Chapman Publishing.

OECD (2001) *Starting Strong: Early childhood care and education*, Paris: OECD.

OMEP France (1999) *L'école Maternelle en France*, Paris: Nathan.

Sigurdardottir, M. and Birgisdottir, S. (1998) 'Play and Print in Iceland', in *International Journal of Early Childhood*, 30, 1 : 9–12.

INDEX